computing ESSENTIALS

Making IT work for you

INTRODUCTORY 2013

· The O'Leary Series

Computing Concepts

- *Computing Essentials 2011* Introductory & Complete Editions
- *Computing Essentials 2012* Introductory & Complete Editions
- *Computing Essentials 2013* Introductory & Complete Editions

Microsoft Office Applications

- *Microsoft® Office 2010: A Case Approach*
- *Microsoft® Office Word 2010: A Case Approach* Introductory & Complete Editions
- *Microsoft® Office Excel 2010: A Case Approach* Introductory & Complete Editions
- *Microsoft® Office Access 2010: A Case Approach* Introductory & Complete Editions
- *Microsoft® Office PowerPoint 2010: A Case Approach* Introductory & Complete Editions
- *Microsoft® Windows 7: A Case Approach*

computing ESSENTIALS

Making IT work for you

INTRODUCTORY 2013

Timothy J. O'Leary

Professor Emeritus
Arizona State University

Linda I. O'Leary

Connect
Learn
Succeed™

COMPUTING ESSENTIALS 2013 INTRODUCTORY EDITION: MAKING IT WORK FOR YOU
Published by McGraw-Hill, a business unit of The McGraw-Hill Companies, Inc., 1221 Avenue
of the Americas, New York, NY, 10020. Copyright © 2013 by The McGraw-Hill Companies, Inc.
All rights reserved. Printed in the United States of America. No part of this publication may
be reproduced or distributed in any form or by any means, or stored in a database or retrieval
system, without the prior written consent of The McGraw-Hill Companies, Inc., including, but
not limited to, in any network or other electronic storage or transmission, or broadcast for
distance learning.

Some ancillaries, including electronic and print components, may not be available to customers
outside the United States.

This book is printed on acid-free paper.

1 2 3 4 5 6 7 8 9 0 QDB/QDB 1 0 9 8 7 6 5 4 3 2

ISBN   978-0-07-753898-9
MHID   0-07-753898-6
ISSN   2159-6336

Vice president/Director of marketing: *Alice Harra*
Publisher: *Scott Davidson*
Sponsoring editor: *Paul Altier*
Director, digital products: *Crystal Szewczyk*
Development editor: *Alan Palmer*
Editorial coordinator: *Allison McCabe*
Marketing manager: *Tiffany Russell*
Digital development editor: *Kevin White*
Director, Editing/Design/Production: *Jess Ann Kosic*
Project manager: *Marlena Pechan*
Senior buyer: *Michael R. McCormick*
Senior designer: *Srdjan Savanovic*
Senior photo research coordinator: *Jeremy Cheshareck*
Photo researcher: *Allison Grimes*
Manager, digital production: *Janean A. Utley*
Media project manager: *Cathy L. Tepper*
Cover design: *Nathan Kirkman*
Typeface: *10/12 New Aster*
Compositor: *Laserwords Private Limited*
Printer: *Quad/Graphics*
Cover credit: ©daboost/Veer
Credits: The credits section for this book begins on page 394 and is considered an extension of
the copyright page.

The Internet addresses listed in the text were accurate at the time of publication. The inclusion
of a Web site does not indicate an endorsement by the authors or McGraw-Hill, and McGraw-
Hill does not guarantee the accuracy of the information presented at these sites.

www.mhhe.com

Dedication

We dedicate this edition to Dan, Nicole, and Katie—our reasons for being.

Brief Contents

1 ● Information Technology, the Internet, and You   2

2 ● The Internet, the Web, and Electronic Commerce   30

3 ● Basic Application Software   70

4 ● Specialized Application Software   106

5 ● System Software   134

6 ● The System Unit   164

7 ● Input and Output   196

8 ● Secondary Storage   232

9 ● Communications and Networks   258

10 ● Privacy, Security, and Ethics   292

11 ● Your Future and Information Technology   328

The Evolution of the Computer Age   350

The Buyer's Guide: How to Buy Your Own Microcomputer System   360

The Upgrader's Guide: How to Upgrade Your Microcomputer System   365

Glossary   369

Credits   394

Index   397

Contents

INFORMATION TECHNOLOGY, THE INTERNET, AND YOU   2

Introduction   4
Information Systems   5
People   6
Software   9
  System Software   9
  Application Software   9
Hardware   10
  Types of Computers   11
  Microcomputer Hardware   12
Data   15
Connectivity, the Wireless Revolution, the Internet, and Cloud Computing   16
Careers in IT   17

A Look to the Future: Using and Understanding Information Technology Means Being Computer Competent   18

> Visual Summary   19
> Key Terms   22
> Making IT Work for You   25
> Explorations   26
> Ethics   27
> Environment   28

THE INTERNET, THE WEB, AND ELECTRONIC COMMERCE   30

Introduction   32
The Internet and the Web   32

Making IT work for you:

iPods and Video from the Internet   34

Access   35
  Providers   35
  Browsers   35
Communication   38
  E-mail   38
  Instant Messaging   39
  Social Networking   40
  Blogs, Microblogs, Webcasts, Podcasts, and Wikis   41

Making IT work for you: Twitter   44
Search Tools   46
  Search Engines   46
  Web Directories   46
  Metasearch Engines   47
  Specialized Search Engines   47
  Content Evaluation   48
Electronic Commerce   49
  Business-to-Consumer E-Commerce   50
  Consumer-to-Consumer E-Commerce   50
  Security   51
Cloud Computing   52
Web Utilities   54
  Plug-ins   54
  Filters   54
  File Transfer Utilities   55
  Internet Security Suites   56
Careers in IT: Webmaster   57

A Look to the Future: Web-Accessible Refrigerators Will Automatically Restock Themselves   58

> Visual Summary   59
> Key Terms   63
> Making IT Work for You   66
> Explorations   67
> Ethics   68
> Environment   69

BASIC APPLICATION SOFTWARE   70

Introduction   72
Application Software   72
  Common Features   72

Making IT work for you:

Speech Recognition   74

Word Processors   76
  Features   76
  Case   76
Spreadsheets   79
  Features   79
  Case   80
Database Management Systems   84
  Features   84
  Case   84
Presentation Graphics   87
  Features   87
  Case   87

Integrated Packages   *89*
   Case   *89*
Software Suites   *90*
   Productivity Suite   *90*
   Cloud Computing   *91*
   Sharing between Programs   *91*
   Specialized and Utility Suites   *91*

Making **work for you:**

Google Docs   *92*

Careers in IT: Computer Trainer   *94*

A Look to the Future: Agents Will Help Write Papers, Pay Bills, and Shop on the Internet   *95*

Visual Summary   *96*
Key Terms   *99*
Making IT Work for You   *102*
Explorations   *103*
Ethics   *104*
Environment   *105*

4

SPECIALIZED APPLICATION SOFTWARE   *106*

Introduction   *108*
Specialized Applications   *108*
Graphics   *109*
   Desktop Publishing   *109*
   Image Editors   *109*
   Illustration Programs   *109*
   Image Galleries   *109*
   Graphics Suites   *111*
Audio and Video   *111*

Making **work for you:**

Digital Video Editing   *112*

Multimedia   *114*
   Links and Buttons   *114*
   Multimedia Authoring Programs   *114*
Web Authoring   *115*
   Web Site Design   *115*
   Web Authoring Programs   *116*
Artificial Intelligence   *116*
   Virtual Reality   *118*
   Knowledge-Based (Expert) Systems   *118*
   Robotics   *119*
Mobile Apps   *120*
   Apps   *120*
   App Stores   *121*
Careers in IT: Desktop Publisher   *122*

A Look to the Future: Robots Can Look, Act, and Think Like Us   *123*

Visual Summary   *124*
Key Terms   *127*
Making IT Work for You   *130*
Explorations   *131*
Ethics   *132*
Environment   *133*

5

SYSTEM SOFTWARE   *134*

Introduction   *136*
System Software   *136*
Operating Systems   *137*
   Functions   *137*
   Features   *138*
   Categories   *139*
Desktop Operating Systems   *140*
   Windows   *140*
   Mac OS   *140*
   UNIX and Linux   *142*
   Virtualization   *142*
Mobile Operating Systems   *143*
Utilities   *144*
   Windows Utilities   *144*
   Utility Suites   *148*
Device Drivers   *148*

Making **work for you:**

Virus Protection   *150*

Careers in IT: Computer Support Specialist   *152*

A Look to the Future: Self-Healing Computers Could Mean an End to Computer Crashes and Performance Problems   *153*

Visual Summary   *154*
Key Terms   *157*
Making IT Work for You   *160*
Explorations   *161*
Ethics   *162*
Environment   *163*

6

THE SYSTEM UNIT   *164*

Introduction   *166*
System Unit   *166*
   Categories   *166*
   Components   *169*
Electronic Data and Instructions   *169*
   Numeric Representation   *170*
   Character Encoding   *170*

System Board *171*
Microprocessor *172*
   Microprocessor Chips *173*
   Specialty Processors *174*
Memory *174*
   RAM *174*
   ROM *175*
   Flash Memory *175*
Expansion Slots and Cards *176*
Bus Lines *177*

Making IT work for you: TV Tuner Cards
and Video Clips *178*
   Expansion Buses *180*
Ports *180*
   Standard Ports *181*
   Specialized Ports *181*
   Legacy Ports *182*
   Cables *182*
Power Supply *183*
Careers in IT: Computer Technician *183*

A Look to the Future: As You Walk out the Door, Don't
Forget Your Computer *185*

Visual Summary *186*
Key Terms *189*
Making IT Work for You *192*
Explorations *193*
Ethics *194*
Environment *195*

7

INPUT AND OUTPUT *196*

Introduction *198*
What Is Input? *198*
Keyboard Entry *198*
   Keyboards *199*
   Features *199*
Pointing Devices *200*
   Mice *200*
   Touch Screens *202*
   Joysticks *202*
   Stylus *202*
Scanning Devices *203*
   Optical Scanners *203*
   Card Readers *204*
   Bar Code Readers *205*
   Character and Mark Recognition
   Devices *205*
Image Capturing Devices *206*
   Digital Cameras *206*
   Digital Video Cameras *206*
Audio-Input Devices *207*
   Voice Recognition Systems *207*

Making IT work for you: WebCams and
Instant Messaging *208*

What Is Output? *210*
Monitors *210*
   Features *210*
      Flat-Panel Monitors *211*
      Cathode-Ray Tubes *211*
      Other Monitors *211*

Making IT work for you:
Using E-Books *213*

Printers *214*
   Features *214*
   Ink-Jet Printers *215*
   Laser Printers *215*
   Other Printers *215*
Audio and Video Devices *217*
   Portable Media Players *217*
Combination Input and Output Devices *217*
   Fax Machines *217*
   Multifunctional Devices *217*
   Internet Telephones *218*
Careers in IT: Technical Writers *219*

A Look to the Future: Crashing through the Foreign
Language Barrier *220*

Visual Summary *221*
Key Terms *224*
Making IT Work for You *227*
Explorations *229*
Ethics *230*
Environment *231*

8

SECONDARY STORAGE *232*

Introduction *234*
Storage *234*
Hard Disks *235*
   Internal Hard Disk *236*
   External Hard Drives *236*
   Performance Enhancements *237*
Optical Discs *238*
   Compact Disc *238*
   Digital Versatile Disc *239*
   Blu-ray Disc *239*
Solid-State Storage *240*
   Solid-State Drives *240*
   Flash Memory *240*
   USB Drives *241*
Cloud Storage *241*

Making IT work for you:
Cloud Storage *242*

Mass Storage Devices *245*
   Enterprise Storage System *245*
   Storage Area Network *246*
Careers in IT: Software Engineer *246*

A Look to the Future: Your Entire Life Recorded on
a Single Disk *247*

Visual Summary *248*
Key Terms *251*
Making IT Work for You *254*
Explorations *255*
Ethics *256*
Environment *257*

COMMUNICATIONS AND NETWORKS *258*

Introduction *260*
Communications *260*
   Connectivity *260*
   The Wireless Revolution *261*
   Communication Systems *261*
Communication Channels *262*
   Physical Connections *262*
   Wireless Connections *263*
Connection Devices *265*
   Modems *265*
   Connection Service *266*
Data Transmission *267*
   Bandwidth *267*
   Protocols *267*
Networks *268*
   Terms *268*
Network Types *270*
   Local Area Networks *270*
   Home Networks *270*
   Wireless LAN *271*

Making IT work for you: Home Networking *272*

   Personal Area Network *274*
   Metropolitan Area Networks *274*
   Wide Area Networks *274*
Network Architecture *275*
   Topologies *275*
   Strategies *276*
Organizational Networks *277*
   Internet Technologies *277*
   Network Security *277*
Careers in IT: Network Administrator *279*

A Look to the Future: Telepresence Lets You Be There
without Actually Being There *280*

Visual Summary *281*
Key Terms *284*
Making IT Work for You *287*
Explorations *288*
Ethics *289*
Environment *290*

PRIVACY, SECURITY, AND ETHICS *292*

Introduction *294*
People *294*
Privacy *295*
   Large Databases *295*
   Private Networks *298*
   The Internet and the Web *299*
   Online Identity *303*
   Major Laws on Privacy *303*

Making IT work for you: Spyware Removal *304*

Security *306*
   Computer Criminals *306*
   Computer Crime *307*
   Other Hazards *310*
   Measures to Protect Computer Security *312*
Ethics *315*
   Copyright and Digital Rights Management *315*
   Plagiarism *316*
Careers in IT: Cryptographer *317*

A Look to the Future: A Webcam on Every Corner *318*

Visual Summary *319*
Key Terms *322*
Making IT Work for You *325*
Explorations *326*
Ethics *327*
Environment *327*

YOUR FUTURE AND INFORMATION TECHNOLOGY *328*

Introduction *330*
Changing Times *330*
Technology and Organizations *331*
   New Products *331*

New Enterprises *332*
New Customer and Supplier Relationships *332*

Technology and People *333*
Cynicism *333*
Naivete *333*
Frustration *333*
Proactivity *333*

How You Can Be a Winner *334*
Stay Current *334*
Maintain Your Computer Competency *335*
Develop Professional Contacts *335*
Develop Specialties *335*

Making IT work for you: Locating Job Opportunities Online *336*
Be Alert for Organizational Change *338*
Look for Innovative Opportunities *338*

Careers in IT *339*

A Look to the Future: Maintaining Computer Competency and Becoming Proactive *340*

Visual Summary *341*
Key Terms *344*
Making IT Work for You *347*
Explorations *348*
Ethics *349*
Environment *349*

The Evolution of the Computer Age *350*

The Buyer's Guide: How to Buy Your Own Microcomputer System *360*

The Upgrader's Guide: How to Upgrade Your Microcomputer System *365*

Glossary 369

Credits 394

Index 397

Every chapter begins with a new, concise "Why Should I Read This Chapter" feature and has all new multiple choice and matching questions. Additionally, four new end-of-chapter features have been added: Making IT Work for You, Explorations, Ethics, and Environment. Each feature provides assignments that expand upon concepts and ideas presented within the text.

Chapter 1   Coverage of Mozilla's Firefox
Expanded discussion of tablet PCs to include traditional and slate computers including iPad2
Updated wireless communication devices

Chapter 2   Updated coverage of the basic parts of a URL
Comparison of client-based versus Web-based e-mail accounts
Expanded coverage of MySpace, Facebook, and LinkedIn
Expanded coverage of streaming technology, Webcasts, and Podcasts
Revised coverage of search engines and Web directories

Chapter 3   Comparison of traditional versus ribbon graphical user interfaces
Improved page layout to improve continuity and comprehension

Chapter 4   Expanded coverage of image editors
Expanded coverage of illustration programs
Expanded and updated coverage of mobile applications

Chapter 5   Expanded coverage of Mac OS
Expanded coverage of mobile operating systems including iOS, WebOS, and Android

Chapter 6   Expanded coverage of traditional and slate tablet PCs
Consolidated coverage of expansion buses

Chapter 7   New coverage of digital interactive whiteboards
New coverage of cloud printers and Google Cloud Print
New discussion of portable media players and Mobile DTV
New coverage of cable Internet telephone service providers including Ooma, Vonage, MagicJack, and Skype

Chapter 8   Revised and repositioned Cloud Storage Making IT Work for You

Chapter 9   More coverage of wireless technologies
Expanded coverage of hotspots
Updated and more concise coverage of network topologies
Updated and more concise coverage of network strategies

Chapter 10   New coverage on privacy modes including InPrivate Browsing and Private Browsing
Expanded coverage of carders
New coverage on cyber-bullying

Preface

The 20th century brought us the dawn of the digital information age and unprecedented changes in information technology. There is no indication that this rapid rate of change will be slowing—it may even be increasing. As we begin the 21st century, computer literacy is undoubtedly becoming a prerequisite in whatever career you choose.

The goal of *Computing Essentials* is to provide you with the basis for understanding the concepts necessary for success. *Computing Essentials* also endeavors to instill an appreciation for the effect of information technology on people and our environment and to give you a basis for building the necessary skill set to succeed in the 21st century.

Times are changing, technology is changing, and this text is changing too. As students of today, you are different from those of yesterday. You put much effort toward the things that interest you and the things that are relevant to you. Your efforts directed at learning application programs and exploring the Web seem, at times, limitless. On the other hand, it is sometimes difficult to engage in other equally important topics such as personal privacy and technological advances.

In this text, we present practical tips related to key concepts through the demonstration of interesting applications that are relevant to your lives. Topics presented focus first on outputs rather than processes. Then, we discuss the concepts and processes.

Motivation and relevance are the keys. This text has several features specifically designed to engage and demonstrate the relevance of technology in your lives. These elements are combined with a thorough coverage of the concepts and sound pedagogical devices.

VISUAL CHAPTER OPENERS

Each chapter begins with a list of chapter competencies or objectives and provides a brief introduction to what will be covered in the chapter. Additionally, the "Why Should I Read This?" feature provides relevance through a brief discussion of the content's historical context.

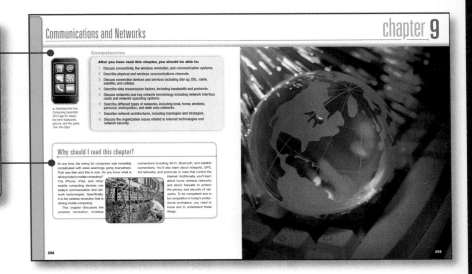

VISUAL SUMMARIES

Visual summaries appear at the end of every chapter and summarize major concepts covered throughout the chapter. Like the chapter openers, these summaries use graphics to reinforce key concepts in an engaging and meaningful way.

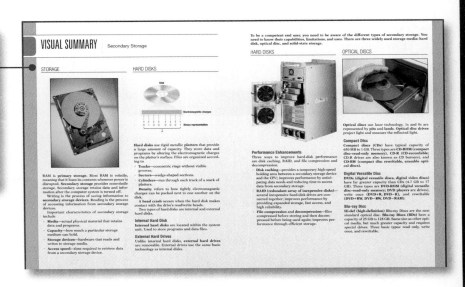

Learning Tools: The CE 2013 App

Download the free *Computing Essentials 2013* App for:

• Key term flash cards

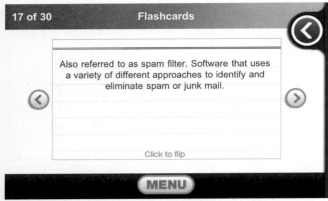

• Quizzes

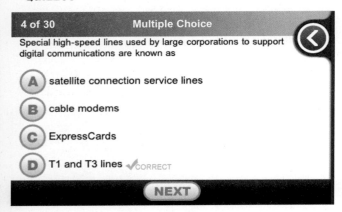

• Game, *Over the Edge*

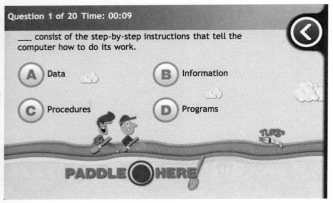

We have specifically designed the end-of-chapter materials to this text to meet the different needs of students and instructors. In addition to the traditional end-of-chapter review materials, you will find four unique categories: (1) Making IT Work for You, which is designed to help students gain a better understanding of how the technology covered in a particular chapter is used today; (2) Explorations, which offers a deeper understanding of selected topics covered in that particular chapter; (3) Ethics, which provides the opportunity to hone essential writing skills while learning about technology issues related to privacy, security, and ethics; and (4) Environment, which explores environmental issues related to technology.

This table offers a glimpse of the unique coverage you can find at the end of each chapter.

END-OF-CHAPTER COVERAGE

Chapter	Making IT Work for You	Explorations	Ethics	Environment
1	iPods and Video from the Internet (p. 25) Google Docs (p. 25) Digital Video Editing (p. 25) Virus Protection and Internet Security (p. 25) Home Networking (p. 25)	How Computer Virus Protection Programs Work (p. 26) How Digital Cameras Work (p. 26) How Internet Telephones Work (p. 26) How Wireless Home Networks Work (p. 26)	Digital Photo Manipulation (p. 27) WebCams (p. 27) Electronic Monitoring (p. 27)	Spam (p. 28) Downloading Music (p. 28) Environmental Utility Software (p. 28) Robots (p. 28)
2	iPods and Video from the Internet (p. 66) Twitter (p. 66)	How Spam Filters Work (p. 67) How Instant Messaging Works (p. 67) Domain Registration (p. 67)	Free Speech Online (p. 68) Digital Divide (p. 68)	Spam (p. 69) CDs and DVDs (p. 69)
3	Speech Recognition (p. 102) Google Docs (p. 102)	How Speech Recognition Works (p. 103) Sharing Data between Applications (p. 103) Shareware (p. 103)	Acquiring Software (p. 104) Audio and Video Clips (p. 104)	Digital Software Distribution (p. 105) Green Software Utilities (p. 105)
4	Digital Video Editing (p. 130) Adobe Flash (p. 130) Streaming Multimedia Players (p. 130)	How Digital Video Editing Works (p. 131) Personal Web Site (p. 131) Streaming Multimedia (p. 131)	Digital Photo Manipulation (p. 132)	Environmental Robots (p. 133)
5	Virus Protection (p. 160) Windows Update (p. 160) Disk Defragmentation (p. 160)	How Virus Protection Programs Work (p. 161) Booting and POST (p. 161) Customized Desktop (p. 161)	Open Source (p. 162)	Power Management (p. 163)
6	TV Tuner Cards and Video Clips (p. 192) Desktop and Notebook Computers (p. 192) Custom System Units (p. 192)	How TV Tuner Cards Work (p. 193) How Virtual Memory Works (p. 193) Binary Numbers (p. 193)	RFIDs (p. 194)	Green PCs (p. 195)
7	WebCams and Instant Messaging (p. 227) E-Book Readers (p. 228)	How Digital Cameras Work (p. 229) How Internet Telephones Work (p. 229) Handwriting Recognition (p. 229)	WebCams (p. 230)	Printing (p. 231) Printer Cartridges (p. 231)
8	Cloud Storage (p. 254) USB Storage Devices (p. 254)	iPod (p. 255) File Compression (p. 255) Cloud Storage Services (p. 255)	CD-R and Music Files (p. 256)	Solid-State Storage (p. 257)
9	Home Networking (p. 287) Distributed Computing (p. 287) Wireless Mobile Devices (p. 287)	How Wireless Home Networks Work (p. 288) BitTorrent (p. 288) Hotspots (p. 288)	Electronic Monitoring (p. 289) Digital Rights Management (p. 289)	GPS (p. 290) iPhone (p. 291)
10	Spyware (p. 325) Personal Firewalls (p. 325) Personal Backups (p. 325)	How Web Bugs Work (p. 326) Mistaken Identity (p. 326) Air Travel Database (p. 326)	Plagiarism (p. 327)	Environmental Scams (p. 327)
11	Jobs Online (p. 347) Maintain Computer Competence (p. 347)	Your Career (p. 348) Resume Advice (p. 348)	Ethical Issues (p. 349)	Environmental Issues (p. 349)

Hands-On

MAKING IT WORK FOR YOU

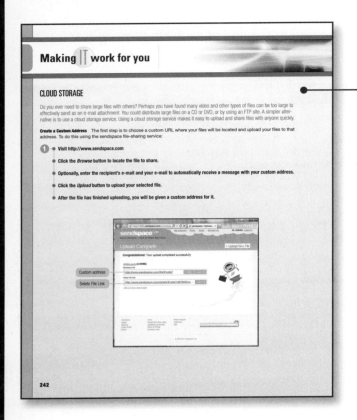

Special-interest topics are presented in the Making IT Work for You section found within nearly every chapter. These topics include using Job Searches, Google Docs, Virus Protection, Internet Security, and Cloud Storage.

Reinforcing Key Concepts

CONCEPT CHECKS

Located at points throughout each chapter, the Concept Check cues you to note which topics have been covered and to self-test your understanding of the material already discussed.

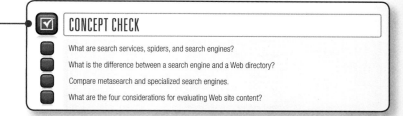

CONCEPT CHECK

☑ What are search services, spiders, and search engines?

What is the difference between a search engine and a Web directory?

Compare metasearch and specialized search engines.

What are the four considerations for evaluating Web site content?

KEY TERMS

Throughout the text, the most important terms are presented in bold and are defined within the text. You will also find a list of key terms at the end of each chapter and in the glossary at the end of the book.

KEY TERMS

address (36, 38)	filter (54)	social networking (40)
Advanced Research	friend (39)	spam (39)
Project Agency Network	header (38)	spam blocker (39)
(ARPANET) (32)	hit (46)	spam filter (39)
AJAX (37)	hyperlink (36)	specialized search
applets (37)	Hypertext Markup	engine (47)
attachment (38)	Language	spider (46)
auction house site (50)	(HTML) (36)	streaming (42)
BitTorrent (55)	instant messaging	subject (38)
blog (42)	(IM) (39)	subject directory (46)
browser (35)	Internet (32)	surf (35)
business-to-business	Internet security	top-level domain
(B2B) (50)	suite (56)	(TLD) (36)
business-to-consumer	Internet service provider	Twitter (42)
(B2C) (49)	(ISP) (35)	uniform resource
cable (35)	Java (37)	locator (URL) (36)
carder (51)	JavaScript (37)	universal instant
Center for European	link (36)	messenger (40)
Nuclear	LinkedIn (41)	uploading (55)
Research (CERN) (32)	location (36)	virus (39)
client-based e-mail	message (39)	Web (32)
account (38)	metasearch	Web 1.0 (32)
cloud computing (52)	engine (47)	Web 2.0 (32)
consumer-to-consumer	microblog (42)	Web 3.0 (32)
(C2C) (50)	mobile browser (37)	Web auction (50)
digital cash (51)	MySpace (40)	Web-based e-mail
domain name (36)	online (32)	account (38)
downloading (55)	online banking (50)	Web-based file
DSL (35)	online shopping (50)	transfer
e-commerce (49)	online stock	services (55)
e-learning (33)	trading (50)	Webcasts (42)
electronic commerce (49)	person-to-person auction	Web directory (46)
electronic mail (38)	site (50)	Web log (42)
e-mail (38)	plug-in (54)	Webmail (38)
e-mail client (38)	podcast (42)	Webmail client (38)
Facebook (40)	protocol (36)	Webmaster (57)
Facebook groups (41)	search engine (46)	Web page (36)
Facebook Pages (40)	search service (46)	Web utility (54)
Facebook Profile (40)	secure file transfer	wiki (43)
file transfer protocol	protocol (SFTP) (55)	Wikipedia (43)
(FTP) (55)	signature (39)	wireless modem (35)

To test your knowledge of these key terms with animated flash cards, visit our Web site at www.computing2013.com and enter the keyword terms2.

CHAPTER REVIEW

Following the Visual Summary, the chapter review includes material designed to review and reinforce chapter content. It includes a Key Terms list that reiterates the terms presented in the chapter, Multiple Choice questions to help test your understanding of information presented in the chapter, Matching exercises to test your recall of terminology presented in the chapter, and Open-Ended questions or statements to help review your understanding of the key concepts presented in the chapter.

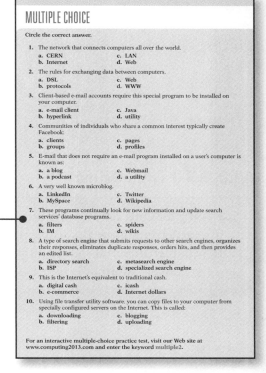

MULTIPLE CHOICE

Circle the correct answer.

1. The network that connects computers all over the world.
   - a. CERN
   - b. Internet
   - c. LAN
   - d. Web

2. The rules for exchanging data between computers.
   - a. DSL
   - b. protocols
   - c. Web
   - d. WWW

3. Client-based e-mail accounts require this special program to be installed on your computer.
   - a. e-mail client
   - b. hyperlink
   - c. Java
   - d. utility

4. Communities of individuals who share a common interest typically create Facebook:
   - a. clients
   - b. groups
   - c. pages
   - d. profiles

5. E-mail that does not require an e-mail program installed on a user's computer is known as:
   - a. a blog
   - b. a podcast
   - c. Webmail
   - d. a utility

6. A very well known microblog.
   - a. LinkedIn
   - b. MySpace
   - c. Twitter
   - d. Wikipedia

7. These programs continually look for new information and update search services' database programs.
   - a. filters
   - b. IM
   - c. spiders
   - d. wikis

8. A type of search engine that submits requests to other search engines, organizes their responses, eliminates duplicate responses, orders hits, and then provides an edited list.
   - a. directory search
   - b. ISP
   - c. metasearch engine
   - d. specialized search engine

9. This is the Internet's equivalent to traditional cash.
   - a. digital cash
   - b. e-commerce
   - c. icash
   - d. Internet dollars

10. Using file transfer utility software, you can copy files to your computer from specially configured servers on the Internet. This is called:
    - a. downloading
    - b. filtering
    - c. blogging
    - d. uploading

For an interactive multiple-choice practice test, visit our Web site at www.computing2013.com and enter the keyword multiple2.

The Future of Information Technology

CAREERS IN IT

> - **RAID systems**—larger versions of the specialized devices discussed earlier in this chapter that enhance organizational security by constantly making backup copies of files moving across the organization's networks.
> - **Tape library**—device that provides automatic access to data archived on a library of tapes.
> - **Organizational cloud storage**—high-speed Internet connection to a dedicated remote organizational cloud storage server.
>
> #### Storage Area Network
> A recent mass storage development is **storage area network (SAN)** systems. SAN is an architecture to link remote computer storage devices, such as enterprise storage systems, to computers such that the devices are as available as locally attached drives. In a SAN system, the user's computer provides the file system for storing data, but the SAN provides the disk space for data.
> The key to a SAN is a high-speed network, connecting individual computers to mass storage devices. Special file systems prevent simultaneous users from interfering with each other. SANs provide the ability to house data in remote locations and still allow efficient and secure access.
>
> **CONCEPT CHECK**
>
> Define mass storage and list five mass storage devices.
>
> What is an enterprise storage system?
>
> What is a storage area network system?
>
>
>
> #### Careers in IT
>
> **Software engineers** analyze users' needs and create application software. Software engineers typically have experience in programming but focus on the design and development of programs using the principles of mathematics and engineering.
> A bachelor's or an advanced specialized associate's degree in computer science or information systems and an extensive knowledge of computers and technology are required by most employers. Internships may provide students with the kinds of experience employers look for in a software engineer. Those with specific experience with networking, the Internet, and Web applications may have an advantage over other applicants. Employers typically look for software engineers with good communication and analytical skills.
> Software engineers can expect to earn an annual salary in the range of $63,000 to $98,500. Advancement opportunities are usually tied to experience. Experienced software engineers may be promoted to project manager or have opportunities in systems design. To learn about other careers in information technology, visit us at www.computing2013.com and enter the keyword careers.
>
> Now that you've learned about secondary storage, let me tell you a little bit about my career as a software engineer.

Some of the fastest-growing career opportunities are in information technology. Each chapter highlights one of the most promising careers in IT by presenting job titles, responsibilities, educational requirements, and salary ranges. Among the careers covered are Webmaster, software engineer, and database administrator. You will learn how the material you are studying relates directly to a potential career path.

A LOOK TO THE FUTURE

Each chapter concludes with a brief discussion of a recent technological advancement related to the chapter material, reinforcing the importance of staying informed.

> ### A LOOK TO THE FUTURE
>
> #### Your Entire Life Recorded on a Single Disk
>
> Imagine if you could store every conversation you ever had on a single disk. What if you could capture your entire life on video stored on just a few discs? What if you could hold in your pocket the contents of the Library of Congress? Innovations in secondary storage capacity using molecular storage promise all of this and more.
> Currently, information is stored on magnetic or optical discs. In the future, the electron state of atoms in a molecule will hold information at a much greater density. Currently, experiments have yielded densities of 200 gigabytes per square inch. If successfully brought to market, such a product would yield two terabytes on one disk, enough to hold every conversation a person has throughout his or her entire lifetime. Experiments with three-dimensional storing (where information is stored in height as well as area) and optical holography (where information is stored by light photons on specially treated crystals) promise to yield even greater storage in smaller packages.
>
> The capability to store vast amounts of data offers a future both tantalizing and problematic. Although having a video of your life would be a wonderful memory tool, how could you sort and use so much information? Imagine having to search through hours of video just to verify the time of a lunch date or to remember where you parked your car. Fortunately, computer scientists are developing computer programs that can rapidly sort through and understand audio and visual material. Great strides have been made in creating programs that can scan photos and videos searching for a particular person's face. This technology is currently being used in airports to identify suspected terrorists. In the future, you may use this technology to search for photos of a loved one or video of the family vacation.
> Is there a downside to recording every event in a person's life? Could your personal video log be used to incriminate you in a court of law? Could someone else's video log be an invasion of your right to privacy? The technology will soon be here. Are you ready for it? Would you use it to record your every move?

MAKING IT WORK FOR YOU

In each chapter, Making IT Work for You presents questions designed to help you gain a better understanding of how technology is being used today. The first question is related directly to the chapter's Making IT Work for You topics. Other questions focus on interesting applications of technology that relate directly to you.

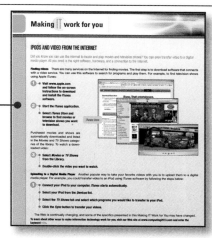

EXPLORATIONS

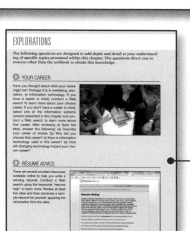

In each chapter, Explorations presents questions that help you gain a deeper understanding of select topics. Typically, one question relates to a topic presented at the book's Web site, www.computing2013.com, such as How Instant Messaging Works, How Streaming Media Works, and How Virus Protection Works. Other questions in Expanding Your Knowledge typically require Web research into carefully selected topics.

ETHICS

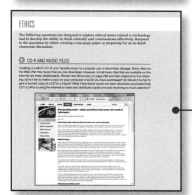

In each chapter, Ethics presents questions designed to explore ethical issues related to technology and to help you develop the ability to think critically and communicate effectively. Typically, the questions relate directly to the Ethics boxes within each chapter. Topics include free speech online, acquiring software, and digital photo manipulation.

ENVIRONMENT

In each chapter, Environment presents questions designed to explore environmental issues related to technology and to help you develop the ability to think critically and communicate effectively. Typically, the questions relate directly to the Environmental boxes within each chapter. Topics include spam, Green pcs, and environmental robots.

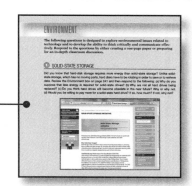

Support Materials

The Instructor's Manual offers lecture outlines with teaching notes and figure references. It provides definitions of key terms and solutions to the end-of-chapter material, including multiple-choice, matching, and open-ended questions.

The PowerPoint slides are designed to provide instructors with a comprehensive resource for lecture use. The slides include a review of key terms and topics, as well as artwork taken from the text to further explain concepts covered in each chapter.

The testbank contains over 2,200 questions categorized by level of learning (definition, concept, and application). This is the same learning scheme that is introduced in the text to provide a valuable testing and reinforcement tool. Text page references have been provided for all questions, including a level-of-difficulty rating. The testbank is offered in Word files, as well as in EZ Test format.

The instructor support materials can be downloaded at www.mhhe.com/ce2013.

The O'Leary Web site

The O'Leary Web site can be found at www.computing2013.com. Students can find a host of additional resources on the Web site, including animations of key concepts, videos relating to select Making IT Work for You applications, and in-depth coverage of select topics.

O'LEARY SERIES

The O'Leary Application Series for Microsoft® Office is available separately or packaged with *Computing Essentials*. The O'Leary Application Series offers a step-by-step approach to learning computer applications and is available in both complete and introductory versions.

SIMNET ONLINE TRAINING AND ASSESSMENT FOR OFFICE APPLICATIONS

SimNet™ Online provides a way for you to test students' software skills in a simulated environment. SimNet is available for Microsoft Office 2010 and will have enhanced concepts coverage coming in 2012! SimNet provides flexibility for you in your applications course by offering:

- Pretesting options

- Posttesting options

- Course placement testing

- Diagnostic capabilities to reinforce skills

- Web delivery of tests

- Learning verification reports

For more information on skills assessment software, please contact your local sales representative, or visit us at www.mhhe.com/simnet2010.

SIMGRADER FOR OFFICE 2010

SimGrader provides automatic grading of projects for Microsoft Office and can be used seamlessly within SimNet Online or can be used separately, if needed. SimGrader offers the widest range of projects from any of our Office series titles. SimNet and SimGrader together provide an ideal, easy-to-use solution for students to gain complete knowledge of Office skills.

Acknowledgments

We would like to extend our thanks to the professors who took time out of their busy schedules to provide us with the feedback necessary to develop the 2013 edition of this text. The following professors offered valuable suggestions on revising the text:

Beverly Amer
Northern Arizona University

Diane Stark
Phoenix College

Mary Locke
Greenville Technical College

Penny Cypert
Tarrant County College

Kin Lam
Medgar Evers College

Charles DeSassure
Tarrant County College

Lissa Whyte-Morazan
Brookline College

Melissa Nemeth
Kelley School of Business Indianapolis

Chris Castillo
Medgar Evers College

Deborah Franklin
Bryant & Stratton College

Emily Holliday
Campbell University

Tamara Butler
Bryant & Stratton College

Mark Renslow
Globe Education Network

Laurence Hitterdale
Glendale Community College

Cynthia Rumney
Middle Georgia Technical College

Lana LaBruyere
Mineral Area College

Jackie Armstrong
Hill College

Paul Schwager
East Carolina University

Laura Ringer
Piedmont Technical College

Cherylee Kushida
Santa Ana College

Barbara Purvis
Centura College

Brenda Abernathy
Northeast State Community College

Jane Liefert
Middlesex County College

David Pence
Moberly Area Community College

Kurt Kominek
Northeast State Community College

Owen Herman
Metropolitan State College Denver

James Gordon Patterson
Paradise Valley Community College

Charulata Trivedi
Quinsigamond Community College

Susan Fuschetto
Cerritos College

Sue Van Boven
Paradise Valley Community College

Patricia Dreven
College of Southern Nevada

Gary Mosley
Southern Wesleyan University

Linda Haberaecker
Davenport University

Herbert Rebhun
University of Houston–Downtown

Carol Grazette
Medgar Evers College

Brenda Killingsworth
East Carolina University

Paulette Comet
Community College of Baltimore County

Jan Kamhotz
Bryant & Stratton College

Linda Kliston
Broward Community College

Marilyn Hibbert
Salt Lake Community College

Beata Lovelace
Pulaski Technical College

Sue McCrory
Missouri State University

Penny Cypert
Tarrant County College

Leticia Kalweit
Bryant & Stratton College

Ella Berenstein
Bryant & Stratton College

Our sincere thanks also go to Gary Sibbitts at Saint Louis Community College at Meramec for taking the screenshots, to Margaret Edmunds at Mount Allison University for revising the Instructor's Manual, and to Laurie Zouharis at Suffolk College for revising the PowerPoint presentations and test bank to accompany this text.

Tim and Linda O'Leary live in the American Southwest and spend much of their time engaging instructors and students in conversation about learning. In fact, they have been talking about learning for over 25 years. Something in those early conversations convinced them to write a book, to bring their interest in the learning process to the printed page. Today, they are as concerned as ever about learning, about technology, and about the challenges of presenting material in new ways, in terms of both content and method of delivery.

A powerful and creative team, Tim combines his 25 years of classroom teaching experience with Linda's background as a consultant and corporate trainer. Tim has taught courses at Stark Technical College in Canton, Ohio, and at Rochester Institute of Technology in upstate New York, and is currently a professor emeritus at Arizona State University in Tempe, Arizona. Linda offered her expertise at ASU for several years as an academic advisor. She also presented and developed materials for major corporations such as Motorola, Intel, Honeywell, and AT&T, as well as various community colleges in the Phoenix area.

Tim and Linda have talked to and taught numerous students, all of them with a desire to learn something about computers and applications that make their lives easier, more interesting, and more productive.

Each new edition of an O'Leary text, supplement, or learning aid has benefited from these students and their instructors who daily stand in front of them (or over their shoulders). *Computing Essentials* is no exception.

Information Technology, the Internet, and You

▲ Download the free *Computing Essentials 2013* app for videos, key term flashcards, quizzes, and the game, *Over the Edge!*

Competencies

After you have read this chapter, you should be able to:

1 Explain the five parts of an information system: people, procedures, software, hardware, and data.

2 Distinguish between system software and application software.

3 Discuss the three kinds of system software programs.

4 Distinguish between basic and specialized application software.

5 Identify the four types of computers and the six types of microcomputers.

6 Describe the different types of computer hardware, including the system unit, input, output, storage, and communication devices.

7 Define data and describe document, worksheet, database, and presentation files.

8 Explain computer connectivity, the wireless revolution, the Internet, smartphone, and cloud computing.

Why should I read this chapter?

When microcomputers were first introduced, they were used by relatively few people to create simple documents and analyze data. These computers were expensive, slow, and difficult to use. Now, microcomputers are used widely throughout the world. Every day billons of people use microcomputers and the Internet socially and professionally. Today's microcomputers are inexpensive, very powerful, and easy to use.

This chapter provides a very concise overview of computing and the organization of this text. It presents the various features of the text including boxes presenting environmental issues and special coverage of how you can make IT work for you. Additionally, an overview of hardware, software, and data is presented. Finally, the concept of connectivity is introduced along with the Internet, Web, the wireless revolution, and cloud computing. To effectively start to use this text, you need to understand these things.

2

chapter 1

Introduction

Welcome to *Computing Essentials.* I'm Alan and I work in information technology. On the following pages, we'll be discussing some of the most exciting new developments in computer technology, especially mobile technologies like Apple's iPad, Motorola's Zoom, and Samsung's Galaxy Tab tablet PCs. Let me begin in this chapter by giving you an overview of the book and showing you some of its special features.

The purpose of this book is to help you become competent with computer technology. **Computer competency** refers to acquiring computer-related skills—indispensable tools for today. They include how to effectively use popular application packages and the Internet.

In this chapter, we present an overview of an information system: people, procedures, software, hardware, and data. It is essential to understand these basic parts and how connectivity through the Internet and the Web expands the role of information technology in our lives. Later, we will describe these parts of an information system in detail.

Fifteen years ago, most people had little to do with computers, at least directly. Of course, they filled out computerized forms, took computerized tests, and paid computerized bills. But the real work was handled by specialists. Then microcomputers came along and changed everything. Today it is easy for nearly everybody to use a computer.

- Microcomputers are common tools in all areas of life. Writers write, artists draw, engineers and scientists calculate—all on microcomputers. Students and businesspeople do all this, and more.

- New forms of learning have developed. People who are homebound, who work odd hours, or who travel frequently may take online courses. A college course need not fit within a quarter or a semester.

People
are end users who use computers to make themselves more productive

Software
provides step-by-step instructions for computer hardware

Procedures
specify rules or guidelines for computer operations

Figure 1-1 The five parts of an information system

- New ways to communicate, to find people with similar interests, and to buy goods are available. People use electronic mail, electronic commerce, and the Internet to meet and to share ideas and products.

To be competent with computer technology, you need to know the five parts of an information system: people, procedures, software, hardware, and data. You also need to understand connectivity, the wireless revolution, the Internet, and the Web and to recognize the role of information technology in your personal life as well as your professional life.

Information Systems

When you think of a microcomputer, perhaps you think of just the equipment itself. That is, you think of the monitor or the keyboard. Yet, there is more to it than that. The way to think about a microcomputer is as part of an information system. An **information system** has five parts: *people, procedures, software, hardware,* and *data.* (See Figure 1-1.)

- **People:** It is easy to overlook people as one of the five parts of an information system. Yet this is what microcomputers are all about—making **people, end users** like you, more productive.
- **Procedures:** The rules or guidelines for people to follow when using software, hardware, and data are **procedures.** These procedures are typically

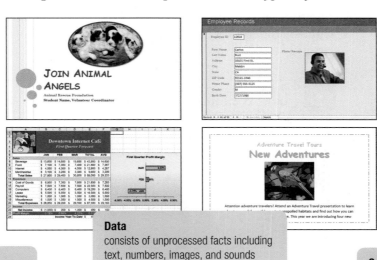

Data
consists of unprocessed facts including text, numbers, images, and sounds

Hardware
includes keyboard, mouse, monitor, system unit, and other devices

Connectivity
allows computers to share information and to connect to the Internet

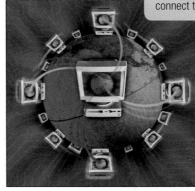

documented in manuals written by computer specialists. Software and hardware manufacturers provide manuals with their products. These manuals are provided in either printed or electronic (web link) form.

- **Software:** A **program** consists of the step-by-step instructions that tell the computer how to do its work. **Software** is another name for a program or programs. The purpose of software is to convert **data** (unprocessed facts) into **information** (processed facts). For example, a payroll program would instruct the computer to take the number of hours you worked in a week (data) and multiply it by your pay rate (data) to determine how much you are paid for the week (information).

- **Hardware:** The equipment that processes the data to create information is called **hardware.** It includes the keyboard, mouse, monitor, system unit, and other devices. Hardware is controlled by software.

- **Data:** The raw, unprocessed facts, including text, numbers, images, and sounds, are called data. Processed data yields information. Using the previous example of a payroll program, the data (number of hours worked and pay rate) is processed (multiplied) to yield information (weekly pay).

Almost all of today's computer systems add an additional part to the information system. This part, called **connectivity,** typically uses the Internet and allows users to greatly expand the capability and usefulness of their information systems.

In large computer systems, there are specialists who write procedures, develop software, and capture data. In microcomputer systems, however, end users often perform these operations. To be a competent end user, you must understand the essentials of **information technology (IT),** including software, hardware, and data.

CONCEPT CHECK

 What are the five parts of an information system?

 What is the difference between data and information?

 What is connectivity?

People

People are surely the most important part of any information system. Our lives are touched every day by computers and information systems. Many times the contact is direct and obvious, such as when we create documents using a word processing program or when we connect to the Internet. Other times, the contact is not as obvious. Consider just the four examples in Figure 1-2.

Throughout this book you will find a variety of features designed to help you become computer competent and knowledgeable. These features include Making IT Work for You, Explorations, Environment, Ethics, Tips, Careers in IT, and the Computing Essentials Web site.

- **Making IT Work for You.** In the chapters that follow, you will find Making IT Work for You features that present numerous interesting and practical IT applications. Using a step-by-step procedure, you are provided

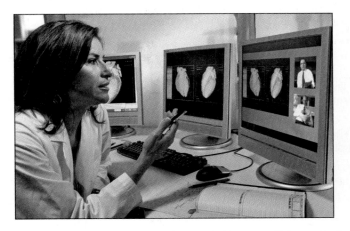

Figure 1-2 **Computers in entertainment, business, medicine, and education**

with specific instructions on how to use each application. For just a few of the Making IT Work for You topics, see Figure 1-3. For a complete list, visit our Web site at www.computing2013.com.

- **Explorations.** The informational content of the Web is limitless; the challenge is to locate the information you are looking for. In this chapter and the ones that follow, you will find Explorations boxes in the margin that direct you to relevant Web information locations.

- **Environment.** Today it is more important than ever that we be aware of our impact on the environment. In this chapter and the following ones, you will find Environment boxes in the margin that present important relevant environmental information.

- **Ethics.** Most people agree that we should behave ethically. That is, we should follow a system of moral principles that direct our everyday lives. However, for any given circumstance, people often do not agree on the ethics of the situation. Throughout this book you will find numerous Ethics boxes posing a variety of different ethical/unethical situations for your consideration.

- **Tips.** We all can benefit from a few tips or suggestions. Throughout this book you will find numerous Tips to make your computing safer, more efficient, and more effective. These tips range from the basics of keeping your computer system running smoothly to how to protect your privacy while

Application	Description
Twitter	Create and use your own microblog to communicate with friends and family. See page 44.
Digital Video Editing	Create, edit, and distribute your own movies. See page 112.
Virus Protection and Internet Security	Protect your computer from catching viruses and from being taken over and controlled by outside forces. See page 150.
E-book	Download and read electronic books using one of the most widely used e-book readers. See page 213.
Cloud Storage	Share large files easily and efficiently with others using the Internet and cloud storage. See page 242.

Figure 1-3 Making IT Work for You applications

To see additional applications, visit our Web site at www.computing2013.com and enter the keyword MIW.

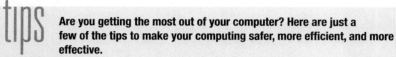

tips

Are you getting the most out of your computer? Here are just a few of the tips to make your computing safer, more efficient, and more effective.

1 **Online shopping.** Have you ever bought anything online? If not, it's likely that in the future you will join the millions who have. Consider a few guidelines to make your shopping easier and safer. See page 49.

2 **Creating and updating Web sites.** Are you thinking about creating your own Web site? Perhaps you already have one and would like to spruce it up a bit. Here are a few suggestions that might help. See page 118.

3 **Buying a new computer.** Are you considering a netbook or notebook? If so, then your decision will most likely be affected by many factors. Here are some to consider. See page 166.

4 **Improving hard-disk performance.** Does your internal hard-disk drive run a lot and seem slow? Are you having problems with lost or corrupted files? To clean up the disk and speed up access, consider defragging. See page 236.

5 **Protecting your privacy.** Are you concerned about your privacy while on the Web? Consider some suggestions for protecting your identity online. See page 41.

To see additional tips, visit our Web site at www.computing2013.com and enter the keyword tips.

Figure 1-4 Selected tips

surfing the Web. For a partial list of the Tips presented in the following chapters, see Figure 1-4. For a complete list, visit our Web site at www .computing2013.com.

- **Careers in IT.** One of the most important decisions of your life is to decide upon your life's work or career. Perhaps you are planning to be a writer, an artist, or an engineer. Or you might become a professional in information technology. Each of the following chapters highlights a specific career in information technology. This feature provides job descriptions, projected employment demands, educational requirements, current salary ranges, and advancement opportunities.

- **Computing Essentials Web site.** Throughout the text you will find numerous text references to the Computing Essentials Web site at www. computing2013.com. This site is carefully integrated with the textbook. At the site, you'll find animations, career information, tips, test review materials, and much more.

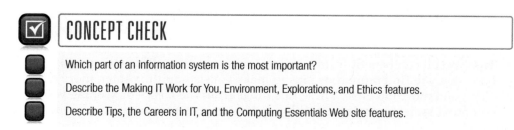

CONCEPT CHECK

Which part of an information system is the most important?

Describe the Making IT Work for You, Environment, Explorations, and Ethics features.

Describe Tips, the Careers in IT, and the Computing Essentials Web site features.

Software

Software, as we mentioned, is another name for programs. Programs are the instructions that tell the computer how to process data into the form you want. In most cases, the words *software* and *programs* are interchangeable. There are two major kinds of software: *system software* and *application software*. You can think of application software as the kind you use. Think of system software as the kind the computer uses.

System Software

The user interacts primarily with application software. **System software** enables the application software to interact with the computer hardware. System software is "background" software that helps the computer manage its own internal resources.

System software is not a single program. Rather it is a collection of programs, including the following:

- **Operating systems** are programs that coordinate computer resources, provide an interface between users and the computer, and run applications. Windows 7, Windows 8, and the Mac OS X are two of the best-known operating systems for today's microcomputer users. (See Figure 1-5 and Figure 1-6.)
- **Utilities** perform specific tasks related to managing computer resources. For example, the Windows utility called Disk Defragmenter locates and eliminates unnecessary file fragments and rearranges files and unused disk space to optimize computer operations.
- **Device drivers** are specialized programs designed to allow particular input or output devices to communicate with the rest of the computer system.

Application Software

Application software might be described as end user software. These programs can be categorized as either *basic* or *specialized applications*.

Basic applications are widely used in nearly all career areas. They are the kinds of programs you have to know to be considered computer competent.

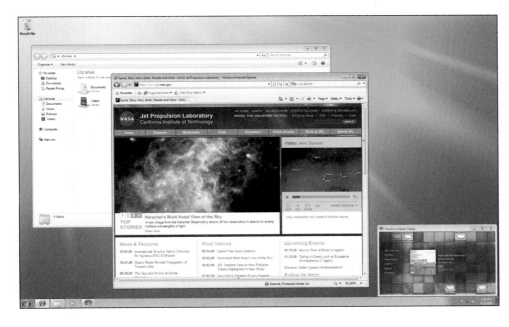

Figure 1-5 Windows 7 operating system

Figure 1-6 Mac OS X operating system

Type	Description
Browsers	Connect to Web sites and display Web pages
Word processors	Prepare written documents
Spreadsheets	Analyze and summarize numerical data
Database management systems	Organize and manage data and information
Presentation graphics	Communicate a message or persuade other people

Figure 1-7 Basic applications

One of these basic applications is a browser to navigate, explore, and find information on the Internet. The three most widely used browsers are Mozilla's Firefox, Microsoft's Internet Explorer, and Google's Chrome. For a summary of the basic applications, see Figure 1-7.

Specialized applications include thousands of other programs that are more narrowly focused on specific disciplines and occupations. Some of the best known are graphics, audio, video, multimedia, Web authoring, artificial intelligence programs, and mobile apps.

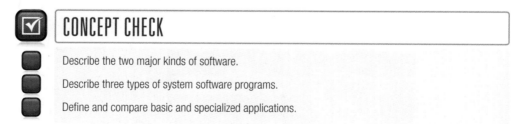

CONCEPT CHECK

Describe the two major kinds of software.

Describe three types of system software programs.

Define and compare basic and specialized applications.

Hardware

Computers are electronic devices that can follow instructions to accept input, process that input, and produce information. This book focuses principally on microcomputers. However, it is almost certain that you will come in contact, at least indirectly, with other types of computers.

Types of Computers

There are four types of computers: supercomputers, mainframe computers, minicomputers, and microcomputers.

- **Supercomputers** are the most powerful type of computer. These machines are special high-capacity computers used by very large organizations. Fujitsu's K computer is one of the fastest computers in the world. (See Figure 1-8.)
- **Mainframe computers** occupy specially wired, air-conditioned rooms. Although not nearly as powerful as supercomputers, mainframe computers are capable of great processing speeds and data storage. For example, insurance companies use mainframes to process information about millions of policyholders.
- **Minicomputers,** also known as **midrange computers,** are refrigerator-sized machines. Medium-sized companies or departments of large companies typically use them for specific purposes. For example, production departments use minicomputers to monitor certain manufacturing processes and assembly-line operations.
- **Microcomputers** are the least powerful, yet the most widely used and fastest-growing type of computer. There are six types of microcomputers: *desktop, media center, notebook, tablet PC, netbook,* and *handheld computers.* (See Figure 1-9.) **Desktop computers** are small enough to fit on top of or alongside a desk yet are too big to carry around. **Media centers** blur the line between desktop computers and dedicated entertainment devices. **Notebook computers,** also known as **laptop computers,** are portable, lightweight, and fit into most briefcases. There are two types of **tablet PCs.** The **traditional tablet PC** is effectively a notebook computer that accepts stylus input. The newer type of tablet PC is sometimes referred to as a **slate computer**. This computer's system unit is a thin slab that is almost all monitor. The best known tablet PCs are Apple's iPad, Motorola's Zoom, and Samsung's Galaxy Tab. **Netbooks** are smaller, lighter, and less expensive than notebook computers. **Handheld computers** are the smallest and are designed to fit into the palm of one hand. These systems contain an entire computer system, including the electronic components, secondary storage,

environment

Did you know that the average American will own nearly 20 computers in his or her lifetime? This means not only will you purchase 20 computers for your use, but you will also discard at least that number. The disposal of old machines is becoming a great concern to communities across the globe, as many machines contain potentially toxic materials. What can you do to responsibly dispose of old technology? Many states now require manufacturers to recycle old machines, so contact them first. If no opportunity is available through the manufacturer, check with your local recycling center, or go online to find a reputable recycling company. To see more environmental facts, visit our Web site at www.computing2013.com.

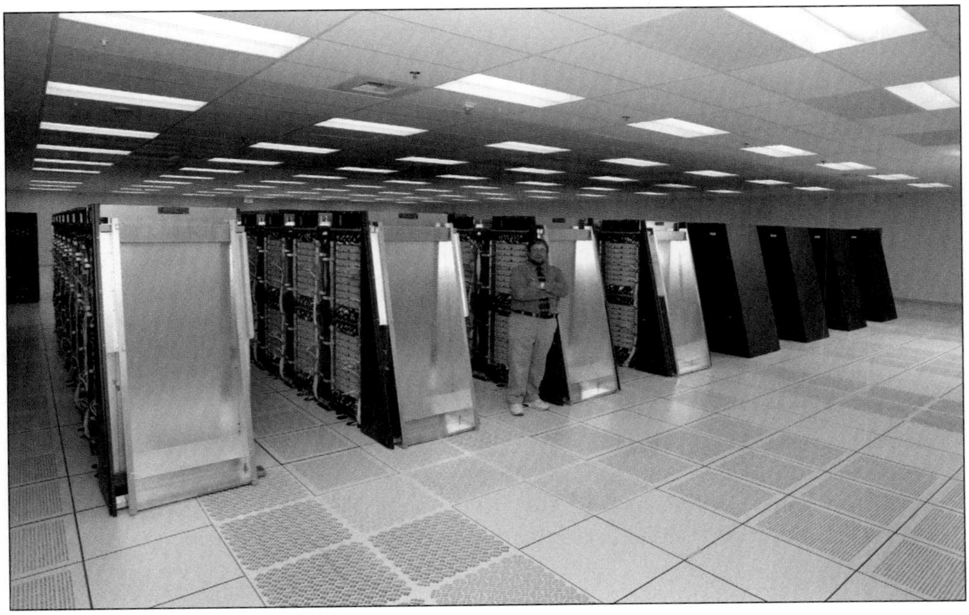

Figure 1-8 IBM's Blue Gene supercomputer

Desktop   **Notebook**   **Media Center**

Tablet PC   **Handheld**   **Netbook**

Figure 1-9 Microcomputers

and input and output devices. **Personal digital assistants (PDAs)** and **smartphones** are the most widely used handheld computers. Smartphones are cell phones with wireless connections to the Internet. Their growth has been explosive in the past few years.

Microcomputer Hardware

Hardware for a microcomputer system consists of a variety of different devices. See Figure 1-10 for a typical desktop system. This physical equipment falls into four basic categories: system unit, input/output, secondary storage, and communication. Because we discuss hardware in detail later in this book, here we will present just a quick overview of the four basic categories.

- **System unit:** The **system unit** is a container that houses most of the electronic components that make up a computer system. Two important components of the system unit are the *microprocessor* and *memory*. (See Figure 1-11.) The **microprocessor** controls and manipulates data to produce information. **Memory** is a holding area for data, instructions, and information. One type, **random-access memory (RAM),** holds the program and data that is currently being processed. This type of memory is sometimes referred to as *temporary storage* because its contents will typically be lost if the electrical power to the computer is disrupted.

- **Input/output: Input devices** translate data and programs that humans can understand into a form that the computer can process. The most common input devices are the **keyboard** and the **mouse. Output devices** translate the processed information from the computer into a form that humans can understand. The most common output devices are **monitors** (see Figure 1-12) and **printers.**

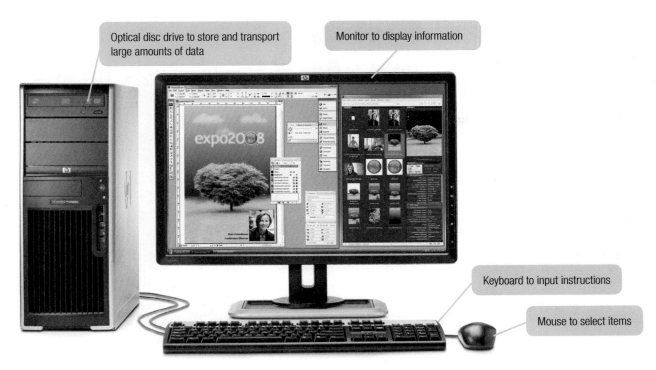

Optical disc drive to store and transport large amounts of data

Monitor to display information

expo2008

Keyboard to input instructions

Mouse to select items

Figure 1-10 **Microcomputer system**

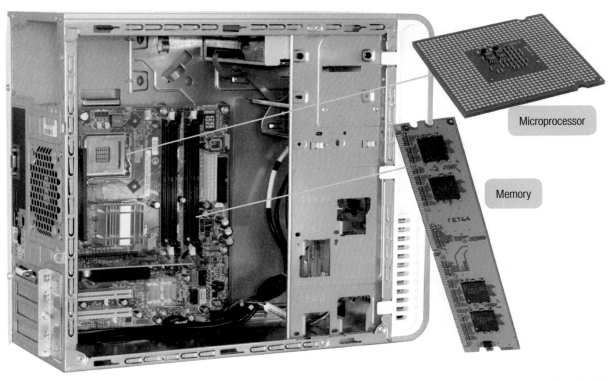

Microprocessor

Memory

Figure 1-11 **System unit**

- **Secondary storage:** Unlike memory, **secondary storage** holds data and programs even after electrical power to the computer system has been turned off. The most important kinds of secondary media are *hard disks, solid-state storage,* and *optical discs.* **Hard disks** are typically used to

Figure 1-12 **Monitor**

Figure 1-13 **Optical disc**

store programs and very large data files. Using rigid metallic platters and read/write heads that move across the platters, data and information are stored using magnetic charges on the disk's surface. In contrast, **solid-state storage** does not have any moving parts, is more reliable, and requires less power. It saves data and information electronically similar to RAM except that it is not volatile. Three types are **solid-state drives (SSDs)** that are used much the same way as an internal hard disk, **flash memory cards** that are widely used in portable devices, and **USB drives** that are a widely used compact storage medium for transporting data and information between computers and a variety of specialty devices. **Optical discs** use laser technology and have the greatest capacity. (See Figure 1-13.) Three types of optical discs are **compact discs (CDs), digital versatile** (or **video**) **discs (DVDs),** and **high-definition (hi def) discs.**

- **Communication:** At one time, it was uncommon for a microcomputer system to communicate with other computer systems. Now, using **communication devices,** a microcomputer can communicate with other computer systems located as near as the next office or as far away as halfway around the world, using the Internet. The most widely used communication device is a **modem,** which modifies telephone communications into a form that can be processed by a computer. Modems also modify computer output into a form that can be transmitted across standard telephone lines.

 ## CONCEPT CHECK

 What are the four types of computers?

 Describe the six types of microcomputers.

 Describe the four basic categories of microcomputer hardware.

Data

Data is raw, unprocessed facts, including text, numbers, images, and sounds. As we mentioned earlier, processed data becomes information. When stored electronically in files, data can be used directly as input for the system unit.

Four common types of files (see Figure 1-14) are

- **Document files,** created by word processors to save documents such as memos, term papers, and letters.
- **Worksheet files,** created by electronic spreadsheets to analyze things like budgets and to predict sales.
- **Database files,** typically created by database management programs to contain highly structured and organized data. For example, an employee database file might contain all the workers' names, Social Security numbers, job titles, and other related pieces of information.
- **Presentation files,** created by presentation graphics programs to save presentation materials. For example, a file might contain audience handouts, speaker notes, and electronic slides.

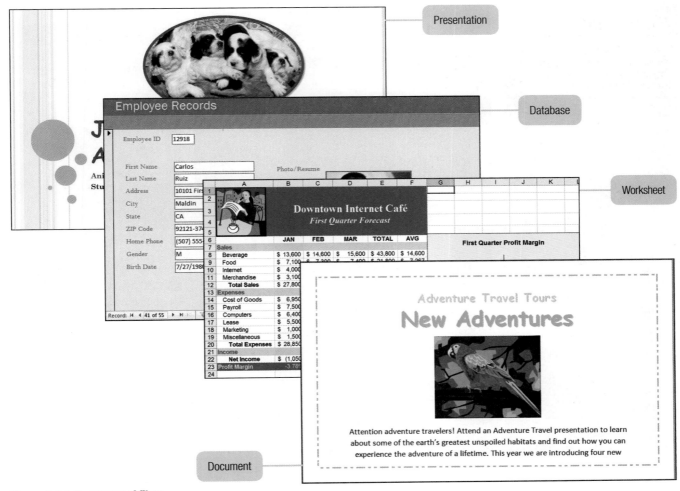

Figure 1-14 Four types of files: presentation, database, worksheet, and document

Connectivity, the Wireless Revolution, the Internet, and Cloud Computing

Connectivity is the capability of your microcomputer to share information with other computers. The two most dramatic changes in connectivity in the past five years have been the widespread use of mobile or wireless communication devices and cloud computing. For just a few of these mobile devices, see Figure 1-15. Many experts predict that these wireless applications are just the beginning of the **wireless revolution,** a revolution that will dramatically affect the way we communicate and use computer technology.

Central to the concept of connectivity is the **network.** A network is a communications system connecting two or more computers. The largest network in the world is the **Internet.** It is like a giant highway that connects you to

Figure 1-15 Wireless communication devices

millions of other people and organizations located throughout the world. The **Web** provides a multimedia interface to the numerous resources available on the Internet. **Cloud computing** uses the Internet and the Web to shift many computer activities from a user's computer to computers on the Internet. The wireless revolution and cloud computing promise the potential to dramatically affect the entire computer industry and how you and I will interact with computers. Each will be discussed in detail in the following chapters.

 CONCEPT CHECK

 Define data. List four common types of files.

 Define connectivity and the wireless revolution.

What is a network? Describe the Internet, Web, and cloud computing.

Careers in IT

As mentioned previously, each of the following chapters highlights a specific career in information technology. Each provides specific job descriptions, salary ranges, advancement opportunities, and more. For a partial list of these careers, see Figure 1-16. For a complete list, visit our Web site at www.computing2013.com and enter the keyword **careers**.

Now that you know the basic outline and important features of this book, I'd like to talk about some of the most exciting and well-paid careers in information technology.

Career	Description
Webmaster	Develops and maintains Web sites and Web resources. See page 57.
Computer trainer	Instructs end users on the latest software or hardware. See page 94.
Desktop publisher	Creates and formats publication-ready books, magazines, newsletters, and newspapers. See page 122.
Computer support specialist	Provides technical support to customers and other users. See page 152.
Computer technician	Repairs and installs computer components and systems. See page 184.
Technical writer	Prepares instruction manuals, technical reports, and other scientific or technical documents. See page 219.
Software engineer	Analyzes users' needs and creates application software. See page 246.
Network administrator	Creates and maintains computer networks. See page 279.

Figure 1-16 Careers in information technology

A LOOK TO THE FUTURE

Using and Understanding Information Technology Means Being Computer Competent

The purpose of this book is to help you use and understand information technology. We want to help you become computer competent in today's world and to provide you with a foundation of knowledge so that you can understand how technology is being used today and anticipate how technology will be used in the future. This will enable you to benefit from six important information technology developments.

The Internet and the Web

The Internet and the Web are considered by most to be the two most important technologies for the 21st century. Understanding how to efficiently and effectively use the Internet to browse the Web, communicate with others, and locate information are indispensable computer competencies. These issues are presented in Chapter 2, The Internet, the Web, and Electronic Commerce.

Powerful Software

The software that is now available can do an extraordinary number of tasks and help you in an endless number of ways. You can create professional-looking documents, analyze massive amounts of data, create dynamic multimedia Web pages, and much more. Today's employers are expecting the people they hire to be able to effectively and efficiently use a variety of different types of software. Basic and specialized applications are presented in Chapters 3 and 4. System software is presented in Chapter 5.

Powerful Hardware

Microcomputers are now much more powerful than they used to be. New communication technologies such as wireless networks are dramatically changing the ways to connect to other computers, networks, and the Internet. However, despite the rapid change of specific equipment, their essential features remain unchanged. Thus, the competent end user should focus on these features. Chapters 6 through 9 explain what you need to know about hardware. A Buyer's Guide and an Upgrader's Guide are presented at the end of this book for those considering the purchase or upgrade of a microcomputer system.

Security and Privacy

What about people? Experts agree that we as a society must be careful about the potential of technology to negatively impact our personal privacy and security. Additionally, we need to be aware of potential physical and mental health risks associated with using technology. Finally, we need to be aware of negative effects on our environment caused by the manufacture of computer-related products. Thus, Chapter 10 explores each of these critical issues in detail.

Organizations

Almost all organizations rely on the quality and flexibility of their information systems to stay competitive. As a member or employee of an organization, you will undoubtedly be involved in these information systems. In order to use, develop, modify, and maintain these systems, you need to understand the basic concepts of information systems and know how to safely, efficiently, and effectively use computers. These concepts are covered throughout this book.

Changing Times

Are the times changing any faster now than they ever have? Almost everyone thinks so. Whatever the answer, it is clear we live in a fast-paced age. The Evolution of the Computer Age section presented at the end of this book tracks the major developments since computers were first introduced.

After reading this book, you will be in a very favorable position compared with many other people in industry today. You not only will learn the basics of hardware, software, connectivity, the Internet, and the Web, but you also will learn the most current technology. You will be able to use these tools to your advantage.

INFORMATION SYSTEMS

The way to think about a microcomputer is to realize that it is one part of an **information system.** There are five parts of an information system:

1. **People** are an essential part of the system. The purpose of information systems is to make people, or **end users** like you, more productive.

2. **Procedures** are rules or guidelines to follow when using software, hardware, and data. They are typically documented in manuals written by computer professionals.

3. **Software (programs)** provides step-by-step instructions to control the computer to convert **data** into **information.**

4. **Hardware** consists of the physical equipment. It is controlled by software and processes data to create information.

5. **Data** consists of unprocessed facts including text, numbers, images, and sound. **Information** is data that has been processed by the computer.

Connectivity is an additional part to today's information systems. It allows computers to connect and share information. To be computer competent, end users need to understand **information technology (IT).**

PEOPLE

People are the most important part of an information system. This book contains several features to demonstrate how people just like you use computers. These features include the following:

- **Making IT Work for You** presents several interesting and practical applications. Topics include using digital video editing and locating job opportunities.

- **Explorations** direct you to important information and Web sites that relate to computers and technology.

- **Environment** discusses important and relevant environmental issues. The impact of computers and other technologies is more critical today than ever before.

- **Ethics** boxes pose a variety of different ethical/unethical situations for your consideration.

- **Tips** offer a variety of suggestions on such practical matters as how to improve slow computer performance and how to protect your privacy while on the Web.

- **Careers in IT** presents job descriptions, employment demands, educational requirements, salary ranges, and advancement opportunities.

- **Computing Essentials Web site** integrates the textbook with information on the Web including animations, career information, tips, test review materials, and much more.

To prepare for your future as a competent end user, you need to understand the basic parts of an information system: people, procedures, software, hardware, and data. Also you need to understand connectivity through the Internet and the Web and to recognize the role of technology in your professional and personal life.

SOFTWARE

Software, or **programs**, consists of system and application software.

System Software

System software enables application software to interact with computer hardware. It consists of a variety of programs:

- **Operating systems** coordinate resources, provide an interface for users and computer hardware, and run applications. Windows 7 and Mac OS X are the best-known microcomputer operating systems.
- **Utilities** perform specific tasks to manage computer resources.
- **Device drivers** are specialized programs to allow input and output devices to communicate with the rest of the computer system.

Application Software

Application software includes basic and specialized applications.

- **Basic applications** are widely used in nearly all career areas. Programs include browsers, word processors, spreadsheets, database management systems, and presentation graphics.
- **Specialized applications** focus on specific disciplines and occupations. These programs include graphics, audio, video, multimedia, Web authoring, and artificial intelligence programs.

HARDWARE

Hardware consists of electronic devices that can follow instructions to accept input, process the input, and produce information.

Types of Computers

Supercomputer, mainframe, minicomputer (midrange), and **microcomputer** are four types of computers. Microcomputers can be **desktop, media center, notebook (laptop computer), tablet PC (traditional** and **slate), netbook,** or **handheld** (**PDAs** and **smartphones** are the most widely used handheld microcomputers).

Microcomputer Hardware

There are four basic categories of hardware devices.

- **System unit** contains electronic circuitry, including the **microprocessor** and **memory**. **Random-access memory (RAM)** holds the program and data currently being processed.
- **Input/output devices** are translators between humans and computers. **Input devices** include the **keyboard** and **mouse. Output devices** include **monitors** and **printers.**
- **Secondary storage** holds data and programs. Typical media include **hard disks, solid-state storage (solid-state drives, flash memory cards,** and **USB drives),** and **optical discs** (**CD, DVD,** and **hi def**).
- **Communication devices** allow microcomputers to communicate with other computer systems. **Modems** modify output for transmission.

DATA

Data are the raw unprocessed facts about something. Common file types include

- **Document files** created by word processors.

- **Worksheet files** created by spreadsheet programs.

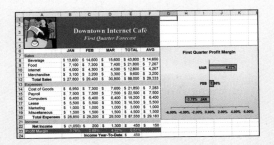

- **Database files** created by database management programs.

- **Presentation files** created by presentation graphics programs.

CONNECTIVITY AND THE INTERNET

Connectivity

Connectivity describes the ability of end users to use resources well beyond their desktops.

The Wireless Revolution

The **wireless revolution** is the widespread and increasing use of mobile (wireless) communication devices.

Internet

The **Internet** is the world's largest computer **network**. The **Web** provides a multimedia interface to resources available on the Internet.

Cloud Computing

Cloud computing uses the Internet and the Web to shift many activities from users' computers to computers on the Internet.

CAREERS IN IT

Career	Description
Webmaster	Develops and maintains Web sites and Web resources. See page 57.
Computer trainer	Instructs end users on the latest software or hardware. See page 94.
Desktop publisher	Creates and formats publication-ready books, magazines, newsletters, and newspapers. See page 122.
Computer support specialist	Provides technical support to customers and other users. See page 152.
Computer technician	Repairs and installs computer components and systems. See page 184.
Technical writer	Prepares instruction manuals, technical reports, and other scientific or technical documents. See page 219.
Software engineer	Analyzes users' needs and creates application software. See page 246.
Network administrator	Creates and maintains computer networks. See page 279.

KEY TERMS

application software (9)
basic application (9)
cloud computing (17)
communication device (14)
compact disc (CD) (14)
computer competency (4)
connectivity (6, 16)
data (6)
database file (15)
desktop computer (11)
device driver (9)
digital versatile disc (DVD) (14)
digital video disc (DVD) (14)
document file (15)
end user (5)
flash memory card (14)
handheld computer (11)
hard disk (13)
hardware (6)
high-definition (hi def) disc (14)
information (6)
information system (5)
information technology (IT) (6)
input device (12)
Internet (16)
keyboard (12)
laptop computer (11)
mainframe computer (11)
media center (11)
memory (12)
microcomputer (11)
microprocessor (12)
midrange computer (11)
minicomputer (11)

modem (14)
monitor (12)
mouse (12)
netbook (11)
network (16)
notebook computer (11)
operating system (9)
optical disc (14)
output device (12)
people (5)
personal digital assistant (PDA) (12)
presentation file (15)
printer (12)
procedures (5)
program (6)
random-access memory (RAM) (12)
secondary storage (13)
slate computer (11)
smartphone (12)
software (6)
solid-state drive (SSD) (14)
solid-state storage (14)
specialized application (10)
supercomputer (11)
system software (9)
system unit (12)
tablet PC (11)
traditional tablet PC (11)
USB drive (14)
utility (9)
Web (17)
wireless revolution (16)
worksheet file (15)

To test your knowledge of these key terms with animated flash cards, visit our Web site at www.computing2013.com and enter the keyword terms1.

MULTIPLE CHOICE

Circle the letter of the correct answer.

1. The keyboard, mouse, monitor, and system unit are:
   - **a.** hardware
   - **b.** output devices
   - **c.** storage devices
   - **d.** software

2. Programs that coordinate computer resources, provide an interface, and run applications are known as:
   - **a.** application programs
   - **b.** operating systems
   - **c.** storage systems
   - **d.** utility programs

3. A browser is an example of a:
   - **a.** basic application
   - **b.** specialized program
   - **c.** system application
   - **d.** utility program

4. Although not as powerful as a supercomputer, this type of computer is capable of great processing speeds and data storage.
   - **a.** mainframe
   - **b.** media center
   - **c.** midrange
   - **d.** netbook

5. The smallest type of microcomputer:
   - **a.** netbook
   - **b.** handheld
   - **c.** midrange
   - **d.** tablet PC

6. RAM is a type of:
   - **a.** computer
   - **b.** memory
   - **c.** network
   - **d.** secondary storage

7. Unlike memory, this type of storage holds data and programs even after electrical power to the computer system has been turned off.
   - **a.** primary
   - **b.** RAM
   - **c.** ROM
   - **d.** secondary

8. The type of file created by word processors to save, for example, memos, term papers, and letters.
   - **a.** database
   - **b.** document
   - **c.** presentation
   - **d.** worksheet

9. The change in connectivity that uses the Internet and the Web to shift many computer activities from a user's computer to computers on the Internet.
   - **a.** cloud computing
   - **b.** high definition
   - **c.** network
   - **d.** USB

10. The largest network in the world is [the]:
    - **a.** Facebook
    - **b.** Internet
    - **c.** Web
    - **d.** USB

For an interactive multiple-choice practice test, visit our Web site at www.computing2013.com and enter the keyword multiple1.

MATCHING

Match each numbered item with the most closely related lettered item. Write your answers in the spaces provided.

a. desktop
b. modem
c. network
d. output
e. presentation
f. program
g. software
h. solid-state
i. system software
j. system unit

_____ 1. Consists of the step-by-step instructions that tell the computer how to do its work.
_____ 2. Another name for a program.
_____ 3. Enables the application software to interact with the computer hardware.
_____ 4. Type of computer that is small enough to fit on top of or alongside a desk yet is too big to carry around.
_____ 5. A container that houses most of the electronic components that make up a computer system.
_____ 6. Devices that translate the processed information from the computer into a form that humans can understand.
_____ 7. Unlike hard disks, this type of storage does not have any moving parts, is more reliable, and requires less power.
_____ 8. The most widely used communication device.
_____ 9. A type of a file that might contain, for example, audience handouts, speaker notes, and electronic slides.
_____10. A communications system connecting two or more computers.

For an interactive matching practice test, visit our Web site at www.computing2013.com and enter the keyword matching1.

OPEN-ENDED

On a separate sheet of paper, respond to each question or statement.

1. Explain the five parts of an information system. What part do people play in this system?
2. What is system software? What kinds of programs are included in system software?
3. Define and compare basic and specialized application software. Describe some different types of basic applications. Describe some types of specialized applications.
4. Describe the different types of computers. What is the most common type? What are the types of microcomputers?
5. What is connectivity? What are wireless devices and the wireless revolution? What is a computer network? What are the Internet and the Web? What is cloud computing?

MAKING IT WORK FOR YOU

Making IT Work for You questions are designed to demonstrate ways that you can effectively use technology today.

Making a habit of keeping current with technology trends is a key to your success with information technology. In each of this book's chapters, the Making IT Work for You feature will present questions designed to help you gain a better understanding of how technology is being used today.

Some of the Making IT Work for You topics are listed below. Select the two that you find the most interesting and then describe why they are of interest to you and how you might use (or are using) those applications.

① IPODS AND VIDEO FROM THE INTERNET

Did you know that you could use the Internet to locate movies and television shows, download them to your computer, and transfer them to a portable media player to watch on the go? All it takes is the right software and hardware and a connection to the Internet. See Making IT Work for You: iPODs and Video from the Internet on page 34.

② GOOGLE DOCS

Do you need to collaborate with others on a document, presentation, or spreadsheet? Do you need access to a document from both home and school? Would you like to try a free alternative to traditional office software suites? If so, a cloud office suite might be for you. Online office suites such as Google Docs allow you to create and edit documents directly though a Web page with no additional software to install on your computer. See Making IT Work for You: Google Docs on pages 92 and 93.

③ DIGITAL VIDEO EDITING

Want to make your own movie? Would you like to edit some home movies and distribute them to family and friends on DVDs? It's easy with the right equipment and software. See Making IT Work for You: Digital Video Editing on pages 112 and 113.

④ VIRUS PROTECTION

Are you worried that a computer virus will erase your personal files? Did you know that others could be intercepting your private e-mail? It is even possible for others to gain access to and control over your computer system. Fortunately, Internet security suites are available to help ensure your safety while you are on the Internet. See Making IT Work for You: Virus Protection and Internet Security on pages 150 and 151.

⑤ HOME NETWORKING

Computer networks are not just for corporations and schools anymore. If you have more than one computer, you can use a wireless home network to share files and printers, to allow multiple users access to the Internet at the same time, and to play interactive computer games. See Making IT Work for You: Home Networking on pages 274 and 275.

EXPLORATIONS

Explorations questions are designed to add depth and detail to your understanding of specific topics presented within this chapter. The questions direct you to sources other than the textbook to obtain this knowledge.

A deeper knowledge of select topics can greatly enhance your understanding of information technology. In each of the following chapters, the Explorations feature presents questions designed to help you gain a deeper understanding of select topics.

Select the two topics that you find the most interesting and then describe why they are of interest to you and why they are important.

1 HOW COMPUTER VIRUS PROTECTION PROGRAMS WORK

Computer viruses are destructive and dangerous programs that can migrate through networks and operating systems. They often attach themselves to other programs, e-mail messages, and databases. It is essential to protect your computer systems from computer viruses. Visit our Web site at www.computing2013.com and enter the keyword virus.

2 HOW DIGITAL CAMERAS WORK

While traditional cameras capture images on film, digital cameras capture images and convert them into a digital form. These images can be viewed immediately and saved to a disk or into the camera's memory. Visit our Web site at www.computing2013.com and enter the keyword photo.

3 HOW INTERNET TELEPHONES WORK

Internet telephones offer a low-cost alternative to making long-distance calls. Using an Internet telephone (or other appropriate audio input and output devices), the Internet, a special service provider, a sound card, and special software, you can place long-distance calls to almost anywhere in the world. Visit our Web site at www.computing2013.com and enter the keyword phone.

4 HOW WIRELESS HOME NETWORKS WORK

Wireless home networks are becoming very popular. They are easy to set up and use. They allow different computers to share resources including a common Internet connection and printer. Visit our Web site at www.computing2013.com and enter the keyword network.

ETHICS

The following questions are designed to explore ethical issues related to technology and to develop the ability to think critically and communicate effectively. Respond to the questions by either creating a one-page paper or preparing for an in-depth classroom discussion.

In each of the following chapters, this Ethics feature will propose ethical questions for your consideration. In addition to exploring critical ethical issues, these ques-

tions are designed to help you develop critical thinking, analysis, and writing skills. Some of the topics are listed below. Select two that you find the most interesting and then describe why they are of interest to you.

1 DIGITAL PHOTO MANIPULATION

Image editing software has made it easy to alter photographs, which in the past were accepted as visual records of real events. In some cases, the purpose of digital editing is humor and exaggeration, while other times subtle changes are used to alter a photo's deeper meaning. Some caution that "seeing is believing" needs to be reconsidered for the digital age and argue that ethical standards need to be clearly established for photo manipulation. See page 132.

2 WEBCAMS

WebCams are almost everywhere, from dorm rooms to parking lots. They are used to communicate face-to-face with friends and family, to catch car thieves, and for any number of other applications. While acknowledging the many very positive applications of WebCams, some argue that their widespread and uncontrolled use has too many cases involving the loss of personal privacy. See page 207.

3 ELECTRONIC MONITORING

Surveillance of individuals occurs more frequently today than ever before. For example, the FBI has proposed the widespread use of a technology known as Carnivore to help them track terrorists. This technology supports widespread monitoring of individual Internet activity and e-mail. Privacy advocates claim that this would be an unnecessary and unneeded invasion of personal privacy. Others believe electronic surveillance is essential to protect national security. See page 289.

ENVIRONMENT

We can all agree that protecting our environment today is more important than ever before. In addition to the Environment boxes located throughout this book, each chapter ends with this Environment feature. This feature will propose environmental questions for your consideration.

In addition to exploring environmental issues, these questions are designed to help you develop critical thinking, analysis, and writing skills. Some of the topics are listed below. Select two that you find the most interesting and then describe why they are of interest to you.

1 SPAM

Spam is any unwelcome and unsolicited e-mail. You may be aware that spam e-mail is often the source of many computer viruses. But did you know that spam also hurts the environment by consuming as much energy as a million cars each year? See page 69.

2 DOWNLOADING MUSIC

Movies, music, instruction manuals, and software programs are typically sold or distributed on CDs and DVDs. In most cases, however, you could use the Internet to receive this content. A recent study by Microsoft concluded that directly downloading music would reduce CO_2 emissions by 80 percent. See page 105.

3 ENVIRONMENTAL UTILITY SOFTWARE

Utility software are programs that typically focus on making computers run safer and easier. Now, many are also looking for ways to make computing more environmentally friendly. These programs automatically monitor computer use and collect data on energy consumption. The programs then analyze the data to determine ways to minimize your computer's energy requirements. See page 105.

4 ROBOTS

Robots are computer-controlled machines that mimic the motor activities of living things. They have been traditionally used to perform a wide range of activities ranging from industrial applications to performing routine household tasks. Now, they are being used to roam the ocean bottom looking for and collecting garbage, oil, and other pollutants. See page 133.

NOTES

The Internet, the Web, and Electronic Commerce

▲ Download the free *Computing Essentials 2013* app for videos, key term flashcards, quizzes, and the game, *Over the Edge!*

Competencies

After you have read this chapter, you should be able to:

1   Discuss the origins of the Internet and the Web.

2   Describe how to access the Web using providers and browsers.

3   Discuss Internet communications, including e-mail, instant messaging, social networking, blogs, microblogs, Webcasts, podcasts, and wikis.

4   Describe search tools, including search engines, Web directories, metasearch engines, and specialized search engines.

5   Evaluate the accuracy of information presented on the Web.

6   Discuss electronic commerce, including B2C, C2C, B2B, and security issues.

7   Describe cloud computing, including the three-way interaction of clients, Internet, and service providers.

8   Describe Web utilities including plug-ins, filters, file transfer utilities, and Internet security suites.

Why should I read this chapter?

The beginning of the Internet can be traced to 1969 when mainframe computers located in different parts of the United States were linked to one another. It was used exclusively to facilitate communication between researchers and was limited to text. That was then and this is now. Now, Internet technologies like Facebook, Twitter, LinkedIn, and cloud computing are changing the way the world works and the way you interact with the world.

This chapter discusses these technologies including the Web; wireless Internet access; and social networking including MySpace, Facebook, and LinkedIn. Additionally, you'll learn about webcasts, streaming technology, podcasts, Twitter, cloud computing, and much more. To be competent and to be competitive in today's professional workplace, you need to know and understand these things.

chapter 2

Hi, I'm Sue, and I'm a Webmaster. I'd like to talk with you about the Internet, the Web, and electronic commerce, things that touch our lives every day. I'd also like to talk with you about the role the Internet plays with Facebook, Twitter, LinkedIn, and cloud computing.

 Explorations

Many individuals and institutions played a part in the development of the Internet and the Web.

To learn more about the history of the Internet and Web, visit our site at www. computing2013.com and enter the keyword history.

Introduction

Want to communicate with a friend across town, in another state, or even in another country? Looking for a long-lost friend? Looking for travel or entertainment information? Perhaps you're researching a term paper or exploring different career paths. Where do you start? For these and other information-related activities, most people use the Internet and the Web.

The Internet is often referred to as the Information Superhighway. In a sense, it is like a highway that connects you to millions of other people and organizations. Unlike typical highways that move people and things from one location to another, the Internet moves your ideas and information. The Web provides an easy-to-use, intuitive, multimedia interface to resources available on the Internet. It has become an everyday tool for all of us to use.

Competent end users need to be aware of the resources available on the Internet and the Web. Additionally, they need to know how to access these resources, to effectively communicate electronically, to efficiently locate information, to understand electronic commerce, and to use Web utilities.

The Internet and the Web

As mentioned earlier, the **Internet** was launched in 1969 when the United States funded a project that developed a national computer network called **Advanced Research Project Agency Network (ARPANET).** The Internet is a large network that connects together smaller networks all over the globe. The **Web** was introduced in 1991 at the **Center for European Nuclear Research (CERN)** in Switzerland. Prior to the Web, the Internet was all text—no graphics, animations, sound, or video. The Web made it possible to include these elements. It provided a multimedia interface to resources available on the Internet.

The first generation of the Web, known as **Web 1.0,** focused on linking existing information. In 2001, the second generation, **Web 2.0,** evolved to support more dynamic content creation and social interaction. Facebook is one of the best known Web 2.0 applications. Some suggest that we have entered into the next generation, **Web 3.0.** It focuses on computer-generated information requiring less human interaction to locate and to integrate information.

It is easy to get the Internet and the Web confused, but they are not the same thing. The Internet is the actual network. It is made up of wires, cables, satellites, and rules for exchanging information between computers connected to the network. Being connected to this network is often described as being **online.** The Internet connects millions of computers and resources throughout the world. The Web is a multimedia interface to the resources available on the Internet. Every day over a billion users from nearly every country in the world use the Internet and the Web. What are they doing? The most common uses are the following:

- **Communicating** is by far the most popular Internet activity. You can exchange e-mail with your family and friends almost anywhere in the

Figure 2-1 Entertainment site

world. You can join and listen to discussions and debates on a wide variety of special-interest topics.

- **Shopping** is one of the fastest-growing Internet applications. You can window shop, look for the latest fashions, search for bargains, and make purchases.
- **Searching** for information has never been more convenient. You can access some of the world's largest libraries directly from your home computer. You can find the latest local, national, and international news.
- **Education** or **e-learning** is another rapidly emerging Web application. You can take classes on almost any subject. There are courses just for fun and there are courses for high school, college, and graduate school credit. Some cost nothing to take and others cost a lot.
- **Entertainment** options are nearly endless. You can find music, movies, magazines, and computer games. You will find live concerts, movie previews, book clubs, and interactive live games. (See Figure 2-1.) To learn more about entertainment options, see Making IT Work for You: iPods and Video from the Internet on page 34.

The first step to using the Internet and the Web is to get connected, or to gain access to the Internet.

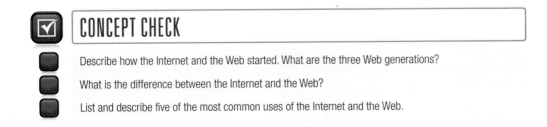

CONCEPT CHECK

Describe how the Internet and the Web started. What are the three Web generations?

What is the difference between the Internet and the Web?

List and describe five of the most common uses of the Internet and the Web.

Making IT work for you

IPODS AND VIDEO FROM THE INTERNET

Did you know you can use the Internet to locate and play movies and television shows? You can even transfer video to a digital media player. All you need is the right software, hardware, and a connection to the Internet.

Finding videos   There are many services on the Internet for finding movies. The first step is to download software that connects with a video service. You can use this software to search for programs and play them. For example, to find television shows using Apple iTunes:

1 ● Visit www.apple.com and follow the on-screen instructions to download and install the iTunes software.

2 ● Start the iTunes application.

● Select *iTunes Store* and browse to find movies or television shows you want to download.

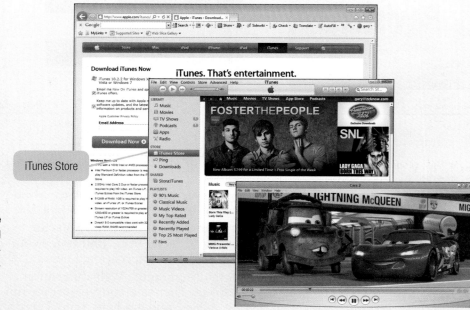

iTunes Store

Purchased movies and shows are automatically downloaded and listed in the *Movies* and *TV Shows* categories of the library. To watch a downloaded video:

3 ● Select *Movies* or *TV Shows* from the Library.

● Double-click the video you want to watch.

Uploading to a Digital Media Player   Another popular way to take your favorite videos with you is to upload them to a digital media player. For example, you could transfer video to an iPod using iTunes software by following the steps below:

1 ● Connect your iPod to your computer. iTunes starts automatically.

● Select your iPod from the *Devices* list.

● Select the *TV Shows* tab and select which programs you would like to transfer to your iPod.

● Click the *Sync* button to transfer your videos.

The Web is continually changing, and some of the specifics presented in this Making IT Work for You may have changed.

To learn about other ways to make information technology work for you, visit our Web site at www.computing2013.com and enter the keyword miw.

Access

The Internet and the telephone system are similar—you can connect a computer to the Internet much like you connect a phone to the telephone system. Once you are on the Internet, your computer becomes an extension of what seems like a giant computer—a computer that branches all over the world. When provided with a connection to the Internet, you can use a browser program to search the Web.

Providers

The most common way to access the Internet is through an **Internet service provider (ISP).** The providers are already connected to the Internet and provide a path or connection for individuals to access the Internet. Your college or university most likely provides you with free access to the Internet. There are also some companies such as Netzero and Juno that offer free Internet access.

The most widely used commercial Internet service providers use telephone lines, cable, and/or wireless connections. Some of the best-known providers are Verizon, AT&T, Sprint, and T-Mobile.

As we will discuss in Chapter 9, users connect to ISPs using one of a variety of connection technologies including **DSL, cable,** and **wireless modems.**

Browsers

Browsers are programs that provide access to Web resources. This software connects you to remote computers, opens and transfers files, displays text, images, and multimedia, and provides in one tool an uncomplicated interface to the Internet and Web documents. Browsers allow you to explore, or to **surf,** the Web by easily moving from one Web site to another. Four well-known browsers are Mozilla Firefox, Apple Safari, Microsoft Internet Explorer, and Google Chrome. (See Figure 2-2.)

Figure 2-2 Browser

Figure 2-3 Basic parts of a URL

For browsers to connect to resources, the **location** or **address** of the resources must be specified. These addresses are called **uniform resource locators (URLs).** All URLs have at least two basic parts. (See Figure 2-3.) The first part presents the protocol used to connect to the resource. As we will discuss in Chapter 9, **protocols** are rules for exchanging data between computers. The protocol *http* is used for Web traffic and is the most widely used Internet protocol. The second part presents the **domain name.** It indicates the specific address where the resource is located. In Figure 2-3 the domain is identified as www.mtv.com. (Many URLs have additional parts specifying directory paths, file names, and pointers.) The last part of the domain name following the dot (.) is the **top-level domain (TLD).** It identifies the type of organization. (See Figure 2-4.) For example, *.com* indicates a commercial site. The URL *http://www.mtv.com* connects your computer to a computer that provides information about MTV.

Domain	Organization Type
.com	Commercial
.edu	Educational
.gov	Government
.mil	U.S. military
.net	Network

Figure 2-4 Top-level domains

Once the browser has connected to the Web site, a document file is sent back to your computer. This document typically contains **Hypertext Markup Language (HTML).** The browser interprets the HTML formatting instructions and displays the document as a **Web page.** For example, when your browser first connects to the Internet, it opens up to a Web page specified in the browser settings. This page presents information about the site along with references and **hyperlinks** or **links** that connect to other documents containing related information—text files, graphic images, audio, and video clips. (See Figure 2-5.)

These documents may be located on a nearby computer system or on one halfway around the world. The links typically appear on the Web page as underlined and colored text and/or images. When your mouse passes over a link, the mouse pointer changes to the shape of a small hand. To access the referenced material, all you do is click on the highlighted text or image. A connection is automatically made to the computer containing the material, and the referenced material appears on your display screen.

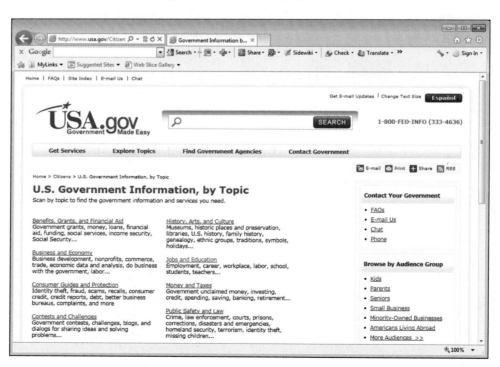

Figure 2-5 Web page

Figure 2-6 **Zoom Web content**

Web pages also can contain special programming to add interest and activity. A language called **JavaScript** is often used to trigger simple interactive features, such as opening new browser windows and checking information entered in online forms. An advanced use of JavaScript called AJAX can be found on many interactive sites. This technology is used to create interactive Web sites that respond quickly, like traditional desktop application software. (Application software will be presented in Chapters 3 and 4.) Applets are written in the Java programming language. (Java and other programming languages will be presented in Chapter 14.) These programs can be downloaded quickly and run by most browsers. Java applets are used to present animation, display graphics, provide interactive games, and much more.

Today it is common to access the Internet from a variety of mobile devices like cell phones. Special browsers called **mobile browsers** are designed to run on these portable devices. Unlike a traditional Web browser that is typically displayed on a large screen, a mobile browser is displayed on a very small screen and special navigational tools are required to conveniently view Web content. The Apple iPhone, for example, enables you to "pinch" or "stretch" the screen with two fingers to zoom Web content in and out. (See Figure 2-6.)

To learn more about browsers, visit our Web site at www.computing2013.com and enter the keyword **browsers.**

 CONCEPT CHECK

What is the function of an ISP? Describe two types of ISPs.

What is the function of a browser? What is the function of a mobile browser?

What are URLs, HTML, Web pages, hyperlinks, JavaScript, AJAX applets, and Java?

Communication

As previously mentioned, communication is the most popular Internet activity, and its impact cannot be overestimated. At a personal level, friends and family can stay in contact with one another even when separated by thousands of miles. At a business level, electronic communication has become a standard, and many times preferred, way to stay in touch with suppliers, employees, and customers. Some popular types of Internet communication are e-mail, instant messaging, social networking, blogs, microblogs, Webcasts, podcasts, and wikis.

E-mail

E-mail or **electronic mail** is the transmission of electronic messages over the Internet. All you need to send and receive e-mail is a computer with an Internet connection and an e-mail account. Using the Internet, your computer connects to an e-mail provider or computer that supports e-mail services. After receiving an e-mail account from the provider, you can begin e-mailing. There are two basic types of e-mail accounts: client based and Web based.

* **Client-based e-mail accounts** require a special program known as an **e-mail client** to be installed on your computer. Before you can begin e-mailing, you need to run the e-mail client from your computer, which communicates with the e-mail service provider. Three of the most widely used e-mail clients are Windows Mail, Mozilla's Thunderbird, and Apple's Mail.

* **Web-based e-mail accounts** do not require an e-mail program to be installed on your computer. Once your computer connects to an e-mail service provider, a special program called a **Webmail client** is run on the e-mail provider's computer and then you can begin e-mailing. This is known as **Webmail.** Most Internet service providers offer Webmail services. Three free Webmail service providers are Google's Gmail, Microsoft's Hotmail, and Yahoo!'s Yahoo!Mail.

For individual use, Webmail is more widely used because it frees the user from installing and maintaining an e-mail client on every computer used to access e-mail. With Webmail, you can access your e-mail from any computer anywhere that has Internet access.

A typical e-mail message has three basic elements: header, message, and signature. (See Figure 2-7.) The **header** appears first and typically includes the following information:

* **Addresses:** Addresses of the persons sending, receiving, and, optionally, anyone else who is to receive copies. E-mail addresses have two basic parts. (See Figure 2-8.) The first part is the user's name and the second part is the domain name, which includes the top-level domain. In our example e-mail, *dcoats* is Dan's user name. The server providing e-mail service for Dan is *usc.edu.* The top-level domain indicates that the provider is an educational institution.

* **Subject:** A one-line description, used to present the topic of the message. Subject lines typically are displayed when a person checks his or her mailbox.

* **Attachments:** Many e-mail programs allow you to attach files such as documents and image files. If a message has an attachment, the file name typically appears on the attachment line.

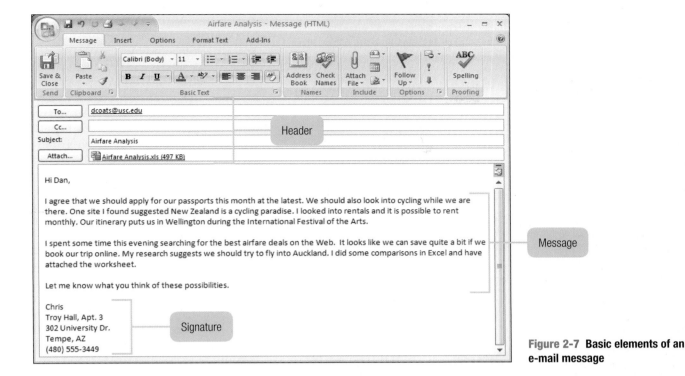

Figure 2-7 Basic elements of an e-mail message

The letter or **message** comes next. Finally, the **signature** provides additional information about the sender. This information may include the sender's name, address, and telephone number.

Figure 2-8 Two parts of an e-mail address

E-mail can be a valuable asset in your personal and professional life. However, like many other valuable technologies, there are drawbacks too. Americans receive billions of unwanted and unsolicited e-mails every year. This unwelcome mail is called **spam.** While spam is indeed a distraction and nuisance, it also can be dangerous. For example, computer **viruses** or destructive programs are often attached to unsolicited e-mail. Computer viruses and ways to protect against them will be discussed in Chapter 5.

In an attempt to control spam, anti-spam laws have been added to our legal system. For example, CAN-SPAM requires that every marketing-related e-mail provide an opt-out option. When the option is selected, the recipient's e-mail address is to be removed from future mailing lists. Failure to do so results in heavy fines. This approach, however, has had minimal impact since over 50 percent of all spam originates from servers outside the United States. A more effective approach has been the development and use of **spam blockers,** also known as **spam filters.** (See Figure 2-9.) These programs use a variety of different approaches to identify and eliminate spam. To learn about these approaches, visit our Web site at www .computing2013.com and enter the keyword spam.

Instant Messaging

Instant messaging (IM) allows two or more people to contact each other via direct, live communication. To use instant messaging, you register with an instant messaging server and then specify a list of **friends.** Whenever you connect to the Internet, special software informs your messaging server that you are online. In response, the server will notify you if any of your friends

tips

Are you tired of sorting through an inbox full of spam? Americans receive over 200 billion spam e-mails every year. Here are a few simple tips to help ensure that your inbox is spam-free:

1 **Choose a complex address.** sally_smith@hotmail.com is much more likely to get spam than 4it3scoq2@hotmail.com. Consider using a more complicated, and less personal, user name.

2 **Keep a low profile.** Many spammers collect e-mail addresses from personal Web sites, chat rooms, and message boards. Use caution when handing out your address and be sure to read the privacy policy of a site before you hand over your address.

3 **Don't ever respond to spam.** Once you respond to spam, either in interest or to opt out of a list, you have confirmed the address is valid. Valid addresses are worth more to spammers, who then sell the addresses to others.

4 **Use e-mail filter options.** Most e-mail programs have a filter option that screens incoming e-mail based on a set of preferences you choose. You can set up your inbox to accept only mail from certain addresses or to block mail from others.

5 **Use spam blockers.** There are plenty of programs available to help protect your inbox. For example, MailWasher provides an effective and free program available at www.mailwasher.com.

To see other tips, visit our Web site at www.computing2013.com and enter the keyword tips.

Spam Blocker	Site
SPAMfighter	www.spamfighter.com
SpamEater	www.spameater.com
Spam Buster	www.spambuster.com

Figure 2-9 Spam blockers

are online. At the same time, it notifies your friends that you are online. You can then send messages directly back and forth to one another. Most instant messaging programs also include video conferencing features, file sharing, and remote assistance. Many businesses routinely use these instant messaging features. To see how instant messaging works, visit our Web site at www.computing2013.com and enter the keyword **im**.

The most widely used instant messaging services are AOL's Instant Messenger, Microsoft's MSN Messenger, Yahoo Messenger, and Google Talk. One limitation, however, is that many instant messaging services do not support communication with other services. For example, at the time of this writing, a user registered with AOL cannot use AOL's Instant Messenger software to communicate with a user registered with Yahoo Messenger. Recently, however, some software companies have started providing **universal instant messenger** programs that overcome this limitation. Three widely used programs are Digsby, Pidgin, and Qnext.

Social Networking

Social networking is one of the fastest-growing and most significant Web 2.0 applications. Social networking sites focus on connecting people and organizations that share a common interest or activity. These sites typically provide a wide array of tools that facilitate meeting, communicating, and sharing. There are hundreds of social networking sites. Three of the best known are MySpace, Facebook, and LinkedIn.

- **MySpace** was one the first large-scale social networking sites. It was introduced in 2005 and rapidly grew into one of the most visited sites on the Web. Reacting to competition and changing user preferences, MySpace has evolved to focus primarily on music, movies, celebrities, and TV for teenage audiences.

- **Facebook** was initially launched by a student at Harvard University for college students in 2004. By 2008 it had replaced MySpace as the most widely used social networking site. It now has well over a half billion users worldwide. Facebook provides a wide array of features and applications including instant messaging, photo and video sharing, games, and much more.

There are three basic categories of Facebook users: individuals, businesses, and communities. Individuals create **Facebook Profiles,** which may include photos, lists of personal interests, contact information, and other personal information. (See Figure 2-10.)

In general, these profiles are available to friends, family members, and others who may be searching for old friends, lost relatives, or people who share a common interest. Businesses create **Facebook Pages** to promote

Figure 2-10 Facebook Profile

products and services. Public figures such as politicians and entertainers frequently use Facebook Pages to connect to their constituents and fans. Communities of individuals who share a common interest create **Facebook groups** to share information. Typically, groups are organized around topics, events, or ideas. Groups allow a number of people to come together online to share information and discuss specific subjects.

- **LinkedIn** started in 2003 and has become the premier business-oriented social networking site. Although not nearly as large as Facebook, it is the largest social networking site focusing on business professionals. It has well over 100 million users. LinkedIn provides tools to maintain business contacts, develop extended business networks, research individual businesses, search for job opportunities, and more.

For a list of some the most popular social networking sites, see Figure 2-11.

tips

Have you ever seen one of those funny or not-so-funny and embarrassing personal videos on the Internet? Unless you are careful, you could be starring in one of these videos. Many of these videos started by individuals posting them to their personal Facebook, Flickr, and YouTube sites. Without explicit privacy settings, images and videos posted to these sites can be viewed and potentially reposted for all to see. To avoid becoming an unwanted video star, protect your privacy by controlling access to your images.

1 If you use Facebook, select Account/Privacy Settings from your Facebook page to review and edit your privacy settings.

2 If you use Flickr, go to its Privacy page to specify who can see your posted images and videos.

3 If you use YouTube, go to www.youtube.com/account#privacy/search to specify who can have access to your posted images and videos.

To see other tips, visit our Web site at www.computing2013.com and enter the keyword tips.

Blogs, Microblogs, Webcasts, Podcasts, and Wikis

In addition to social networking sites, there are other Web 2.0 applications that help ordinary people communicate across the Web including blogs, microblogs, Webcasts, podcasts, and wikis.

Organization	Site
Facebook	www.facebook.com
LinkedIn	www.linkedin.com
MySpace	www.myspace.com
Google+	www.google.com/+

Figure 2-11 Social networking sites

Many individuals create personal Web sites, called **Web logs** or **blogs,** to keep in touch with friends and family. Blog postings are time-stamped and arranged with the newest item first. Often, readers of these sites are allowed to comment. Some blogs are like online diaries with personal information; others focus on information about a hobby or theme, such as knitting, electronic devices, or good books. Although most are written by individual bloggers, there are also group blogs with multiple contributors. Some businesses and newspapers also have started blogging as a quick publishing method. Several sites provide tools to create blogs. Two of the most widely used are Blogger and WordPress. (See Figure 2-12.)

A **microblog** publishes short sentences that only take a few seconds to write, rather than long stories or posts like a traditional blog. Microblogs are designed to keep friends and other contacts up-to-date on your interests and activities. The most popular microblogging site, **Twitter,** enables you to add new content from your browser, instant messaging application, or even a mobile phone. To learn more about Twitter, see Making IT Work for You: Twitter on pages 44 and 45.

Both Webcasts and podcasts deliver media content such as music and movies over the Internet to your computer. **Webcasts** use **streaming** technology in which audio and video files are continuously downloaded to your computer while you are listening to and/or viewing the file content. After a Webcast has been completed, there are no files remaining on your computer. Webcasts typically broadcast live events. For example, the popular Web site YouTube.com as well as other sites routinely Webcast live movie premiers and sporting events.

Podcasts do not use streaming technology. Before a podcast can be run, the media files have to be downloaded and saved to your computer. Once downloaded, you can run the files to listen to music or watch a movie as often as you would like. The media files also can be transferred from your computer to a media player such as an iPod. Podcasts are widely used to download music,

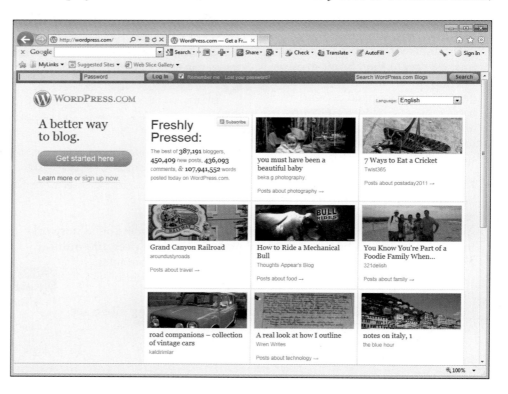

Figure 2-12 Blog creation site

tutorials, and educational training. To learn more about how to use a media player to view podcast movies and TV shows, see Making IT Work for You: iPods and Video from the Internet on page 66.

A **wiki** is a Web site specially designed to allow visitors to fill in missing information or correct inaccuracies. "Wiki" comes from the Hawaiian word for fast, which describes the simplicity of editing and publishing through wiki software. Wikis support collaborative writing in which there isn't a single expert author, but rather a community of interested people that builds knowledge over time. Perhaps the most famous example is **Wikipedia,** an online encyclopedia, written and edited by anyone who wants to contribute, that has millions of entries in over 20 languages. (See Figure 2-13.)

Creating blogs and wikis are examples of Web authoring. We will discuss Web authoring software in detail in Chapter 4. To learn more about creating your own personal Web site, visit us at www.computing2013.com and enter the keyword **blog.**

☑ CONCEPT CHECK

⬤ Define e-mail. What is the difference between client- and Web-based e-mail accounts? What is Webmail?

⬤ What is instant messaging? How is it different from e-mail?

⬤ What is social networking? Describe three well-known sites.

⬤ Describe the differences among blogs, microblogs, Webcasts, podcasts, and wikis.

Figure 2-13 Wikipedia

Making IT work for you

TWITTER

Would you like your own microblog? A microblog can help you stay in touch with friends and family, or coordinate a project with other students. It's easy using the free Twitter microblogging service.

Sign Up To create a new Twitter account:

1
- Visit http://www.twitter.com.
- Click the *Sign up* button.

2
- Follow the on-screen instructions to create an account.

Sign up button

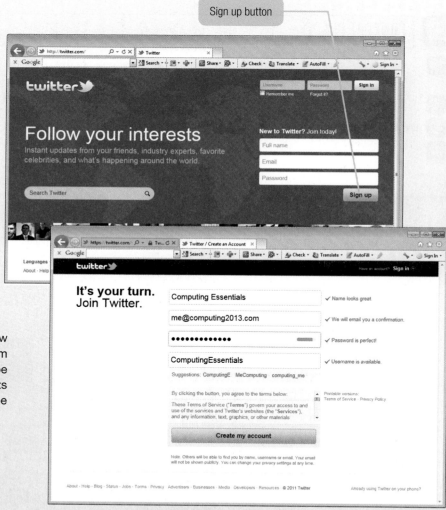

The username you select for your new account will be used to create a custom blog address where your posts can be viewed by others. For example, tweets posted by the user **computing2013** can be seen at **http://twitter.com/computing2013**.

Posting and Following   Using Twitter involves posting short messages about your current status. Following others allows you to see their messages each time they post an update. To post an update to Twitter:

1
● Enter a short message in the *What's happening?* text box.

● Click the *Tweet* button.

Your text is immediately visible at your custom Twitter page. In addition to tweeting directly from the Twitter Web site, there are also options to tweet by sending a text message from a mobile phone, or using other software such as instant messaging applications.

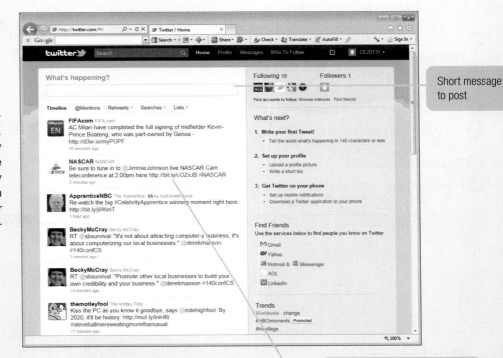

Short message to post

Posts by others you are following

To follow updates by other people, simply visit their custom blog address and click the *Follow* button.

Follow button

The Web is continually changing, and some of the specifics presented in Making IT Work for You may have changed.

To learn about other ways to make information technology work for you, visit our Web site at www.computing2013.com and enter the keyword miw.

Search Tools

The Web can be an incredible resource, providing information on nearly any topic imaginable. Are you planning a trip? Writing an economics paper? Looking for a movie review? Trying to locate a long-lost friend? Information sources related to these questions, and much, much more, are available on the Web.

With over 20 billion pages and more being added daily, the Web is a massive collection of interrelated pages. With so much available information, locating the precise information you need can be difficult. Fortunately, a number of organizations called **search services** operate Web sites that can help you locate the information you need. They maintain huge databases relating to information provided on the Web and the Internet. The information stored at these databases includes addresses, content descriptions or classifications, and keywords appearing on Web pages and other Internet informational resources. Special programs called **spiders** continually look for new information and update the search services' databases. Additionally, search services provide special programs called *search engines* that you can use to locate specific information on the Web.

Are you going to use a search tool to locate some information? Here are a few tips that might help.

1 Start with the right approach. For general information, use a direct search. For specific information, use a keyword search.

2 Be as precise as possible. Use specific keywords that relate directly to the topic.

3 Use multiple words. Use quotation marks to identify key phrases.

4 Use Boolean operators. Typically, these include words such as "and," "not," and "or."

5 Check your spelling. Misspelling is one of the most common problems.

6 Keep moving. Look only at the first page of search results. If necessary, try another search using different keywords.

To see other tips, visit our Web site at www.computing2013.com and enter the keyword tips.

Search Engines

Search engines are specialized programs that assist you in locating information on the Web and the Internet. To find information, you go to a search service's Web site and use its search engine. For example, see Figure 2-14 for Google's search engine.

To use a search Web site, you enter a keyword or phrase reflecting the information you want. The search engine compares your entry against its database and returns a list of **hits,** or sites that contain the keywords. Each hit includes a link to the referenced Web page (or other resource) along with a brief discussion of the information contained at that location. Many searches result in a large number of hits. For example, if you were to enter the keyword *music,* you would get billions of hits. Search engines order the hits according to those sites that most likely contain the information requested and present the list to you in that order, usually in groups of 10. See Figure 2-15 for a list of commonly used search engines.

Search engines are designed to find specific information. For example, if you were looking for a specific music file, you would enter the album title and/or the artist's name. If you were looking for more general information such as rock music, you might want to use a Web directory.

Web Directories

Web directories, also known as **subject directories,** organize information according to categories or topics such as Arts, Games, and News. They are designed to find general information about a topic. To find information at a Web directory site, you select a category or topic that fits the information

Figure 2-14 **Google search engine**

that you want. Another list of subtopics related to the topic you selected appears. You select the subtopic that best relates to your topic and another subtopic list appears. You continue to narrow your search in this manner until a list of Web sites appears. This list corresponds to the hit list previously discussed. Two well-known Web directory sites are dir.yahoo.com and www.dmoz.org.

A recent study by the NEC Research Institute found that any one search approach will only locate a fraction of the informational sources on the Web. Therefore, it is highly recommended that you use more than one search engine or Web directory when researching important topics. Or you could use a special type of search engine called a metasearch engine.

Search Service	Site
AOL Search	search.aol.com
Ask	www.ask.com
Bing	www.bing.com
Google	www.google.com
Yahoo!	www.yahoo.com

Figure 2-15 **Search engines**

Metasearch Engines

One way to research a topic is to visit the Web sites for several individual search engines. At each site, you would enter the search instructions, wait for the hits to appear, review the list, and visit selected sites. This process can be quite time-consuming and duplicate responses from different search engines are inevitable. Metasearch engines offer an alternative.

Metasearch engines are programs that automatically submit your search request to several search engines simultaneously. The metasearch engine receives the results, eliminates duplicates, orders the hits, and then provides the edited list to you. See Figure 2-16 for a list of several metasearch engines available on the Web. One of the best known is Dogpile; see Figure 2-17.

Metasearch Service	Site
Dogpile	www.dogpile.com
Ixquick	www.ixquick.com
MetaCrawler	www.metacrawler.com
Search	www.search.com
Clusty	www.clusty.com

Figure 2-16 **Metasearch sites**

Specialized Search Engines

Specialized search engines focus on subject-specific Web sites. Specialized sites can potentially save you time by narrowing your search. For a list of just a few selected specialized search engines, see Figure 2-18. For example,

Figure 2-17 Dogpile metasearch site

Topic	Site
Environment	www.eco-web.com
Fashion	www.infomat.com
History	www.historynet.com
Law	www.lawcrawler.com
Medicine	www.medscape.com

Figure 2-18 Select specialized search engines

let's say you are researching a paper about the fashion industry. You could begin with a general search engine like Yahoo! Or you could go to a search engine that specializes specifically in fashion, such as www.infomat.com.

Content Evaluation

Search engines are excellent tools to locate information on the Web. Be careful, however, how you use the information you find. Unlike most published material found in newspapers, journals, and textbooks, not all the information you find on the Web has been subjected to strict guidelines to ensure accuracy. In fact, anyone can publish content on the Web. Many sites, such as Wikipedia.com, allow anyone to post new material, sometimes anonymously and without critical evaluation. To learn how you can publish on the Web, visit our Web site at www.computing2013.com and enter the keyword **blog**.

To evaluate the accuracy of information you find on the Web, consider the following:

- **Authority.** Is the author an expert in the subject area? Is the site an official site for the information presented, or is the site an individual's personal Web site?
- **Accuracy.** Has the information been critically reviewed for correctness prior to posting on the Web? Does the Web site provide a method to report inaccurate information to the author?
- **Objectivity.** Is the information factually reported or does the author have a bias? Does the author appear to have a personal agenda aimed at convincing or changing the reader's opinion?
- **Currency.** Is the information up to date? Does the site specify the date when the site was updated?

☑

- What are search services, spiders, and search engines?
- What is the difference between a search engine and a Web directory?
- Compare metasearch and specialized search engines.
- What are the four considerations for evaluating Web site content?

Electronic Commerce

Electronic commerce, also known as **e-commerce,** is the buying and selling of goods over the Internet. Have you ever bought anything over the Internet? If you have not, there is a very good chance that you will within the next year or two. Shopping on the Internet is growing rapidly and there seems to be no end in sight.

The underlying reason for the rapid growth in e-commerce is that it provides incentives for both buyers and sellers. From the buyer's perspective, goods and services can be purchased at any time of day or night.

Have you ever bought anything online? If not, it's likely that in the future you will join the millions that have. Here are a few suggestions on how to shop online:

1 **Consult product review sites.** To get evaluations or opinions on products, visit one of the many review sites on the Web such as www.consumersearch.com and www.epinions.com.

2 **Use a shopping bot.** Once you have selected a specific product, enlist a shopping bot or automated shopping assistants to compare prices. Two well-known shopping bots are located at www.mysimon.com and www.pricegrabber.com.

3 **Consult vendor review sites.** Of course, price is not everything. Before placing an order with a vendor, check its reputation by visiting vendor review sites such as www.resellerratings.com and www.bizrate.com.

To see other tips, visit our Web site at www.computing2013.com and enter the keyword tips.

Traditional commerce is typically limited to standard business hours when the seller is open. Additionally, buyers no longer have to physically travel to the seller's location. For example, busy parents with small children do not need to coordinate their separate schedules or to arrange for a babysitter whenever they want to visit the mall. From the seller's perspective, the costs associated with owning and operating a retail outlet can be eliminated. For example, a music store can operate entirely on the Web without an actual physical store and without a large sales staff. Another advantage is reduced inventory. Traditional stores maintain an inventory of goods in their stores and periodically replenish this inventory from warehouses. With e-commerce, there is no in-store inventory and products are shipped directly from warehouses.

While there are numerous advantages to e-commerce, there are disadvantages as well. Some of these disadvantages include the inability to provide immediate delivery of goods, the inability to "try on" prospective purchases, and questions relating to the security of online payments. Although these issues are being addressed, very few observers suggest that e-commerce will replace bricks-and-mortar businesses entirely. It is clear that both will coexist and that e-commerce will continue to grow.

Just like any other type of commerce, electronic commerce involves two parties: businesses and consumers. There are three basic types of electronic commerce:

- **Business-to-consumer (B2C)** involves the sale of a product or service to the general public or end users. Oftentimes this arrangement eliminates the wholesaler by allowing manufacturers to sell directly to customers. Other times, existing retail stores use B2C e-commerce to create a presence on the Web as another way to reach customers.

- **Consumer-to-consumer (C2C)** involves individuals selling to individuals. This often takes the form of an electronic version of the classified ads or an auction.
- **Business-to-business (B2B)** involves the sale of a product or service from one business to another. This is typically a manufacturer–supplier relationship. For example, a furniture manufacturer requires raw materials such as wood, paint, and varnish.

Business-to-Consumer E-Commerce

The fastest-growing type of e-commerce is business-to-consumer. It is used by large corporations, small corporations, and start-up businesses. Whether large or small, nearly every existing corporation in the United States provides some type of B2C support as another means to connect to customers. Because extensive investments are not required to create traditional retail outlets and to maintain large marketing and sales staffs, e-commerce allows start-up companies to compete with larger established firms.

The three most widely used B2C applications are for online banking, financial trading, and shopping.

- **Online banking** is becoming a standard feature of banking institutions. Customers are able to go online with a standard browser to perform many banking operations. These online operations include accessing account information, balancing checkbooks, transferring funds, paying bills, and applying for loans.
- **Online stock trading** allows investors to research, buy, and sell stocks and bonds over the Internet. While e-trading is more convenient than using a traditional full-service broker, the greatest advantage is cost.
- **Online shopping** includes the buying and selling of a wide range of consumer goods over the Internet. (See Figure 2-19.) There are thousands of e-commerce applications in this area. Fortunately, there are numerous Web sites that provide support for consumers looking to compare products and to locate bargains. (See Figure 2-20.)

Consumer-to-Consumer E-Commerce

A trend in C2C e-commerce is the growing popularity of Web auctions. **Web auctions** are similar to traditional auctions except that buyers and sellers seldom, if ever, meet face-to-face. Sellers post descriptions of products at a Web site and buyers submit bids electronically. Like traditional auctions, sometimes the bidding becomes highly competitive and enthusiastic. There are two basic types of Web auction sites:

- **Auction house sites** sell a wide range of merchandise directly to bidders. The auction house owner presents merchandise that is typically from a company's surplus stock. These sites operate like a traditional auction, and bargain prices are not uncommon. Auction house sites are generally considered safe places to shop.
- **Person-to-person auction sites** operate more like flea markets. The owner of the site provides a forum for numerous buyers and sellers to gather. While the owners of these sites typically facilitate the bidding process, they are not involved in completing transactions or in verifying the authenticity of the goods sold. As with purchases at a flea market, buyers and sellers need to be cautious.

For a list of the most popular Web auction sites, see Figure 2-21.

Figure 2-19 Online shopping site

Security

The single greatest challenge for e-commerce is the development of fast, secure, and reliable payment methods for purchased goods. The three basic payment options are check, credit card, and digital cash. ✳

- Checks are the most traditional. Unfortunately, check purchases require the longest time to complete. After selecting an item, the buyer sends a check through the mail. Upon receipt of the check, the seller verifies that the check is good. If it is good, then the purchased item is sent out.

- Credit card purchases are faster and more convenient than check purchases. Credit card fraud, however, is a major concern for both buyers and sellers. Criminals known as **carders** specialize in stealing, trading, and using stolen credit cards over the Internet. We will discuss this and other privacy and security issues related to the Internet in Chapter 10.

- **Digital cash** is the Internet's equivalent to traditional cash. Buyers purchase digital cash from a third party (a bank that specializes in electronic currency) and use it (see Figure 2-22) to purchase goods. Sellers convert the digital cash to traditional currency through the third party. Although not as convenient as credit card purchases, digital cash is more secure. For a list of digital cash providers, see Figure 2-23.

Support	Site
Product comparisons	www.shopping.com
Locating closeouts	www.overstock.com
Finding coupons	www.ebates.com

Figure 2-20 Consumer support sites

Organization	Site
Amazon	www.auctions.amazon.com
WeBidz	www.webidz.com
eBay	www.ebay.com
Overstock	auctions.overstock.com

Figure 2-21 Auction sites

Figure 2-22 PayPal offers digital cash

Organization	Site
ECash	www.ecash.com
Google	checkout.google.com
Internet Cash	www.internetcash.com
PayPal	www.paypal.com

Figure 2-23 Digital cash providers

CONCEPT CHECK

What is electronic commerce?

What are the three basic types of e-commerce?

What are the three basic options for electronic payment?

Cloud Computing

Typically, application programs are owned by individuals or organizations and stored on their computer system's hard disks. As discussed in Chapter 1, **cloud computing** uses the Internet and the Web to shift many of these computer activities from the user's computer to other computers on the Internet.

While some suggest that the term *cloud computing* is merely a marketing term designed to promote new products, many others see cloud computing as a new model for computing that frees users from owning, maintaining,

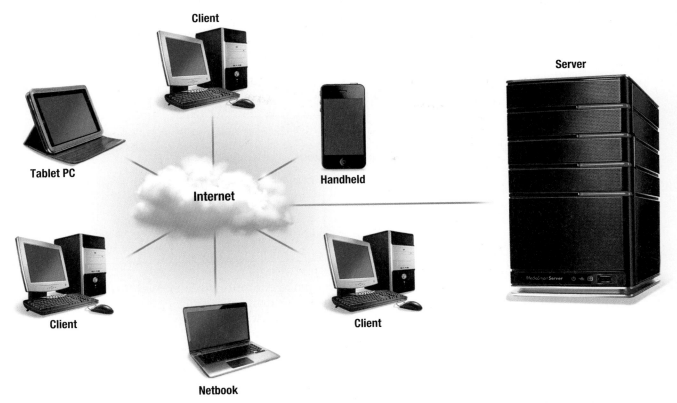

Figure 2-24 Cloud Computing

and storing software and data. It further provides access to these services from anywhere through an Internet connection. Several prominent firms are aggressively pursuing this new concept. These firms include Google, IBM, Intel, and Microsoft to name just a few.

The basic components to cloud computing are clients, the Internet, and service providers. (See Figure 2-24.)

- Clients are corporations and end users who want access to data, programs, and storage. This access is to be available anywhere and anytime that a connection to the Internet is available. End users do not need to buy, install, and maintain application programs and data.

- The Internet provides the connection between the clients and the providers. Two of the most critical factors determining the efficiency of cloud computing are (1) the speed and reliability of the user's access to the Internet and (2) the Internet's capability to provide safe and reliable transmission of data and programs.

- Service providers are organizations with computers connected to the Internet that are willing to provide access to software, data, and storage. These providers may charge a fee or may be free. For example, Google Apps provides free access to programs with capabilities similar to Microsoft's Word, Excel, and PowerPoint. (See Figure 2-25.)

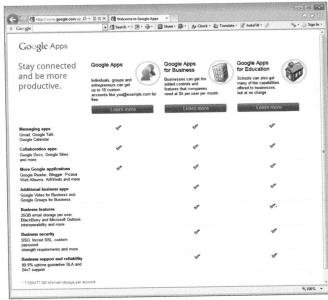

Figure 2-25 Web-based service (Google Apps)

In the following chapters, you will learn more about the services provided through cloud computing. You will also learn about security and privacy challenges associated with cloud computing.

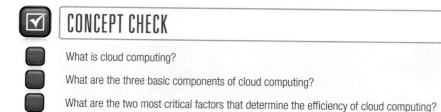

CONCEPT CHECK

What is cloud computing?

What are the three basic components of cloud computing?

What are the two most critical factors that determine the efficiency of cloud computing?

Web Utilities

Utilities are programs that make computing easier. **Web utilities** are specialized utility programs that make using the Internet and the Web easier and safer. Some of these utilities are browser-related programs that either become part of your browser or are executed from your browser. Others are designed to protect children from dangerous and inappropriate Web site material. File transfer utilities allow you to efficiently copy files to and from your computer across the Internet.

Plug-ins

Plug-ins are programs that are automatically started and operate as a part of your browser. Many Web sites require you to have one or more plug-ins to fully experience their content. Some widely used plug-ins include

- Acrobat Reader from Adobe—for viewing and printing a variety of standard forms and other documents saved in a special format called PDF.
- Windows Media Player from Microsoft—for playing audio files, video files, and much more.
- QuickTime from Apple—for playing audio and video files. (See Figure 2-26.)
- RealPlayer from RealNetworks—for playing audio and video files.
- Shockwave from Adobe—for playing Web-based games and viewing concerts and dynamic animations.

Some of these utilities are included in many of today's browsers and operating systems. Others must be installed before they can be used by your browser. To learn more about plug-ins and how to download them, visit some of the sites listed in Figure 2-27.

Filters

Filters block access to selected sites. The Internet is an interesting and multifaceted arena. But one of those facets is a dark and seamy one. Parents, in particular, are concerned about children roaming unrestricted across the Internet. (See Figure 2-28.) Filter programs allow parents as well as organizations to block out selected sites and set time limits. (See Figure 2-29.) Additionally, these programs can monitor use and generate reports detailing the total time spent on the Internet and the time spent at individual Web sites, chat groups, and newsgroups. For a list of some of the best-known filters, see Figure 2-30.

Explorations

Some privacy groups object to the use of Web filtering programs on the grounds that they accidentally censor valuable Web content.

To learn more about this issue, visit our Web site at www.computing2013.com and enter the keyword filter.

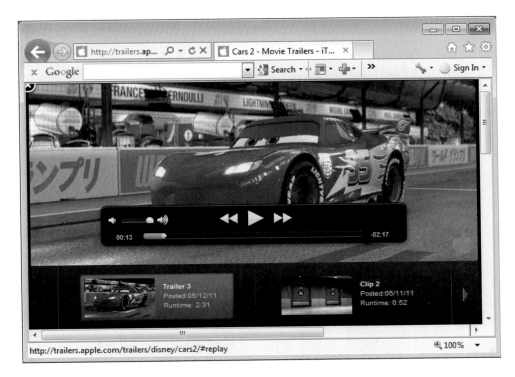

Figure 2-26 **QuickTime movie at Apple.com**

http://trailers.apple.com/trailers/disney/cars2/#replay   🔍 100% ▼

Plug-in	Source
Acrobat Reader	www.adobe.com
Flash	www.adobeflash.com
QuickTime	www.apple.com
RealPlayer	www.service.real.com
Silverlight	www.silverlight.net

Figure 2-27 **Plug-in sites**

Figure 2-28 **Parents play an important role in Internet supervision**

File Transfer Utilities

Using file transfer utility software, you can copy files to your computer from specially configured servers. This is called **downloading.** You also can use file transfer utility software to copy files from your computer to another computer on the Internet. This is called **uploading.** Three popular types of file transfer are FTP, Web-based, and BitTorrent.

- **File transfer protocol (FTP)** and **secure file transfer protocol (SFTP)** allow you to efficiently copy files to and from your computer across the Internet, and are frequently used for uploading changes to a Web site hosted by an Internet service provider. FTP has been used for decades and still remains one of the most popular methods of file transfer.
- **Web-based file transfer services** make use of a Web browser to upload and download files. This eliminates the need for any custom software to be installed. A popular Web-based file transfer service is drop.io.
- **BitTorrent** distributes file transfers across many different computers for more efficient downloads, unlike other transfer technologies where a file

Figure 2-29 Net Nanny is a Web filter

is copied from one computer on the Internet to another. A single file might be located on dozens of individual computers. When you download the file, each computer sends you a tiny piece of the larger file, making BitTorrent well-suited for transferring very large files. Unfortunately, BitTorrent technology often has been used for distributing unauthorized copies of copyrighted music and video.

Filter	Site
CyberPatrol	www.cyberpatrol.com
Cybersitter	www.cybersitter.com
iProtectYou Pro Web Filter	www.softforyou.com
Net Nanny	www.netnanny.com
Safe Eyes Platinum	www.safeeyes.com

Figure 2-30 Filters

Internet Security Suites

An **Internet security suite** is a collection of utility programs designed to maintain your security and privacy while you are on the Web. These programs control spam, protect against computer viruses, provide filters, and much more. You could buy each program separately; however, the cost of the suite is typically much less. Two of the best-known Internet security suites are McAfee's Internet Security and Symantec's Norton Internet Security. (See Figure 2-31.) To learn more about Internet security suites, see Making IT Work for You: Virus Protection on pages 150 and 151.

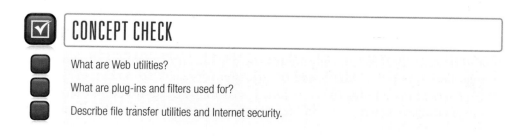

CONCEPT CHECK

- What are Web utilities?
- What are plug-ins and filters used for?
- Describe file transfer utilities and Internet security.

Figure 2-31 **McAfee Antivirus**

Careers in IT

Webmasters develop and maintain Web sites and resources. The job may include backup of the company Web site, updating resources, or development of new resources. Webmasters are often involved in the design and development of the Web site. Some Webmasters monitor traffic on the site and take steps to encourage users to visit the site. Webmasters also may work with marketing personnel to increase site traffic and may be involved in development of Web promotions.

Employers look for candidates with a bachelor's or associate's degree in computer science or information systems and knowledge of common programming languages and Web development software. Knowledge of HTML is considered essential. Those with experience using Web authoring software and programs like Adobe Illustrator and Adobe Flash are often preferred. Good communication and organizational skills are vital in this position.

Webmasters can expect to earn an annual salary of $49,500 to $82,500. This position is relatively new in many corporations and tends to have fluid responsibilities. With technological advances and increasing corporate emphasis on a Web presence, experience in this field could lead to managerial opportunities. To learn about other careers in IT, visit us at www.computing2013.com and enter the keyword **careers.**

Now that you've learned about the Internet, the Web, and electronic commerce, I'd like to tell you about my career as a Webmaster.

A LOOK TO THE FUTURE

Web-Accessible Refrigerators Will Automatically Restock Themselves

What if you could virtually tour your home from anywhere using the Web? What if your refrigerator knew what it contained and could create a grocery list to restock itself? What if you could remotely check to see if you left your wallet on the bedside table or make sure you remembered to turn the oven off? In the future, this will almost certainly be the case, as every aspect of the modern home becomes Web accessible.

Web-accessible home appliances are not a new idea. Several companies offer kitchen appliances that connect to the Internet. At present these appliances are passive, meaning that they do not have any knowledge of what food items they contain and are therefore not able to actively act to restock. In the future, however, appliances will be much more active. Refrigerators could know

what food they contain and what food is needed to be fully stocked and automatically will place orders over the Internet to restock missing items. Also, every appliance in your home might have its own Web page. Through such a Web page, you will be able to actively interact and control these appliances.

The home of the future will include more than just smart appliances. Internet cameras, high-speed Internet, and wireless technologies are converging to offer an inexpensive way to virtually visit your home from anywhere with Internet access. You will be able to follow pets to make sure they stay off the couch or search for a missing wallet you may have left on the nightstand. Coupled with Internet appliances, you could review your pantry using Internet cameras and your refrigerator's Web site to create a grocery list. You could have this list e-mailed to your grocery store and then pick up the groceries on the way home.

Could there be a downside to all this? Currently, many people's computers are infested with Internet viruses and spyware. What could happen if these malicious programs infested your home's appliances? Would it be possible that your every move in your own home could be broadcast to others over the Internet?

INTERNET AND WEB

ACCESS

Internet

Launched in 1969 with **ARPANET,** the **Internet** consists of the actual physical network.

Web

Introduced in 1991 at **CERN,** the **Web** provides a multimedia interface to Internet resources. Three generations: **Web 1.0** (existing information), **Web 2.0** (content creation and social interaction), **Web 3.0** (computer-generated information).

Common Uses

The most common uses of the Internet and the Web include

- Communication—the most popular Internet activity.
- Shopping—one of the fastest-growing Internet activities.
- Searching—access libraries and local, national, and international news.
- Education—**e-learning** or taking online courses.
- Entertainment—music, movies, magazines, and computer games.

Once connected to the Internet, your computer seemingly becomes an extension of a giant computer that branches all over the world.

Providers

Internet service providers are connected to the Internet, providing a path for individuals to access the Internet. Connection technologies include **DSL, cable,** and **wireless modems.**

Browsers

Browsers access the Web allowing you to **surf** or explore. Some related terms are

- **URLs—locations** or **addresses** to Web resources; two parts are **protocol** and **domain name; top-level domain (TLD)** identifies type of organization.
- **HTML**—commands to display **Web pages; hyperlinks (links)** are connections.
- **JavaScript**—a scripting language that adds basic interactivity and form checking to Web pages. **AJAX** allows rapid response time.
- **Applets**—special programs linked to Web pages; typically written in **Java.**
- **Mobile browsers**—run on portable devices; display on very small screens; provide special navigational tools.

To be a competent end user, you need to be aware of resources available on the Internet and Web, to be able to access these resources, to effectively communicate electronically, to efficiently locate information, to understand electronic commerce, and to use Web utilities.

COMMUNICATION

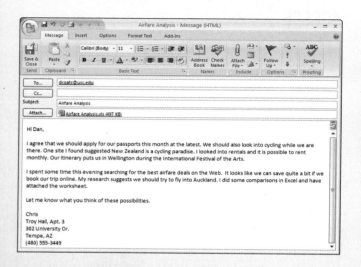

E-mail

E-mail (electronic mail) is the transmission of electronic messages. There are two basic types of e-mail accounts:

* **Client-based e-mail accounts** use **e-mail clients** installed on your computer.
* **Web-based e-mail accounts** use **Webmail clients** located on the e-mail providers's computer. This is known as **Webmail.**

A typical e-mail has three basic elements: **header** (including **address, subject,** and perhaps **attachment**), **message**, and **signature.**

Spam is unwanted and unsolicited e-mail that may include a **computer virus** or destructive programs often attached to unsolicited e-mail. **Spam blockers,** also known as **spam filters,** are programs that identify and eliminate spam.

Instant Messaging

Instant messaging (IM) supports live communication with **friends. Universal instant messengers** support communication with other services.

COMMUNICATION

Social Networking

Social networks connect individuals to one another. Many sites support a variety of different activites. Three of the best known are **MySpace, Facebook** (provides access to **Facebook Profiles, Facebook Pages,** and **Facebook groups**), and **LinkedIn.**

Blogs, Webcasts, and Wikis

Other sites that help individuals communicate across the Web are blogs, microblogs, Webcasts, podcasts, and wikis.

* **Blogs (Web logs) and microblogs** are online journals that support chronological postings. Unlike blogs that often contain detailed postings, **microblogs** publish short, concise sentences. **Twitter** is the most popular microblogging site.
* **Webcasts** and **podcasts** deliver audio, video, and other media content over the Internet. Unlike podcasts, Webcasts use **streaming** technology.
* A **wiki** is a Web site designed to allow visitors to fill in missing information or correct inaccuracies. It allows people to edit or contribute to it by directly editing the pages. Wikis are often used to support collaborative writing in which there is a community of interested contributors. **Wikipedia** is one of the most popular wikis.

Search services maintain huge databases relating to Web site content. **Spiders** are programs that update these databases.

Search Engines

Search engines are specialized programs to help locate information. To use, enter a keyword or phrase and a list of **hits** or links to references is displayed. Good to find specific information.

Web Directories

Web directories (subject directories) are organized by categories or topics. To use, select a topic, then select subtopics until a list of hits appears. Good to find general information.

Metasearch Engines

Metasearch engines submit to several search engines simultaneously. Duplicate sites are eliminated, hits are ordered, and composite hits are presented.

Specialized Search Engines

Specialized search engines focus on subject-specific Web sites.

Content Evaluation

The Web is an excellent source of information, however, it is essential to evaluate the accuracy of the information. Consider the site's authority, accuracy, objectivity, and currency.

Electronic commerce, or **e-commerce**, is the buying and selling of goods over the Internet. Three basic types of e-commerce are **business-to-consumer**, **business-to-business**, and **consumer-to-consumer**.

Business-to-Consumer E-Commerce

Most widely used **business-to-consumer (B2C)** applications are online **banking**, **online stock trading**, and **online shopping**.

Consumer-to-Consumer E-Commerce

Web auctions are a growing **consumer-to-consumer (C2C)** application. Two basic types are **auction house sites** and **person-to-person auction sites**.

Security

Security is the greatest challenge for online banking, online stock trading, and online shopping. Three basic payment options are check, credit card, and **digital cash**. Buyers purchase digital cash from a third party and use it to purchase goods. Sellers accept digital cash and convert to traditional currency through the third party.

CLOUD COMPUTING

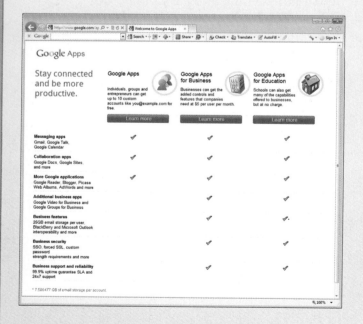

Cloud computing uses the Internet and the Web to shift many computer activities from the user's computer to other computers on the Internet.

Components

There are three basic components to cloud computing:

- Clients are corporations and end users who want access to data, programs, and storage.
- The Internet provides the connection between the clients and providers. Two critical factors are the speed and reliability of the user's access and the Internet's capability to provide safe and reliable access.
- Service providers are organizations with computers connected to the Internet that are willing to provide access to software, data, and storage.

WEB UTILITIES

Plug-in	Source
Acrobat Reader	www.adobe.com
Flash	www.adobeflash.com
QuickTime	www.apple.com
RealPlayer	www.service.real.com
Silverlight	www.silverlight.net

Web utilities are specialized utility programs that make using the Internet and the Web easier and safer.

Plug-ins

Plug-ins are automatically loaded and operate as part of a browser. Many Web sites require specific plug-ins to fully experience their content. Some plug-ins are included in many of today's browsers; others must be installed.

Filters

Filters are used by parents and organizations to block certain sites and to monitor use of the Internet and the Web.

File Transfer Utilities

File transfer utilities copy files to (**downloading**) and from (**uploading**) your computer. Three types are

- **File transfer protocol (FTP)** and **secure file transfer protocol (SFTP)** allow you to efficiently copy files across the Internet.
- **Web-based file transfer services** make use of a Web browser to upload and download files.
- **BitTorrent** distributes file transfers across many different computers.

Internet Security Suite

An **Internet security suite** is a collection of utility programs designed to protect your privacy and security on the Internet.

CAREERS IN IT

Webmasters develop and maintain Web sites and Web resources. Bachelor's or associate's degree in computer science or information systems and knowledge of common programming languages and Web development software are required. Salary range is $49,500 to $82,500.

KEY TERMS

address (36, 38)
Advanced Research
   Project Agency Network
   (ARPANET) (32)
AJAX (37)
applets (37)
attachment (38)
auction house site (50)
BitTorrent (55)
blog (42)
browser (35)
business-to-business
  (B2B) (50)
business-to-consumer
  (B2C) (49)
cable (35)
carder (51)
Center for European
  Nuclear
  Research (CERN) (32)
client-based e-mail
  account (38)
cloud computing (52)
consumer-to-consumer
  (C2C) (50)
digital cash (51)
domain name (36)
downloading (55)
DSL (35)
e-commerce (49)
e-learning (33)
electronic commerce (49)
electronic mail (38)
e-mail (38)
e-mail client (38)
Facebook (40)
Facebook groups (41)
Facebook Pages (40)
Facebook Profile (40)
file transfer protocol
  (FTP) (55)

filter (54)
friend (39)
header (38)
hit (46)
hyperlink (36)
Hypertext Markup
  Language
  (HTML) (36)
instant messaging
  (IM) (39)
Internet (32)
Internet security
  suite (56)
Internet service provider
  (ISP) (35)
Java (37)
JavaScript (37)
link (36)
LinkedIn (41)
location (36)
message (39)
metasearch
  engine (47)
microblog (42)
mobile browser (37)
MySpace (40)
online (32)
online banking (50)
online shopping (50)
online stock
  trading (50)
person-to-person auction
  site (50)
plug-in (54)
podcast (42)
protocol (36)
search engine (46)
search service (46)
secure file transfer
  protocol (SFTP) (55)
signature (39)

social networking (40)
spam (39)
spam blocker (39)
spam filter (39)
specialized search
  engine (47)
spider (46)
streaming (42)
subject (38)
subject directory (46)
surf (35)
top-level domain
  (TLD) (36)
Twitter (42)
uniform resource
  locator (URL) (36)
universal instant
  messenger (40)
uploading (55)
virus (39)
Web (32)
Web 1.0 (32)
Web 2.0 (32)
Web 3.0 (32)
Web auction (50)
Web-based e-mail
  account (38)
Web-based file
  transfer
  services (55)
Webcasts (42)
Web directory (46)
Web log (42)
Webmail (38)
Webmail client (38)
Webmaster (57)
Web page (36)
Web utility (54)
wiki (43)
Wikipedia (43)
wireless modem (35)

To test your knowledge of these key terms with animated flash cards, visit our Web site at www.computing2013.com and enter the keyword terms2.

MULTIPLE CHOICE

Circle the correct answer.

1. The network that connects computers all over the world.
   - **a.** CERN
   - **b.** Internet
   - **c.** LAN
   - **d.** Web

2. The rules for exchanging data between computers.
   - **a.** DSL
   - **b.** protocols
   - **c.** Web
   - **d.** WWW

3. Client-based e-mail accounts require this special program to be installed on your computer.
   - **a.** e-mail client
   - **b.** hyperlink
   - **c.** Java
   - **d.** utility

4. Communities of individuals who share a common interest typically create Facebook:
   - **a.** clients
   - **b.** groups
   - **c.** pages
   - **d.** profiles

5. E-mail that does not require an e-mail program installed on a user's computer is known as:
   - **a.** a blog
   - **b.** a podcast
   - **c.** Webmail
   - **d.** a utility

6. A very well known microblog.
   - **a.** LinkedIn
   - **b.** MySpace
   - **c.** Twitter
   - **d.** Wikipedia

7. These programs continually look for new information and update search services' database programs.
   - **a.** filters
   - **b.** IM
   - **c.** spiders
   - **d.** wikis

8. A type of search engine that submits requests to other search engines, organizes their responses, eliminates duplicate responses, orders hits, and then provides an edited list.
   - **a.** directory search
   - **b.** ISP
   - **c.** metasearch engine
   - **d.** specialized search engine

9. This is the Internet's equivalent to traditional cash.
   - **a.** digital cash
   - **b.** e-commerce
   - **c.** icash
   - **d.** Internet dollars

10. Using file transfer utility software, you can copy files to your computer from specially configured servers on the Internet. This is called:
    - **a.** downloading
    - **b.** filtering
    - **c.** blogging
    - **d.** uploading

For an interactive multiple-choice practice test, visit our Web site at www.computing2013.com and enter the keyword multiple2.

MATCHING

Match each numbered item with the most closely related lettered item. Write your answers in the spaces provided.

a.	communicating	_____**1.**	The most popular Internet activity.
b.	C2C	_____**2.**	The most common way to access the Internet is through a(n).
c.	e-mail		
d.	Internet	_____**3.**	Transmission of electronic messages over the Internet.
e.	ISP		
f.	LinkedIn	_____**4.**	Type of instant messaging service that supports a variety of different IM services.
g.	microblog		
h.	search services	_____**5.**	The premier business-oriented social networking site.
i.	universal	_____**6.**	Another name for a blog.
j.	Web log	_____**7.**	Publishes short sentences that only take a few seconds to write.

_____**8.** Maintain huge databases relating to information provided on the Web and the Internet.

_____**9.** Electronic commerce involving individuals selling to individuals.

_____**10.** The basic components of cloud computing are clients, service providers, and the _____.

For an interactive matching practice test, visit our Web site at www.computing2013 .com and enter the keyword matching2.

OPEN-ENDED

On a separate sheet of paper, respond to each question or statement.

1. Discuss the Internet, including its origins, the three generations of the Web, and the most common uses.
2. Describe how to access the Internet. What are providers? Define browsers and discuss URLs, HTML, JavaScript, Applets, and mobile browsers.
3. Discuss Internet communications including client-based and Web-based e-mail, instant messaging, social networking, blogs, microblogs, WebCasts, podcasts, and wikis.
4. Define search tools including search services. Discuss search engines, Web directories, metasearch engines, and specialized search engines. Describe how to evaluate the content of a Web site
5. Describe electronic commerce including business-to-consumer, consumer-to-consumer, and business-to-business e-commerce, and security.
6. What is cloud computing? Describe the three basic components of cloud computing.
7. What are Web utilities? Discuss plug-ins, filters, file transfer utilities, and Internet security suites.

MAKING IT WORK FOR YOU

The following questions are designed to demonstrate ways that you can effectively use technology today.

1 IPODS AND VIDEO FROM THE INTERNET

Did you know that you could use the Internet to locate movies and television shows, download them to your computer to view and/or transfer them to a portable media player to watch on the go? All it takes is the right software, hardware, and a connection to the Internet. To learn more about using portable media players, review Making IT Work for You: iPods and Video from the Internet on page 34. Then answer the following questions: (a) What item is clicked in the iTunes application to locate movies and television shows? (b) Which television show was selected for purchase in the Making IT Work for You feature? (c) Describe the procedure to transfer video from the iTunes application to an iPod.

2 TWITTER

Would you like to create your own microblog? A microblog can help you stay in touch with friends and family, or coordinate a project with other students. It's easy using the free Twitter microblogging service. All it takes is a computer connected to the Internet and the right software. To learn more about creating, posting, and receiving tweets (posted messages), review Making IT Work for You: Twitter on page 44. If you do not already have a Twitter account, create one and use it. Then answer the following questions: (a) What computing device did you use to set up and use your Twitter account? (b) What is your Twitter address? (c) What was the first message you

posted? (d) Have you visited other people's Twitter accounts? If yes, whose and how often? Do you automatically receive tweets from others? If so, from whom?

EXPLORATIONS

The following questions are designed to add depth and detail to your understanding of specific topics presented within this chapter. The questions direct you to sources other than the textbook to obtain this knowledge.

1 HOW SPAM FILTERS WORK

Spam is an ongoing problem for e-mail users everywhere. Spam is cheap, easy to send, and difficult to track, so the problem is unlikely to disappear soon. Fortunately, spam-blocking software is available. To learn "How Spam Filters Work," visit our Web site at www.computing2013.com and enter the keyword spam. Then answer the following questions: (a) Briefly describe an advantage and a disadvantage to using each of the three types of filters to stop spam. (b) Choose one of the filters and draw a diagram depicting a spam e-mail going through this filter. Be sure to label each step. (c) Modify the diagram to show an e-mail from a friend.

2 HOW INSTANT MESSAGING WORKS

One of the fastest-growing applications on the Internet is instant messaging. This extension to e-mail provides a way for friends and colleagues to communicate and share information from almost anywhere in the world. To learn "How Instant Messaging Works," visit our Web site at www.computing2013.com and enter the keyword im. Then answer the following:

As described in Step 4: Communicate, Linda, Steve, and Chris agree to meet for a movie. Then Chris tells them that he has to leave for school and disconnects. Linda and Steve continue talking, with Linda asking Steve, "Have you seen any good movies lately?" On a single page of paper, create a drawing based on the animation that describes these events beginning with Step 5 when Chris says, "Bye for now—I have to leave for school."

3 DOMAIN REGISTRATION

Individuals and businesses do not *own* domain names. Instead, names such as "yahoo.com" are *registered* with a domain name registrar for an annual fee. Conduct a Web search to locate a domain name registrar site. Review the process for registering a domain name and address the following questions: (a) List the steps involved in registering a domain name. (b) What is the cost for registering a domain name? (c) How long can a domain name be registered for?

ETHICS

The following questions are designed to explore ethical issues related to technology and to develop the ability to think critically and communicate effectively. Respond to the questions by either creating a one-page paper or preparing for an in-depth classroom discussion.

1 FREE SPEECH ONLINE

Some feel that there is too much objectionable material allowed on the Internet, whereas others argue that the Internet should be completely uncensored. Review the Ethics box on page 43. Then respond to the following: (a) Should religious groups be allowed to distribute information over the Internet? What about groups that advocate hatred or oppression? (b) Is there any material you feel should not be freely available on the Web? What about child pornography? (c) If you think some regulation is required, who should determine what restrictions should be imposed? (d) The Internet is not owned by a particular group or country. What limitations does this impose on enforcement of restrictions?

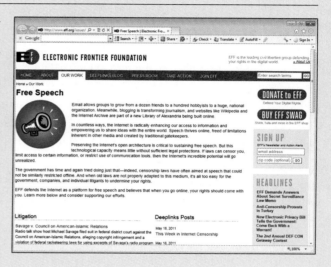

2 DIGITAL DIVIDE

The phrase "digital divide" describes the gap between people who have access to digital information via the Internet and people who lack effective access. Lack of access may stem from a physical lack of technology or from an inability to use available technology. Research two or three articles about the digital divide and address the following items: (a) Summarize some factors that influence unequal Internet access for some members of society. Which ones seem the hardest to overcome and why? (b) What are some social or economic benefits brought by access to the Internet? (c) Make a prediction about the severity of the digital divide. Will it increase or decrease as new Internet-related technologies become available? Explain your answer.

ENVIRONMENT

The following questions are designed to explore environmental issues related to technology and to develop the ability to think critically and communicate effectively. Respond to the questions by either creating a one-page paper or preparing for an in-depth classroom discussion.

1 SPAM

Did you know that spam or unwanted e-mail has an environmental cost? McAfee, an antivirus and spam filter software provider, estimates that spam e-mail consumes the equivalent energy of over a million cars driving around each year. What can you do to help limit this consumption? Review the Environment box on page 38 and then respond to the following: (a) How much spam e-mail do you receive in a typical day? (b) What can you do to reduce the spam? (c) Which of the ways to limit spam you identified in part (b) are you currently doing? (d) If you did all you could to limit spam, how much do you think it would reduce spam in your mail box?

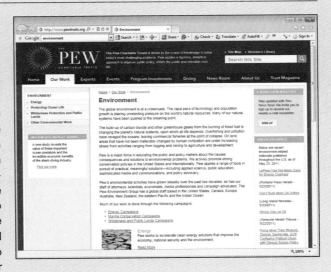

2 CDs AND DVDs

Did you know that CDs and DVDs can take over one million years to degrade in a landfill? The migration of many applications to the Web has had a measurable impact on the environment, as fewer obsolete compact discs end up in landfills. For example, most software developers provide their programs directly over the Web as well as on CDs or DVDs. Review the Environment box on page 50 and then respond to the following: (a) How many CDs and DVDs do you current own that you will probably never use again? (b) Have you ever thrown out any CDs or DVDs in the garbage? (c) What can you do to reduce the future effect of CDs and DVDs on landfills? (d) List three disc recycling companies. (e) What can companies do?

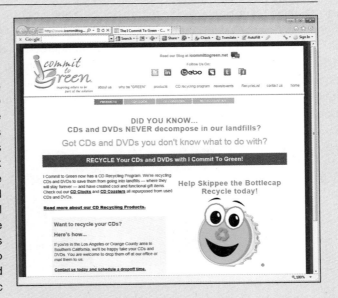

Basic Application Software

▲ Download the free *Computing Essentials 2013* app for videos, key term flashcards, quizzes, and the game, *Over the Edge!*

Competencies

After you have read this chapter, you should be able to:

1 Discuss common features of most software applications.

2 Discuss word processors and word processing features.

3 Describe spreadsheets and spreadsheet features.

4 Discuss database management systems and database management features.

5 Describe presentation graphics and presentation graphics features.

6 Discuss integrated packages.

7 Describe software suites including office suites, cloud suites, specialized suites, and utility suites.

Why should I read this chapter?

At one time all document preparation was a manual process performed by clerical staff. That was then and this is now. Now, a required skill for nearly every profession is the ability to create documents, to analyze data, to develop presentations, and to store and retrieve information. Professionals need to know how to use software applications on their desktops or from the cloud to perform these activities.

This chapter discusses these applications including word processors, spreadsheets, database management systems, and presentation graphics. Additionally, you'll learn about cloud computing applications, integrated packages, and software suites. To be competent and to be competitive in today's professional workplace, you need to know and to understand these things.

chapter 3

71

Hi, I'm Juan and I'm a computer trainer. I'd like to talk with you about basic application software . . . programs that we all need to know. I'd also like to talk with you about how to access and use these traditional programs using cloud computing.

Introduction

Not long ago, trained specialists were required to perform many of the operations you can now do with a microcomputer. Market analysts used calculators to project sales. Graphic artists created designs by hand. Data processing clerks created electronic files to be stored on large computers. Now you can do all these tasks—and many others—with a microcomputer and the appropriate application software.

Think of the microcomputer as an electronic tool. You may not consider yourself very good at typing, calculating, organizing, presenting, or managing information. However, a microcomputer can help you do all these things and much more. All it takes is the right kinds of software.

Competent end users need to understand the capabilities of basic application software, which includes word processors, spreadsheets, database management systems, and presentation programs. They need to know about integrated packages and software suites.

Application Software

As we discussed in Chapter 1, there are two kinds of software. **System software** works with end users, application software, and computer hardware to handle the majority of technical details. **Application software,** also known simply as **apps,** can be described as end-user software and is used to accomplish a variety of tasks.

Application software, in turn, can be divided into two categories. One category, **basic applications,** is the focus of this chapter. They include word processors, spreadsheets, database management systems, and presentation graphics. The other category, **specialized applications,** includes thousands of other programs that tend to be more narrowly focused and used in specific disciplines and occupations. Specialized applications are presented in Chapter 4.

Common Features

A **user interface** is the portion of the application that allows you to control and to interact with the program. Almost all applications use a **graphical user interface (gui)** that displays graphical elements called **icons** to represent familiar objects and a mouse. The mouse controls a **pointer** on the screen that is used to select items such as icons. Another feature is the use of windows to display information. A **window** is simply a rectangular area that can contain a document, program, or message. (Do not confuse the term *window* with the various versions of Microsoft's Windows operating systems, which are programs.) More than one window can be opened and displayed on the computer screen at one time.

Traditionally, most software programs use a system of menus, toolbars, and dialog boxes. (See Figure 3-1.)

- **Menus** present commands that are typically displayed in a **menu bar** at the top of the screen.
- **Toolbars** typically appear below the menu bar and include small graphic elements called **buttons** that provide shortcuts for quick access to commonly used commands.
- **Dialog boxes** provide additional information and request user input.

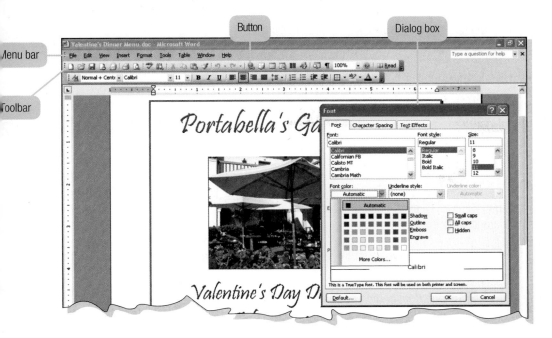

Button

Dialog box

Menu bar

Toolbar

Figure 3-1 Traditional graphical user interface

Many Microsoft and other applications use an interface known as the **ribbon gui.** Designed to make it easier to find and use all the features of an application, this gui uses a system of ribbons, tabs, and galleries. (See Figure 3-2.)

- **Ribbons** replace menus and toolbars by organizing commonly used commands into a set of tabs. These tabs display command buttons that are the most relevant to the tasks being performed by the user.
- **Tabs** are used to divide the ribbon into major activity areas. Each tab is then organized into **groups** that contain related items. Some tabs, called **contextual tabs,** only appear when they are needed and anticipate the next operations to be performed by the user.
- **Galleries** simplify the process of making a selection from a list of alternatives. This is accomplished by graphically displaying the effect of alternatives before being selected.

Many applications support **speech recognition,** the ability to accept voice input to select menu options and dictate text. See Making IT Work for You: Speech Recognition on pages 74 and 75. To learn more about how speech recognition works, visit our Web site at www.computing2013.com and enter the keyword **speech.**

Gallery

Tab

Ribbons

Groups

Figure 3-2 Ribbon gui

Making IT work for you

SPEECH RECOGNITION

Tired of using your keyboard to type term papers? Have you ever thought about using your voice to control application software? Perhaps speech recognition is just what you are looking for.

Training the Software   The first step is to set up your microphone and train your software to recognize your voice. Using the Microsoft Windows 7 operating system:

1 • Click *Start/Control Panel/Ease of Access/Speech Recognition Options.*

• Click *Start Speech Recognition.*

2 • Complete the Microphone Setup Wizard to adjust your microphone for Speech Recognition.

3 • Click *Start/Control Panel/Ease of Access/Speech Recognition.*

• Click *Train your computer to better understand you.*

• Read the text presented to teach the software your unique speech patterns.

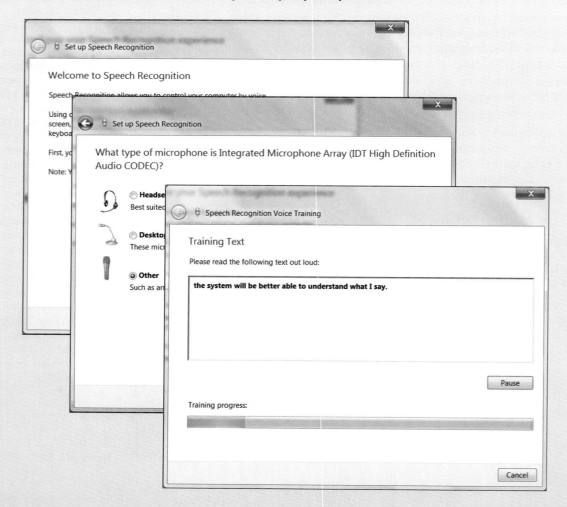

Controlling a Program   Once the software is trained, you can control many computer operations with just your voice. The Speech Reference Card is a handy guide to the commands your computer will understand. To open the Speech Reference Card:

1 ● Click *Start/Control Panel/ Ease of Access/ Speech Recognition.*

● Click *Open the Speech Reference Card.*

● Click *Show All* to display a complete list of speech shortcuts, or click the print icon to print the list.

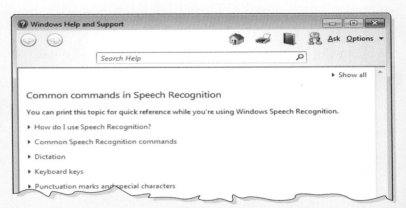

Dictating a Document   You can also dictate text using the Language bar. For example, to insert text into a Microsoft Word document:

1 ● Say, "Open Word," to open a new Microsoft Word document.

● Dictate the text you want to appear in the document.

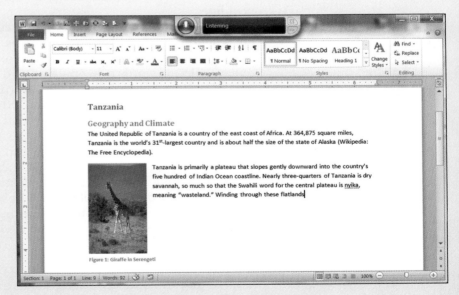

Although speech recognition technology continues to improve, speech recognition is not yet ready for completely hands-free operation. You will get the best results if you use a combination of your voice and the mouse or keyboard.

The Web is continually changing, and some of the specifics presented in the Making IT Work for You section may have changed.

To learn about other ways to make information technology work for you, visit our Web site at www.computing2013.com and enter the keyword miw.

CONCEPT CHECK

What is the difference between basic and specialized applications?

List some common features of most programs including those with a traditional gui.

Discuss the ribbon gui including ribbons, tabs, groups, contextual tabs, and galleries.

Word Processors

Explorations

Microsoft is one of the leaders in creating software applications.

To learn more about the company, visit our Web site at www.computing2013. com and enter the keyword microsoft.

Word processors create text-based **documents** and are one of the most flexible and widely used software tools. All types of people and organizations use word processors to create memos, letters, and faxes. Organizations create newsletters, manuals, and brochures to provide information to their customers. Students and researchers use word processors to create reports. Word processors can even be used to create personalized Web pages.

Microsoft Word is the most widely used word processor. Other popular word processors include Corel WordPerfect, Apple Pages, Open Office, and Google Docs.

Features

Word processors provide a variety of features to make entering, editing, and formatting documents easy. One of the most basic features for entering text is **word wrap.** This feature automatically moves the insertion point to the next line once the current line is full. As you type, the words wrap around to the next line.

There are numerous features designed to support **editing** or modifying a document. One of these is a **thesaurus** that provides synonyms, antonyms, and related words for a selected word or phrase. You can quickly locate and replace selected words using the **find and replace** feature. **Spelling** and **grammar checkers** look for misspelled words and problems with capitalization, punctuation, and sentence structure. Other features are designed to improve the **format** or appearance of a document. One of the most basic is the **font** or design of the characters. (See Figure 3-3.) The height of a character is its **font size.** The appearance of characters can be enhanced using such **character effects** as **bold,** *italic,* and **colors.** Rather than individually selecting specific fonts, sizes, and formats, the **styles** feature, found in most word processors, enables users to quickly apply a predefined set of formatting characteristics to text in one easy step. **Bulleted** and **numbered lists** can make a sequence of topics easy to read.

Font	Sample
Calibri	A B C a b c
Impact	**A B C a b c**
Cambria	A B C a b c
Broadway	**A B C a b c**

Figure 3-3 Sample fonts

Case

Assume that you have accepted a job as an advertising coordinator for Adventure Travel Tours, a travel agency specializing in active adventure vacations. Your primary responsibilities are to create and coordinate the company's promotional materials, including flyers and travel reports. To see how you could use Microsoft Word as the advertising coordinator for the Adventure Travel Tours, see Figures 3-4 and 3-5.

creating a flyer

You have been asked to create a promotional advertising flyer. After discussing the flyer's contents and basic structure with your supervisor, you start to enter the flyer's text. As you enter the text, *words wrap* automatically at the end of each line. Also, while entering the text, the *spelling checker* and *grammar checker* catch spelling and grammatical errors. Once the text has been entered, you focus your attention on enhancing the visual aspects of the flyer. You add an interesting graphic and experiment with different character and paragraph formats including *fonts, font sizes, colors,* and *alignments.* See Figure 3-4. ●

Spelling Checker
Correcting spelling and typing errors identified by the **spelling checker** creates an error-free and professional-looking document.

Center-Aligning
Center-aligning all of the text in the flyer creates a comfortable, balanced appearance.

Fonts and Font Size
Using interesting **fonts** and a large **font size** in the flyer's title grab the reader's attention.

Word Wrap
The **word wrap** feature automatically determines where to end one line of text and to begin the next.

Adventure Travel Tours
New Adventures

Attention adventure travelers! Attend an Adventure presentation to learn about some of the earth's greatest unspoiled habitats and find out how you can experience the adventure of a lifetime. This year we are offering four new tours:

- India Wildlife Adventure
- Inca Trail to Machu Picchu
- Safari in Tanzania
- Costa Rica Rivers and Rainforests

Call Student Name at 1-800-555-0004 for presentation locations, full color brochures, itinerary information, costs, and trip dates.

Character Effects
Adding **character effects** such as bold and color make important information stand out and make the flyer more visually interesting.

Grammar Checker
Incomplete sentences, awkward wording, and incorrect punctuation are identified and corrections are offered by the **grammar checker**.

Figure 3-4 Flyer

creating a report

Your next assignment is to create a report on Tanzania and Peru. After conducting your research, you start writing your paper. As you enter the text for the report, you notice that the *AutoCorrect* feature automatically corrects some grammar and punctuation errors. Your report includes several figures and *tables*. You use the *captions* feature to keep track of figure and table numbers, to enter the caption text, and to position the captions. When referencing figures or tables from the text, you use the *cross-reference* feature. *Footnotes* are used to further explain or comment on information in the report. You then carefully document your sources using *citations*. Finally, you prepare the report for printing by adding *header* and *footer* information. See Figure 3-5. ●

Captions and Cross-References
Identifying figures with **captions** and using **cross-references** in a report make the report easier to read and more professional.

AutoCorrect
As you enter text, you occasionally forget to capitalize the first word in a sentence. Fortunately, **Auto-Correct** recognizes the error and automatically capitalizes the word.

Citations
The sources of information you used in developing the report appear in **citations**.

Header or Footer
Page numbers and other document-related information can be included in a **header** or **footer**.

Footnote
To include a note about Mt. Kilimanjaro, you use the footnote feature. This feature inserts the **footnote** superscript number and automatically formats the bottom of the page to contain the footnote text.

Tanzania & Peru

Tanzania

Geography and Climate

"In the midst of a great wilderness, full of wild beasts...I fancied I saw a summit...covered with a dazzlingly white cloud (qtd. in Cole 56). This is how Johann Krapf, the first outsider to witness the splendor of Africa's highest mountain, described Kilimanjaro. The peak was real, though the white clouds he "fancied" he saw were the dense layer of snow that coats the mountain.[1]

Tanzania is primarily a plateau that slopes gently downward into the country's five hundred miles of Indian Ocean coastline. Nearly three-quarters of Tanzania is dry savannah, so much so that the Swahili word for the central plateau is *nyika*, meaning "wasteland." Winding through these flatlands is the Great Rift Valley, which forms narrow and shallow lakes in its long path. Several of these great lakes form a belt-like oasis of green vegetation. Contrasting with the severity of the plains are the coastal areas, which are lush with ample rainfall. In the north the plateau slopes dramatically into Mt. Kilimanjaro.

Ngorongoro Conservation Area

Some of Tanzania's most distinguishing geographical features are found in the Ngorongoro Conservation Area.[2] The park is composed of many craters and gorges, as well as lakes, forest, and plains. Among these features is the area's namesake, the Ngorongoro Crater. The Crater is a huge expanse, covering more than one hundred square miles. On the Crater's floor, grasslands blend into swamps, lakes, rivers, and woodland. Also within the Conservation Area's perimeter is the Olduvai Gorge, commonly referred to as the "Cradle of Mankind," where in 1931 the stone

FIGURE 1 GIRAFFE IN SERENGETI

---

[1] Mt. Kilimanjaro is 19,340 feet high, making it the fourth tallest mountain in the world.

[2] The Conservation Area is a national preserve spanning 3,196 square miles.

Tanzania & Peru

2

Figure 3-5 Report

CONCEPT CHECK

What do word processors do? What is word wrap?

Describe the following editing features: thesaurus, find and replace, spelling and grammar checkers.

Describe the following formatting features: font, font size, character effects, styles, numbered and bulleted lists.

Spreadsheets

Spreadsheet programs organize, analyze, and graph numeric data such as budgets and financial reports. Once used exclusively by accountants, spreadsheets are widely used by nearly every profession. Marketing professionals analyze sales trends. Financial analysts evaluate and graph stock market trends. Students and teachers record grades and calculate grade point averages.

The most widely used spreadsheet program is Microsoft Excel. Other spreadsheet applications include Apple iWork's Numbers and Corel Quattro Pro.

Features

Unlike word processors, which manipulate text and create text documents, spreadsheet programs manipulate numeric data and create workbook files. **Workbook files** consist of one or more related worksheets. A **worksheet,** also known as a **spreadsheet** or **sheet,** is a rectangular grid of **rows** and **columns.** For example, in Figure 3-6, the columns are identified by letters and the rows are identified by numbers. The intersection of a row and column creates a **cell.** For example, the cell D8 is formed by the intersection of column D and row 8.

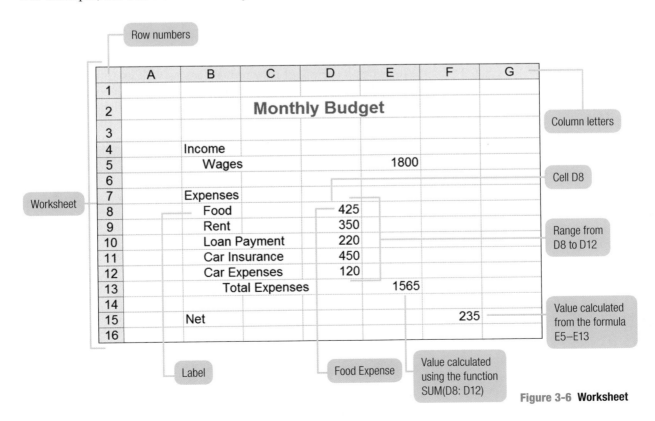

Figure 3-6 **Worksheet**

A cell can contain text or numeric entries. **Text entries** or **labels** provide structure to a worksheet by describing the contents of rows and columns. For example, in Figure 3-6, cell B8 contains the label Food. The cell D8 contains a number identified as the food expense.

A **numeric entry** can be a number or a formula. A **formula** is an instruction to calculate or process. For example, the cell F15 contains the formula = E5–E13. This formula will calculate a value and display that value in cell F15. The value is calculated by taking the value in cell E5 and subtracting the value in cell E13. **Functions** are prewritten formulas provided by the spreadsheet program that perform calculations such as adding a series of cells. For example, the cell E13 contains the function SUM(D8:D12), which adds the values in the range from D8 to D12. A **range** is a series of continuous cells. In this case, the range includes D8, D9, D10, D11, and D12. The sum of the values in this range is displayed in cell E13. Spreadsheet programs typically provide a variety of different types of functions, including financial, mathematical, statistical, and logical functions. Some of these functions are presented in Figure 3-7.

Analytical graphs or **charts** are visual representations of data in a spreadsheet. You can readily create graphs in a spreadsheet program by selecting the cells containing the data to be charted and then selecting the type of chart to display. If you change one or more numbers in your spreadsheet, all related formulas will automatically recalculate and charts will be recreated. This is called **recalculation.** The process of observing the effect of changing one or more cells is often referred to as **what-if analysis.** For example, to analyze the effect of a rent increase in the Monthly Budget worksheet in Figure 3-6, all you would need to do is replace the contents in cell D9. The entire spreadsheet, including any charts that had been created, would be recalculated automatically.

tips

Have you ever wanted to draw attention to a cell in a spreadsheet? Shapes make it easy to emphasize the contents of your worksheet. If you are using Excel 2010:

1 Select *Shapes* from the *Illustrations* group on the *Insert* tab.

2 Choose a shape from the menu, click on the worksheet, and drag to create the shape.

3 While the shape is selected on the worksheet, use the *Shape Styles* gallery on the *Drawing Tools Format* tab to modify its appearance.

To see additional tips, visit our Web site at www.computing2013.com and enter the keyword tips.

Case

Assume that you have just accepted a job as manager of the Downtown Internet Café. This café provides a variety of flavored coffees as well as Internet access. One of your responsibilities is to create a financial plan for the next year. To see how you could use Microsoft Excel, the most widely used spreadsheet program, as the manager for the Downtown Internet Café, see Figures 3-8 through 3-10.

Type	Function	Calculates
Financial	PMT	Size of loan payments
	PV	Present value for an investment
Mathematical	SUM	Sum of the numbers in a range of cells
	ABS	Absolute value of a number
Statistical	AVERAGE	Average or mean of the numbers in a range of cells
	MAX	Largest number in a range of cells
Logical	IF	Whether a condition is true; if true, a specified value is displayed; if not true, then a different specified value is displayed
	AND	Whether two conditions are true; if both are true, then a specified value is displayed; if either one or both are not true, then a different specified value is displayed

Figure 3-7 Selected spreadsheet functions

Your first project is to develop a first-quarter sales forecast for the café. You begin by studying sales data and talking with several managers. After obtaining sales and expense estimates, you are ready to create the first-quarter forecast. You start structuring the *worksheet* by inserting descriptive *text entries* for the row and column headings. Next, you insert *numeric entries,* including *formulas* and *functions* to perform calculations. To test the accuracy of the worksheet, you change the values in some cells and compare the recalculated spreadsheet results with hand calculations. See Figure 3-8. ●

Worksheets
Worksheets are used for a wide range of different applications. One of the most common uses is to create, analyze, and forecast budgets.

Text Entries
Text entries provide meaning to the values in the worksheet. The rows are labeled to identify the various sales and expense items. The columns are labeled to specify the months.

	A	B	C	D	E	F
1						
2						
3		**Downtown Internet Café**				
4		*First Quarter Forecast*				
5						
6		JAN	FEB	MAR	TOTAL	AVG
7	**Sales**					
8	Beverage	$ 13,600	$ 14,600	$ 15,600	$ 43,800	$ 14,600
9	Food	$ 7,100	$ 7,300	$ 7,400	$ 21,800	$ 7,267
10	Internet	$ 4,000	$ 4,300	$ 4,500	$ 12,800	$ 4,267
11	Merchandise	$ 3,100	$ 3,200	$ 3,300	$ 9,600	$ 3,200
12	Total Sales	$ 27,800	$ 29,400	$ 30,800	$ 8?	
13	**Expenses**					
14	Cost of Goods	$ 6,950	$ 7,300	$ 7,600	$ 2	
15	Payroll	$ 7,500	$ 7,500	$ 7,500	$ 2	
16	Computers	$ 6,400	$ 6,400	$ 6,400	$ 1	
17	Lease	$ 5,500	$ 5,500	$ 5,500	$ 1	
18	Marketing	$ 1,000	$ 1,000	$ 1,000	$	
19	Miscellaneous	$ 1,500	$ 1,500	$ 1,500	$	
20	Total Expenses	$ 28,850	$ 29,200	$ 29,500	$ 87,550	$ 29,183
21	**Income**					
22	Net Income	$ (1,050)	$ 200	$ 1,300	$ 450	$ 150
23	Profit Margin	-3.78%	0.68%	4.22%	0.51%	
24				Income Year-To-Date	$ 450	

Cells
Cells can contain labels, numbers, formulas, and functions. A cell's content is indicated by the row and column labels. For example, cell D15 contains a number for the Payroll expense expected for March.

Functions
One advantage of using **functions** rather than entering formulas is that they are easier to enter. In this case, cell C20 (Total Expenses for February) contains the function SUM(C14: C19) rather than the formula =C14+C15+ C16+C17+C18+C19.

Formulas
Formulas Formulas provide a way to perform calculations in the worksheet. In this case, cell C22 (Net Income for February) contains the formula =C12 (Total Sales for February) – C20 (Total Expenses for February) contains a number for the Payroll expense expected for March.

Figure 3-8 **Worksheet**

After completing the First-Quarter Forecast for the Downtown Internet Café, you decide to *chart* the sales data to better visualize the projected growth in sales. You select the 3D column *chart type* to show each month's projected sales category. Using a variety of chart options, you enter descriptive *titles* for the chart, the x-axis, and the y-axis. Then you use *data labels* to focus attention on the growing Internet sales. Finally, you insert a *legend* to define the chart's different columns. See Figure 3-9. ●

Chart Titles
Including a **chart title** and subtitle as well as titles along the x-axis and y-axis make the chart easier to read and understand.

Chart Types
To display the monthly expenses over the quarter, you consider several different **chart types** before selecting the 3D column chart. The 3D variation of the chart provides an interesting depth perception to the columns.

Chart
Once data is in the worksheet, it is very easy to **chart** the data. All you need to do is to select the data to chart, select the chart type, and add some descriptive text.

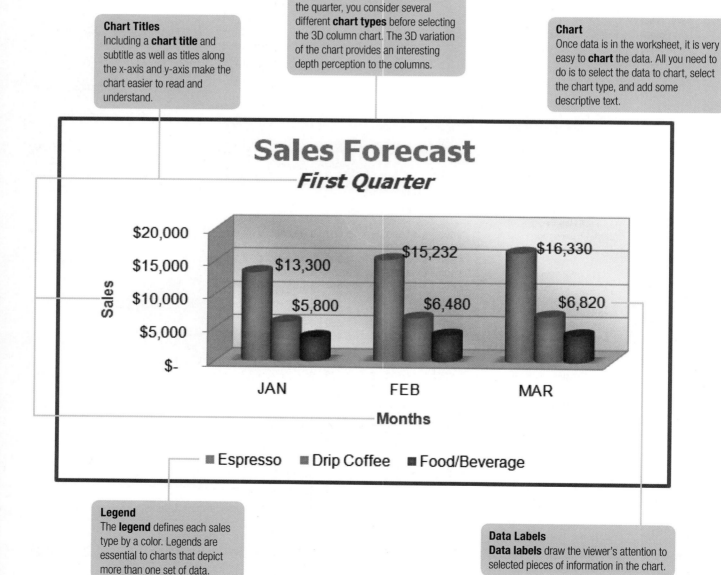

Legend
The **legend** defines each sales type by a color. Legends are essential to charts that depict more than one set of data.

Data Labels
Data labels draw the viewer's attention to selected pieces of information in the chart.

Figure 3-9 Chart

After presenting the First-Quarter Forecast to the owner, you revise the format and expand the *workbook* to include worksheets for each quarter and an annual forecast summary. You give each worksheet a descriptive *sheet name.* At the request of the owner, you perform a *what-if analysis* to test the effect of different estimates for payroll, and you use *Goal Seek* to determine how much Total Internet Sales would have to increase to produce a profit margin of 15 percent for the first quarter. See Figure 3-10. ●

Workbook
The first worksheet in a **workbook** is often a summary of the following worksheets. In this case, the first worksheet presents the entire year's forecast. The subsequent worksheets provide the details.

Downtown Internet Café
2006 Annual Forecast

	JAN	FEB	MAR	APR	MAY	JUN	JUL	AUG	SEP
Sales									
Beverage	$18,000	$ 17,500	$ 17,200	$18,039	$ 17,940	$19,074	$10,993	$ 9,099	$12,909
Food	$ 8,500	$ 8,200	$ 8,000	$ 8,123	$ 9,231	$ 7,001	$ 6,912	$ 5,500	$ 8,700
Internet	$ 5,700	$ 7,400	$ 7,200	$ 8,021	$ 6,751	$ 5,781	$ 4,510	$ 8,233	$ 7,811
Merchandise	$ 3,600	$ 3,500	$ 3,300	$ 2,390	$ 1,290	$ 1,592	$ 1,677	$ 3,008	$ 2,987
Total Sales	$35,800	$ 36,600	$ 35,700	$36,573	$ 35,212	$33,448	$24,092	$25,840	$32,407
Expenses									
Cost of Goods	$ 8,750	$ 8,475	$ 8,300	$ 8,750	$ 8,475	$ 8,300	$ 8,750	$ 8,475	$ 8,300
Payroll	$ 9,398	$ 8,700	$ 8,100	$ 9,398	$ 8,700	$ 8,100	$ 9,398	$ 8,700	$ 8,100
Computers	$ 6,400	$ 6,400	$ 6,400	$ 6,400	$ 6,400	$ 6,400	$ 6,400	$ 6,400	$ 6,400
Lease	$ 6,000	$ 6,000	$ 6,000	$ 6,000	$ 6,000	$ 6,000	$ 6,000	$ 6,000	$ 6,000
Advertising	$ 1,000	$ 1,000	$ 1,000	$ 1,000	$ 1,000	$ 1,000	$ 1,000	$ 1,000	$ 1,000
Miscellaneous	$ 1,500	$ 1,500	$ 1,500	$ 1,500	$ 1,500	$ 1,500	$ 1,500	$ 1,500	$ 1,500
Total Expenses	$33,048	$ 32,075	$ 31,300	$33,048	$ 32,075	$31,300	$33,048	$32,075	$31,300
Income									
Net Income	$ 2,752	$ 4,525	$ 4,400	$ 2,752	$ 4,525	$ 4,400	$ 2,752	$ 4,525	$ 4,400
Profit Margin	7.69%	12.36%	12.32%	7.69%	12.36%	12.32%	7.69%	12.36%	12.32%
Quarter Profit Margin			10.80%			10.80%			10.80%
Income Year-To-Date			$ 11,677			$ 23,353			$ 35,030

Year / First Quarter / Second Quarter / Third Quarter / Fourth Quarter / Scenario Summary / D

Sheet Name
Each worksheet has a unique **sheet name**. To make the workbook easy to navigate, it is a good practice to always use simple yet descriptive names for each worksheet.

What-If Analysis
What-if analysis is a very powerful and simple tool to test the effects of different assumptions in a spreadsheet.

E10 ▾ ƒx =E22/E12

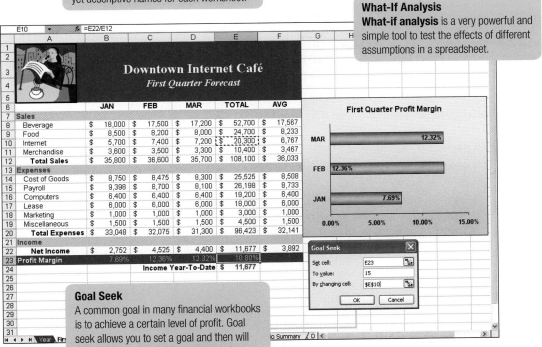

Goal Seek
A common goal in many financial workbooks is to achieve a certain level of profit. Goal seek allows you to set a goal and then will analyze other parts of the workbook that would need to be adjusted to meet that goal.

Figure 3-10 **Workbook**

CONCEPT CHECK

What are spreadsheets used for? What is a workbook file? What is a worksheet?

Define rows, columns, cells, ranges, text, and numeric entries.

Describe the following spreadsheet features: formulas, functions, charts, recalculation, and what-if analysis.

Database Management Systems

A **database** is a collection of related data. It is the electronic equivalent of a file cabinet. A **database management system (DBMS)** or **database manager** is a program that sets up, or structures, a database. It also provides tools to enter, edit, and retrieve data from the database. All kinds of individuals use databases, from teachers recording grades to police officers checking criminal histories. Colleges and universities use databases to keep records on their students, instructors, and courses. Organizations of all types maintain employee databases.

The most widely used database management system designed for microcomputers is Microsoft Access.

Explorations

Adobe is one of the leaders in software development.

To learn more about the company, visit our Web site at www.computing2013 .com and enter the keyword adobe.

tips

Are you overwhelmed by your collection of music, videos, and books? Would you like some help getting your life in order? Fortunately, Microsoft provides a variety of Access templates that might be just right for you. Here's how to find them:

1 Connect to office.microsoft.com.

2 Click the *Templates* tab to display the Templates Web page. Type Access in the Templates search box and click the Search button.

3 Look through the templates and select the ones that might be valuable to you.

To see more tips, visit our Web site at www.computing2013.com and enter the keyword tips.

Features

The **relational database** is the most widely used database structure. Data is organized into related **tables.** Each table is made up of rows called **records** and columns called **fields.** Each record contains fields of data about some specific person, place, or thing.

A DBMS provides a variety of tools to create and use databases. A **sort** tool will quickly rearrange a table's records according to a selected field. A **filter** tool will display only those records meeting the conditions you specify.

The greatest power of a DBMS, however, comes from its ability to find and bring together information stored in separate tables using queries, forms, and reports. A **query** is a request for specific data contained in a database. Database **forms** look similar to traditional printed forms. These electronic forms are displayed on the computer monitor and typically reflect the contents for one record in a table. They are primarily used to enter new records and to make changes to existing records. Data from tables and queries can be printed in a variety of different types of **reports** from a simple listing of one field in a table to a list of selected fields based on a query involving several tables.

Case

Assume that you have accepted a job as an employment administrator for the Lifestyle Fitness Club. One of your responsibilities is to create a database management system to replace the club's manual system for recording employee information. To see how you could use Microsoft Access, one of the most widely used relational DBMS programs, as the employment administrator for the Lifestyle Fitness Club, see Figures 3-11 and 3-12.

creating a database

The first step in creating the database management system is to plan. You study the existing manual system focusing on how and what data is collected and how it is used. Next, you design the basic structure or organization of the new database system to have two related *tables,* which will make entering data and using the database more efficient. Focusing on the first table, Employees, you create the table structure by specifying the *fields,* and *primary key* field. To make the process faster and more accurate, you create a *form* and enter the data for each employee as a *record* in the table. See Figure 3-11. ●

Primary Key
The primary key is the unique employee identification number. You considered using the last name field as the primary key but realized that more than one employee could have the same last name. Primary keys are often used to link tables.

Fields
Fields are given field names that are displayed at the top of each table. You select the field names to describe their contents.

Table
Tables make up the basic structure of a relational database with columns containing field data and rows containing record information. This table records basic information about each employee, including name, address, and telephone number.

Record
Each record contains information about one employee. A record often includes a combination of numeric, text, and object data types.

Employee ID	Last Name					ZIP Code	Home Phone	Gender	Birth Date	
12920	Larson					92121-3740	(941) 555-7717	F	6/21/1983	Ⓤ(0)
13416	Lembi					92120-3741	(941) 555-4747	M	9/12/1979	Ⓤ(0)
11747	Lettow					92120-3740	(507) 555-2805	M	11/15/1981	Ⓤ(0)
22085	Lindau					92120-3741	(941) 555-6363	F	2/24/1977	Ⓤ(0)
03406	Lopez					92121-3740	(507) 555-5050	F	2/25/1977	Ⓤ(0)
04731	Marchant					92120-3741	(507) 555-6707	F	5/13/1980	Ⓤ(2)
13543	Martinez	Julie	1920 First Ave.	Maldin	CA	92121-3740	(941) 555-1044	F	12/10/1983	Ⓤ(0)
13635	Martinez	Juan	7115 E Roosevelt Dr.	Maldin	CA	92121-3740	(507) 555-2935	M	12/10/1983	Ⓤ(0)
22407	Mazeau	Rebecca	7383 Oak Dr.	Landis	CA	92120-3741	(941) 555-1093	F	9/23/1979	Ⓤ(0)
03225	Morgan	Dan	564 S. Lemon Dr.	Maldin	CA	92121	(507) 555-5567	M	3/5/1975	Ⓤ(0)
99999	Name	Student	1234 N. Fifth St.	Chesterfield	CA	92122-1268	(507) 555-1234	F	4/1/1982	Ⓤ(0)
00617	Nichols	Cathy	75 Brooklea Dr.	Landis	CA	92120-3741	(507) 555-0001	F	5/19/1965	Ⓤ(0)
00907	Pennington	Mark	23 Mill Ave.	Landis	CA	92120-3741	(507) 555-3333	M	7/7/1969	Ⓤ(0)
12194	Polonsky	Mitch	8701 E. Sheridan	Maldin	CA	92121-3740	(507) 555-1018	M	3/13/1980	Ⓤ(0)
12247	Rath	Kathy	87 E. Aurora Ave.	Chesterfield	CA	92122-1268	(507) 555-9797	F	5/30/1978	Ⓤ(0)
12594	Reddie	Mark	900 W. Campus Dr.	Maldin	CA	92121	(507) 555-1139	M	11/5/1983	Ⓤ(0)
12230	Reddie	Suzanne	932 E. Parkway Dr.	Landis	CA	92120-3741	(507) 555-1191	F	7/14/1978	Ⓤ(0)
13005	Reilly	Emily	125 N. Marigold St.	Maldin	CA	92121-3740	(941) 555-6532	F	5/21/1985	Ⓤ(0)
12612	Richards	Melissa	5522 W. Marin Lane	River Mist	CA	92123	(507) 555-7789	F	9/30/1978	Ⓤ(0)
06000	Robertson	Kirk	832 S. William Ave.	Maldin	CA	92121	(507) 555-3730	M	4/5/1974	Ⓤ(0)
22297	Rogondino	Patricia	7583 Turquoise	Chesterfield	CA	92122-1268	(941) 555-7539	F	8/30/1977	Ⓤ(0)
07287	Roman	Anita	2348 S. Bala Dr.	Maldin	CA	92121-3740	(507) 555-9870	F	3/15/1981	Ⓤ(0)
12918	Ruiz	Carlos	10101 First St.	Maldin	CA	92121-3740	(507) 555-5125	M	7/27/1980	Ⓤ(1)
08391	Ruiz	Enrique	35 Palm St.	Chesterfield	CA	92122-1268	(507) 555-0091	M	12/10/1973	Ⓤ(0)
04321	Sabin	Greg	90 E. Rawhide Ave							
00212	Schiff	Chad	235 N. Cactus Dr.							
22114	Schneider	Paul	1731 Jackson Ave							
01421	Spehr	Timothy	90 Royal Dr.							
12366	Stacey	David	737 S. College Rd							
13497	Steele	Jeff	1011 E. Holly Ln.							
12668	Stueland	Valerie	34 University Dr.							
12583	Sullivan	Marie	78 Omega Drive							
12867	Talic	Elvis	21 Oasis St.							
03890	Thi	Erona	7867 Forest Ave.							
22304	Torcivia	Peter	904 S. Dorsey Dr.							
			289 E. Heather Av							

Form
Like printed paper forms, electronic forms should be designed to be easy to read and use. This form makes it easy to enter and view all employees' data, including their photographs.

Employee Records

Employee ID	12918
First Name	Carlos
Last Name	Ruiz
Address	10101 First St.
City	Maldin
State	CA
ZIP Code	92121-3740
Home Phone	(507) 555-5125
Gender	M
Birth Date	7/27/1980

Photo/Resume

Record: 14 ◄ 41 of 55 ► ►I   No Filter   Search

Figure 3-11 Table and form

creating a query

You have continued to build the database by creating a second table named Job containing information about each employee's work location and job title. This table is linked or *joined* with the Employee Records table by the common field, Employee ID. After you completed this second table, you received a request to create car pool information for those employees who live in either Maldin or Chesterfield and work in Landis. You created a *query* using the appropriate *criteria* to create the car pool list. Then *sorting* alphabetically according to city, you created a *report* to distribute to interested employees. See Figure 3-12. ●

Query
Your query requests the names, addresses, and telephone numbers of all employees living in Maldin or Chesterfield who work in Landis.

Joined
Since the query involves three tables, they must be linked or joined by common fields. You chose to link the tables by the key field Employee ID.

Criteria
The query criteria to produce the car pool list require that both the Employee Records table and the Jobs table be consulted. The criteria identify all employees who work at Landis and live either in Maldin or Chesterfield.

Report
From a variety of different report formats, you selected this format to display the names, addresses, and telephone numbers of all employees who might commute from either Maldin or Chesterfield to Landis.

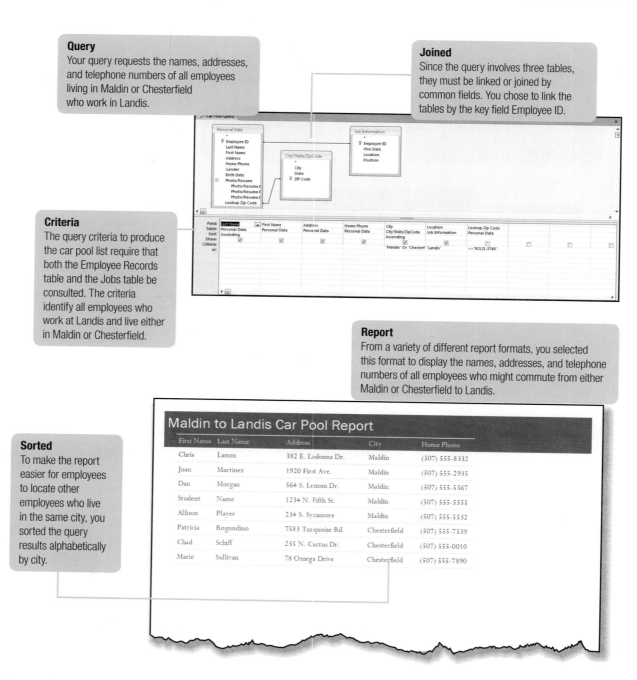

Sorted
To make the report easier for employees to locate other employees who live in the same city, you sorted the query results alphabetically by city.

Maldin to Landis Car Pool Report

First Name	Last Name	Address	City	Home Phone
Chris	Lamm	382 E. Ladonna Dr.	Maldin	(507) 555-8332
Juan	Martinez	1920 First Ave.	Maldin	(507) 555-2935
Dan	Morgan	564 S. Lemon Dr.	Maldin	(507) 555-5567
Student	Name	1234 N. Fifth St.	Maldin	(507) 555-5555
Allison	Player	234 S. Sycamore	Maldin	(507) 555-5532
Patricia	Rogondino	7583 Turquoise Rd.	Chesterfield	(507) 555-7539
Chad	Schiff	235 N. Cactus Dr.	Chesterfield	(507) 555-0010
Marie	Sullivan	78 Omega Drive	Chesterfield	(507) 555-7890

Figure 3-12 Query and report

CONCEPT CHECK

- What is a database? What is a DBMS? A relational database?
- What are tables, records, and fields?
- Describe the following DBMS features: sort, filter, query, form, and report.

Presentation Graphics

Research shows that people learn better when information is presented visually. A picture is indeed worth a thousand words or numbers. **Presentation graphics** are programs that combine a variety of visual objects to create attractive, visually interesting presentations. They are excellent tools to communicate a message and to persuade people.

People in a variety of settings and situations use presentation graphics programs to make their presentations more interesting and professional. For example, marketing managers use presentation graphics to present proposed marketing strategies to their superiors. Salespeople use these programs to demonstrate products and encourage customers to make purchases. Students use presentation graphics programs to create high-quality class presentations.

Three of the most widely used presentation graphics programs are Microsoft PowerPoint, Corel Presentations, and Apple Keynote.

Features

An electronic presentation consists of a series of **slides** or **pages.** Presentation programs include a variety of features to help you create effective dynamic presentations. Most include design and content templates that help you quickly create a professional-looking presentation. **Design templates** provide professionally selected combinations of color schemes, slide layouts, and special effects. **Content templates** include suggested content for each slide. Other features include tools to select alternative color schemes and slide layouts, to create animated graphics and charts, and to help you rehearse the presentation.

More advanced features include the capability to insert video and audio clips as well as **animations** or special effects that add action to text and graphics on a slide. Additionally, **transitions** can be used to animate how the presentation moves from one slide to the next. Other features allow you to print slides, create speaker notes, and provide handouts for your audience.

Case

Assume that you have volunteered for the Animal Rescue Foundation, a local animal rescue agency. You have been asked to create a powerful and persuasive presentation to encourage other members from your community to volunteer. To see how you could use Microsoft PowerPoint, one of the most widely used presentation graphics programs, as a volunteer for the Animal Rescue Foundation, see Figures 3-13 and 3-14.

Explorations

Lotus is one of the leaders in developing presentation graphics.

To learn more about the company, visit our Web site at www.computing2013 .com and enter the keyword lotus.

creating a presentation

You start creating the presentation using the Presentation on Product or Service *template*. The template consists of a sample presentation containing suggested content in each slide and uses a consistent design style throughout. After replacing the sample content, you are on your way to the director's office to show what you have. See Figure 3-13. •

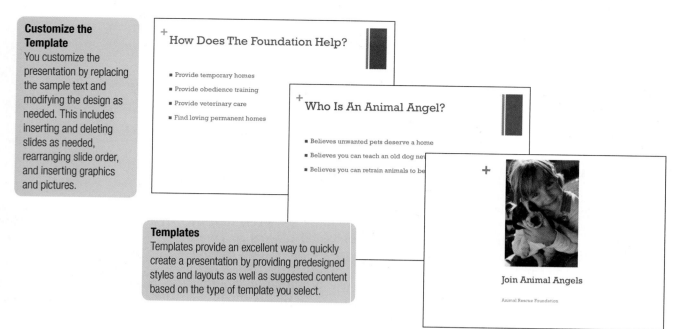

Customize the Template
You customize the presentation by replacing the sample text and modifying the design as needed. This includes inserting and deleting slides as needed, rearranging slide order, and inserting graphics and pictures.

Templates
Templates provide an excellent way to quickly create a presentation by providing predesigned styles and layouts as well as suggested content based on the type of template you select.

Figure 3-13 Presentation

updating a presentation

After discussing the presentation with the director, you have some ideas to enhance the effectiveness of the message. First, you select a different document theme to change the colors, fonts, and effects used throughout the presentation. Then to add interest to the presentation as it is running, you add animation and transition effects. Then you add animations to selected objects and add slide transition effects. Finally, you practice or rehearse the presentation, create speaker notes, and print out audience handouts. You're ready to give a professionally designed, dynamic presentation. See Figure 3-14.

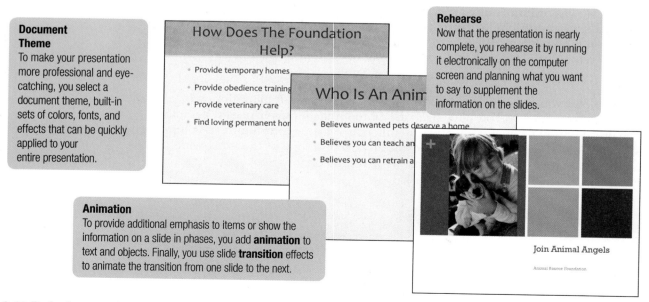

Document Theme
To make your presentation more professional and eye-catching, you select a document theme, built-in sets of colors, fonts, and effects that can be quickly applied to your entire presentation.

Rehearse
Now that the presentation is nearly complete, you rehearse it by running it electronically on the computer screen and planning what you want to say to supplement the information on the slides.

Animation
To provide additional emphasis to items or show the information on a slide in phases, you add **animation** to text and objects. Finally, you use slide **transition** effects to animate the transition from one slide to the next.

Figure 3-14 Revised presentation

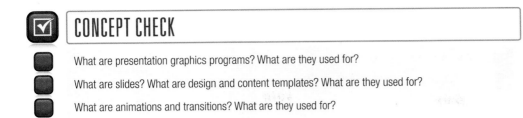

CONCEPT CHECK

- What are presentation graphics programs? What are they used for?

- What are slides? What are design and content templates? What are they used for?

- What are animations and transitions? What are they used for?

Integrated Packages

An **integrated package** is a single program that provides the *functionality* of a word processor, spreadsheet, database manager, and more. The primary disadvantage of an integrated package is that the capabilities of each function (such as word processing) are not as extensive as in the individual programs (such as Microsoft Word). The primary advantages are cost and simplicity. The cost of an integrated package is much less than the cost of the individual powerful, professional-grade application programs discussed thus far in this chapter.

Integrated packages are popular with many home users and are sometimes classified as **personal** or **home software.** The most widely used integrated package is Microsoft Works. See Figure 3-15. AppleWorks is also widely used.

Figure 3-15 Microsoft Works

Case

Assume that you publish a gardening newsletter that you distribute to members of the Desert Gardening Club. Using the word processing function, you entered text, formatted titles and subtitles, and inserted several photographs. (See Figure 3-16.) Using the spreadsheet function, you analyzed daily rainfall for the feature article and included a chart. After completing the newsletter, you will use the database function and the membership database to print mailing labels.

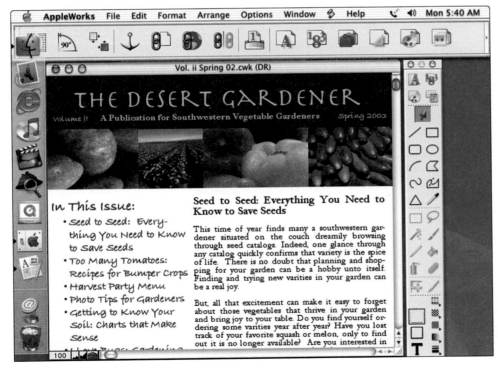

Figure 3-16 Integrated package (AppleWorks)

Figure 3-17 Microsoft Office

Figure 3-18 Office for Mac

Software Suites

A **software suite** is a collection of separate application programs bundled together and made available as a group. While the applications function exactly the same whether purchased in a suite or separately, it is significantly less expensive to buy a suite of applications than to buy each application separately.

Productivity Suite

Productivity suites, also known as **office software suites** or simply **office suites,** contain professional-grade application programs that are typically used in a business situation. Productivity suites commonly include a word processor, spreadsheet, database manager, and a presentation application. The best known is Microsoft Office. (See Figure 3-17.) Other well-known productivity suites are Apple iWork, Lotus SmartSuite, Microsoft Office for Mac, and Sun StarOffice. (See Figure 3-18.)

Traditionally, when you purchase an office suite, you are licensed to use the application and a copy of the software is stored on your computer. Recently, however, several alternative office suites have been made available for free as downloadable software. Popular downloadable office suites include IBM Lotus Symphony, OpenOffice, and SoftMaker Office. (See Figure 3-19.)

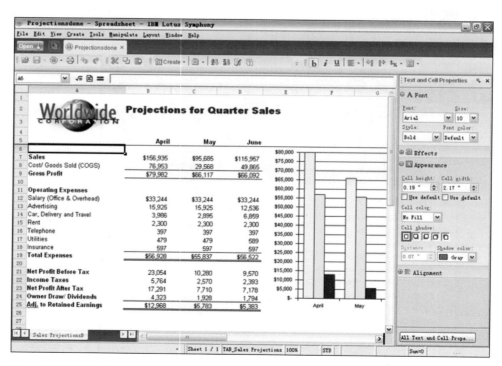

Figure 3-19 IBM Lotus Symphony

Cloud Computing

Cloud suites or **online office suites** are stored at a server on the Internet and are available anywhere you can access the Internet. Documents created using online applications also can be stored online, making it easy to share and collaborate on documents with others. One downside to cloud applications is that you are dependent upon the server providing the application to be available whenever you need it. For this reason, when using online applications, it is important to have backup copies of your documents on your computer and to have a desktop office application available to use. Popular online office suites include Google Docs, Zoho, and Microsoft Office Web Apps. To learn more about one of the most widely used online office suites, see Making IT Work for You: Google Docs on pages 92 and 93.

Sharing between Programs

Many times it is convenient to share data between applications. For example, when writing a report, it may be useful to include a chart from a spreadsheet or data from a database. Data created by one application can be shared with another application in a variety of different ways, including copying and pasting, object linking, and object embedding. To learn more about sharing data between applications, visit us on the Web at www.computing2013.com and enter the keyword sharing.

Specialized and Utility Suites

Two other types of suites that are more narrowly focused are specialized suites and utility suites.

- **Specialized suites** focus on specific applications. These include graphics suites, financial planning suites, and many others. (Graphics suites will be discussed in Chapter 4.)
- **Utility suites** include a variety of programs designed to make computing easier and safer. Two of the best known are Norton SystemWorks and Norton Internet Security Suite. (Utility suites will be discussed in detail in Chapter 5.)

environment

Did you know that software is going green? While utility software used to focus solely on making computing safer and easier, new utility software is focusing on making computers more environmentally friendly. These utility programs track your computer use and your computer's operations. The programs then analyze the data for ways to minimize your computer's energy consumption. The results are then presented and suggestions made to make your computing greener. Environmental utility programs are expected to quickly become a standard part in all utility suites. For additional discussion of this issue, see GREEN SOFTWARE UTILITIES on page 105. To see more environmental facts, visit our Web site at www.computing2013.com and enter the keyword environment.

☑ CONCEPT CHECK

- What is a software suite? What are the advantages of purchasing a suite?
- What is the difference between a traditional office suite and a cloud or online suite?
- How can data be shared between applications?
- What is the difference between a specialized suite and a utility suite?

Making **IT** work for you

GOOGLE DOCS

Do you need to collaborate with others on a document, presentation, or spreadsheet? Do you need access to a document from both home and school? Would you like to try a free alternative to traditional office software suites? If so, an online office suite might be for you. Online office suites, such as Google Docs, allow you to create and edit documents directly though a Web page with no additional software to install on your computer.

Creating a Document   To create a new online document:

1
  ● Visit http://docs.google.com. Follow the on-screen instructions to create a free Google account if you do not already have one.

  ● Click the *Create new* button.

  ● Select the type of document you want to create, such as a word processing document, presentation, or spreadsheet.

The new document is displayed and can be edited directly through the Web page.

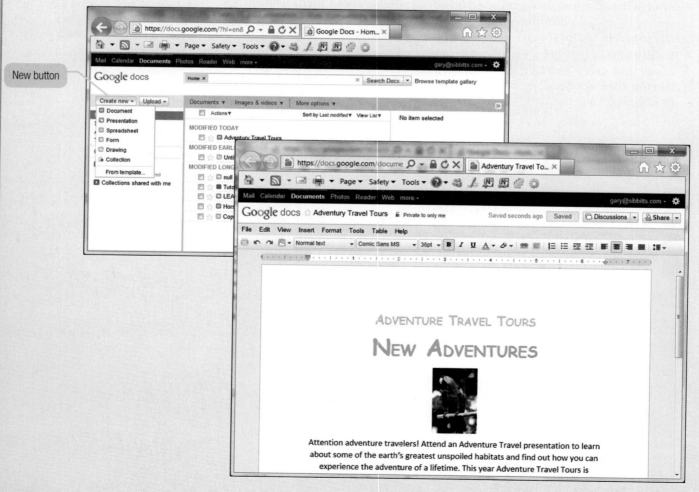

Sharing a Document   To give others access to view and edit your document:

1 ● Click the *Share* button.

 ● Select *Share . . .*

2 ● Enter the e-mail addresses of people to invite.

 ● Optionally enter a brief message to the people you are inviting.

 ● Click the *Share* button.

The people you invited will receive an e-mail with instructions for accessing your document. You will be able to see any changes others make to the document, and they will see yours.

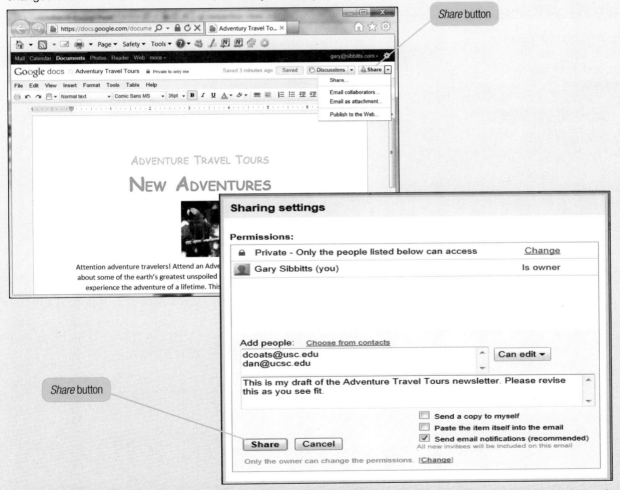

The Web is continually changing, and some of the specifics presented in Making IT Work for You may have changed.
To learn about other ways to make information technology work for you, visit our Web site at www.computing2013.com and enter the keyword miw.

Now, that you have learned about basic application software, I'd like to tell you about my career as a computer trainer.

Computer trainers instruct new users on the latest software or hardware. Many computer training positions are offered to those with experience with the most popular business software.

Employers look for good communication skills and teaching experience. Though a teaching degree may not be required, it may be preferred. Experience with the latest software and/or hardware is essential, but this varies depending on the position. Employers often seek detail-oriented individuals with IT experience.

Computer trainers can expect to earn an annual salary of $25,000 to $50,500. However, salary is dependent on experience and may vary drastically. Responsibilities typically include preparation of course materials, grading coursework, and continuing education in the field. Opportunities for advancement include management of other trainers and consulting work. To learn more about other careers in information technology, visit us at www.computing2013.com and enter the keyword **careers**.

A LOOK TO THE FUTURE

Agents Will Help Write Papers, Pay Bills, and Shop on the Internet

Wouldn't it be great to have your own personal assistant? Your assistant could research topics for a term paper, collect relevant information, and even suggest famous quotes that apply to your topic. Your assistant could monitor your personal budget using a spreadsheet and even evaluate the impact of a rental income. Or your assistant could add interest to a classroom presentation by suggesting and locating relevant photos and videos. All this is likely with special programs called *agents.*

An agent is an intelligent program that can understand your needs and act to fulfill those needs. Today, primitive agents already exist in many help tools to interpret user questions and to formulate appropriate responses. Computer scientists at the University of Maryland are working on the next-generation agents that may provide the most efficient way to locate information on the Web. These agents promise to understand words and the context in which they are used. They will locate Web sites that not only have the *words* you are looking for but also the *meaning.* This future is not far off, and as agent technology improves, it is only a matter of time until agents act in more autonomous ways and can help you use basic applications to do complex tasks, like prepare an essay, a budget, or a presentation.

What do you think? Should we all have our own personal agent to help us write papers, pay bills, and shop on the Internet?

APPLICATION SOFTWARE

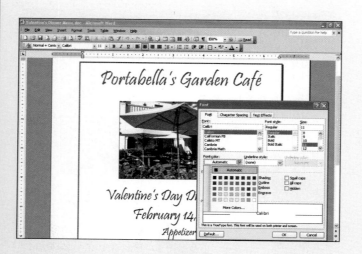

There are two basic types of software. **System software** focuses on handling technical details. **Application software** focuses on completing specific tasks or applications. Two categories are **basic applications** and **specialized applications.**

Common Features

You control and interact with a program using a **user interface.** A **graphical user interface (gui)** uses **icons** selected by a mouse-controlled **pointer.** A **window** contains a document, program, or message. Software programs with a traditional gui have:

- **Menus**—present commands listed on the **menu bar.**
- **Dialog box**—provides additional information or requests user input.
- **Toolbars**—contain **buttons** for quick access to commonly used commands.

Software programs with a **ribbon gui** have

- **Ribbons**—replace menus and toolbars.
- **Tabs**—divide ribbons into major activity areas organized into **groups. Contextual tabs** automatically appear when needed.
- **Galleries**—graphically display alternatives before they are selected.

Some applications support **speech recognition** by allowing voice input.

WORD PROCESSORS

Word processors allow you to create, edit, save, and print text-based **documents,** including flyers, reports, newsletters, and Web pages.

Features

Word wrap is a basic feature that automatically determines where to end one line and begin the next. **Editing** features include

- **Thesaurus**—provides synonyms, antonyms, and related words.
- **Find and replace**—locates (finds), removes, and inserts (replaces) another word(s).
- **Spelling** and **grammar checkers**—locate spelling and grammatical problems.

Formatting features include

- **Font**—design of characters. **Font size** is the height of characters.
- **Character effects**—include **bold,** *italic,* and **colors.**
- **Styles**—feature that quickly applies predefined formats.
- **Bulleted** and **numbered lists**—used to present sequences of topics or steps.

To be a competent end user, you need to understand the capabilities of basic application software, which includes word processors, spreadsheets, database management systems, and presentation programs. You need to know how to use these applications and how data can be shared between them.

SPREADSHEETS

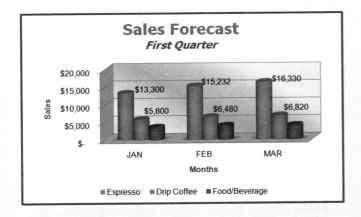

Spreadsheet programs are used to organize, analyze, and graph numeric data.

Features

Principal spreadsheet features include the following:

- **Workbook files** consist of one or more related worksheets.
- **Worksheets,** also known as **spreadsheets** or **sheets,** are rectangular grids of **rows** and **columns.** Rows are identified by numbers, columns by letters.
- **Cells** are formed by the intersection of a row and column; used to hold text and numeric entries.
- **Text entries (labels)** provide structure and **numeric entries** can be numbers or formulas.
- **Formulas** are instructions for calculations. **Functions** are prewritten formulas.
- **Range** is a series of cells.
- **Analytical graphs (charts)** represent data visually.
- **Recalculation** occurs whenever a value changes in one cell that affects another cell(s).
- **What-if analysis** is the process of observing the effect of changing one or more values.

DATABASE MANAGEMENT SYSTEMS

A **database** is a collection of related data. A **database management system (DBMS),** also known as a **database manager,** structures a database and provides tools for manipulating data.

Features

Principal database management system features include the following:

- **Relational database** organizes data into related tables.
- **Tables** have rows (**records**) and columns (**fields**).
- **Sort** is a tool to rearrange records.
- **Filter** is a tool to display only those records meeting specified conditions.
- **Query** is a question or request for specific data contained in a database.
- **Forms** are used to enter and edit records.
- **Reports** are printed output in a variety of forms.

PRESENTATION GRAPHICS

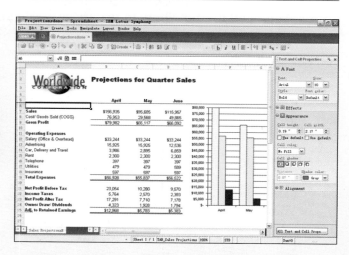

Join Animal Angels

Animal Rescue Foundation

Presentation graphics combine a variety of visual objects to create attractive, visually interesting presentations. They are excellent tools to communicate a message and to persuade people.

Features

Principal presentation graphics features include the following:

- **Slides**—individual **pages** or screens of a presentation.
- **Design templates**—professionally selected combination of color schemes, slide layouts, and special effects.
- **Content templates**—provide suggested content for each slide.
- **Animation**—adds action to text and graphics.
- **Transitions**—animate moving from one slide to the next.

INTEGRATED PACKAGES

An **integrated package**, also known as **personal** or **home software**, is a single program that provides the functionality of several application packages. Some important characteristics include

- Functions that typically include word processing, spreadsheet, database manager, and more. Each function is not as extensive or powerful as a single-function application program.
- Less expensive than purchasing several individual application programs and simple to use.
- Popular with home users who are willing to sacrifice some advanced features for cost and simplicity.

SOFTWARE SUITES

A **software suite** is a collection of individual application packages sold together.

- **Productivity suites (office software suites** or **office suites)** contain professional-grade application programs.
- **Cloud suites (online office suites)** are stored on servers and available through the Internet.
- **Specialized suites** focus on specific applications such as graphics.
- **Utility suites** include a variety of programs designed to make computing easier and safer.

CAREERS IN IT

Computer trainers instruct new users on the latest software or hardware. Teaching degree is preferred and experience with latest software and/or hardware is essential. Salary range $25,000 to $50,500.

KEY TERMS

analytical graph   (80)
animation   (87)
app   (72)
application software   (72)
basic application   (72)
bulleted list   (76)
button   (72)
cell   (79)
character effect   (76)
chart   (80)
cloud suite   (91)
column   (79)
computer trainer   (94)
content template   (87)
contextual tab   (73)
database   (84)
database management system
   (DBMS)   (84)
database manager   (84)
design template   (87)
dialog box   (72)
document   (76)
editing   (76)
field   (84)
find and replace   (76)
filter   (84)
font   (76)
font size   (76)
form   (84)
format   (76)
formula   (80)
function   (80)
gallery   (73)
grammar checker   (76)
graphical user interface (gui)   (72)
group   (73)
home software   (89)
icon   (72)
integrated package   (89)
label   (80)
menu   (72)
menu bar   (72)
numbered list   (76)

numeric entry   (80)
office software suite   (90)
office suite   (90)
online office suite   (91)
page   (87)
personal software   (89)
pointer   (72)
presentation graphics   (87)
productivity suite   (90)
query   (84)
range   (80)
recalculation   (80)
record   (84)
relational database   (84)
report   (84)
ribbon   (73)
ribbon gui   (73)
row   (79)
sheet   (79)
slide   (87)
software suite   (90)
sort   (84)
specialized application   (72)
specialized suite   (91)
speech recognition   (73)
spelling checker   (76)
spreadsheet   (79)
styles   (76)
system software   (72)
tab   (73)
table   (84)
text entry   (80)
thesaurus   (76)
toolbar   (72)
transition   (87)
user interface   (72)
utility suite   (91)
what-if analysis   (80)
window   (72)
word processor   (76)
word wrap   (76)
workbook file   (79)
worksheet   (79)

To test your knowledge of these key terms with animated flash cards, visit our Web site at www.computing2013.com and enter the keyword terms3.

MULTIPLE CHOICE

Circle the correct answer.

1. This type of software works with end users, application software, and computer hardware to handle the majority of technical details.
   a. application
   b. general purpose
   c. system
   d. utility

2. A rectangular area that can contain a document, program, or message.
   a. dialog box
   b. form
   c. frame
   d. window

3. Programs that create text-based documents.
   a. DBMS
   b. suites
   c. spreadsheets
   d. word processors

4. Programs that organize, analyze, and graph numeric data such as budgets and financial reports.
   a. DBMS
   b. suites
   c. spreadsheets
   d. word processors

5. In a spreadsheet, the intersection of a row and column creates a:
   a. cell
   b. formula
   c. function
   d. label

6. A collection of related data that is the electronic equivalent of a file cabinet.
   a. cell
   b. database
   c. document
   d. table

7. A database tool that will quickly rearrange a table's records according to a selected field.
   a. filter
   b. sort
   c. spreadsheet
   d. word processor

8. Programs that combine a variety of visual objects to create attractive, visually interesting presentations.
   a. DBMS
   b. presentation graphics
   c. spreadsheet
   d. word processor

9. The primary disadvantage of this type of package is that the capabilities of each function are not as extensive as in individual programs.
   a. integrated
   b. office
   c. software
   d. utility

10. A type of suite stored at a server on the Internet and available anywhere through Internet access.
    a. cloud
    b. integrated
    c. office
    d. utility

For an interactive multiple-choice practice test, visit our Web site at www.computing2013.com and enter the keyword multiple3.

MATCHING

Match each numbered item with the most closely related lettered item. Write your answers in the spaces provided.

a. bulleted list
b. dialog box
c. function
d. galleries
e. grammar
f. integrated
g. software suite
h. tables
i. design templates
j. worksheet

_____ 1. Provides additional information and requests user input.

_____ 2. Simplifies the process of making a selection by graphically displaying the effect of alternatives.

_____ 3. Checker that looks for problems with capitalization, punctuation, and sentence structure.

_____ 4. In a spreadsheet, the grid of rows and columns is called a _____.

_____ 5. A rectangular grid of rows and columns.

_____ 6. Prewritten formula.

_____ 7. In a relational database, data is organized into related _____.

_____ 8. Provides selected combinations of color schemes, slide layouts, and special effects.

_____ 9. Package that is also known as personal or home software.

_____10. A collection of separate application programs bundled together and made available as a group.

For an interactive matching practice test, visit our Web site at www.computing2013.com and enter the keyword matching3.

OPEN-ENDED

On a separate sheet of paper, respond to each question or statement.

1. Explain the difference between general-purpose and special-purpose applications. Also discuss the common features of application programs, including those with traditional and ribbon graphical user interfaces.

2. Define word processors and discuss their basic, editing, and formating features.

3. Discuss spreadsheets and define workbook files, worksheets, cells, text entries, formulas, functions, ranges, graphs, recalculation, and what-if analysis.

4. What are databases and database management systems? Define relational databases, tables, sorting, filtering, querying, forms, and reports.

5. What are presentation programs and what are they used for? Define slides, design templates, content templates, animation, and transitions.

6. What is the difference between integrated packages and software suites? Discuss productivity, cloud, and specialized suites.

MAKING IT WORK FOR YOU

The following questions are designed to demonstrate ways that you can effectively use technology today.

① SPEECH RECOGNITION

Tired of using your keyboard? Have you ever thought about speaking to your computer? Perhaps speech recognition is for you. To learn more about speech recognition, review Making IT Work for You: Speech Recognition on pages 74 and 75. Then answer the following questions: (a) What menu item is selected to begin training the software? (b) What are the verbal commands to start the Microsoft Word application? (c) Have you ever used speech recognition? If you have, describe how you used it and discuss how

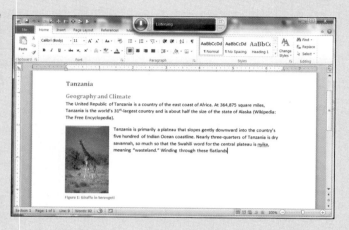

effective it was for you. If you have not, discuss how you might use it in the future. Be specific.

② GOOGLE DOCS

Do you need to collaborate with others on a document, presentation, or spreadsheet? Do you need access to a document from both home and school? Would you like to try a free alternative to traditional office software suites? If so, a cloud office suite might be for you. Online office suites, such as Google Docs, allow you to create and edit documents directly though a Web page with no additional software to install on your computer. To learn how to access, use, and collaborate with others using Google Docs, review Making IT Work for You: Google Docs on pages 92 and 93. Create your own

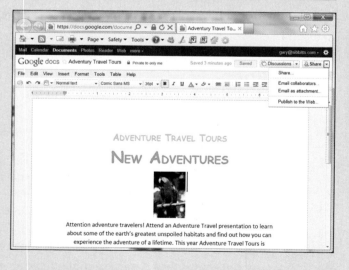

Google account and use it to collaborate with others. Then answer the following: (a) Describe the steps you used to create a new document with Google Docs. (b) Describe how to send an e-mail within Google Docs. (c) Have you ever used Google Docs or any other cloud application before? If so, describe what you used and how you used it. If not, do you think that you might in the future? How would you anticipate using Google Docs or some other cloud application?

EXPLORATIONS

The following questions are designed to add depth and detail to your understanding of specific topics presented within this chapter. The questions direct you to sources other than the textbook to obtain this knowledge.

1 HOW SPEECH RECOGNITION WORKS

Speech recognition is an emerging technology. To learn how speech recognition works, visit our Web site at www.computing2013.com and enter the keyword speech. Then answer the following: (a) Create a drawing similar to the one on our Web site that would represent dictating a mailing address for an address label. (b) What hardware is required to use voice recognition software? (c) Describe how speech recognition could enhance your use of each of the following types of applications: word processing, spreadsheet, and presentation. (d) Describe a profession that could benefit from speech recognition software. Be specific.

2 SHARING DATA BETWEEN APPLICATIONS

Sharing data between applications can be very convenient and can greatly increase your productivity. The three most common ways to share information are copy and paste, object linking, and object embedding. To learn more about sharing data between applications, visit our Web site at www.computing2013.com and enter the keyword sharing. Then respond to the following: (a) Discuss how copy and paste works. Provide a specific example. (b) What is the difference between object linking and object embedding? Provide specific examples. (c) Describe a specific situation in which you might use all three types of sharing data between applications.

3 SHAREWARE

One way to acquire new application software is by downloading shareware. Conduct a Web search for shareware programs. Connect to and explore a shareware site offering a program that might interest you. Then respond to the following: (a) What is shareware? Who creates it? (b) What does shareware cost to use? What about support if you have a problem using it? (c) What are the risks of using shareware? Be thorough. (d) Would you use shareware? Why or why not?

ETHICS

The following questions are designed to explore ethical issues related to technology and to develop the ability to think critically and communicate effectively. Respond to the questions by either creating a one-page paper or preparing for an in-depth classroom discussion.

1 ACQUIRING SOFTWARE

There are three common ways to obtain new software: use public domain software, use shareware, buy commercial software. In addition to these three ways, two others are to copy programs from a friend or to purchase unauthorized copies of programs. Review the Ethics box on page 72. Then respond to the following: (a) Define and discuss each option. Be sure to discuss both the advantages and disadvantages of each. (b) Which seems like the best method to you? Why? (c) Do you think there is anything wrong with obtaining and using unauthorized software? Identify and explore the key issues.

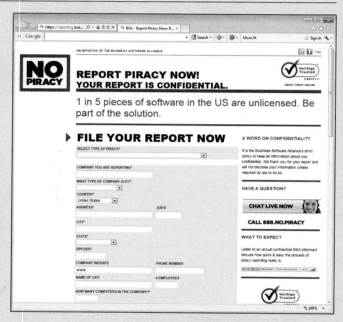

2 AUDIO AND VIDEO CLIPS

One of the more powerful features of many applications is the ability to insert audio and video clips. The Making IT Work for You: TV Tuner Cards and Video Clips on pages 178 and 179 demonstrate just how easy it is to insert a video clip into a PowerPoint presentation. Millions of video clips are available on the Internet from video-sharing sites to individual Facebook pages. (a) Have you ever copied a video clip from the Internet? If so, what did you copy and how did you use it? (b) Do you see anything wrong with copying and using video clips from the Internet? (c) Do you think that it can be a violation of copyright law to copy video clips? If so, under what circumstances might it be illegal? (d) Do you think it is illegal to copy all or part of a recently released movie and distribute it to others? Why or why not? (e) Would you consider it either illegal or unethical for a person to copy a video or picture from someone's (perhaps your) Facebook page and distribute it to thousands of others over the Internet? Why or why not?

ENVIRONMENT

The following questions are designed to explore environmental issues related to technology and to develop the ability to think critically and communicate effectively. Respond to the questions by either creating a one-page paper or preparing for an in-depth classroom discussion.

1 DIGITAL SOFTWARE DISTRIBUTION

Did you know that downloading software and other types of files rather than buying them on CDs or DVDs can actually generate energy savings? Microsoft compared the impact of downloading music directly to a computer or music player via the Internet versus using a CD and found an 80-percent reduction in CO_2 emissions. Review the Environment box on page 73. Locate and review Microsoft's report "Benefits of Digital Software Distribution" and then respond to the following: (a) What is digital software distribution? (b) Did

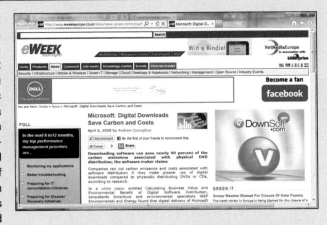

you locate the report "Benefits of Digital Software Distribution"? If so, please summarize its findings. If not, discuss what you did find out about digital software distribution and the environment. (c) Have you downloaded software from the Internet? If so, what did you download and describe the downloading process? If you have not downloaded software, do you anticipate that you will in the near future? Why or why not? (d) What can you do to encourage software companies and others to distribute software and other types of files over the Internet?

2 GREEN SOFTWARE UTILITIES

Some software manufacturers are creating green utility software that focuses on making computers more environmentally friendly. These utility programs track your computer use and your computer's operations. The programs then analyze the data for ways to minimize energy consumption. Review the Environment box on page 91 and then locate a green software utility. (Hint: You might try Green Pulse Software Utility.) Then respond to the following: (a) What is green software? (b) Did you locate the Green Pulse Software Utility? If you did, describe the program. If you

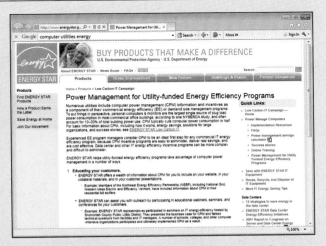

did not locate Green Pulse, describe another green software utility. (c) Have you ever used a green software utility? If so, what have you used and was it effective? If not, do you foresee yourself using one in the future? Why or why not?

Specialized Application Software

▲ Download the free *Computing Essentials 2013* app for videos, key term flashcards, quizzes, and the game, *Over the Edge!*

Competencies

After you have read this chapter, you should be able to:

1 Describe graphics software, including desktop publishing, image editors, illustration programs, image galleries, and graphics suites.

2 Discuss audio and video editing software.

3 Describe multimedia, including links, buttons, and multimedia authoring programs.

4 Explain Web authoring, Web site design, and Web authoring programs.

5 Describe artificial intelligence including virtual reality, knowledge-based systems, and robotics.

6 Discuss mobile apps and apps stores.

Why should I read this chapter?

A few years ago, specialized applications required large, powerful computers and were only available to specialists in specific professions. For example, to produce an album you would need an expensive recording studio, professional musicians, and experts to run the equipment. That was then and this is now. Now with powerful desktop and mobile computers, professionals in every profession can tap the power of specialized applications once reserved for musicians, Web page designers, and other specialists.

This chapter discusses image editing, digital video editing, Web authoring, artificial intelligence including virtual reality, expert systems, and robotics. Additionally, you'll learn about mobile apps and where to go to get the most current apps. To be competent and to be competitive in today's professional workplace, you need to know and to understand these things.

Hi, I'm Katie and I'm a desktop publisher. I'd like to talk with you about some very interesting specialized applications . . . including desktop publishing. I'd also like to talk with you about some of the most useful mobile apps.

Introduction

Expect exciting surprises and positive opportunities. The latest technological developments offer you new opportunities to extend your range of computer competency. As we show in this chapter, software that for years was available only for larger computers has become available for microcomputers and mobile devices like smartphones and tablets.

For example, it is now quite common for people to create their own Web sites. Home users also have access to software that helps manipulate and create graphic images. Many musicians and artists work from home to create complex and beautiful work using specialized applications. You can use your smartphone to surf the Web, scan documents, even update your blog from almost any location.

Some of these same technological advances have allowed researchers and computer scientists to make advances in the field of artificial intelligence that previously were envisioned only in science fiction. Robots now provide security and assistance in homes. Virtual reality is providing opportunities in the fields of medicine and science but also commonly appears in video games. The wireless revolution has brought even more exciting applications to smartphones and other mobile devices.

Competent end users need to be aware of specialized applications. They need to know who uses them, what they are used for, and how they are used. These advanced applications include graphics programs, audio and video editing software, multimedia, Web authoring, and artificial intelligence. Additionally, competent end users need to be aware of and know how to use some of the most dynamic mobile applications.

Specialized Applications

In the previous chapter, we discussed basic applications that are widely used in nearly every profession. This chapter focuses on specialized applications that are widely used within specific professions. (See Figure 4-1.) Specifically, we will examine

- Graphics programs for creating professional-looking published documents, for creating and editing images, and for locating and inserting graphics.
- Audio and video software to create, edit, and play music and videos.
- Multimedia programs to create dynamic interactive presentations.

Figure 4-1 Specialized applications

- Web authoring programs to create, edit, and design Web sites.
- Artificial intelligence, including virtual reality, knowledge-based systems, and robotics.

Graphics

In Chapter 3, we discussed analytical and presentation graphics, which are widely used to analyze data and to create professional-looking presentations. Here we focus on more specialized graphics programs used by professionals in the graphic arts profession.

Desktop Publishing

Desktop publishing programs, or **page layout programs,** allow you to mix text and graphics to create publications of professional quality. While word processors focus on creating text and have the ability to combine text and graphics, desktop publishers focus on page design and layout and provide greater flexibility. Professional graphic artists use desktop publishing programs to create documents such as brochures, newsletters, newspapers, and textbooks.

Popular desktop publishing programs include Adobe InDesign, Microsoft Publisher, and QuarkXPress. While these programs provide the capability to create text and graphics, typically graphic artists import these elements from other sources, including word processors, digital cameras, scanners, image editors, illustration programs, and image galleries.

Image Editors

One of the most common types of graphic files is bitmap. **Bitmap images,** also known as **raster images,** use thousands of dots or **pixels** to represent images. Each dot has a specific location, color, and shade. One limitation of bitmap images, however, is that when they are expanded, the images can become pixilated, or jagged on the edges. For example, when the letter A in Figure 4-2 is expanded, the borders of the letter appear jagged, as indicated by the expanded view.

Image editors, also known as **photo editors,** are specialized graphics programs for editing or modifying digital photographs. They are often used to touch up photographs to remove scratches and other imperfections. Popular image editors include Adobe Photoshop, Corel Paint Shop Pro, and Paint.NET. (See Figure 4-3.)

Illustration Programs

Vector is another common type of graphic file. While bitmap images use pixels to represent images, **vector images,** also known as **vector illustrations,** use geometric shapes or objects. (See Figure 4-4.) These objects are created by connecting lines and curves. Because these objects can be defined by mathematical equations, they can be rapidly and easily resized, colored, textured, and manipulated. An image is a combination of several objects. **Illustration programs,** also known as **drawing programs,** are used to create and edit vector images. They are often used for graphic design, page layout, and creating sharp artistic images.

Popular illustration programs include Adobe Illustrator, CorelDRAW, and Inkscape. (See Figure 4-5.)

Image Galleries

Image galleries are libraries of electronic images. These images are used for a wide variety of applications from illustrating

Letter A

Expanded view

Figure 4-2 Bitmap image

Paint Tools

Selection tool

Brush

Pen

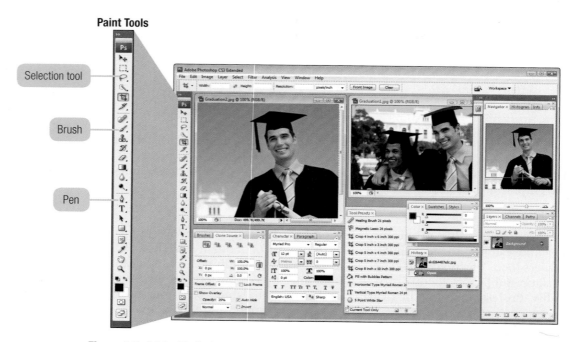

Figure 4-3 Adobe Photoshop

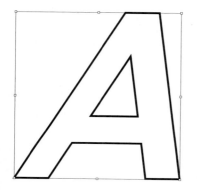

Figure 4-4 Vector image

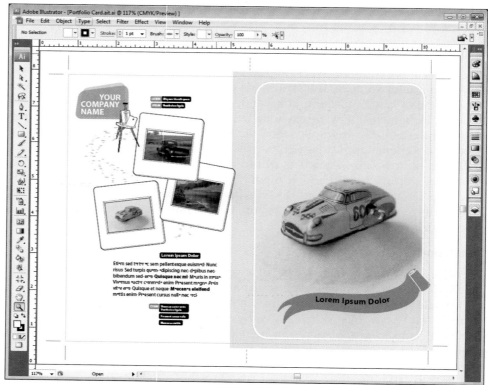

Figure 4-5 Adobe Illustrator

textbooks to providing visual interest to presentations. There are two basic types of electronic images in these galleries:

- **Stock photographs**—photographs on a variety of subject material from people to landscapes.
- **Clip art**—graphic illustrations representing a wide range of topics. Most applications provide access to a limited selection of free clip art. For example,

in Microsoft Word, you can gain access to several pieces of clip art by issuing the command Insert>Clip Art.

There are numerous Web image galleries. (See Figure 4-6.) Some of these sites offer free images and clip art while others charge a fee.

Graphics Suites

Some companies have combined or bundled their separate graphics programs in groups called **graphics suites.** The advantage of the graphics suites is that you can buy a larger variety of graphics programs at a lower cost than if purchased separately.

Two popular suites are CorelDRAW Graphics Suite and Adobe Creative Suite. CorelDRAW Graphics Suite includes five individual graphics programs plus a large library of clip art, media clips, and fonts. (See Figure 4-7.)

Organization	Site
Classroom Clipart	www.classroomclipart.com
ClipArt.com	www.clipart.com
Graphics Factory	www.graphicsfactory.com
MS Office clip art	office.microsoft.com/clipart
iStockphoto	istockphoto.com
Flickr Creative Commons	www.flickr.com/creativecommons

Figure 4-6 Select Web image galleries

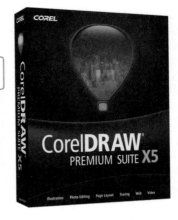

Figure 4-7 CorelDRAW Graphics Suite

☑ CONCEPT CHECK

What is desktop publishing?

What is the difference between an image editor and an illustration program?

Describe image galleries. What are graphics suites?

Audio and Video

In the past, professional-quality editing of home audio and video was a job for professional photo labs or studios. For example, if you wanted to assemble footage from all your Fourth of July picnics, you sent all the tapes to a lab and waited for a compilation tape. Now, using audio and video editing software, you can create your own compilation movies.

- **Video editing software** allows you to reorganize, add effects, and more to your digital video footage. Two commonly used video editing software programs are Apple iMovie and Windows Movie Maker. (See Figure 4-8.) These programs are designed to allow you to assemble and edit new home videos and movies from raw digital video footage. To see how digital video editors work, visit our Web site at www.computing2013.com and enter the keyword video. To learn how to use a digital video editor, see Making IT Work for You: Digital Video Editing on pages 112 and 113.

- **Audio editing software** allows you to create and edit audio clips. Most audio editing software also has features that allow you to add audio effects, like filters, to your tracks. For example, you can use this type of software to filter out pops or scratches in an old recording. You can even use this software to create your own MP3s. Some commonly used audio editing software programs are Apple Garage-Band and Sony ACID. (See Figure 4-9.)

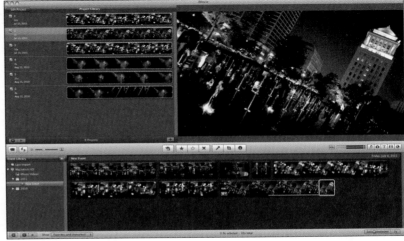

Figure 4-8 Apple iMovie

Making IT work for you

DIGITAL VIDEO EDITING

Do you want to make your own movie? Would you like to edit some home movies and distribute them to family and friends on DVDs? It's easy with the right equipment and software.

Capturing Video   You can capture video to your computer from a device such as a digital camcorder. Once captured, the video can be edited using digital video editing software. Follow the steps below to capture video from a digital camcorder using Windows 7. If Windows Live Movie Maker is not already installed on your computer, you can download it for free from **http://explore.live.com/windows-live-movie-maker**.

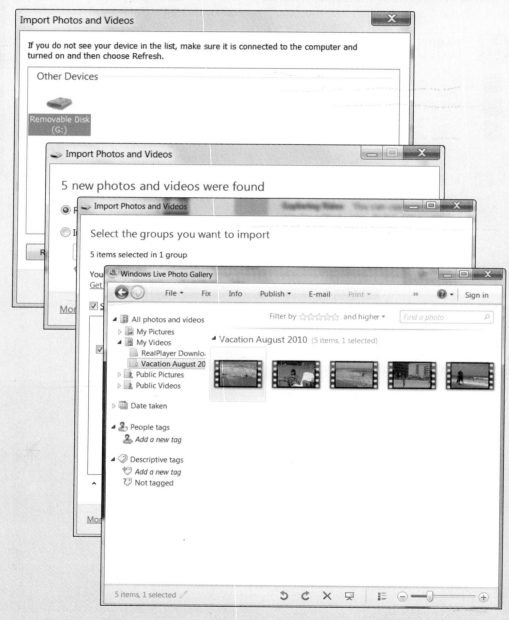

1 ● Connect the digital camcorder to your computer and turn it on.

● Select *Import*.

● Enter a name and select a location to save the imported video.

2 ● Select the video files to import. You can import all new files or selected files.

3 ● If you choose to import only a few files, select the check boxes for the files you want and select *Import*.

4 ● Preview the video files you have imported as they appear in the location you specified.

Editing a Movie Windows Live Movie Maker divides your captured video into clips, or scenes that make up your movie. Follow the steps below to create a movie by arranging clips and adding special effects.

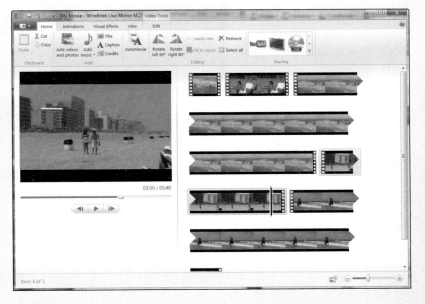

1 • Drag movie clips from the Clipboard Pane and arrange them in the Storyboard. Add movie clips by clicking on *Add videos and photos* on the Home tab.

• Use the options in the Visual Effects tab to add sounds, transitions, and effects to your movie. Titles, captions, and credits can be added from the Add group on the Home tab.

• Use the Preview Monitor to preview your movie.

Creating a DVD Once you have edited your movies, you can create a DVD to share with friends and family. You will need a DVD writer and a blank writable DVD. Follow the steps below to design a menu, add movies, and create your DVD.

1 • Launch Windows DVD Maker, and click the *Choose Photos and Videos* button.

• Select the video file you created with Windows Live Movie Maker in the previous step.

• Click the *Next* button.

2 • Select a menu style that will be displayed when your DVD is played.

• Insert a writable DVD in your DVD drive and click the *Burn* button to create your DVD.

The Web is continually changing, and some of the specifics presented in this Making IT Work for You may have changed.

To learn about other ways to make information technology work for you, visit our Web site at www.computing2013.com and enter the keyword miw.

Figure 4-9 Apple GarageBand

Multimedia

Multimedia is the integration of all sorts of media into one presentation. For example, a multimedia presentation may include video, music, voice, graphics, and text. You may have seen multimedia applied in video games, Web presentations, or even a word processing document. Many of the basic application software programs you learned about in Chapter 3 include features that make the incorporation of multimedia in documents easy. Although these applications include multimedia features, they create documents that are generally accessed in a linear fashion and provide very limited user interaction.

Effective multimedia presentations incorporate user participation or interactivity. **Interactivity** allows the user to choose the information to view, to control the pace and flow of information, and to respond to items and receive feedback. When experiencing an interactive multimedia presentation, users customize the presentation to their needs. For example, Figure 4-10 presents an opening page of a multimedia presentation. Users are able to select the language to be used and decide whether to include sound.

Once used almost exclusively for computer games, interactive multimedia is now widely used in business, education, and the home. Business uses include high-quality interactive presentations, product demonstrations, and Web page design. In education, interactive multimedia is used for in-class presentations and demonstrations, distance education, and online testing. In the home, multimedia is frequently used for entertainment.

Links and Buttons

An interactive multimedia presentation is typically organized as a series of related pages. Each page presents information and provides **links,** or connections, to related information. These links can be to video, sound, graphics, and text files, and to other pages and resources. By clicking special areas called **buttons** on a page, you can make appropriate links and navigate through a presentation to locate and discover information. Typically, there are several buttons on a page. You can select one, several, or none of them. You are in control. You direct the flow and content of the presentation. (See Figure 4-10.)

Multimedia Authoring Programs

Multimedia authoring programs are special programs used to create multimedia presentations. They bring together all the video, audio, graphics, and text elements into an interactive framework. Widely used authoring programs include Adobe Director and Toolbook.

Explorations

To learn more about a leading company that develops multimedia authoring programs, visit our Web site at www.computing2013.com and enter the keyword multimedia.

CONCEPT CHECK

- What is video editing software? What is audio editing software?
- What are multimedia, interactivity, links, and buttons?
- What are multimedia authoring programs?

Figure 4-10 **Opening page of a multimedia presentation**

✳ Web Authoring

There are over a billion Web sites on the Internet, and more are being added every day. Corporations use the Web to reach new customers and to promote their products. (See Figure 4-11.) Individuals create their own personal sites, called blogs. Creating a site is called **Web authoring.** It begins with site design followed by creation of a document file that displays the Web site's content.

Web Site Design

A Web site is an interactive multimedia form of communication. Designing a Web site begins with determining the site's overall content. The content is

Figure 4-11 **Flora Photographs Web site**

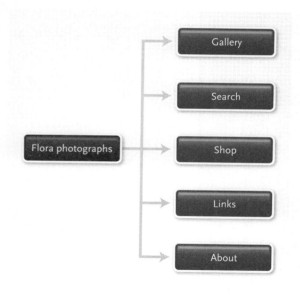

Figure 4-12 Partial graphical map for the Flora Photographs Web site

then broken down into a series of related pieces of information. The overall site design is commonly represented in a **graphical map.** (See Figure 4-12.)

Notice that in the graphical map shown in Figure 4-12 each block in the map represents a Web page. Lines joining the blocks represent links to related pages of information that make up the Web site. The first page, or home page, typically serves as an introduction and supplies a table of contents. The following pages present the specific pieces or blocks of information.

Multimedia elements are added to individual pages to enhance interest and interactivity. One multimedia element found on many Web sites is moving graphics called **animations.** These animations can be simple moving text or complicated interactive features. There are many specialized programs available to aid in the creation of animation. One type of interactive animation is produced using software called Adobe Flash. **Flash** movies can be inserted as a part of the page or encompass the entire screen.

Web Authoring Programs

As we mentioned in Chapter 2, Web pages are typically HTML (Hyper Text Markup Language) documents. With knowledge of HTML and a simple text editor, you can create Web pages. Even without knowledge of HTML, you can create simple Web pages using a word processing package like Microsoft Word.

More specialized and powerful programs, called **Web authoring programs,** are typically used to create sophisticated commercial sites. Also known as **Web page editors** and **HTML editors,** these programs provide support for Web site design and HTML coding. Some Web authoring programs are **WYSIWYG (what you see is what you get) editors,** which means you can build a page without interacting directly with HTML code. WYSIWYG editors preview the page described by HTML code. Widely used Web authoring programs include Adobe Dreamweaver, NetObjects Fusion, and Microsoft Expression. The Web site depicted in Figure 4-11 was created using Adobe Dreamweaver. (See Figure 4-13.)

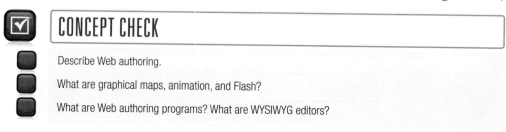

CONCEPT CHECK

● Describe Web authoring.

● What are graphical maps, animation, and Flash?

● What are Web authoring programs? What are WYSIWYG editors?

Explorations

Many people believe that the next big leap forward in computing will involve artificial intelligence.

To learn about a leading developer of artificial intelligence software, visit our Web site at www.computing2013.com and enter the keyword ai.

Artificial Intelligence

The field of computer science known as **artificial intelligence (AI)** attempts to develop computer systems that can mimic or simulate human senses, thought processes, and actions. These include reasoning, learning from past actions, and using senses such as vision and touch. Artificial intelligence that corresponds to human intelligence is still a long way off. However, several tools that emulate human senses, problem solving, and information processing have been developed.

These modern applications of artificial intelligence are designed to help people and organizations become more productive. Many of these tools have practical applications for business, medicine, law, and so on. In the past,

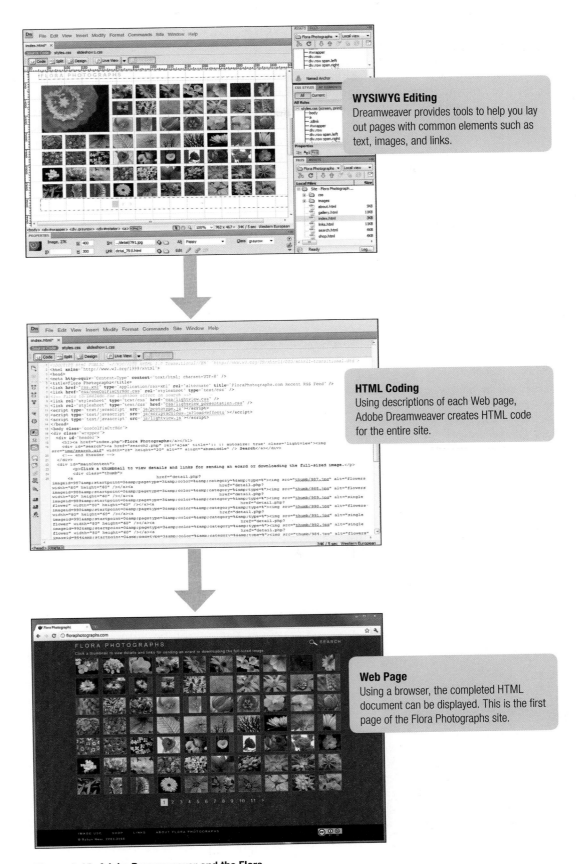

WYSIWYG Editing
Dreamweaver provides tools to help you lay out pages with common elements such as text, images, and links.

HTML Coding
Using descriptions of each Web page, Adobe Dreamweaver creates HTML code for the entire site.

Web Page
Using a browser, the completed HTML document can be displayed. This is the first page of the Flora Photographs site.

Figure 4-13 Adobe Dreamweaver and the Flora Photographs Web site

computers used calculating power to solve structured problems, which can be broken down into a series of well-defined steps. People—using intuition, reasoning, and memory—were better at solving unstructured problems, whether building a product or approving a loan. Organizations have long been able to computerize the tasks once performed by clerks. Now knowledge-intensive work and unstructured problems, such as activities performed by many managers, are being automated. Let us now consider three areas in which human talents and abilities have been enhanced with "computerized intelligence": virtual reality, knowledge-based systems, and robotics.

tips

Are you thinking about creating your own Web site? Perhaps you already have one and would like to spruce it up a bit? Here are a few suggestions that might help.

1 **Use a common design and theme.** Consistency in the use of colors, fonts, background designs, and navigation features gives a Web site a unified feeling and makes it easier to use.

2 **Use graphics and animations to add interest.** Graphics and animations add interest and focus the user's attention. However, they can take time to download, and the wait frustrates users. Be selective and limit the size of graphics. Also, reuse graphics from one page to another.

3 **Make navigating your Web site easy.** Create a simple method of navigating that allows users to get to their desired information as quickly as possible. None of your content should be more than three clicks from the home page.

4 **Design your site for a standard display.** To maximize the impact of your site for the largest number of users, design it to be viewed on a monitor with a standard 1024 × 768 resolution.

To see additional tips, visit us at www.computing2013.com and enter the keyword tips.

Virtual Reality

Suppose you could create and virtually experience any new form of reality you wished. You could see the world through the eyes of a child, a robot—or even a lobster. You could explore faraway resorts, the moon, or inside a nuclear waste dump without leaving your chair. This simulated experience is possible with virtual reality.

Virtual reality is an artificial, or simulated, reality generated in 3-D by a computer. Virtual reality is also commonly known as **VR, artificial reality,** or **virtual environments.** In some cases, to navigate in a virtual space, you use virtual reality hardware including headgear and gloves. The headgear has earphones and three-dimensional stereoscopic screens (one type is called Eyephones). The gloves have sensors that collect data about your hand movements (one type is called DataGlove). Coupled with software, this interactive sensory equipment lets you immerse yourself in a computer-generated world. (See Figure 4-14.)

Creating virtual reality programs once required very-high-end software costing several thousands of dollars. Recently, several lower-cost yet powerful authoring programs have been introduced. One of the best known is Second Life from Linden Labs, which allows users to create animated characters to represent themselves and to develop their own environment.

There are any number of possible applications for virtual reality. The ultimate recreational use might be something resembling a giant virtual amusement park. More serious applications can simulate important experiences or training environments such as in aviation, surgical operations, spaceship repair, or nuclear disaster cleanup. Some virtual reality strives to be an **immersive experience,** allowing a user to walk into a virtual reality room or view simulations on a **virtual reality wall.** (See Figure 4-15.)

Figure 4-14 Virtual reality

Knowledge-Based (Expert) Systems

People who are expert in a particular area—certain kinds of medicine, accounting, engineering, and so on—are generally well paid for their specialized knowledge. Unfortunately for their clients and customers, these experts are expensive, not always available, and hard to replace when they move on.

Figure 4-15 **Virtual reality wall**

Figure 4-16 **Asimo**

What if you were to somehow capture the knowledge of a human expert and make it accessible to everyone through a computer program? This is exactly what is being done with so-called knowledge-based or expert systems. **Knowledge-based systems,** also known as **expert systems,** are a type of artificial intelligence that uses a database to provide assistance to users. These systems use a database or **knowledge base** that contains specific facts, rules to relate these facts, and user input to formulate recommendations and decisions. The sequence of processing is determined by the interaction of the user and the knowledge base. Many expert systems use so-called **fuzzy logic,** which allows a system to respond to questions in a very humanlike way. For example, if an expert system asked how your classes were going, you could respond, "great," "OK," "terrible," and so on, and the system would understand your statement.

Over the past decade, expert systems have been developed in areas such as medicine, geology, architecture, and nature. There are expert systems with such names as Oil Spill Advisor, Bird Species Identification, and even Midwives Assistant. A system called Grain Marketing Advisor helps farmers select the best way to market their grain.

Robotics

Robotics is the field of study concerned with developing and using robots. **Robots** are computer-controlled machines that mimic the motor activities of living things. For example, Honda's Asimo robot resembles a human and is capable of walking upstairs, dancing, shaking hands, and much more. (See Figure 4-16.) Some robots can even solve unstructured problems using artificial intelligence.

Robots are used in factories, manufacturing, home security, the military, and many other fields of human endeavor. They differ from other assembly-line machines because they can be reprogrammed to do more than one task. Robots often are used to handle dangerous, repetitive tasks. There are four types of robots.

- **Perception systems: Perception system robots** imitate some of the human senses. For example, robots with television-camera vision systems are particularly useful. They can guide machine tools, inspect products, and secure homes.
- **Industrial robots: Industrial robots** are used to perform a variety of tasks. Examples are machines used in automobile plants to do welding, polishing, and painting. Some types of robots have claws for picking up objects and handling dangerous materials. (See Figure 4-17.)

ex.
put in systems
get response
according to
relatability

environment

Did you know that robots may someday help clear our oceans of pollution? Investigators are currently exploring the use of robots and special companion ocean vessels for just that purpose. The robots would roam the ocean bottom looking for garbage, oil, and other pollutants. Once located, the robots would either clean up the mess on their own or radio other robots for assistance. When full, the robots would resurface and deposit the offensive materials on the companion vessel and then go back for more. The future of robotics promises many opportunities for this kind of robotic cleanup. For additional discussion of this issue, see ENVIRONMENTAL ROBOTS on page 133. To see more environmental facts, visit our Web site at www .computing2013.com and enter the keyword environment.

- **Mobile robots: Mobile robots** act as transports and are widely used for a variety of different tasks. For example, the police and military use them to locate and disarm explosive devices. In the early 2000s, mobile robots entered the world of entertainment with their own television program, called *Battlebots.* You can even build your own mobile robot from a kit.
- **Household robots: Household robots** are now widely available and are designed to vacuum or scrub floors, mow lawns, patrol the house, or simply provide entertainment.

Figure 4-17 Industrial robot

☑ CONCEPT CHECK

Define artificial intelligence. What are virtual reality and virtual reality walls?

Describe knowledge-based systems and fuzzy logic.

Describe four types of robots.

Mobile Apps

Mobile apps or **mobile applications** are add-on features for a variety of mobile devices including smartphones, netbooks, and tablets. Mobile apps have been widely used for years. The traditional applications include address books, to-do lists, alarms, and message lists. With the introduction of smartphones and wireless connections to the Internet, mobile capabilities have exploded. Now, any number of specialized applications are available.

Apps

The breadth and scope of available specialized applications for smartphones and other mobile devices is ever expanding. There are over 350,000 apps just for Apple's iPhone alone. Some of the most widely used mobile apps are text messaging, Internet browsing, and connecting to social networks. See Figure 4-18 for a list of some specialized apps.

One of the fastest growing apps is QR code readers. These readers allow mobile devices to use their digital cameras to scan QR codes. **QR codes,** also known as **Quick Response codes,** are graphics that typically appear as black and white boxes that automatically link mobile devices to a variety of different

App	Description	Site
Facebook	Connects to Facebook	facebook.com
Gmail	Access e-mail from any computer	mail.google.com
Games.com	Access to single- and multiplayer games	www.games.com
Photoshop Express	Photo sharing and editing site	www.photoshop.com/express
ESPN	Sports information and scores	www.espn.go.com

Figure 4-18 Specialized apps

content including games, text, videos, and Web sites. You likely have seen QR codes in magazines, newspapers, and even in books. See Figure 4-19.

Many apps are written for a particular type of mobile device and will not run on other types. For example, an app designed for Apple's iPhone may not work with Google's Android. So, before obtaining or installing a mobile app, be sure that it is intended to work with your particular mobile device and that your mobile device has the capability to support the app.

App Stores

An **app store** is typically a Web site that provides access to specific mobile apps that can be downloaded either for a nominal fee or free of charge. Two of the best-known stores are Apple's App Store and Android Market. (See Figure 4-20.) Although most of the best-known app stores specialize in applications for a particular line of mobile device, other less-well-known stores provide apps for a wide variety of mobile devices. For a list of some more widely used app stores, see Figure 4-21.

Figure 4-19 QR Code

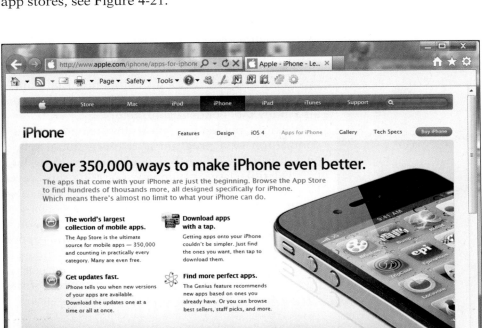

Figure 4-20 Apple's App Store

App	Focus	Site
Apple App Store	iPhone	www.appstore.com
Android Market	Smartphones using Android operating system	www.android.com/market
BlackBerry App World	BlackBerry products	www.appworld.com
GetJar	Variety	www.getjar.com
Handango	Variety	www.handango.com
Windows Phone Store	Smartphones using Windows Phone 7 operating system	www.microsoft.com/WindowsPhone

Figure 4-21 App Stores

☑ CONCEPT CHECK

 What are mobile apps? What impact have smartphones, netbooks and tablets had?

 What are some of the most common applications? What are QR codes and QR code readers?

 What are app stores?

Careers in IT

Now that you have learned about some of the most important specialized applications, let me tell you about my job in desktop publishing.

Desktop publishers use computers to format and create publication-ready material. They may create books, magazines, newsletters, and newspapers on home computers using special application software. A large part of the job is designing page layout, importing text, and manipulating graphics. Most desktop publishers work for companies that handle commercial printing accounts. However, there are also many independent contractors.

Desktop publishing positions usually require completion of a program at a professional school or a university. Internships and part-time work can be a valuable asset to someone pursuing this career. Employers typically look for individuals with good communication skills and artistic ability.

Desktop publishers can expect to earn an annual salary of $26,500 to $44,500. Advancement opportunities include management positions or independent contracting. To learn about other careers in information technology, visit us at www.computing 2013.com and enter the keyword **careers**.

A LOOK TO THE FUTURE

Robots Can Look, Act, and Think Like Us

Would you like to talk with your mom through a robot that both resembles you and demonstrates your emotions on its rubber face? What if you received a companion robot with a set of moral values? Would you trust a robot to trade the stocks in your portfolio? Researchers are currently at work on robots with the artificial intelligence needed to perform these tasks and more.

The Saya robot, with its artificial skin and muscles, was recently unveiled in Tokyo. Researchers hope that eventually it will be used as a communication device similar to a current Web cam. For example, you could connect to a robot that resembles you at your mother's house and communicate through it with her. You would see your mother through the robot's visual system. Your mother would hear your voice come from the robot and your emotions would be displayed on its face.

Other research is being conducted that will give robots a sense of values. It is hoped that these robots will be able to make decisions independently based on this set of values. Researchers in California are creating robots that act as surveillance instruments, capable of following a target without direction from a human. The robots can predict potential escape routes and pursue a subject through crowded areas.

The Feelix Growing project, a European research project, is developing robots that detect human emotions using simple video cameras and sensors combined with sophisticated software. These robots can then be programmed to respond with similar emotional cues. These robots recognize faces and respond to stimuli like a person would with emotions ranging from surprise to disgust. These robots might be used to help children with developmental disabilities in the near future. Someday, you might interact with a robot that can respond to how you are feeling.

All of these projects are designed to move beyond simple computing and into a decidedly human realm of emotional intelligence. Some experts have even suggested that human intelligence relies on emotional input for all important decision making. Thus, by definition, for a machine to approximate human intelligence, it would have to understand and rely on emotions. If computers could read human emotions, and had emotional intelligence of their own, it could be possible for your computer to act as a stress counselor when you stay up all night working on a project.

Computers with their own emotional intelligence could be the ultimate human companions. Computer scientists have suggested they may read your mood and play music accordingly. Or they could search through audio and video files for media you would find moving, funny, or dramatic. If computers had their own emotional sense, it is possible that they, like the humans they emulate, would require interaction for mental health.

Would you use a robot as a communication device? Do you think we should build robots with a sense of moral values? Some researchers have suggested that robots with artificial intelligence could serve as ideal supervisors and managers. What do you think? Would you like to have an "emotional" robot for a boss?

GRAPHICS

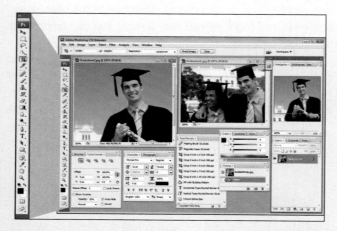

Professionals in graphic arts use specialized graphics programs.

Desktop Publishing

Desktop publishing programs (page layout programs) mix text and graphics to create professional publications.

Image Editors

Image editors (photo editors) create and modify **bitmap (raster) image** files. Images are recorded as dots or **pixels.**

Illustration Programs

Illustration programs, also known as **drawing programs,** modify **vector images (vector illustrations).** In a vector file, images are recorded as a collection of objects such as lines, rectangles, and ovals.

Image Galleries

Image galleries are libraries of electronic images, widely available from the Web. Two types are **stock photographs** and **clip art.**

Graphics Suites

A **graphics suite** is a collection of individual graphics programs sold as a unit.

AUDIO AND VIDEO

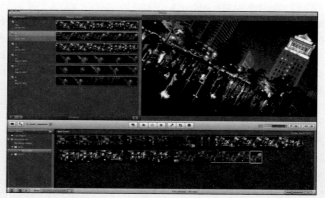

Recent advances in video and audio technology allow individuals to assemble near-professional-quality video and audio footage. You can create your own compilation movies.

Video Software

Video editing software allows you to reorganize, add effects, and more to digital video. Apple iMovie and Windows Movie Maker are commonly used video editing programs.

Audio Software

Audio editing software allows you to create and edit audio clips. You can add audio effects, like filters, to your tracks. You can filter out pops or scratches in an old recording. You can create MP3s. Apple GarageBand and Sony ACID are commonly used audio editing programs.

To be a competent end user, you need to be aware of specialized applications. You need to know who uses them, what they are used for, and how they are used. Specialized applications include graphics programs, audio and video editing software, multimedia, Web authoring, artificial intelligence, and mobile apps.

MULTIMEDIA

Multimedia integrates all sorts of media into one presentation. An essential feature is user participation or **interactivity.**

Links and Buttons

A multimedia presentation is organized as a series of related pages connected by links and buttons.

- **Links** are connections to related information, which can be video, sound, graphics, text files, pages, and other resources.
- **Buttons** are special areas on a page that can make appropriate links and navigate through a presentation to locate and discover information.

Multimedia Authoring Programs

Multimedia authoring programs bring together video, audio, graphics, and text elements in an interactive framework.

WEB AUTHORING

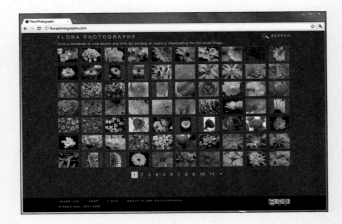

Blogs are personal Web sites. Creating Web sites is called **Web authoring.** It begins with Web site design, followed by creating a document file that displays the Web site content.

Web Site Design

Web sites are an interactive multimedia form of communication.

Graphical maps use linked blocks to represent a Web site's overall content. Typically, blocks represent individual Web pages and links indicate relationships between related pages.

The first Web page (home page) usually introduces the site and supplies a table of contents. Multimedia elements are added to pages. **Animations** are moving graphics. **Flash** is a widely used application for Web animation.

Web Authoring Programs

Web sites can be created using a simple text editor or word processor. **Web authoring programs,** also known as **Web page editors** or **HTML editors,** are specifically designed to create Web sites. They provide support for Web site design and HTML coding. Some offer **WYSIWYG (what you see is what you get) editors.**

ARTIFICIAL INTELLIGENCE

Artificial intelligence (AI) attempts to develop computer systems that mimic human senses, thought processes, and actions.

Virtual Reality

Virtual reality (VR, artificial reality, or virtual environments) creates a computer-generated simulated environment using sensory equipment, including head gear and gloves.

Applications include recreational and other areas such as aviation, surgical operations, spaceship repair, and nuclear disaster cleanup. Some applications strive for immersive experiences and can be viewed on virtual reality walls.

Knowlege-Based (Expert) Systems

Knowledge-based (expert) systems are programs that duplicate the knowledge that humans use to perform specific tasks. Knowledge bases are databases containing facts and rules. Fuzzy logic allows a system to respond to questions in a very humanlike way.

Robotics

Robotics is concerned with developing and using robots. Robots are computer-controlled machines that mimic the motor activities of living things. There are four types of robots.

- **Perception system robots** imitate some of the human senses.
- **Industrial robots** perform a variety of tasks including welding, polishing, and painting.
- **Mobile robots** act as transports and are widely used for a variety of different tasks including locating and disarming explosive devices.
- **Household robots** perform activities around the home including vacuuming or scrubbing floors, mowing lawns, patrolling the house, or providing entertainment.

MOBILE APPS

Mobile apps, also known as mobile applications, are add-on features that perform a variety of tasks not associated with typical cell phone use. Introduction of smartphones and wireless Internet connections have expanded mobile capabilities and the number of specialized apps.

Apps

Some of the most widespread mobile apps are for text messaging, Internet browsing, and connecting to social networks. Thousands of other specialized apps are available. QR code readers are one of the fastest growing apps.

- **QR code readers** allow mobile devices to use digital cameras to scan QR codes.
- **QR codes (Quick Response codes)** provide links to a variety of different content.

App Stores

App stores are typically Web sites providing access to specific apps for a fee or free. The two best-known stores are Apple's App Store and Android Market. Many app stores focus on apps for particular lines of mobile device. Other stores provide apps for a variety of mobile devices.

CAREERS IN IT

Desktop publishers use computers to format and create publication-ready material. Vocational or university degree is preferred plus good communication skills and artistic ability. Salary range is $26,500 to $44,500.

KEY TERMS

animation   (116)
app store   (121)
artificial intelligence (AI)   (116)
artificial reality   (118)
audio editing software   (111)
bitmap image   (109)
blog   (115)
button   (114)
clip art   (110)
desktop publisher   (122)
desktop publishing program   (109)
drawing program   (109)
expert system   (119)
Flash   (116)
fuzzy logic   (119)
graphical map   (116)
graphics suite   (111)
household robot   (120)
HTML editor   (116)
illustration program   (109)
image editor   (109)
image gallery   (109)
immersive experience   (118)
industrial robot   (119)
interactivity   (114)
knowledge base   (119)
knowledge-based system   (119)
link   (114)

mobile app   (120)
mobile application   (120)
mobile robot   (120)
multimedia   (114)
multimedia authoring program   (114)
page layout program   (109)
perception system robot   (119)
photo editor   (109)
pixel   (109)
QR code   (120)
QR code reader   (120)
raster image   (109)
robot   (119)
robotics   (119)
stock photograph   (110)
vector   (109)
vector illustration   (109)
vector image   (109)
video editing software   (111)
virtual environment   (118)
virtual reality   (118)
virtual reality wall   (118)
VR   (118)
Web authoring   (115)
Web authoring program   (116)
Web page editor   (116)
WYSIWIG editor   (116)

To test your knowledge of these key terms with animated flash cards, visit our Web site at www.computing2013.com and enter the keyword **terms4**.

MULTIPLE CHOICE

Circle the correct answer.

1. These specialized graphics programs combine text and graphics to create publications of professional quality.
   a. desktop publishing programs
   b. image editors
   c. image galleries
   d. illustration programs

2. Also known as drawing programs.
   a. desktop publishing programs
   b. image editors
   c. image galleries
   d. illustration programs

3. Graphics programs used to create and edit vector images.
   a. desktop publishing programs
   b. image editors
   c. image galleries
   d. illustration programs

4. An essential multimedia feature that allows user participation.
   a. Flash
   b. interactivity
   c. immersion
   d. raster

5. Special programs used to create multimedia presentations.
   a. desktop publishing programs
   b. Flash editors
   c. image editors
   d. multimedia authoring programs

6. A widely used interactive animation application from Adobe.
   a. ACTION
   b. Flash
   c. Fuzzy
   d. WYSIWYG

7. Programs for Web site design and HTML coding are called Web page editors or
   a. apps
   b. HTML editors
   c. VR programs
   d. Web editors

8. This area of artificial intelligence is also known as expert systems.
   a. acoustics
   b. knowledge-based systems
   c. robotics
   d. virtual reality

9. A type of artificial intelligence that uses a database to provide assistance to users.
   a. acoustics
   b. expert systems
   c. robotics
   d. virtual reality

10. Another name for the database used in expert systems that contains specific facts and rules.
    a. access table
    b. expert table
    c. knowledge base
    d. rule base

For an interactive multiple-choice practice test, visit our Web site at www.computing2013.com and enter the keyword multiple4.

MATCHING

Match each numbered item with the most closely related lettered item. Write your answers in the spaces provided.

a.	audio editing	____ 1. Specialized graphics programs for editing or modifying digital images.
b.	bitmap images	____ 2. Another name for raster images.
c.	blog	____ 3. Raster images contain thousands of dots known as ____.
d.	button	
e.	image editors	____ 4. Type of software used to create and edit audio clips.
f.	mobile	____ 5. A link on a multimedia page used to locate and discover information.
g.	pixels	
h.	virtual reality	____ 6. Personal Web site created by an individual.
i.	robots	____ 7. The process of creating a Web site.
j.	Web authoring	____ 8. Also known as artificial reality or virtual environments.
		____ 9. Computer-controlled machines that mimic human activities.
		____ 10. The type of app designed for smartphones, netbooks, and tablets.

For an interactive matching practice test, visit our Web site at www.computing2013 .com and enter the keyword matching4.

OPEN-ENDED

On a separate sheet of paper, respond to each question or statement.

1. Describe graphics, including desktop publishers, image editors, illustration programs, image galleries, and graphics suites.
2. Discuss audio and video editing software.
3. What is multimedia? Discuss interactivity, links, buttons, and multimedia authoring programs.
4. Describe Web authoring, including Web site design, graphical maps, animations, flash, Web authoring programs, Web page editors, and WYSIWYG editors.
5. Discuss artificial intelligence including virtual reality, knowledge-based (expert) systems, and robotics.
6. What are mobile apps? Discuss QR code readers, QR codes, and app stores.

MAKING IT WORK FOR YOU

The following questions are designed to demonstrate ways that you can effectively use technology today.

① DIGITAL VIDEO EDITING

Have you ever thought of making your own movie? Would you like to edit some home videos and distribute them to family and friends on DVDs? It's easy with the right equipment and software. To learn more about digital video editing, review Making IT Work for You: Digital Video Editing, on pages 112 and 113. Then answer the following questions: (a) Briefly describe the steps necessary to begin transferring video from a camcorder to your computer. (b) Where can you preview your movie in Windows Live Movie Maker? (c) What is Windows DVD Maker and what is it used for?

② ADOBE FLASH

Web sites aren't all just text and pictures anymore. Many are taking advantage of browser plug-ins that add new functionality and display abilities to Web browsers, as we discussed in Chapter 2. One of the most popular plug-ins is Adobe Flash. Visit our Web site at www.computing2013.com and enter the keyword flash for a link to the Adobe site. Once connected, read about Flash and answer the following questions: (a) What is Flash? What types of content can it display? (b) How is the Flash plug-in obtained? (c) What types of companies are using Flash in their Web page designs? (d) Do you think Flash is a valuable Web page addition or just a flashy distraction? Explain your answer.

③ STREAMING MULTIMEDIA PLAYERS

Streaming multimedia files come in many varieties. There are several formats for streaming audio and video files available, each with its own advantage. To play these files, a user needs software known as a *player,* which must support the type of file the user wishes to play. Visit our Web site at www.computing2013.com and enter the keyword streaming for a link to a popular streaming multimedia player. Read about the player and then answer the following questions: (a) What types of streaming multimedia files can be played with this player? (b) How does the user receive and install the player? (c) As streaming multimedia becomes more widely available on the Internet, how might the role of player software change? Be specific.

EXPLORATIONS

The following questions are designed to add depth and detail to your understanding of specific topics presented within this chapter. The questions direct you to sources other than the textbook to obtain this knowledge.

1 HOW DIGITAL VIDEO EDITING WORKS

The falling prices of digital camcorders and improvements in computer technology have made digital video editing affordable for individuals. To learn more about digital video editing, visit our Web site at www.computing2013.com and enter the keyword video. Then answer the following questions: (a) What hardware is needed to capture video from a VCR tape? Why is this hardware necessary? (b) How can video editing software be used to improve a video? (c) What are some common ways to share videos?

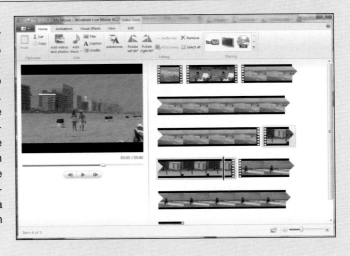

2 PERSONAL WEB SITE

Would you like a personal Web site but don't want to deal with learning HTML? There are many services available to get you started. To learn more about personal Web sites, visit our Web site at www.computing2013.com and enter the keyword blog. Then answer the following questions: (a) What are Web logs? What are they used for? (b) What is Blogger.com? Describe the following features provided by Blogger.com: templates, upload file, hyperlink, post, publish, and view Web page. (c) Have you ever created a Web log or other types of personal Web site? If you have, describe how you created it and what you used it for. If you have not, discuss why and how you might use one.

3 STREAMING MULTIMEDIA

Many Web sites are now enhanced with streaming multimedia. Some sites offer streaming audio or video to augment text, such as news sites with file footage. For others, the content *is* the streaming multimedia, such as Internet radio or animation sites. Locate several Web sites that offer streaming multimedia and pick one to review. Then answer the following: (a) Define "streaming multimedia." (b) What type of streaming multimedia did the site offer? Who is the intended audience? (c) In what ways was the experience limited? Be specific.

ETHICS

The following question is designed to explore ethical issues related to technology and to develop the ability to think critically and communicate effectively. Respond to the questions by either creating a one-page paper or preparing for an in-depth classroom discussion.

1 DIGITAL PHOTO MANIPULATION

Image editing software has made it easy to alter photographs, which in the past were accepted as visual records of real events. In some cases, the purpose of digital editing is humor and exaggeration, while other times subtle changes are used to alter a photo's deeper meaning. Review the Ethics box on page 109. Research examples of digital photo editing that resulted in controversy and then respond to the following: (a) Do you see any ethical issues related to altering photographs? (b) What do you consider the boundary between acceptable photo editing and deceptive or misleading practices? (c) Do you feel the old saying "seeing is believing" needs to be reconsidered for the digital age? Defend your answers.

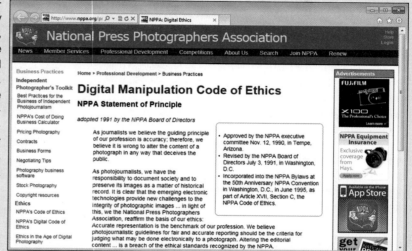

ENVIRONMENT

The following question is designed to explore environmental issues related to technology and to develop the ability to think critically and communicate effectively. Respond to the question by either creating a one-page paper or preparing for an in-depth classroom discussion.

1 ENVIRONMENTAL ROBOTS

Environmental robots are protecting our environment. For example, robots roam the ocean looking for and cleaning up garbage, oil spills, and other pollutants. Review the Environment box on page 119. Research environmental robots and then respond to the following: (a) Define environmental robots. (b) Describe one type of environmental robot. What does it do? Where is it used? (c) Have you ever seen an environmental robot? If so, how was it used? If not, describe some areas where environmental robots would be effective. (d) Do you see any disadvantages to using environmental robots? Do you think more will be used in the future? Why or why not?

System Software

▲ Download the free *Computing Essentials 2013* app for videos, key term flashcards, quizzes, and the game, *Over the Edge!*

Competencies

After you have read this chapter, you should be able to:

1 Describe the differences between system software and application software.

2 Discuss the four types of system software.

3 Discuss the basic functions, features, and categories of operating systems.

4 Describe Windows, Mac OS, UNIX, Linux, and virtualization.

5 Describe the purpose of utilities and utility suites.

6 Discuss mobile operating systems including BlackBerry OS, iOS, Android, Windows Phone 7, and WebOS.

7 Identify the five most essential utilities.

8 Discuss Windows utility programs.

9 Describe device drivers, including Windows' Add a Device Wizard and Update.

Why should I read this chapter?

Many years ago, microcomputers were very limited in what they could do. A major limitation was their operating systems, which often required computer specialists to keep them running. That was then and this is now. Now, the possibilities seem limitless with the powerful operating systems of today. These programs make it easy and safe for any of us to use computers, the Internet, and the Web.

This chapter discusses a variety of operating systems for desktop computers including Windows 7 and Mac OS X. Additionally, you'll learn about mobile operating systems including Apple's iOS, Android, and Windows Phone 7. You also will learn about how to use programs that recognize and correct computer problems and use programs that guard your computer against viruses. To be competent and to be competitive in today's professional workplace, you need to know and to understand these things.

chapter 5

Hi, I'm Ann and I'm a computer support specialist. I'd like to talk with you about system software, programs that do a lot of the work behind the scenes so that you can run applications and surf the Web. I'd also like to talk about the mobile operating systems that control smartphones and other small portable computers.

Introduction

When most people think about computers, they think about surfing the Web, creating reports, analyzing data, storing information, making presentations, and any number of other valuable applications. We typically think about applications and application software. Computers and computer applications have become a part of the fabric of our everyday lives. Most of us agree that they are great . . . as long as they are working.

We usually do not think about the more mundane and behind-the-scenes computer activities: loading and running programs, coordinating networks that share resources, organizing files, protecting our computers from viruses, performing periodic maintenance to avoid problems, and controlling hardware devices so that they can communicate with one another. Typically, these activities go on behind the scenes without our help.

That is the way it should be, and the way it is, as long as everything is working perfectly. But what if new application programs are not compatible and will not run on our current computer system? What if we get a computer virus? What if our hard disk fails? What if we buy a new digital video camera and can't store and edit the images on our computer system? What if our computer starts to run slower and slower?

These issues may seem mundane, but they are critical. This chapter covers the vital activities that go on behind the scenes. A little knowledge about these activities can go a long way to making your computing life easier. To effectively use computers, competent end users need to understand the functionality of system software, including operating systems, utility programs, and device drivers.

System Software

End users use application software to accomplish specific tasks. For example, we use word processors to create letters, documents, and reports. However, end users also use system software. **System software** works with end users, application software, and computer hardware to handle the majority of technical details. For example, system software controls where a word processing program is stored in memory, how commands are converted so that the system unit can process them, and where a completed document or file is saved. See Figure 5-1.

System software is not a single program. Rather it is a collection or a system of programs that handle hundreds of technical details with little or no user intervention. System software consists of four types of programs:

- **Operating systems** coordinate computer resources, provide an interface between users and the computer, and run applications.
- **Utilities** perform specific tasks related to managing computer resources.
- **Device drivers** are specialized programs that allow particular input or output devices to communicate with the rest of the computer system.
- **Language translators** convert the programming instructions written by programmers into a language that computers understand and process.

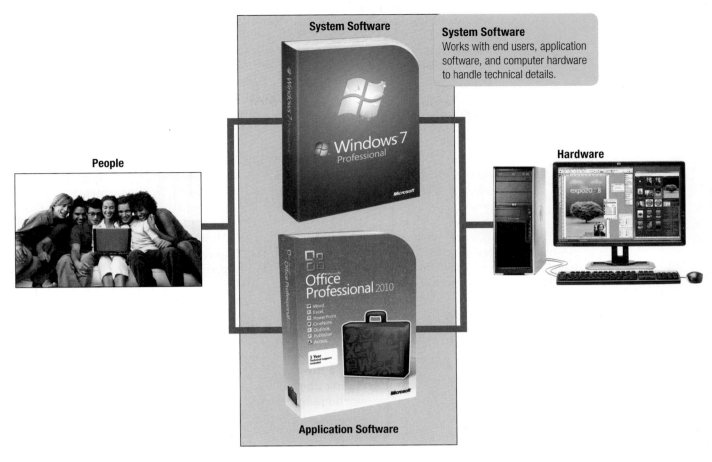

System Software
Works with end users, application software, and computer hardware to handle technical details.

People

Hardware

Application Software

Figure 5-1 System software handles technical details

Operating Systems

An **operating system** is a collection of programs that handle many of the technical details related to using a computer. In many ways, an operating system is the most important type of computer program. Without a functioning operating system, your computer would be useless.

Functions

Every computer has an operating system and every operating system performs a variety of functions. These functions can be classified into three groups:

- **Managing resources:** Operating systems coordinate all the computer's resources including memory, processing, storage, and devices such as printers and monitors. They also monitor system performance, schedule tasks, provide security, and start up the computer.
- **Providing user interface:** Operating systems allow users to interact with application programs and computer hardware through a **user interface.** Many older operating systems used a character-based interface in which users communicated with the operating system through written commands such as "Copy A: assign.doc C:". Almost all newer operating systems use a **graphical user interface (gui).** As we discussed in Chapter 3, a graphical user interface uses graphical elements such as icons and windows.

- **Running applications:** Operating systems load and run applications such as word processors and spreadsheets. Most operating systems support **multitasking,** or the ability to switch between different applications stored in memory. With multitasking, you could have Word and Excel running at the same time and switch easily between the two applications. The program that you are currently working on is described as running in the **foreground.** The other program or programs are running in the **background.**

Features

Starting or restarting a computer is called **booting** the system. There are two ways to boot a computer: a warm boot and a cold boot. A **warm boot** occurs when the computer is already on and you restart it without turning off the power. A warm boot can be accomplished in several ways. For many computer systems, they can be restarted by simply pressing a sequence of keys. Starting a computer that has been turned off is called a **cold boot.** To learn more about booting your computer system and POST (power on self-test), visit our Web site at www.computing2013.com and enter the keyword **boot.**

You typically interact with the operating system through the graphical user interface. Most provide a place, called the **desktop,** that provides access to computer resources. (See Figure 5-2.) Operating systems have several features in common with application programs, including

- **Icons**—graphic representations for a program, type of file, or function.
- **Pointer**—controlled by a mouse, trackpad, or touchscreen, the pointer changes shape depending upon its current function. For example, when shaped like an arrow, the pointer can be used to select items such as an icon.
- **Windows**—rectangular areas for displaying information and running programs.

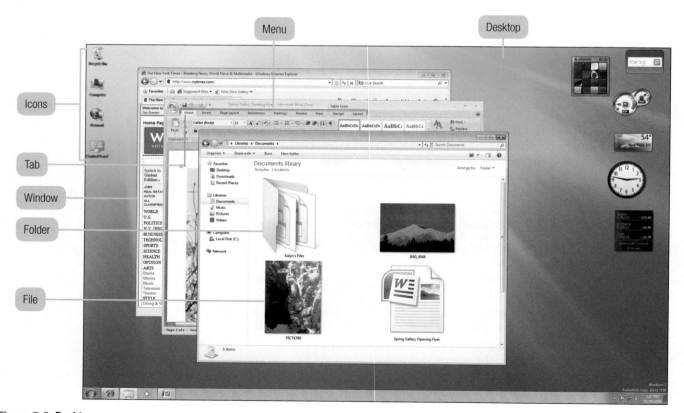

Figure 5-2 Desktop

- **Menus**—provide a list of options or commands.
- **Tabs**—divide menus into major activity areas.
- **Dialog boxes**—provide information or request input.
- **Help**—provides online assistance for operating system functions and procedures.

Most operating systems store data and programs in a system of files and folders. **Files** are used to store data and programs. Related files are stored within a **folder** and, for organizational purposes, a folder can contain other folders. For example, you might organize your electronic files in the *Documents* folder on your hard disk. This folder could contain other folders, each named to indicate its contents. One might be "Computers" and could contain all the files you have created (or will create) for this course.

Categories

While there are hundreds of different operating systems, there are only three basic categories: embedded, network, or stand-alone.

Figure 5-3 Handheld devices have embedded operating systems

- **Embedded operating systems** are used for handheld devices such as smartphones, cable and satellite television tuner boxes, video game systems, and other small electronics. (See Figure 5-3.) The entire operating system is stored within or embedded in the device. The operating system programs are permanently stored on **ROM**, or read-only memory, chips.
- **Network operating systems (NOS)** are used to control and coordinate computers that are networked or linked together. Many networks are small and connect only a limited number of microcomputers. Other networks, like those at colleges and universities, are very large and complex. These networks may include other smaller networks and typically connect a variety of different types of computers.

  Network operating systems are typically located on one of the connected computers' hard disks. Called the **network server,** this computer coordinates all communication between the other computers. Popular network operating systems include NetWare, Windows Server, and UNIX.
- **Stand-alone operating systems,** also called **desktop operating systems,** control a single desktop or notebook computer. (See Figure 5-4.) These operating systems are located on the computer's hard disk. Often desktop computers and notebooks are part of a network. In these cases, the desktop operating system works with the network's NOS to share and coordinate resources. In these situations, the desktop operating system is referred to as the *client operating system.*

Figure 5-4 Stand-alone operating system

The operating system is often referred to as the **software environment** or **platform.** Almost all application programs are designed to run with a specific platform. For example, Apple's iMovie software is designed to run with the Mac OS environment. Many applications, however, have different versions, each designed to operate with a particular platform. For example, one version of Microsoft Office is designed to operate with Windows. Another version is designed to operate with Mac OS.

 CONCEPT CHECK

 What is system software? What are the four kinds of system software programs?

 What is an operating system? Discuss operating system functions and features.

Describe each of the three categories of operating systems.

DESKTOP OPERATING SYSTEMS

Every microcomputer has an operating system controlling its operations. The most widely used operating systems are Windows, Mac OS, Unix, and Linux.

Windows

Microsoft's **Windows** is by far the most popular microcomputer operating system today with nearly 90 percent of the market. Because its market share is so large, more application programs are developed to run under Windows than any other operating system. Windows comes in a variety of different versions and is designed to run with Intel and Intel-compatible microprocessors such as the Core 2 Quad and Atom series. For a summary of Microsoft's desktop operating systems, see Figure 5-5.

There are many versions of Windows. The latest, **Windows 7,** was released in 2009. (See Figure 5-6.) Compared to the previous system, **Windows Vista,** Windows 7 provides several improvements, including

- Improved handwriting recognition for tablet computers.
- A taskbar that features previews, large icons, and personalization features.
- Advanced searching capabilities for finding files and content on your computer.

Mac OS

Apple introduced its Macintosh microcomputer and operating system in 1984. It provided one of the first guis, making it easy even for novice computer users to move and delete files. Designed to run with Apple computers, **Mac OS** is not as widely used as the Windows operating system. As a result, fewer application

Figure 5-5 Microsoft desktop operating systems

Name	Description
Windows XP	Upgrade to a previous Windows version, Windows 2000, with improved interface, stability, and reliability
Windows Vista	Upgrade to Windows XP with improved security, three-dimensional workspace, and filtering capabilities
Windows 7	Microsoft's latest operating system with improved user experience, speed, and stability

Figure 5-6 Windows 7

programs have been written for it. With increasing sales of Apple computers, however, the use of Mac OS is increasing and is widely recognized as one of the most innovative operating systems. It is a powerful, easy-to-use operating system that is popular with professional graphic designers, desktop publishers, and many home users.

Mac OS X is the most widely used Mac OS. (See Figure 5-7.) This operating system provides a wide array of powerful features including Spotlight and Dashboard Widgets. **Spotlight** is an advanced search tool that can rapidly locate files, folders, e-mail messages, addresses, and much more. **Dashboard Widgets** are a collection of specialized programs that will constantly update and display information. Some versions of Mac OS X also include **Boot Camp,** which allows Macintosh computers to run both Mac OS and the Windows operating system.

The most recent version, **Mac OS 10.7,** is known as **Lion** and has introduced some exciting features including Launchpad, Mission Control, and gesture support:

- **Launchpad** displays and provides direct access to all apps installed on your computer.

Have you ever thought about updating your current operating system? Keeping your computer updated with the latest security features and corrections is essential to avoiding viruses and other security problems. You can keep Windows 7 up to date automatically by following these steps:

1 Click *Start*, point to *All Programs*, and then click *Windows Update*.

2 In the left pane, click *Change settings*.

3 Select *Install updates automatically (recommended)*.

4 Under *Recommended updates*, select the check box labeled *Give me recommended updates the same way I receive important updates*, and then click *OK*.

To see additional tips, visit our Web site at www.computing2013.com and enter the keyword tips.

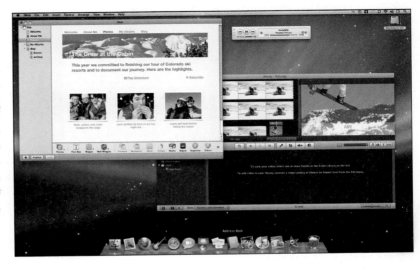

Figure 5-7 Mac OS X

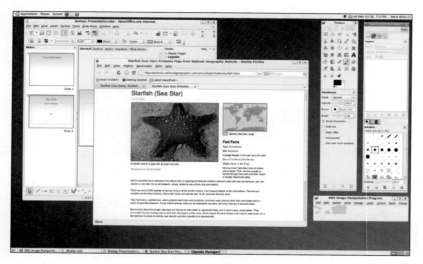

Figure 5-8 Linux

- **Mission Control** displays all running programs at one time.
- **Gestures** allow you to use your fingers to run programs and to control the content of your display screen.

UNIX and Linux

The **UNIX** operating system was originally designed to run on minicomputers in network environments. Now, it is widely widely used by servers on the Web, mainframe computers, and very powerful microcomputers. There are a large number of different versions of UNIX. One receiving a great deal of attention today is **Linux.**

Linux was originally developed by a graduate student at the University of Helsinki, Linus Torvalds, in 1991. He allowed free distribution of the operating system code and encouraged others to modify and further develop the code. Programs released in this way are called **open source.** Linux is a popular and powerful alternative to the Windows operating system. (See Figure 5-8.)

Linux has been the basis of several other operating systems. For example, Google's **Chrome OS** is based on Linux. This operating system is designed for netbook computers and other mobile devices. Chrome OS focuses on Internet connectivity and cloud computing.

Virtualization

As we have discussed, application programs are designed to run with particular operating systems. What if you wanted to run two or more applications each requiring a different operating system? One solution would be to install each of the operating systems on a different computer. There is, however, a way in which a single physical computer can support multiple operating systems that operate independently. This approach is called **virtualization.**

When a single physical computer runs a special program known as **virtualization software,** it operates as though it were two or more separate and independent computers known as **virtual machines.** Each virtual machine appears to the user as a separate independent computer with its own operating system. The operating system of the physical machine is known as the **host operating system.** The operating system for each virtual machine is known as the **guest operating system.** Users can readily switch between virtual computers and programs running on them. (See Figure 5-9.)

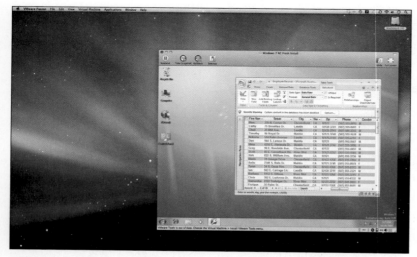

Figure 5-9 Windows 7 running within a window on the Mac OS X operating system

What is Windows? What is Windows 7?

 What are Mac OS and Lion? Spotlight? Dashboard Widgets? Boot Camp? Launchpad? Mission Control? Gestures?

 What is UNIX? What is Linux? What is Chrome?

 What are virtualization and virtualization software? What are host and guest operating systems?

Mobile Operating Systems

Mobile operating systems, also known as **mobile OS,** are a type of embedded operating system. Just like other computer systems, mobile computers including smartphones and tablets require an operating system. These mobile operating systems are less complicated and more specialized for wireless communication. They control mobile devices just as Windows or Mac OS controls desktop computer operations.

While there are numerous mobile operating systems, some of the best known are Android, BlackBerry OS, iOS, Web OS, and Windows Phone 7.

- **Android** was introduced in 2007. It was originally developed by Android Inc. and later purchased by Google. Android is widely used in many of today's smartphones. Like iOS, Android is one of the fastest-growing mobile operating systems.

- **BlackBerry OS,** also known as **RIM OS,** was first introduced in 1999 by a small Canadian firm called Research In Motion. Originally designed as the platform for the BlackBerry handheld computer, it has evolved into a powerful mobile phone operating system.

- **iOS,** formerly known as **iPhone OS,** was originally developed in 2007 by Apple. It is based on Mac OS and is used as the platform for Apple's iPhone, iPod Touch, and iPad. iOS is one of the fastest-growing mobile operating systems. See Figure 5-10.

- **WebOS** was originally developed in 2009 by Palm, Inc. and later purchased by the Hewlett-Packard Company. Originally developed for

Figure 5-10 Apple iPhone

Palm's handheld computers, it has evolved to support Hewlett-Packard's smartphones and tablet computers.

- **Windows Phone 7** was originally developed in 2010 by Microsoft to support a variety of portable devices. It was designed for users actively involved in social networking and instant messaging.

In the last chapter, we discussed that not all mobile applications will run on all cell phones. That is because a cell phone app is designed to run on a particular platform or operating system. Before downloading an app, be sure that it is designed to run with the mobile operating system on your cell phone.

CONCEPT CHECK

 What is a mobile operating system?

 What are the six most widely used mobile operating systems?

Which mobile operating systems control the most smartphones? Which ones are the fastest growing?

Utilities

Ideally, microcomputers would continuously run without problems. However, that simply is not the case. All kinds of things can happen—internal hard disks can crash, computers can freeze up, operations can slow down, and so on. These events can make computing very frustrating. That's where utilities come in. **Utilities** are specialized programs designed to make computing easier. There are hundreds of different utility programs. The most essential are

- **Troubleshooting** or **diagnostic programs** that recognize and correct problems, ideally before they become serious.
- **Antivirus programs** that guard your computer system against viruses or other damaging programs that can invade your computer system.
- **Uninstall programs** that allow you to safely and completely remove unneeded programs and related files from your hard disk.
- **Backup programs** that make copies of files to be used in case the originals are lost or damaged.
- **File compression programs** that reduce the size of files so they require less storage space and can be sent more efficiently over the Internet.

Most operating systems provide some utility programs. Even more powerful utility programs can be purchased separately or in utility suites.

tips

Did you know you can search the content of e-mail messages, files, notes, and contacts all at once using a simple utility in Windows 7? Here's how:

1 Click the *Start* button in the lower-left corner of your screen and begin typing the term you want to search for into the *Search programs and files* blank.

2 As you type, a list of files and other items containing your search term is displayed.

3 Continue typing to further narrow the list, or click an item in the list to view it instantly.

To see additional tips, visit our Web site at www.computing2013.com and enter the keyword tips.

Windows Utilities

The Windows operating systems are accompanied by several utility programs, including Backup and Restore, Disk Cleanup, and Disk Defragmenter.

Backup and Restore is a utility program included with the many versions of Windows that makes a copy of all files or selected files that have been saved onto a disk. It helps to protect you from the effects of a disk failure. For example, you can select *Backup and Restore* from the Windows 7 Maintenance menu to create a backup for your hard disk as shown in Figure 5-11.

When you surf the Web, a variety of programs and files are saved on your hard disk. Many of

1 ● Click *Start*, and then select *Maintenance* from the *All Programs* menu.

● Select *Backup and Restore*, and then click *Set up backup*.

● Choose the destination for the backup.

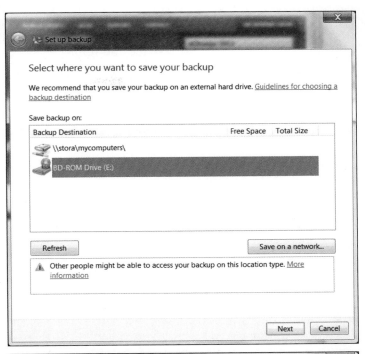

2 ● Choose the files you want to back up.

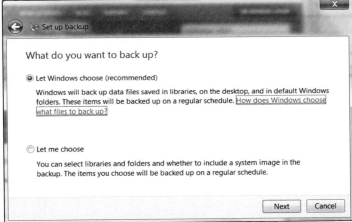

3 ● Set up Backup Wizard to back up the selected files.

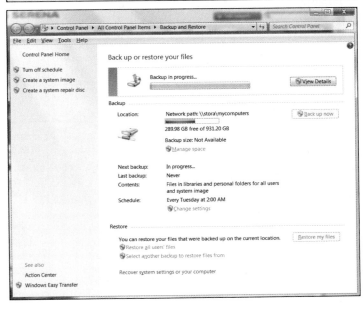

Figure 5-11 Backup and Restore utility

these and other files are not essential. **Disk Cleanup** is a troubleshooting utility that identifies and eliminates nonessential files. This frees up valuable disk space and improves system performance.

For example, by selecting Disk Cleanup from the Windows 7 System Tools menu, you can eliminate unneeded files on your hard disk as shown in Figure 5-12.

1 Click *Start*, and then select *Accessories* from the *All Programs* menu.

Select *Disk Cleanup* from the *System Tools* menu.

Review the files suggested for cleanup, and then click *OK*.

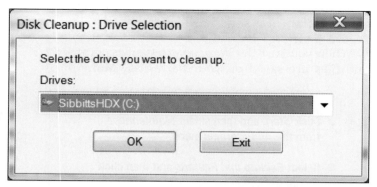

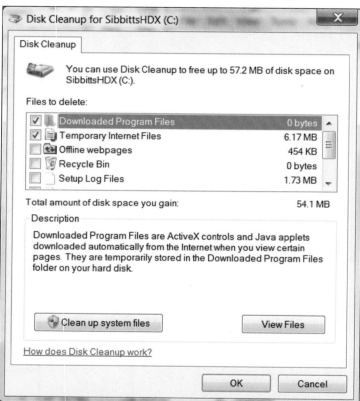

2 The utility cleans the selected files.

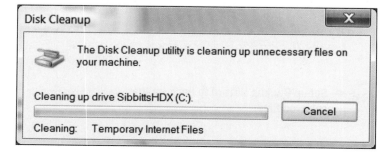

Figure 5-12 Disk Cleanup utility

As we will discuss in detail in Chapter 8, files are stored and organized on a disk according to tracks and sectors. A **track** is a concentric ring. Each track is divided into wedge-shaped sections called **sectors.** (See Figure 5-13.) The operating system tries to save a file on a single track across contiguous sectors. Often, however, this is not possible and the file has to be broken up, or **fragmented,** into small parts that are stored wherever space is available. Whenever a file is retrieved, it is reconstructed from the fragments. After a period of time, a hard disk becomes highly fragmented, slowing operations.

Disk Defragmenter is a utility program that locates and eliminates unnecessary fragments and rearranges files and unused disk space to optimize operations. For example, by selecting Disk Defragmenter from the Windows 7 System Tools menu, you can defrag your hard disk as shown in Figure 5-14.

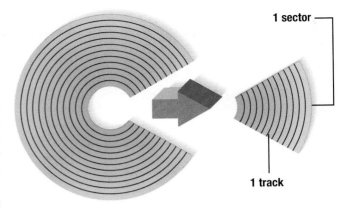

Figure 5-13 **Tracks and sectors**

1 • Click *Start.*

• Select *Accessories* from the *All Programs* menu.

• Select *Disk Defragmenter* from the *System Tools* menu. If necessary, click *Continue.*

2 • Click the *Defragment disk* button to begin defragging.

• If necessary, choose the drive you want to defragment.

• When defragmentation is complete for the selected drive, view the report or close the window.

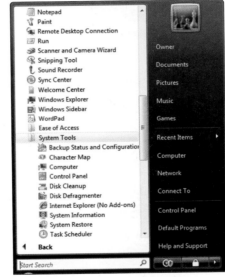

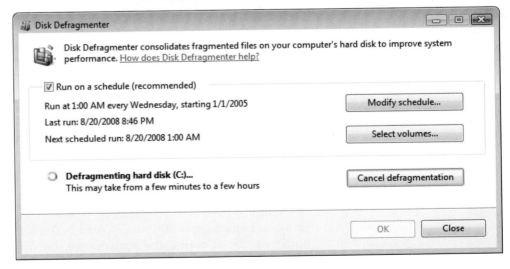

Figure 5-14 **Disk Defragmenter utility**

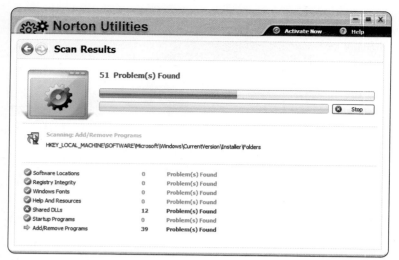

Figure 5-15 Norton Utilities

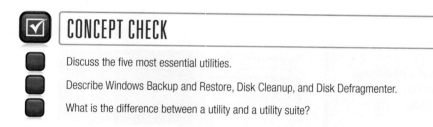

Program	Location
Avast Free Antivirus	www.avast.com/free-antivirus-download
Avira AntiVir Personal	www.free-av.com
Microsoft Security Essentials	www.microsoft.com/security_essentials
Panda Cloud Antivirus	www.cloudantivirus.com

Figure 5-16 Free Antivirus programs

Utility Suites

Like application software suites, **utility suites** combine several programs into one package. Buying the package is less expensive than buying the programs separately. The three best-known utility suites are McAfee Office, Norton 360, and V Communications SystemSuite. (See Figure 5-15.) These suites provide a variety of utilities, including programs that will protect your system from dangerous programs called computer **viruses.** You can "catch" a computer virus many ways, including by opening attachments to e-mail messages and downloading software from the Internet. (We will discuss computer viruses in detail in Chapter 10.) See Figure 5-16 for some highly regarded antivirus programs that are free on the Web.

To learn more about virus protection, visit our Web site at www.computing2013.com and enter the keyword **virus.** Also see Making IT Work for You: Virus Protection on pages 150 and 151.

CONCEPT CHECK

Discuss the five most essential utilities.

Describe Windows Backup and Restore, Disk Cleanup, and Disk Defragmenter.

What is the difference between a utility and a utility suite?

Explorations

Utility software can make your computer faster, safer, and more productive.

To learn more about a market leader of utility software, visit our Web site at www.computing2013.com and enter the keyword utility.

Device Drivers

Every device, such as a mouse or printer, that is connected to a computer system has a special program associated with it. This program, called a **device driver** or simply a **driver,** works with the operating system to allow communication between the device and the rest of the computer system. Each time the computer system is started, the operating system loads all of the device drivers into memory.

Whenever a new device is added to a computer system, a new device driver must be installed before the device can be used. Windows supplies hundreds of different device drivers with its system software. For many devices, the appropriate drivers are automatically selected and installed when the device is first connected to the computer system. For others, the device driver must be manually installed. Fortunately, Windows provides wizards to assist in this process. For example, Windows' **Add a Device Wizard** provides step-by-step guidance for selecting the appropriate hardware driver and installing that driver. If a particular device driver is not included with the Windows system software, the product's manufacturer will supply one. Many times these drivers are available directly from the manufacturer's Web site.

You probably never think about the device drivers in your computer. However, when your computer behaves unpredictably, you may find reinstalling or updating your device drivers solves your problems. Windows makes it easy to update the drivers on your computer using **Windows Update,** as shown in Figure 5-17.

☑ CONCEPT CHECK

What are device drivers and what do they do?

What is Windows' Add a Device Wizard and what does it do?

What is Windows Update? What does it do?

1 • Access *Windows Update* from the *All Programs* list of the *Start* menu.

• Click *Check for updates.*

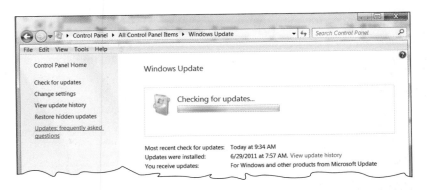

2 • Review the list of recommended updates.

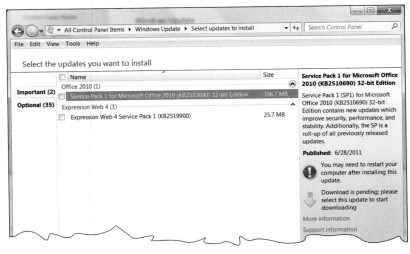

3 • Click *Install updates* to download updates to your computer.

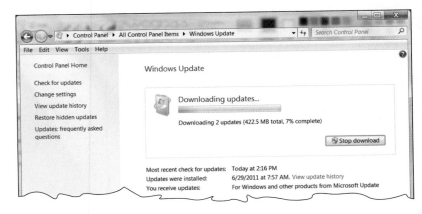

Figure 5-17 Using Windows Update

Making IT work for you

VIRUS PROTECTION

Are you worried that a computer virus will erase your personal files? Did you know that others could be intercepting your private e-mail? It is even possible for others to gain access to and control over your computer system. Fortunately, Internet security suites are available to help ensure your safety while you are on the Internet.

Getting Started   The first step would be to purchase and install an Internet security suite. Once installed, the software will continually work to ensure security and privacy. For example, to purchase and install McAfee Security Center, follow the instructions below.

1 ● Connect to www.mcafee.com and locate their virus protection programs.

2 ● Follow the instructions at the Web site to download and install a free 30-day trial for McAfee AntiVirus Plus to your computer.

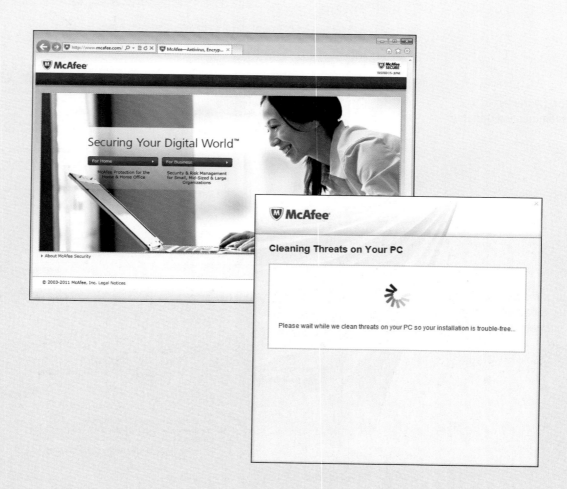

SecurityCenter McAfee SecurityCenter runs a number of programs continually to monitor your computer. Some of Security Center's most powerful features include VirusScan, PersonalFirewall, and SiteAdvisor. You can modify the way these programs run with the McAfee SecurityCenter.

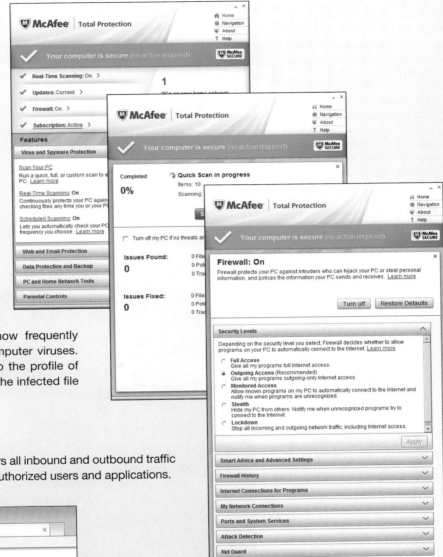

VirusScan is a program that controls how frequently the computer system is searched for computer viruses. When a file is checked, it is compared to the profile of known viruses. Once a virus is detected, the infected file is quarantined or deleted.

PersonalFirewall is a program that monitors all inbound and outbound traffic to a computer system. It limits access to authorized users and applications.

SiteAdvisor is a program that helps protect your privacy online. It installs in your Web browser and warns you of potentially harmful Web sites as you surf.

The Web is continually changing, and some of the specifics presented in this Making IT Work for You may have changed.

To learn about other ways to make information technology work for you, visit our Web site at www.computing2013.com and enter the keyword miw.

Careers in IT

Computer support specialists provide technical support to customers and other users. They also may be called technical support specialists or help-desk technicians. Computer support specialists manage the everyday technical problems faced by computer users. They resolve common networking problems and may use troubleshooting programs to diagnose problems. Most computer support specialists are hired to work within a company and provide technical support for other employees and divisions. However, it is increasingly common for companies to provide technical support as an outsourced service.

Employers generally look for individuals with either an advanced associate's degree or a bachelor's degree to fill computer support specialist positions. Degrees in computer science or information systems may be preferred. However, because demand for qualified applicants is so high, those with practical experience and certification from a training program increasingly fill these positions. Employers seek individuals with good analytical and communication skills. Those with good people skills and customer service experience have an advantage in this field.

Computer support specialists can expect to earn an annual salary of $32,000 to $53,500. Opportunities for advancement are very good and may involve design and implementation of new systems. To learn about other careers in information systems, visit us at www.computing2013.com and enter the keyword **careers**.

Now that you know about system software, I'd like to tell you about my career as a computer support specialist.

A LOOK TO THE FUTURE

Self-Healing Computers Could Mean an End to Computer Crashes and Performance Problems

Wouldn't it be nice if computers could fix themselves? What if you never had to worry about installing or updating software? What if your computer could continually fine-tune its operations to maintain peak performance? What if your computer could fight off viruses and malicious attacks from outsiders? For many people, this sounds too good to be true. Maintenance and security tasks like these can be time-consuming and frustrating.

Now imagine you run a business and unless these tasks are performed, you will lose valuable time and money. It is not a pleasant daydream and it quickly becomes a nightmare without properly trained systems administrators to keep servers running smoothly. Yet many experts predict that supercomputers and business systems are not far from becoming too complex for humans to oversee. Recent news from IBM makes the dream of a self-repairing, self-updating, and self-protecting server seem ever closer.

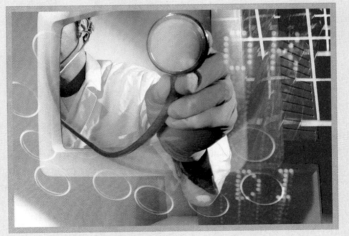

IBM has announced plans to concentrate research efforts on developing just such a server. The project, called the Autonomic Computing Initiative (ACI), hopes to free businesses from the time-consuming maintenance and the complexity of business infrastructure. IBM hopes the new system will be self-regulating and virtually invisible. They believe ACI has the potential to revolutionize the way businesses run.

Autonomic computing is a system that allows machines to run with little human intervention. Such computers would not have self-awareness, but rather would be self-correcting. Autonomic processes in machines are modeled after autonomic processes in the human body. For example, you are not consciously breathing as you read this. Instead, your body monitors and maintains your respiration without your constant input. Scientists hope autonomic computing will behave in a similar manner and maintain self-regulating systems without intervention.

Autonomic machines would be able to sense security flaws and repair them. They would be able to sense slow computer operations and take corrective action. They would be able to sense new equipment, format it, and test it. These goals are impressive and the autonomic computer is still in development.

As technology continues to develop, many computer systems have become too complex for human maintenance. This progress makes autonomic computing more valuable now than ever. However, it is important to note that autonomic computing is not artificial intelligence because autonomic machines do not have human cognitive abilities or intelligence. Instead, these machines have knowledge of their own systems and the capability to learn from experiences to correct errors in such systems.

Given the potential for a self-maintaining server, the possibility of a similar system designed for a microcomputer seems less like a dream and more like a reality. What do you think—will microcomputers someday care for themselves?

SYSTEM SOFTWARE

System software works with end users, application programs, and computer hardware to handle many details relating to computer operations.

Not a single program but a collection or system of programs, these programs handle hundreds of technical details with little or no user intervention.

Four kinds of systems programs are operating systems, utilities, device drivers, and language translators.

- **Operating systems** coordinate resources, provide an interface between users and the computer, and run programs.
- **Utilities** perform specific tasks related to managing computer resources.
- **Device drivers** allow particular input or output devices to communicate with the rest of the computer system.
- **Language translators** convert programming instructions written by programmers into a language that computers can understand and process.

OPERATING SYSTEMS

Operating systems (software environments, platforms) handle technical details.

Functions

Functions include managing resources, providing a **user interface** (most newer operating systems use a **graphical user interface, or gui**), and running applications. **Multitasking** allows switching between different applications stored in memory; current programs run in **foreground**; other programs run in **background**.

Features

Booting starts (**cold**) or restarts (**warm**) a computer system. The **desktop** provides access to computer resources. Common features include **icons, pointers, windows, menus, tabs, dialog boxes**, and **Help**. Data and programs are stored in a system of **files** and **folders**.

Categories

Three categories of operating systems are

- **Embedded**—used with handheld computers; operating system stored within device.
- **Network (NOS)**—controls and coordinates networked computers; located on the **network server**.
- **Stand-alone (desktop)**—controls a single computer; located on the hard disk.

Operating systems are often called **software environments** or **platforms**.

To effectively use computers, competent end users need to understand the functionality of system software, including operating systems, utility programs, and device drivers.

DESKTOP OPERATING SYSTEMS

Windows

Windows, the most widely used operating system, is designed to run with Intel and Intel-compatible microprocessors. There are numerous versions of Windows. **Windows 7** is the most recent version of Windows. It provides improved handwriting recognition; taskbar with previews, large icons, and personalization features; and advanced search capabilities.

Mac OS

Mac OS, an innovative, powerful, easy-to-use operating system, runs on Macintosh computers. Recent versions provide **Spotlight,** an advanced search tool, and **Dashboard Widgets,** a collection of specialized programs. Some versions of **Mac OS X** come with **Boot Camp,** which allows Macintosh computers to run both Mac OS and Windows operating systems.

The most recent version is **Mac OS 10.7 (Lion),** which introduced some exciting features including

- **Launchpad,** to display and access installed apps.
- **Mission Control,** to display all running programs at one time.
- **Gestures,** to allow use of fingers to run programs and to control the content of the display screen.

DESKTOP OPERATING SYSTEMS

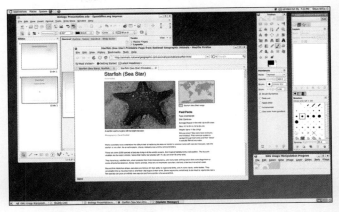

UNIX and Linux

UNIX was originally designed to run on minicomputers in network environments. Now, it is widely used by servers on the Web, mainframe computers, and very powerful microcomputers. There are many different versions of UNIX. One version, **Linux,** a popular and powerful alternative to the Windows operating system, is **open source** software. Google's **Chrome OS** is based on Linux and designed for netbooks and other mobile devices. Chrome OS focuses on Internet connectivity and cloud computing.

Virtualization

Virtualization is a process that allows a single physical computer to support multiple operating systems. A single physical computer runs a special program (**virtualization software**) that allows the single physical computer to operate as two or more separate and independent computers known as **virtual machines. Host operating systems** run on the physical machine. **Guest operating systems** operate on virtual machines.

MOBILE OPERATING SYSTEMS

Mobile operating systems (mobile OS) are embedded in every smartphone. These systems are less complicated and more specialized for wireless communication than desktop operating systems.

Some of the best known are BlackBerry, iOS (iPhone OS), Android, Windows Phone 7, and WebOS.

- **Android** was originally developed by Android Inc. and later purchased by Google. It is one of the fastest-growing mobile OS.
- **BlackBerry OS (RIM OS)** originated in Canada. It was designed as the platform for BlackBerry handheld computers.
- **iOS (iPhone OS)** was developed by Apple to support iPhone, iPod Touch, and iPad. It is one of the fastest-growing mobile OS.
- **WebOS** was developed by Palm, Inc. and later purchased by HP. It has evolved into the operating system for many of HP's mobile devices.
- **Windows Phone 7** was developed by Microsoft. It is designed to support a variety of portable devices focusing on social networking and instant messaging.

UTILITIES

Utilities make computing easier. The most essential are **troubleshooting (diagnostic), antivirus, uninstall, backup,** and **file compression.**

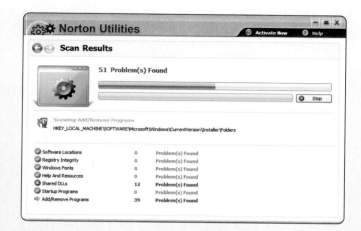

Windows Utilities

Windows operating systems are accompanied by several utility programs, including **Backup and Restore, Disk Cleanup,** and **Disk Defragmenter** (eliminates unnecessary **fragments; tracks** are concentric rings; **sectors** are wedge-shaped).

Utility Suites

Utility suites combine several programs into one package. Computer **viruses** are dangerous programs.

DEVICE DRIVERS

Device drivers (drivers) allow communication between hardware devices. **Add a Device Wizard** gives step-by-step guidance to install printer drivers. **Windows Update** automates the process of updating device drivers.

CAREERS IN IT

Computer support specialists provide technical support to customers and other users. Degrees in computer science or information systems are preferred plus good analytical and communication skills. Salary range is $32,000 to $53,500.

KEY TERMS

Add a Device Wizard   (148)
Android   (143)
antivirus program   (144)
background   (138)
Backup and Restore   (145)
backup program   (144)
BlackBerry OS   (143)
Boot Camp   (141)
booting   (138)
Chrome OS   (142)
cold boot   (138)
computer support specialist   (152)
Dashboard Widgets   (141)
desktop   (138)
desktop operating system   (139)
device driver   (148)
diagnostic program   (144)
dialog box   (139)
Disk Cleanup   (146)
Disk Defragmenter   (147)
driver   (148)
embedded operating system   (139)
file   (139)
file compression program   (144)
folder   (139)
foreground   (138)
fragmented   (147)
gestures   (142)
graphical user interface (gui)   (137)
guest operating system   (142)
Help   (139)
host operating system   (142)
icon   (138)
iOS   (143)
iPhone OS   (143)
Launchpad   (141)
language translator   (136)
Linux   (142)
Lion   (141)
Mac OS   (140)

Mac OS 10.7   (141)
Mac OS X   (141)
menu   (139)
Mission Control   (143)
mobile OS   (143)
mobile operating system   (143)
multitasking   (138)
network operating system (NOS)   (139)
network server   (139)
open source   (142)
operating system   (137)
platform   (140)
pointer   (138)
RIM OS   (143)
sector   (147)
software environment   (140)
Spotlight   (141)
stand-alone operating system   (139)
system software   (136)
tab   (139)
track   (147)
troubleshooting program   (144)
uninstall program   (144)
UNIX   (142)
user interface   (137)
Utilities   (136, 144)
utility suite   (148)
virtual machine   (142)
virtualization   (142)
virtualization software   (142)
virus   (148)
warm boot   (138)
WebOS   (143)
window   (138)
Windows   (140)
Windows 7   (140)
Windows Phone 7   (144)
Windows Update   (149)
Windows Vista   (140)

To test your knowledge of these key terms with animated flash cards, visit our Web site at www.computing2013.com and enter the keyword terms5.

MULTIPLE CHOICE

Circle the correct answer.

1. What type of software works with users, application software, and computer hardware to handle the majority of technical details?
   a. application
   b. desktop
   c. Linux
   d. system

2. The programs that convert programming instructions written by programmers into a language that computers understand and process are language:
   a. converters
   b. linguists
   c. managers
   d. translators

3. The ability to switch between different applications stored in memory is called:
   a. diversion
   b. multitasking
   c. operational interference
   d. programming

4. Graphic representations for a program, type of file, or function:
   a. app
   b. icon
   c. image
   d. software

5. This operating system feature is controlled by a mouse and changes shape depending on its current function.
   a. dialog box
   b. menu
   c. mouse
   d. pointer

6. The operating system based on Linux, designed for Netbook computers, and focused on Internet connectivity through cloud computing:
   a. Chrome
   b. Mac
   c. UNIX
   d. Windows

7. The mobile operating system developed by Apple and originally called iPhone OS:
   a. Android
   b. BlackBerry OS
   c. iOS
   d. Mac OS

8. A utility program that makes copies of files to be used in case the originals are lost or damaged:
   a. Backup and Restore
   b. Disk Cleanup
   c. Disk Defragmenter
   d. Compactor

9. A troubleshooting utility that identifies and eliminates nonessential files, frees up valuable disk space, and improves system performance:
   a. Backup and Restore
   b. Disk Cleanup
   c. Disk Defragmenter
   d. Compactor

10. Windows makes it easy to update drivers with Windows:
    a. Backup
    b. Restore
    c. Driver
    d. Update

For an interactive multiple-choice practice test, visit our Web site at www.computing2013.com and enter the keyword multiple5.

MATCHING

Match each numbered item with the most closely related lettered item. Write your answers in the spaces provided.

a. antivirus
b. Boot Camp
c. driver
d. fragmented
e. NOS
f. platform
g. Android
h. utilities
i. virtualization
j. warm boot

_____ 1. Programs that perform specific tasks related to managing computer resources.

_____ 2. Restarting a running computer without turning off the power.

_____ 3. Type of operating system that controls and coordinates networked computers.

_____ 4. An operating system is often referred to as the software environment or _____.

_____ 5. Allows Macintosh computers to run both Mac OS and the Windows operating system.

_____ 6. A type of software that allows a single physical computer to operate as though it were two or more separate and independent computers.

_____ 7. Mobile operating system that is owned by Google and is one of the fastest-growing mobile operating systems.

_____ 8. Type of program that guards computer systems from viruses and other damaging programs.

_____ 9. If a file cannot be saved on a single track, it has to be _____.

_____10. Program that works with the operating system to allow communication between a device and the rest of a computer system is called a device _____.

For an interactive matching practice test, visit our Web site at www.computing2013 .com and enter the keyword matching5.

OPEN-ENDED

On a separate sheet of paper, respond to each question or statement.

1. Describe system software. Discuss each of the four types of system programs.
2. Define operating systems. Describe the basic features and the three categories of operating systems.
3. What are desktop operating systems? Compare Windows, Mac OS, Linux, and Chrome OS. Discuss visualization.
4. What are mobile operating systems? Describe six leading mobile operating systems.
5. Discuss utilities. What are the five most essential utilities? What is a utility suite?
6. Explain the role of device drivers. Discuss the Add a Device Wizard and Windows Update.

MAKING IT WORK FOR YOU

The following questions are designed to demonstrate ways that you can effectively use technology today.

1 VIRUS PROTECTION

Worried about computer viruses? Did you know that others could be intercepting your private e-mail? It is even possible for them to gain access and control over your computer systems. Fortunately, Internet security suites are available to help ensure your safety while you are on the Internet. To learn more about virus protection, review Making IT Work for You: Virus Protection on pages 150 and 151. Then answer the following questions: (a) What are viruses? What are Internet security suites? What do they do? (b) Have you ever experienced a computer virus? If you have, describe the virus, how you got it, and what you did to get rid of it. If you have not, have you taken any special precautions? Discuss the precautions. Do you think it's possible that you may have one now and not know it, or do you think that you have just been lucky? (c) What is a personal firewall? What does it do?

2 WINDOWS UPDATE

Windows Update is a utility built into Windows that monitors and controls the process of keeping the computer up-to-date. Connect to our Web site at www.computing2013.com and enter the keyword update to link to the Windows Update Web site. Read the information about Windows Update. Then answer the following questions: (a) How does Windows Update work? (b) How does a user know when he or she requires an update? (c) What is the process for initiating an update using Windows Update? (d) In what ways can Windows Update be automated?

3 DISK DEFRAGMENTATION

In addition to the Disk Defragmenter utility built in to Windows, several products are available to perform this task and help improve your computer's performance. Visit our Web site at www.computing2013.com and enter the keyword defrag to learn more about one of these utilities. Then answer the following: (a) What is fragmentation? (b) How does this utility correct fragmentation? (b) Can this utility be automated to run on a regular schedule? (d) What is the procedure to automate this utility? Be specific.

EXPLORATIONS

The following questions are designed to add depth and detail to your understanding of specific topics presented within this chapter. The questions direct you to sources other than the textbook to obtain this knowledge.

1 HOW VIRUS PROTECTION PROGRAMS WORK

Computer viruses are destructive and dangerous programs that can migrate through networks and operating systems. They often attach themselves to other programs, e-mail messages, and databases. It is essential to protect your computer system from computer viruses. To learn how virus protection programs work, visit our Web site at www.computing2013.com and enter the keyword virus. Then answer the following: (a) Briefly describe the four steps taken by virus protection programs. (b) What is signature scanning? (c) What is heuristic detection

and how is it different from signature scanning? (d) Do you use a virus protection program? If yes, what program(s) do you use and has it been effective? If no, do you plan to in the near future? Why or why not?

2 BOOTING AND POST

Computers do a considerable amount of work before a user even hits a key. Knowing how a computer starts up can be an invaluable tool for fixing a broken computer or getting working computers to run at peak efficiency. To learn how a computer starts up, visit our Web site at www.computing2013.com and enter the keyword boot. Then answer the following: (a) Briefly describe the four steps of a cold boot. (b) When booting up, what does the microprocessor do first? (c) What does BIOS stand for? (d) Advanced users often customize their BIOS and POST. What benefits can users achieve by modifying their BIOS or POST?

3 CUSTOMIZED DESKTOP

There are several ways to customize your computer's desktop to make it more interesting, informative, or efficient. To learn about customizations, connect to our Web site at www.computing2013.com and enter the keyword desktop, and then address the following: (a) Summarize some of the customizations you found. (b) Briefly explain how these customizations are added to a user's computer. (c) Explain how customization could make your computing experience more enjoyable or productive.

ETHICS

The following questions are designed to explore ethical issues related to technology and to develop the ability to think critically and communicate effectively. Respond to the questions by either creating a one-page paper or preparing for an in-depth classroom discussion.

1 OPEN SOURCE

Most programs are protected by copyright laws that prohibit unauthorized copying or use. Some argue that this restriction is too limiting and inhibits improvement of existing programs. Some programs such as the Linux operating system are open source, meaning that the program is freely available to other computer programmers to improve and redistribute it. Review the Ethics box on page 152 and research open source. Then answer the following: (a) Why are some programs copyright protected? (b) Do you think it is fair and/or ethical for a software

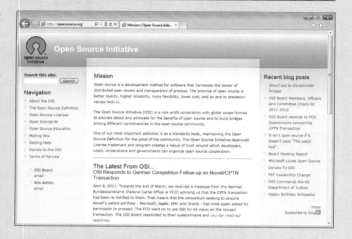

manufacturer to sell a program to you but not allow you to change or modify it? Why or why not? (c) If you purchase a copyright-protected program, do you think it is fair and/or ethical to change the program to meet your needs? Why or why not? (d) What is an open source program? (e) Why do you suppose that some programmers will allow their programs to be modified without permission? (f) Have you ever used an open source program? If so, what program did you use and what did you use it for? (g) Do you think all programs should be open source? Why or why not?

ENVIRONMENT

The following questions are designed to explore environmental issues related to technology and to develop the ability to think critically and communicate effectively. Respond to the questions by either creating a one-page paper or preparing for an in-depth classroom discussion.

1 POWER MANAGEMENT

Windows 7 is designed to do more computing with less energy. For example, it has a new power management system that uses fewer system programs that run automatically, dims the screen to minimize energy use, and turns off power to unused ports on your machine. Review the Environment box on page 140. Research Windows 7 Power Management and then respond to the following: (a) What is Windows 7 Power Management? (b) Do you think the Power Management system will have an impact on the environment? Why or why not? (c) Have you ever used any power management programs? If so, what have you used and how effective were they? If you have not used a power management program, identify one and describe it. (d) Do you think that you will be using a power management system in the future? Why or why not?

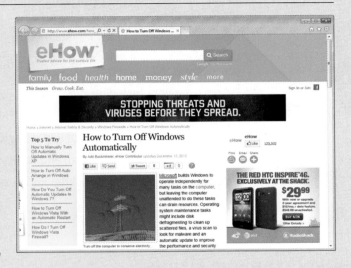

The System Unit

▲ Download the free *Computing Essentials 2013* app for videos, key term flashcards, quizzes, and the game, *Over the Edge!*

Competencies

After you have read this chapter, you should be able to:

1 Describe the six basic types of system units.

2 Discuss how a computer can represent numbers and encode characters electronically.

3 Describe each of the major system unit components.

4 Discuss microprocessors, including microprocessor chips and specialty processors.

5 Discuss memory including RAM, ROM, and flash memory.

6 Discuss expansion slots and cards.

7 Describe five principal types of expansion buses.

8 Compare standard, specialized, and legacy ports.

9 Discuss power supply for desktop and notebook computers.

Why should I read this chapter?

The first computers ever built were too big to fit into a modern home. That was then and this is now. Today's microcomputers fit onto a desk, onto a lap, and even in a hand. They can go almost anywhere and do almost anything. And they are many, many times more powerful than computers of only a few years ago.

This chapter discusses a variety of different types of microcomputers including notebooks, tablet PCs like the iPad,

and handheld computers including smartphones like the iPhone. You will learn about the most important computer components including microprocessors and memory. Additionally, you'll learn how to connect external devices like a digital video camera and how you can upgrade your computer's speed and power. To be competent and to be competitive in today's professional workplace, you need to know and to understand these things.

chapter 6

165

Introduction

Hi, I'm Liz, and I'm a computer technician. I'd like to talk with you about the system unit, all that electronic stuff that makes your computer work. I'd also like to talk about the changing tablet PC including the very portable slate computers like the Apple iPad.

Why are some microcomputers more powerful than others? The answer lies in three words: speed, capacity, and flexibility. After reading this chapter, you will be able to judge how fast, powerful, and versatile a particular microcomputer is. As you might expect, this knowledge is valuable if you are planning to buy a new microcomputer system or to upgrade an existing system. (The Buyer's Guide and the Upgrader's Guide at the end of this book provide additional information.) This knowledge will help you to evaluate whether or not an existing microcomputer system is powerful enough for today's new and exciting applications. For example, with the right hardware, you can use your computer to watch TV and to capture video clips for class presentations.

Sometime you may get the chance to watch when a technician opens up a microcomputer. You will see that it is basically a collection of electronic circuitry. While there is no need to understand how all these components work, it is important to understand the principles. Once you do, you will be able to determine how powerful a particular microcomputer is. This will help you judge whether it can run particular kinds of programs and can meet your needs as a user.

Competent end users need to understand the functionality of the basic components in the system unit, including the system board, microprocessor, memory, expansion slots and cards, bus lines, ports, cables, and power supply units.

System Unit

The **system unit,** also known as the **system chassis,** is a container that houses most of the electronic components that make up a computer system. There are a variety of different categories or types of system units.

Categories

All computer systems have a system unit. For microcomputers, there are six basic types (see Figure 6-1):

- **Desktop system units** typically contain the system's electronic components and selected secondary storage devices. Input and output devices, such as a mouse, keyboard, and monitor, are located outside the system unit. This type of system unit is designed to be placed either horizontally or vertically.

- **Media center system units** blur the line between desktop computers and dedicated entertainment devices. Media center system units use powerful desktop system hardware with specialized graphics cards for interfacing

Desktop

Media Center

Notebook

Netbook

Tablet PC

Handheld

Figure 6-1 Basic types of system units

with televisions and other home entertainment devices. A special operating system like Microsoft Windows Media Center provides on-demand TV programs, movies, music, and games.

- **Notebook system units** are portable and much smaller. These system units contain the electronic components, selected secondary storage devices, and input devices (keyboard and pointing device). Located outside the system unit, the monitor is attached by hinges. Notebook system units are often called **laptops.**

- **Netbook system units** are similar to notebook system units. They are, however, smaller, less powerful, and less expensive. **Netbooks** are designed to support on-the-go Web browsing and e-mail access. They reduce space and weight by leaving out components such as optical drives.

- Traditionally, **tablet PC system units** were similar to notebook system units. Since the introduction of Apple's iPad, however, the definition of **tablet PCs** has evolved. Now there are basically two types. The first type is the **traditional tablet PC** that is effectively a notebook computer that accepts stylus input and has a monitor that swivels and folds onto its keyboard as shown in Figure 6-1. These devices use traditional desktop operating systems and provide all the functionality of a notebook computer to create documents, connect to the Internet, and much more.

  The other newer type of tablet PC is better described as a **slate computer.** This computer's system unit is effectively a thin slab that is almost all monitor. (See Figure 6-2.) It is a very portable device that uses mobile operating systems, accepts gesture input, and is designed to display content such as movies and information downloaded from the Internet. Although they can, slate computers are not designed to create information. They are designed to display content.

- **Handheld computer system units** are the smallest and are designed to fit into the palm of one hand. These systems contain an entire computer system, including the electronic components, secondary storage, and input and output devices. **Personal digital assistants (PDAs)** and **smartphones** are the most widely used handheld computers.

Figure 6-2 Slate computer

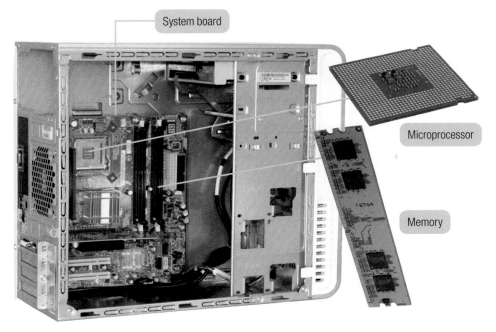

System board

Microprocessor

Memory

Figure 6-3 System unit components

Components

While the actual size may vary, each type of system unit has the same basic system components including system board, microprocessor, and memory. (See Figure 6-3.) Before considering these components, however, a more basic issue must be addressed. How are data and instructions represented electronically?

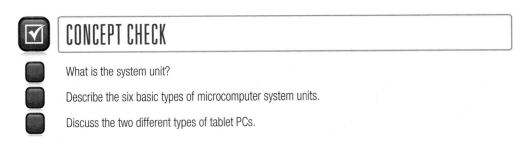

CONCEPT CHECK

What is the system unit?

Describe the six basic types of microcomputer system units.

Discuss the two different types of tablet PCs.

Electronic Data and Instructions

Have you ever wondered why it is said that we live in a digital world? It's because computers cannot recognize information the same way you and I can. People follow instructions and process data using letters, numbers, and special characters. For example, if we wanted someone to add the numbers 3 and 5 together and record the answer, we might say "please add 3 and 5." The system unit, however, is electronic circuitry and cannot directly process such a request.

Our voices create **analog,** or continuous, signals that vary to represent different tones, pitches, and volume. Computers, however, can recognize only **digital** electronic signals. Before any processing can occur within the system unit, a conversion must occur from what we understand to what the system unit can electronically process.

Decimal	Binary	Hex
00	00000000	00
01	00000001	01
02	00000010	02
03	00000011	03
04	00000100	04
05	00000101	05
06	00000110	06
07	00000111	07
08	00001000	08
09	00001001	09
10	00001010	0A
11	00001011	0B
12	00001100	0C
13	00001101	0D
14	00001110	0E
15	00001111	0F

Figure 6-4 Numeric representations

Numeric Representation

What is the most fundamental statement you can make about electricity? It is simply this: It can be either on or off. Indeed, there are many forms of technology that can make use of this two-state on/off, yes/no, present/absent arrangement. For instance, a light switch may be on or off, or an electric circuit open or closed. A specific location on a tape or disk may have a positive charge or a negative charge. This is the reason, then, that a two-state or binary system is used to represent data and instructions.

The decimal system that we are all familiar with has 10 digits (0, 1, 2, 3, 4, 5, 6, 7, 8, 9). The **binary system,** however, consists of only two digits—0 and 1. Each 0 or 1 is called a **bit**—short for binary digit. In the system unit, the 1 can be represented by a positive charge and the 0 by no electrical charge. In order to represent numbers, letters, and special characters, bits are combined into groups of eight called **bytes.** Whenever you enter a number into a computer system, that number must be converted into a binary number before it can be processed. To learn more about binary systems and binary arithmetic, visit our Web site at www.computing2013.com and enter the keyword **binary.**

Any number can be expressed as a binary number. Binary numbers, however, are difficult for humans to work with because they require so many digits. Instead, binary numbers are often represented in a format more readable by humans. The **hexadecimal system,** or **hex,** uses 16 digits (0, 1, 2, 3, 4, 5, 6, 7, 8, 9, A, B, C, D, E, F) to represent binary numbers. Each hex digit represents four binary digits, and two hex digits are commonly used together to represent 1 byte (8 binary digits). (See Figure 6-4.) You may have already seen hex when selecting a color in a Web site design or drawing application, or when entering the password for access to a wireless network.

Character Encoding

As we've seen, computers must represent all numbers with the binary system internally. What about text? How can a computer provide representations of the nonnumeric characters we use to communicate, such as the sentence you are reading now? The answer is character encoding schemes or standards.

Character encoding standards assign a unique sequence of bits to each character. Historically, microcomputers used the **ASCII (American Standard Code for Information Interchange)** to represent characters while mainframe computers used **EBCDIC (Extended Binary Coded Decimal Interchange Code).** These schemes were quite effective; however, they are limited. ASCII, for example, only uses 7 bits to represent each character, which means that only 128 total characters could be represented. This was fine for most characters in the English language but was not large enough to support other languages such as Chinese and Japanese. These languages have too many characters to be represented by the 7-bit ASCII code.

The explosion of the Internet and subsequent globalization of computing has led to a new character encoding called **Unicode.** The Unicode standard is the most widely used character encoding standard and is recognized by virtually every computer system. The first 128 characters are assigned the same sequence of bits as ASCII to maintain compatibility with older ASCII-formatted information. However, Unicode uses a variable number of bits to represent each character, which allows non-English characters and special characters to be represented.

CONCEPT CHECK

What is the difference between an analog and a digital electronic signal?

What are decimal and binary systems? How are they different?

Compare EBCDIC, ASCII, and Unicode.

System Board

The **system board** is also known as the **main** or **motherboard.** The system board controls communications for the entire computer system. Every component within the system unit connects to the system board. All external devices including the keyboard, mouse, and monitor connect to the system board. It acts as a data path and traffic monitor, allowing the various components to communicate efficiently with one another.

On a desktop computer, the system board is typically located at the bottom of the system unit or along one side. It is a large flat circuit board covered with a variety of different electronic components including sockets, slots, and bus lines. (See Figure 6-5.)

Explorations

Improvements in system unit components are being made every day.

To learn more about a company on the forefront of these technologies, visit our Web site at www.computing2013.com and enter the keyword component.

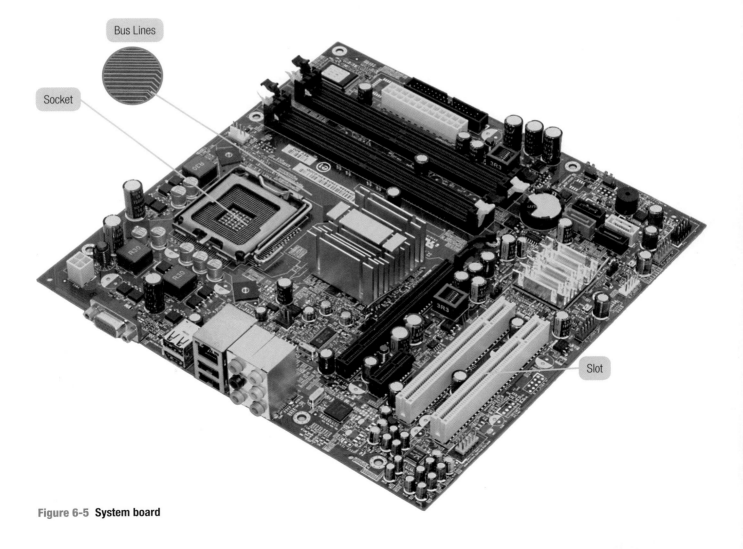

Figure 6-5 **System board**

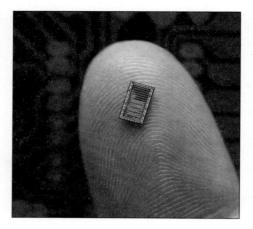

Figure 6-6 Chip

Figure 6-7 Chip mounted onto a carrier package

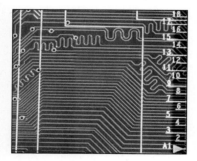

Figure 6-8 Bus lines

- **Sockets** provide a connection point for small specialized electronic parts called chips. **Chips** consist of tiny circuit boards etched onto squares of sandlike material called silicon. These circuit boards can be smaller than the tip of your finger. (See Figure 6-6.) A chip is also called a **silicon chip, semiconductor,** or **integrated circuit.** Chips are mounted on **carrier packages.** (See Figure 6-7.) These packages plug either directly into sockets on the system board or onto cards that are then plugged into slots on the system board. Sockets are used to connect the system board to a variety of different types of chips, including microprocessor and memory chips.
- **Slots** provide a connection point for specialized cards or circuit boards. These cards provide expansion capability for a computer system. For example, a wireless networking card plugs into a slot on the system board to provide a connection to a local area network.
- Connecting lines called **bus lines** provide pathways that support communication among the various electronic components that are either located on the system board or attached to the system board. (See Figure 6-8.)

Notebook, tablet PC, and handheld system boards are smaller than desktop system boards. However, they perform the same functions as desktop system boards.

☑ CONCEPT CHECK

 What is the system board and what does it do?

 Define and describe sockets, slots, and bus lines.

 What are chips? How are chips attached to the system board?

Microprocessor

In a microcomputer system, the **central processing unit (CPU)** or **processor** is contained on a single chip called the **microprocessor.** The microprocessor is the "brains" of the computer system. It has two basic components: the control unit and the arithmetic-logic unit.

- **Control unit:** The **control unit** tells the rest of the computer system how to carry out a program's instructions. It directs the movement of electronic signals between memory, which temporarily holds data, instructions, and processed information, and the arithmetic-logic unit. It also directs these control signals between the CPU and input and output devices.

- **Arithmetic-logic unit:** The **arithmetic-logic unit,** usually called the **ALU,** performs two types of operations: arithmetic and logical. **Arithmetic operations** are, as you might expect, the fundamental math operations: addition, subtraction, multiplication, and division. **Logical operations** consist of comparisons. That is, two pieces of data are compared to see whether one is equal to ($=$), less than ($<$), or greater than ($>$) the other.

Unit	Speed
Microsecond	Millionth of a second
Nanosecond	Billionth of a second
Picosecond	Trillionth of a second

Figure 6-9 Processing speeds

Microprocessor Chips

Chip processing capacities are often expressed in word sizes. A **word** is the number of bits (such as 16, 32, or 64) that can be accessed at one time by the CPU. The more bits in a word, the more data a computer can process at one time. As mentioned previously, eight bits group together to form a byte. A 32-bit-word computer can access 4 bytes at a time. A 64-bit-word computer can access 8 bytes at a time. Therefore, the computer designed to process 64-bit words has greater processing capacity. Other factors affect a computer's processing capability including how fast it can process data and instructions.

The processing speed of a microprocessor is typically represented by its **clock speed,** which is related to the number of times the CPU can fetch and process data or instructions in a second. Older microcomputers typically process data and instructions in millionths of a second, or microseconds. Newer microcomputers are much faster and process data and instructions in billionths of a second, or nanoseconds. Supercomputers, by contrast, operate at speeds measured in picoseconds—1,000 times as fast as microcomputers. (See Figure 6-9.) Logically, the higher a microprocessor's clock speed, the faster the microprocessor. However, some processors can handle multiple instructions per cycle or tick of the clock; this means that clock speed comparisons can only be made between processors that work the same way.

The two most significant recent developments in microprocessors are the 64-bit processor and the multicore chip. Until recently, 64-bit processors were primarily used in large mainframe and supercomputers. All of that is changing as 64-bit processors have become standard for most of today's desktop and laptop computers.

The other recent development is the multicore chip. As mentioned previously, a traditional microcomputer's CPU is typically contained on a single microprocessor chip. A new type of chip, the **multicore chip,** can provide two or more separate and independent CPUs. These chips allow a single computer to run two or more operations at the same time. For example, a dual-core process could have one core computing a complex Excel spreadsheet while the other is running a multimedia presentation. More significantly, however, is the potential for microcomputers to run very large, complex programs that previously required expensive and specialized hardware.

For multicore processors to be used effectively, computers must understand how to divide tasks into parts that can be distributed across each core—an operation called **parallel processing.** Operating systems such as Windows 7 and Mac OS X support parallel processing. Software developers use this technology for a wide range of applications from scientific programs to sophisticated computer games.

See Figure 6-10 for a table of popular microprocessors.

Did you ever wonder what your computer microprocessor's clock speed is? It's easy to find. If you are using Windows Vista or Windows 7:

1 Click *Start*.

2 In the *Search Programs and Files* box, enter msinfo32.

3 If necessary, scroll the System Information window to locate Processor.

To see additional tips, visit our Web site at www.computing2013.com and enter the keyword tips.

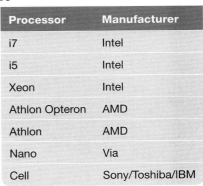

Processor	Manufacturer
i7	Intel
i5	Intel
Xeon	Intel
Athlon Opteron	AMD
Athlon	AMD
Nano	Via
Cell	Sony/Toshiba/IBM

Figure 6-10 Popular microprocessors

Specialty Processors

In addition to microprocessor chips, a variety of more specialized processing chips have been developed.

- **Coprocessors** are specialty chips designed to improve specific computing operations. One of the most widely used is the **graphics coprocessor,** also called a **GPU (graphics processing unit).** These processors are designed to handle a variety of specialized tasks such as displaying 3-D images and encrypting data.
- **Smart cards** are plastic cards the size of a regular credit card that have an embedded specialty chip. Many colleges and universities provide smart cards to their students for identification.
- Many cars have as many as 70 separate specialty processors to control nearly everything from fuel efficiency to satellite entertainment and tracking systems.
- **RFID tags** are specialty chips embedded in merchandise to track their location. The International Civil Aviation Organization has proposed inserting RFID chips in over a billion passports to track visitors as they enter or leave the United States.

 CONCEPT CHECK

 Name and describe the two components of a microprocessor.

 Define word, clock speed, multicore chip, and parallel processing.

 What are specialty processors? Describe coprocessors, smart cards, and RFID tags.

Memory

Memory is a holding area for data, instructions, and information. Like microprocessors, **memory** is contained on chips connected to the system board. There are three well-known types of memory chips: random-access memory (RAM), read-only memory (ROM), and flash memory.

RAM

Random-access memory (RAM) chips hold the program (sequence of instructions) and data that the CPU is presently processing. (See Figure 6-11.) RAM is called temporary or volatile storage because everything in most types of RAM is lost as soon as the microcomputer is turned off. It is also lost if there is a power failure or other disruption of the electric current going to the microcomputer. Secondary storage, which we shall describe in Chapter 8, does not lose its contents. It is permanent or nonvolatile storage, such as the data stored on a hard disk. For this reason, as we mentioned earlier, it is a good idea to frequently save your work in progress to a secondary storage device. That is, if you are working on a document or a spreadsheet, every few minutes you should save, or store, the material.

Cache (pronounced "cash") **memory** improves processing by acting as a temporary high-speed holding area between the memory and the CPU. The computer detects which information in RAM is most frequently

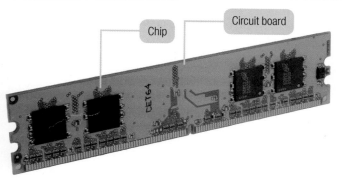

Figure 6-11 RAM chips mounted on circuit board

Chip

Circuit board

used and then copies that information into the cache. When needed, the CPU can quickly access the information from the cache.

Having enough RAM is important! For example, to use Microsoft Office 2010 effectively, you need a minimum of 256 MB of RAM to hold the program, 512 MB to support graphical features, and another 512 MB–1024 MB of RAM for the operating system.

Some applications, such as photo editing software, may require even more. Fortunately, additional RAM can be added to a computer system by inserting an expansion module called a **DIMM (dual in-line memory module)** into the system board. The capacity or amount of RAM is expressed in bytes. There are three commonly used units of measurement to describe memory capacity. (See Figure 6-12.)

Other types of RAM include DRAM, SDRAM, DDR, and Direct RDRAM. To learn more about these other types of RAM, visit our Web site at www.computing2013.com and enter the keyword **ram.**

Even if your computer does not have enough RAM to hold a program, it might be able to run the program using **virtual memory.** Most of today's operating systems support virtual memory. With virtual memory, large programs are divided into parts and the parts are stored on a secondary device, usually a hard disk. Each part is then read into RAM only when needed. In this way, computer systems are able to run very large programs. To learn more about how virtual memory works, visit our Web site at www.computing2013.com and enter the keyword **memory.**

Unit	Capacity
Megabyte (MB)	1 million bytes
Gigabyte (GB)	1 billion bytes
Terabyte (TB)	1 trillion bytes

Figure 6-12 Memory capacity

Type	Use
RAM	Programs and data
ROM	Fixed start-up instructions
Flash	Flexible start-up instructions

Figure 6-13 Memory

ROM

Read-only memory (ROM) chips have information stored in them by the manufacturer. Unlike RAM chips, ROM chips are not volatile and cannot be changed by the user. "Read only" means that the CPU can read, or retrieve, data and programs written on the ROM chip. However, the computer cannot write—encode or change—the information or instructions in ROM.

ROM chips typically contain special instructions for basic computer operations. For example, ROM instructions are needed to start a computer, to access memory, and to handle keyboard input.

Flash Memory

Flash memory offers a combination of the features of RAM and ROM. Like RAM, it can be updated to store new information. Like ROM, it does not lose that information when power to the computer system is turned off.

Flash memory is used for a wide range of applications. For example, it is used to store the startup instructions for a computer. This information would include the specifics concerning the amount of RAM and the type of keyboard, mouse, and secondary storage devices connected to the system unit. If changes are made to the computer system, these changes are reflected in flash memory.

See Figure 6-13 for a summary of the three types of memory.

 CONCEPT CHECK

What is memory? Name and describe three types.

What are cache memory, DIMM, and virtual memory?

Define ROM and flash memory.

Expansion Slots and Cards

Most microcomputers allow users to expand their systems by providing **expansion slots** on the system board. Users can insert optional devices known as **expansion cards** into these slots. (See Figure 6-14.) Ports on the cards allow cables to be connected from the expansion cards to devices outside the system unit. (See Figure 6-15.) There are a wide range of different types of expansion cards. Some of the most commonly used expansion cards are

- **Advanced graphics cards** provide high-quality 3D graphics and animation for games and simulations.
- **Sound cards** accept audio input from a microphone and convert it into a form that can be processed by the computer. Also, these cards convert internal electronic signals to audio signals so they can be heard from external speakers or home theater systems.
- **Network interface cards (NIC),** also known as **network adapter cards,** are used to connect a computer to a network. (See Figure 6-16.) The network allows connected computers to share data, programs, and hardware. The network adapter card typically connects the system unit to a cable that connects to the network.
- **Wireless network cards** allow computers to be connected without cables.
- Now you can watch television, capture video, and surf the Internet at the same time. **TV tuner cards** contain a TV tuner and a video converter that changes a traditional TV signal into one that can be displayed on your monitor. To see how TV tuner cards work, visit our

Slot

Figure 6-14 Expansion cards fit into slots on the system board

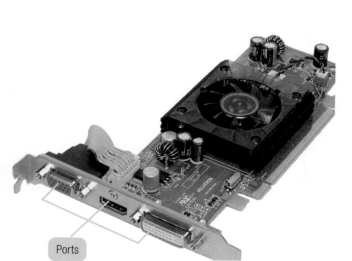

Ports

Figure 6-15 Expansion card with three ports

Figure 6-16 Network interface card

Figure 6-17 PC Card

Web site at www.computing2013.com and enter the keyword **tv.** To learn about using TV tuner cards, see Making IT Work for You: TV Tuner Cards and Video Clips on pages 178 and 179.

Plug and Play was originally a set of specific hardware and software standards developed by Intel, Microsoft, and others. As hardware and software have evolved, however, Plug and Play has become a generic term that is associated with the ability to plug any device such as a printer or monitor into a computer and have it play or work immediately. Some devices, however, are not Plug and Play and require that new device drivers be installed, as discussed in Chapter 5.

To meet the size constraints of notebook and handheld computers, small credit card–sized expansion cards have been developed. These cards plug into **PCMCIA** slots (called **PC Card slots**) or, most recently, **ExpressCard** slots. (See Figure 6-17.)

CONCEPT CHECK

 What are expansion slots and cards? Name five expansion cards.

 Discuss Plug and Play.

 What are PC Card and ExpressCard slots?

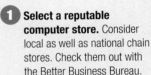
Bus Lines

A **bus line**—also known simply as a **bus**—connects the parts of the CPU to each other. Buses also link the CPU to various other components on the system board. (See Figure 6-18.) A bus is a pathway for bits representing data and instructions. The number of bits that can travel simultaneously down a bus is known as the **bus width.**

A bus is similar to a multilane highway that moves bits rather than cars from one location to another. The number of traffic lanes determines the bus

Making IT work for you

TV TUNER CARDS AND VIDEO CLIPS

Want to watch your favorite television program from your computer? Perhaps you would like to include a video clip from television in a class presentation. It's easy using a TV tuner card.

Viewing Once a TV tuner card has been installed, you can view your favorite TV shows, even while running other applications such as PowerPoint. For example, you could use a Hauppauge TV tuner product and Hauppauge software as shown below.

1 • **Launch the WinTV application.**

• **Size and move the television application window.**

• **Select a channel to view.**

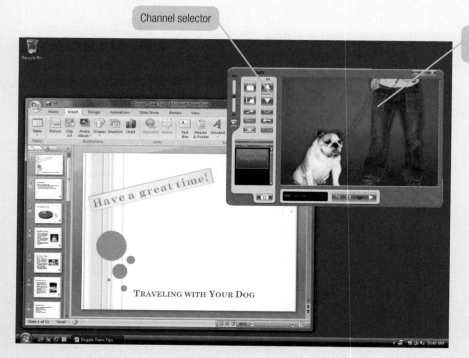

Channel selector

Television applications window

Capturing   You can capture the video playing in the TV window into a digital file by following the steps shown below.

1 ● Click the *Record* button to begin recording.

● Click the *Stop* button to stop recording.

● Select a location and name to save your captured video file.

Record/Stop button

Using   Once captured in a file, a video can be used in any number of ways. It can be added to a Web page*, attached to an e-mail, or added to a class presentation. For example, you could include a video clip in a PowerPoint presentation by following the steps below.

1 ● Select the *Insert* tab, and then select *Movie* from the Media Clips group.

● Select the video file you saved in the previous step.

● Choose whether the video file should start automatically, or only when you click it during your presentation.

● Drag and resize the inserted movie clip as needed.

Inserted movie clip

TV tuner cards are relatively inexpensive and easy to install. Some factors limiting their performance on your computer are the speed of your processor, the amount of memory, and secondary storage capacity.

TV tuner cards are continually changing, and some of the specifics presented in this Making IT Work for You may have changed.

*Some video content may be copyrighted, so make sure you have obtained permission to use it.

To learn about other ways to make information technology work for you, visit our Web site at www.computing2013.com and enter the keyword miw.

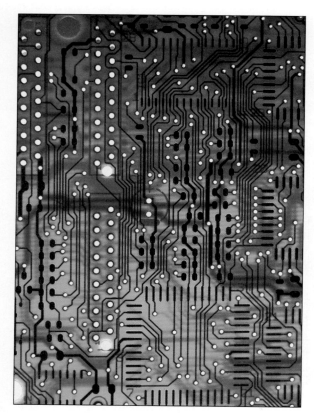

Figure 6-18 Bus is a pathway for bits

width. A highway (bus line) with more traffic lanes (bus width) can move traffic (data and instructions) more efficiently. For example, a 64-bit bus can move twice as much information at a time as a 32-bit bus. Why should you even care about what a bus line is? Because as microprocessor chips have changed, so have bus lines. Bus design or bus architecture is an important factor relating to the speed and power for a particular computer. Additionally, many devices, such as expansion boards, will work with only one type of bus.

Every computer system has two basic categories of buses. One category, called **system buses,** connects the CPU to memory on the system board. The other category, called **expansion buses,** connects the CPU to other components on the system board, including expansion slots.

Expansion Buses

Computer systems typically have a combination of different types of expansion buses. The principal types are USB, Firewire, and PCIe.

- **Universal serial bus (USB)** is widely used today. External USB devices are connected from one to another or to a common point or hub and then onto the USB bus. The USB bus then connects to the PCI bus on the system board. The current USB standard is USB 3.0.
- **FireWire buses** are similar to USB buses but more specialized. They are used primarily to connect audio and video equipment to the system board.
- **PCI Express (PCIe)** is widely used in many of today's most powerful computers. Unlike most other buses that share a single bus line or path with several devices, the PCIe bus provides a single dedicated path for each connected device.

 CONCEPT CHECK

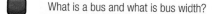

What is a bus and what is bus width?

What is the difference between a system and an expansion bus?

Discuss three types of expansion buses.

Ports

A **port** is a socket for external devices to connect to the system unit. (See Figure 6-19.) Some ports connect directly to the system board while others connect to cards that are inserted into slots on the system board. Some ports are standard features of most computer systems and others are more specialized.

Figure 6-19 Ports

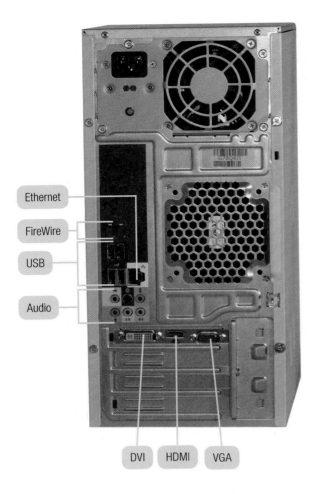

Ethernet

FireWire

USB

Audio

DVI HDMI VGA

Standard Ports

Most microcomputers come with a standard set of ports for connecting a monitor, keyboard, and other peripheral devices. The most common ports include

- **VGA (Video Graphics Adapter)** and **DVI (Digital Video Interface) ports** provide connections to analog and digital monitors, respectively. DVI has become the most commonly used standard, but VGA ports are still provided on almost all systems for compatibility with older/lower-cost monitors.
- **Universal serial bus (USB) ports** can be used to connect several devices to the system unit and are widely used to connect keyboards, mice, printers, and storage devices to the system unit. A single USB port can be used to connect many USB devices to the system unit.
- **FireWire ports** provide high-speed connections to specialized FireWire devices such as camcorders and storage devices.
- **Ethernet ports** are a high-speed networking port that has become a standard for many of today's computers. Ethernet allows you to connect multiple computers for sharing files, or to a DSL or cable modem for high-speed Internet access.

Specialized Ports

In addition to standard ports, there are numerous specialty ports including S/PDIF, HDMI, and MIDI.

- **Sony/Philips Digital Interconnect Format (S/PDIF)** ports are also known as **optical audio connections.** These ports are used to integrate computers into high-end audio and home theater systems.
- **High Definition Multimedia Interface (HDMI)** ports provide high-definition video and audio, making it possible to use a computer as a video jukebox or an HD video recorder.
- **Musical instrument digital interface (MIDI)** ports are a special type of serial port for connecting musical instruments like an electronic keyboard to a sound card. The sound card converts the music into a series of digital instructions. These instructions can be processed immediately to reproduce the music or saved to a file for later processing.

Legacy Ports

In the past, additional ports were common on microcomputer systems to connect specific types of devices. These older ports, known as **legacy ports,** have largely been replaced by faster, more flexible ports such as the universal serial bus (USB).

- **Serial ports** were used for a wide variety of purposes, such as connecting a mouse, keyboard, modem, and many other devices to the system unit. Serial ports sent data one bit at a time and were good for sending information over long distances.
- **Parallel ports** were used to connect external devices that needed to send or receive a lot of data over a short distance. These ports typically sent eight bits of data simultaneously across eight parallel wires. Parallel ports were mostly used to connect printers to the system unit.
- **Keyboard** and **mouse ports** were used to connect keyboards and mice to the system unit. Different types of keyboard ports existed for different types of keyboards, making some keyboards incompatible with some system units.
- **Infrared Data Association (IrDA) ports** were used to provide a wireless mechanism for transferring data between devices. Instead of cables, the IrDA ports from each device were directly aligned and infrared light waves were used to transmit data. One of the most common applications was to transfer data from either a handheld or notebook computer to a desktop computer.
- **Game ports** were used to connect video game controllers and joysticks.

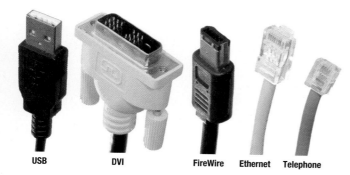

USB   DVI   FireWire   Ethernet   Telephone

Figure 6-20 Cables

Cables

Cables are used to connect exterior devices to the system unit via the ports. One end of the cable is attached to the device and the other end has a connector that is attached to a matching connector on the port. (See Figure 6-20.)

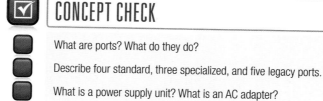

CONCEPT CHECK

What are ports? What do they do?

Describe four standard, three specialized, and five legacy ports.

What is a power supply unit? What is an AC adapter?

Figure 6-21 **Power supply unit**

Figure 6-22 **AC adapter**

Power Supply

Computers require direct current (DC) to power their electronic components and to represent data and instructions. DC power can be provided indirectly by converting alternating current (AC) from standard wall outlets or directly from batteries.

- Desktop computers have a **power supply unit** located within the system unit. (See Figure 6-21.) This unit plugs into a standard wall outlet, converts AC to DC, and provides the power to drive all of the system unit components.
- Notebook and tablet PCs use **AC adapters** that are typically located outside the system unit. (See Figure 6-22.) AC adapters plug into a standard wall outlet, convert AC to DC, provide power to drive the system unit components, and can recharge the batteries. These computers can be operated either using an AC adapter plugged into a wall outlet or using battery power. Their batteries typically provide sufficient power for four to six hours before they need to be recharged.
- Like notebook and tablet PCs, netbook and handheld computers use AC adapters located outside the system unit. Unlike notebook and tablet PCs, however, netbook and handheld computers typically operate only using battery power. The AC adapter is used to recharge the batteries.

Careers in IT

Computer technicians repair and install computer components and systems. They may work on everything from personal computers and mainframe servers to printers. Some computer technicians are responsible for setting up and maintaining computer networks. Experienced computer technicians may work with computer engineers to diagnose problems and run routine maintenance on complex systems. Job growth is expected in this field as computer equipment becomes more complicated and technology expands.

Now that you know about system units, I'd like to tell you about
my career as a computer technician.

Employers look for those with certification in computer repair or associate
degrees from professional schools. Computer technicians also can expect to
continue their education to keep up with technological changes. Good communication skills are important in this field.

Computer technicians can expect an hourly wage of $13.50 to $22.50.
Opportunities for advancement typically come in the form of work on more
advanced computer systems. Some computer technicians move into customer service positions or go into sales. To learn more about other careers
in information technology, visit us at www.computing2013.com and enter the
keyword **careers**.

A LOOK TO THE FUTURE

As You Walk Out the Door, Don't Forget Your Computer

Wouldn't it be nice if you could conveniently access the Internet wirelessly at any time during the day? What if you could send and receive e-mail while jogging without touching a screen, or send a friend live video of what you are looking at? What if a computer on your body could help you remember the names of people at a party? Of course, many people currently use wireless phone technology when they are away from their home or office. What if these users could accomplish these tasks with an even smaller, more portable, and less intrusive system? Will people be wearing computers rather than carrying them?

Wearable computers already exist for specialized military and industrial use. Imagine using your hands to prepare a meal or work on a car with instructions and diagrams instantly available in your line of sight. Some of these systems are composed of a computer that is worn inside a jacket or in a belt and a head-mounted display. The display allows you to see the equivalent of a desktop monitor via a small screen that is worn in front of one eye or projected onto the inside of a regular pair of eyeglasses. Such devices might be used in airports by security personnel. These devices are currently being used by the U.S. Department of Defense for military applications and by the Toronto Blue Jays to end long lines at ticket windows. When coupled with face recognition technology, these products provide security personnel portable and instant communication with the command center. Police and security officers may someday use this technology to check IDs and verify your identity.

Experts say that wearable computers will be used by surgeons in operating rooms to "view" their patients. Will we be wearing computers soon? Some of us already are. And some experts predict the majority of us will employ a wearable computer before the end of the decade. Many computer manufacturers are currently working on wearable computers, and there is even a wearable computer fashion show that showcases the latest designs.

Many people are already wearing their computers, and making use of this mobile technology to read e-mail while waiting in lines or even studying their notes for the next exam. What do you think? Will people someday grab their keys and their computers before they leave the house? Will your computer one day be housed in your jacket? Do you see any potential issues that might come up if wearable computers were widespread?

SYSTEM UNIT

System unit (**system chassis**) contains electronic components.

Categories

There are six basic categories of system units: **desktop, media center, notebook (laptop), netbook, tablet PC** (**traditional** and **slate**), and **handheld**.

Components

Each type of system unit has the same basic components including system board, microprocessor, and memory.

ELECTRONIC REPRESENTATION

Human voices create **analog** (continuous) signals; computers only recognize **digital** electronic signals.

Numeric Representation

Data and instructions can be represented electronically with a two-state or **binary system** of numbers (0 and 1). Each 0 or 1 is called a **bit**. A **byte** consists of eight bits. **Hexadecimal system** (**hex**) uses 16 digits to represent binary numbers.

Character Encoding

Character encoding standards assign unique sequences of bits to each character. Three standards are **ASCII** (**American Standard Code for Information Interchange**), **EBCDIC** (**Extended Binary Coded Decimal Interchange Code**), and **Unicode**.

SYSTEM BOARD

The **system board** (**main board** or **motherboard**) connects all system components and allows input and output devices to communicate with the system unit. It is a flat circuit board covered with these electronic components:

- **Sockets** provide connection points for **chips** (**silicon chips, semiconductors, integrated circuits**). Chips are mounted on **carrier packages**.
- **Slots** provide connection points for specialized cards or circuit boards.
- **Bus lines** provide pathways to support communication.

To be a competent end user, you need to understand how data and programs are represented electronically. Additionally, you need to understand the functionality of the basic components in the system unit: system board, microprocessor, memory, expansion slots and cards, bus lines, and ports and cables.

MICROPROCESSOR

Processor	Manufacturer
i7	Intel
i5	Intel
Xeon	Intel
Athlon Opteron	AMD
Athlon	AMD
Nano	Via
Cell	Sony/Toshiba/IBM

The **microprocessor** is a single chip that contains the **central processing unit (CPU)** or **microprocessor**. It has two basic components:

- **Control unit** tells the computer system how to carry out program instructions.
- **Arithmetic-logic unit (ALU)** performs **arithmetic** and **logical operations.**

Microprocessor Chips

A **word** is the number of bits that can be accessed by the microprocessor at one time. **Clock speed** represents the number of times the CPU can fetch and process data or instructions in a second. Older microprocessors process data and instructions in microseconds; newer ones process in nanoseconds. Supercomputers process in picoseconds.

The two most significant developments are 64-bit processors and **multicore chips. Parallel processing** requires programs that allow multiple processors to work together to run large complex programs.

Specialty Processors

Specialty processors include **graphics coprocessors** also known as **GPU** or **graphics processing unit** (process graphic images), **smart cards** (plastic cards containing embedded chips), processors in automobiles (monitor fuel efficiency, satellite entertainment, and tracking systems), and **RFID tags** (track merchandise).

MEMORY

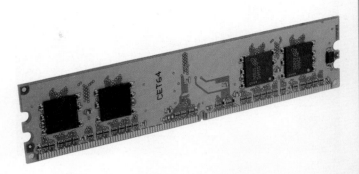

Memory holds data, instructions, and information. There are three types of memory chips: RAM, ROM, and flash memory.

RAM

RAM (random-access memory) chips are called temporary or volatile storage because their contents are lost if power is disrupted.

- **Cache memory** is a high-speed holding area for frequently used data and information.
- **DIMM (dual in-line memory module)** is used to expand memory.
- **Virtual memory** divides large programs into parts that are read into RAM as needed.

ROM

ROM (read-only memory) chips are nonvolatile storage and control essential system operations.

Flash Memory

Flash memory does not lose its contents when power is removed. It is used to store information about a computer's configuration.

Unit	Capacity
Megabyte (MB)	1 million bytes
Gigabyte (GB)	1 billion bytes
Terabyte (TB)	1 trillion bytes

EXPANSION SLOTS AND CARDS

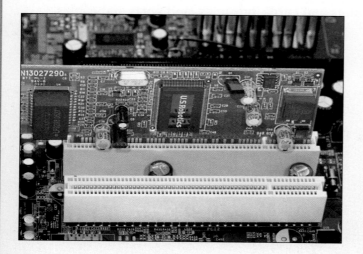

Most computers allow users to expand their systems by providing **expansion slots** on their system boards to accept **expansion cards**.

Examples of expansion cards include **advanced graphics cards**, **sound cards**, **network interface cards (NIC; network adapter cards)**, **wireless network cards**, and **TV tuner cards**.

Plug and Play is the ability for a computer to recognize and configure a device without human interaction.

PC Card (PCMCIA) and **ExpressCard** slots accept credit card–sized expansion cards in notebook computers.

BUS LINES

Bus lines, also known as **buses,** provide data pathways that connect various system components. **Bus width** is the number of bits that can travel simultaneously.

System buses connect CPU and memory. **Expansion buses** connect CPU and slots.

Expansion Buses

Three principal expansion bus types are

- **USB (universal serial bus)** widely used today; external USB devices connect from one to another or to a common point (hub) and then onto the system board.
- **FireWire bus** similar to USB bus but more specialized; used to connect digital camcorders and video editing equipment to system board.
- **PCIe (PCI Express) bus** widely used; provides a single dedicated path for each connected device.

PORTS

Ports are connecting sockets on the outside of the system unit.

Standard Ports

Four standard ports are

- **VGA (Video Graphics Adapter)** and **DVI (Digital Video Interface)**—provide connections to monitors.
- **USB (universal serial bus)**—widely used to connect keyboards, mice, printers, and storage devices; one port can connect several devices to system unit.
- **FireWire**—provides high-speed connections to specialized FireWire devices such as camcorders and storage devices.
- **Ethernet**—high-speed networking port that has become a standard for many of today's computers.

Specialized Ports

Three specialty ports are **S/PDIF (Sony/Philips Digital Interface)** for high-end audio and home theater systems, **HDMI (High Definition Multimedia Interface)** for high-definition digital audio *and* video, and **MIDI** for digital music.

Legacy Ports

Legacy ports have largely been replaced by faster, more flexible ports such as the universal serial bus (USB). These ports include **serial, parallel, keyboard, mouse,** and **Infrared Data Association (IrDA).**

Cables

Cables are used to connect external devices to the system unit via ports.

POWER SUPPLY

Power supply units convert AC to DC; they are located within the desktop computer's system unit. **AC adapters** power notebook computers and tablet PCs and recharge batteries.

CAREERS IN IT

Computer technicians repair and install computer components and systems. Certification in computer repair or associate degree from professional schools required. Hourly wage is $13.50 to $22.50.

KEY TERMS

AC adapter (183)
advanced graphics
  card (176)
analog (169)
arithmetic-logic unit
  (ALU) (173)
arithmetic
  operation (173)
ASCII (170)
binary system (170)
bit (170)
bus (177)
bus line (172, 177)
bus width (177)
byte (170)
cable (182)
cache memory (174)
carrier package (172)
central processing unit
  (CPU) (172)
character encoding
  standards (170)
chip (172)
clock speed (173)
computer
  technician (183)
control unit (172)
coprocessor (174)
desktop system
  unit (166)
digital (169)
DIMM (175)
DVI (Digital Video
  Interface) port (181)
EBCDIC (170)
Ethernet port (181)
expansion bus (180)
expansion card (176)
expansion slot (176)
ExpressCard (177)
FireWire bus (180)
FireWire port (181)
flash memory (175)
game port (182)
GPU (174)

graphics
  coprocessor (174)
handheld computer
  system unit (168)
hexadecimal system
  (hex) (170)
High Definition
  Multimedia Interface
  (HDMI) (182)
Infrared Data Association
  (IrDA) port (182)
integrated circuit (172)
keyboard port (182)
laptop (167)
legacy port (182)
logical operation (173)
main board (171)
media center system
  unit (166)
memory (174)
microprocessor (172)
motherboard (171)
mouse port (182)
multicore chip (173)
musical instrument
  digital interface
  (MIDI) (182)
netbook (168)
netbook system
  unit (168)
network adapter
  card (176)
network interface card
  (NIC) (176)
notebook system
  unit (167)
optical audio
  connections (182)
parallel port (182)
parallel processing (173)
PC Card slot (177)
PCI Express
  (PCIe) (180)
PCMCIA slot (177)

personal digital assistant
  (PDA) (168)
Plug and Play (177)
port (180)
power supply unit (183)
processor (172)
random-access memory
  (RAM) (174)
read-only memory
  (ROM) (175)
RFID tag (174)
semiconductor (172)
serial port (182)
silicon chip (172)
slate computer (168)
slot (172)
smart card (174)
smartphone (168)
socket (172)
Sony/Philips Digital
  Interconnect Format
  (S/PDIF) (182)
sound card (176)
system board (171)
system bus (180)
system chassis (166)
system unit (166)
tablet PC (168)
tablet PC system
  unit (168)
traditional tablet
  PC (168)
TV tuner card (176)
Unicode (170)
universal serial bus (180)
universal serial bus
  (USB) port (181)
VGA (Video Graphics
  Adapter) port (181)
virtual memory (175)
wireless network
  card (176)
word (173)

To test your knowledge of these key terms with animated flash cards, visit our Web site at www.computing2013.com and enter the keyword terms6.

MULTIPLE CHOICE

Circle the letter or fill in the correct answer.

1. This container houses most of the electrical components for a computer system.
   a. carrier package
   b. system board
   c. system unit
   d. TV tuner

2. Similar to notebooks, this system unit specializes in on-the-go Web browsing and e-mail access.
   a. chassis
   b. desktop
   c. media center
   d. netbook

3. Computers can only recognize this type of electronic signal.
   a. analog
   b. bus
   c. digital
   d. maximum

4. The main or motherboard is also known as the:
   a. computer
   b. board processor
   c. mobile system
   d. system board

5. How many bytes can a 32-bit-word computer access at one time?
   a. 1
   b. 4
   c. 8
   d. 16

6. In a microcomputer system, the central processing unit is contained on a single:
   a. bus
   b. chip
   c. module
   d. RAM

7. This type of memory divides large programs into parts and stores the parts on a secondary storage device.
   a. direct
   b. expanded
   c. random-access
   d. virtual

8. Also known as NIC, this adapter card is used to connect a computer to a:
   a. AIA
   b. expansion
   c. graphics
   d. network

9. This provides a pathway to connect parts of the CPU to each other.
   a. bus
   b. Plug and Play
   c. wired
   d. wireless

10. Older ports that have largely been replaced by faster, more flexible ports are called:
    a. buses
    b. expandable
    c. legacy
    d. rendered

For an interactive multiple-choice practice test, visit our Web site at www.computing2013.com and enter the keyword multiple6.

MATCHING

Match each numbered item with the most closely related lettered item. Write your answers in the spaces provided.

a. cache
b. flash
c. media center
d. Plug and Play
e. power supply
f. slate
g. slots
h. smart cards
i. system
j. USB

_____ 1. The category of system units that blurs the line between desktop computers and dedicated entertainment devices.

_____ 2. The newer type of tablet PC that is almost all monitor.

_____ 3. System board component that provides a connection point for specialized cards or circuit boards.

_____ 4. Plastic cards the size of a regular credit card that have an embedded specialty chip.

_____ 5. A type of memory that improves processing by acting as a temporary high-speed holding area between the memory and the CPU.

_____ 6. A type of memory that provides a combination of features of RAM and ROM.

_____ 7. A generic term that is associated with the ability to attach any device onto a computer and have it play or work immediately.

_____ 8. This bus connects the CPU to memory on the system board.

_____ 9. This port can be used to connect many USB devices to the system.

_____10. This unit plugs into a standard wall outlet and converts AC to DC.

For an interactive matching practice test, visit our Web site at www.computing2013 .com and enter the keyword matching6.

OPEN-ENDED

On a separate sheet of paper, respond to each question or statement.

1. Describe the six basic types of systems units.
2. Discuss electronic data and instructions.
3. Describe system boards including sockets, chips, carrier packages, slots, and bus lines.
4. Discuss microprocessors components, chips, and specialty processors.
5. Define computer memory including RAM, ROM, and flash memory.
6. Define expansion slots, cards, Plug and Play, PCMCIA, and ExpressCard.
7. Describe bus lines, bus width, system bus, and expansion bus.
8. Define ports including standard, specialized, and legacy ports. Give examples of each.
9. Describe power supply including power supply units and AC adapters.

MAKING IT WORK FOR YOU

The following questions are designed to demonstrate ways that you can effectively use technology today.

1 TV TUNER CARDS AND VIDEO CLIPS

Want to watch your favorite television program while you work? Perhaps you would like to include a video clip in a class presentation. It's easy using a video TV card. To learn more about this technology, review Making IT Work for You: TV Tuner Cards and Video Clips on pages 178 and 179. Then visit our Web site at www.computing2013.com and enter the keyword tuner. Play the video and answer the following: (a) Describe the two windows that open when the TV icon is selected. (b) What are the basic functions of the control box? (c) What is the command sequence to insert a video clip into a PowerPoint presentation?

2 DESKTOP AND NOTEBOOK COMPUTERS

Are you thinking about purchasing a new computer? Visit our Web site at www.computing2013.com and enter the keyword computer to link to a site that presents information about the newest desktop and notebook computers. Check out different desktop and notebook models and then answer the following questions: (a) If you were to purchase a desktop computer, which one would you select? Describe how it would fit your needs and print out its specifications. (b) If you were to purchase a notebook computer, which one would you select? Describe how it would fit your needs and print out its specifications. (c) If you had to choose between the desktop and notebook, which one would you choose? Why?

3 CUSTOM SYSTEM UNITS

When it is time for you to purchase your next computer, you might consider shopping online. A big advantage to choosing a computer online instead of in a store is that many computer manufacturers allow you to customize your new computer and build it to order. Visit our Web site at www.computing2013.com and enter the keyword custom to connect to a retailer of customized computers and use their online tools to customize and price a computer that meets your current needs. Then answer the following questions: (a) Which of the three types of system units did you configure? (b) What microprocessor did you choose? (c) How much and what type of memory option did you choose? (d) Would you purchase the computer you customized? Why or why not?

EXPLORATIONS

The following questions are designed to add depth and detail to your understanding of specific topics presented within this chapter. The questions direct you to sources other than the textbook to obtain this knowledge.

1 HOW TV TUNER CARDS WORK

The advent of digital TV and the success of digital video recorders have made TV tuner cards a popular addition to many computers. TV tuner cards allow you to watch and record TV shows on your computer, even while running other applications. To learn more about how TV tuner cards work, visit our Web site at www.computing2013.com and enter the keyword tv. Then answer the following questions: (a) What are some examples of inputs to a TV tuner card? (b) What is the function of a TV tuner card? (c) Where can the TV tuner card send the video signal once it is converted?

2 HOW VIRTUAL MEMORY WORKS

Typically before a program can be executed, it must be read into RAM. Many programs, however, are too large to fit into many computer systems' RAM. One option is to increase the RAM in the system. Another way is to use virtual memory. To learn more about how virtual memory works, visit our Web site at www.computing2013.com and enter the keyword memory. Then answer the following: (a) What is virtual memory? (b) Define page file, page, and paging. (c) What is thrashing?

3 BINARY NUMBERS

Binary numbers are the most basic unit that computers use to perform tasks. To learn more about how binary numbers work, visit our Web site at www.computing2013.com and enter the keyword binary. Then answer the following questions: (a) What character is represented by the binary number 01000011 in ASCII code? (b) What is the binary result of 1011 + 0010? What is the decimal equivalent to this number? (c) How many numbers can be represented with 1 bit (one binary "place")? How many by 2 bits? How many by 3 bits?

ETHICS

The following questions are designed to explore ethical issues related to technology and to develop the ability to think critically and communicate effectively. Respond to the questions by either creating a one-page paper or preparing for an in-depth classroom discussion.

 RFIDS

RFIDs have been touted by the media as an up-and-coming technology for several years. These tiny chips (that can be embedded in virtually everything) can be used to identify groceries, vehicles, and even people! Without knowing where RFID readers are placed and where RFID chips are embedded, it is unclear what information we might be sharing about ourselves and who we might be sharing it with. Write a one-page paper that addresses the following items: (a) What benefits do you see in using RFIDs in daily life? Explain your answers. (b) What privacy issues does an RFID raise for consumers? (c) Describe how RFIDs might be misused.

ENVIRONMENT

The following questions are designed to explore environmental issues related to technology and to develop the ability to think critically and communicate effectively. Respond to the questions by either creating a one-page paper or preparing for an in-depth classroom discussion.

1 GREEN PCS

A marketing and manufacturing race is now on to create the greenest computer available to consumers. Some manufacturers are going to great lengths to make computer components from recycled materials and to make computers that are completely recyclable. Review the Environment box on page 168 and research green PCs. Then respond to the following: (a) What does it mean to be a green PC? (b) Do you have a green PC? If so, who is the manufacturer and describe how it helps to protect the environment. If you do not have a green PC, locate and describe a well-known PC that is considered "green." (c) What can you do to encourage manufacturers to produce the "greenest" PC.

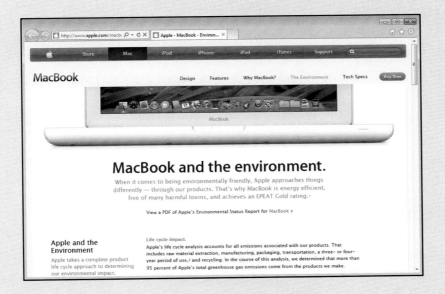

Input and Output

▲ Download the free *Computing Essentials 2013* app for videos, key term flashcards, quizzes, and the game, *Over the Edge!*

Competencies

After you have read this chapter, you should be able to:

1 Define input.

2 Describe keyboard entry including the different types of keyboards and keyboard features.

3 Discuss pointing devices including mice, touch screens, joysticks, and styluses.

4 Describe scanning devices including optical scanners and card readers.

5 Discuss image-capturing devices including digital cameras, digital video cameras and WebCams.

6 Define output.

7 Discuss monitor features, flat-panel, CRT, e-book readers, data projectors, and HDTVs.

8 Define printing features as well as ink-jet, laser, cloud, thermal, plotter, photo, and portable printers.

9 Discuss audio and video devices including portable media devices, and Mobile DTV.

10 Define combination input and output devices including fax machine, multifunctional devices, and Internet telephones.

Why should I read this chapter?

Years ago the only way to interact with a computer was through a keyboard, a monitor, and a printer. That was then and this is now. Now, we can input data in a wide variety of ways including pointing, scanning, and photographing. Computers can provide output in many different ways including humanlike voices, monitors that are almost as thin as a piece of paper, and inexpensive high-speed printers.

This chapter discusses a variety of input devices including wireless and virtual keyboards, touch screens, digital interactive white boards, portable scanners, WebCams, and voice recognition systems. Additionally, you'll learn about output devices including e-books, HDTV, cloud printers, photo printers, and portable media players. To be competent and to be competitive in today's professional workplace, you need to know and to understand these things.

chapter 7

Hi, I'm Marie, and I'm a technical writer. I'd like to talk with you about input and output devices. . . all those devices that help us to communicate with a computer. I'd also like to talk about e-books, portable media players, and cloud printing.

Introduction

How do you send instructions and information to the CPU? How do you get information out? Here we describe one of the most important places where computers interface with people. We input text, music, and even speech, but we probably never think about the relationship between what we enter and what the computer processes. People understand language, which is constructed of letters, numbers, and punctuation marks. However, at a basic level, computers can understand only the binary machine language of 0s and 1s. Input devices are essentially translators. Input devices translate numbers, letters, and actions that people understand into a form that computers can process.

Have you ever wondered how information processed by the system unit is converted into a form that you can use? That is the role of output devices. While input devices convert what we understand into what the system unit can process, output devices convert what the system unit has processed into a form that we can understand. Output devices translate machine language into letters, numbers, sounds, and images that people can understand.

Competent end users need to know about the most commonly used input devices, including keyboards, mice, scanners, digital cameras, voice recognition, and audio-input devices. Additionally, they need to know about the most commonly used output devices, including monitors, printers, and audio output devices. And end users need to be aware of combination input and output devices such as fax machines, multifunctional devices, and Internet telephones.

What Is Input?

Input is any data or instructions that are used by a computer. They can come directly from you or from other sources. You provide input whenever you use system or application programs. For example, when using a word processing program, you enter data in the form of numbers and letters and issue commands such as to save and to print documents. You also can enter data and issue commands by pointing to items, or using your voice. Other sources of input include scanned or photographed images.

Input devices are hardware used to translate words, sounds, images, and actions that people understand into a form that the system unit can process. For example, when using a word processor, you typically use a keyboard to enter text and a mouse to issue commands. In addition to keyboards and mice, there are a wide variety of other input devices. These include pointing, scanning, image capturing, and audio-input devices.

Keyboard Entry

One of the most common ways to input data is by **keyboard.** As mentioned in Chapter 6, keyboards convert numbers, letters, and special characters that people understand into electrical signals. These signals are sent to, and

Figure 7-1 **Ergonomic keyboard**

processed by, the system unit. Most keyboards use an arrangement of keys given the name QWERTY. This name reflects the keyboard layout by taking the letters of the first six alphabetic characters found on the top row of keys displaying letters.

Keyboards

There are a wide variety of different keyboard designs. They range from the full-sized to miniature and from rigid to flexible. There are even virtual keyboards that project an interactive key layout onto a flat surface. The most common types are

- **Traditional keyboards**—full-sized, rigid, rectangular keyboards that include function, navigational, and numeric keys.

- **Ergonomic keyboards**—similar to traditional keyboards. The keyboard arrangement, however, is not rectangular and a palm rest is provided. They are designed specifically to alleviate wrist strain associated with the repetitive movements of typing. (See Figure 7-1.)

- **Wireless keyboards**—transmit input to the system unit through the air. By eliminating connecting wires to the system unit, these keyboards provide greater flexibility and convenience.

- **PDA keyboards**—miniature keyboards for PDAs and smartphones to send e-mail, create documents, and more. (See Figure 7-2.)

- **Virtual keyboards**—display an image of a keyboard on a touch screen device. The screen functions as the actual input device, which is why the keyboard is considered virtual. Virtual keyboards are common on tablet computers and mobile devices. Another less widely used variation of the virtual keyboard displays the image of the keyboard onto a desktop.

Features

A computer keyboard combines a typewriter keyboard with a **numeric keypad,** used to enter numbers and arithmetic symbols. It also has many special-purpose keys. Some keys, such as the CAPS LOCK key, are **toggle keys.**

Explorations

People are spending more time at their computers than ever before. Consequently, the need for ergonomic keyboards is increasing.

To learn more about one manufacturer of ergonomic keyboards, visit our Web site at www.computing2013.com and enter the keyword ergonomic.

Figure 7-2 **PDA keyboard**

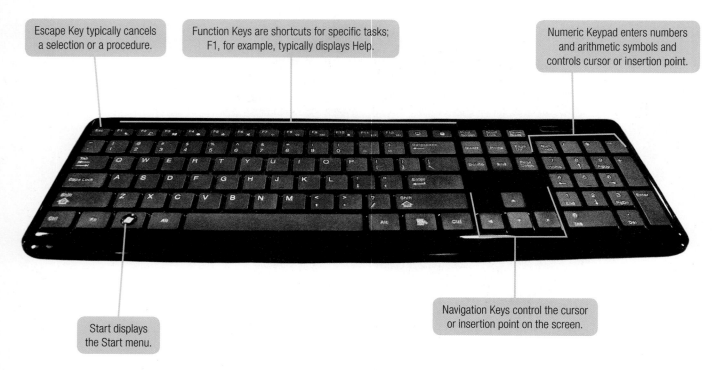

Escape Key typically cancels a selection or a procedure.

Function Keys are shortcuts for specific tasks; F1, for example, typically displays Help.

Numeric Keypad enters numbers and arithmetic symbols and controls cursor or insertion point.

Start displays the Start menu.

Navigation Keys control the cursor or insertion point on the screen.

Figure 7-3 Keyboard features

These keys turn a feature on or off. Others, such as the CTRL key, are **combination keys,** which perform an action when held down in combination with another key. To learn more about keyboard features, see Figure 7-3.

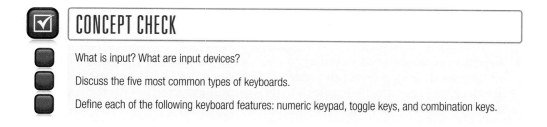

CONCEPT CHECK

What is input? What are input devices?

Discuss the five most common types of keyboards.

Define each of the following keyboard features: numeric keypad, toggle keys, and combination keys.

Pointing Devices

Pointing is one of the most natural of all human gestures. Pointing devices provide an intuitive interface with the system unit by accepting pointing gestures and converting them into machine-readable input. There are a wide variety of different pointing devices, including the mouse, joystick, touch screen, and stylus.

Mice

A **mouse** controls a pointer that is displayed on the monitor. The **mouse pointer** usually appears in the shape of an arrow. It frequently changes

Figure 7-4 Optical mouse

Figure 7-5 Trackball

shape, however, depending on the application. A mouse can have one, two, or more buttons, which are used to select command options and to control the mouse pointer on the monitor. Some mice have a **wheel button** that can be rotated to scroll through information that is displayed on the monitor. Although there are several different mouse types, there are three basic designs:

- **Optical mouse** has no moving parts and is currently the most widely used. It emits and senses light to detect mouse movement. An optical mouse can be used on almost any surface with high precision. (See Figure 7-4.)

- **Mechanical mouse** has a ball on the bottom and is attached with a cord to the system unit. As you move the mouse across a smooth surface, the roller rotates and controls the pointer on the screen.

- **Cordless** or **wireless mouse** is a battery-pow-ered device that typically uses radio waves or infrared light waves to communicate with the system unit. These devices eliminate the mouse cord and free up desk space.

Three devices similar to a mouse are trackballs, touch pads, and pointing sticks. You can use the **trackball,** also known as the **roller ball,** to control the pointer by rotating a ball with your thumb. (See Figure 7-5.) You can use **touch pads** to control the pointer by moving and tapping your finger on the sur-face of a pad. (See Figure 7-6.) You can use a **point-ing stick,** located in the middle of the keyboard, to control the pointer by directing the stick with one finger. (See Figure 7-7.)

Figure 7-6 Touch pad

Figure 7-7 Pointing stick

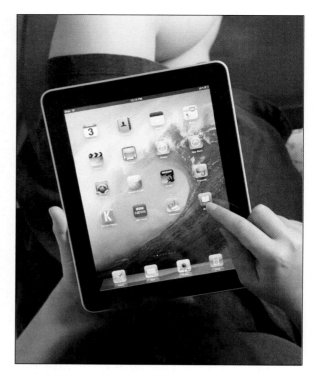

Figure 7-8 A touch screen

Touch Screens

A **touch screen** allows users to select actions or commands by touching the screen with a finger or penlike device. Touch screens are easy to use, especially when people need information quickly. They are widely used with tablet PCs, netbooks, and smartphones. Touch screens are also commonly used at restaurants, automated teller machines (ATMs), and information centers. (See Figure 7-8.)

Multitouch screens can be touched with more than one finger, which allows for interactions such as rotating graphical objects on the screen with your hand or zooming in and out by pinching and stretching your fingers. Multitouch screens are commonly used on mobile devices such as the Apple iPhone, as well as some notebook computers and desktop monitors. (See Figure 7-9.)

Joysticks

The **joystick** is a popular input device for computer games. You control game actions by varying the pressure, speed, and direction of the joystick. Additional controls, such as buttons and triggers, are used to specify commands or initiate specific actions. (See Figure 7-10.)

Stylus

A **stylus** is a penlike device commonly used with tablet PCs and PDAs. (See Figure 7-11.) A stylus uses pressure to draw images on a screen. Often, a

Figure 7-9 Multitouch screen

Figure 7-10 Joystick

Figure 7-11 Stylus

stylus interacts with the computer through handwriting recognition software. **Handwriting recognition software** translates handwritten notes into a form that the system unit can process.

 CONCEPT CHECK

 What is a pointing device? Describe four pointing devices.

 Describe three basic mouse designs.

 Define touch screens, joysticks, and styluses.

Scanning Devices

Scanners move across text and images. Scanning devices convert scanned text and images into a form that the system unit can process. There are four types of scanning devices: optical scanners, card readers, bar code readers, and character and mark recognition devices.

Optical Scanners

An **optical scanner,** also known simply as a **scanner,** accepts documents consisting of text and/or images and converts them to machine-readable form. These devices do not recognize individual letters or images. Rather, they recognize light, dark, and colored areas that make up individual letters or images. Typically, scanned documents are saved in files that can be further processed, displayed, printed, or stored for later use. There are three basic types of optical scanners: flatbed, document, and portable. (See Figure 7-12.)

- **Flatbed scanner** is much like a copy machine. The image to be scanned is placed on a glass surface and the scanner records the image from below.
- **Document scanner** is similar to a flatbed scanner except that it can quickly scan multipage documents. It automatically feeds one page of a document at a time through a scanning surface.

Flatbed scanner

Portable scanner

Document scanner

Figure 7-12 Three types of scanners

- **Portable scanner** is typically a handheld device that slides across the image, making direct contact.

    Optical scanners are powerful tools for a wide variety of end users, including graphics and advertising professionals who scan images and combine them with text. Lawyers and students use portable scanners as a valuable research tool to record information.

Card Readers

Nearly everyone uses a credit card, debit card, access (parking or building) card, and/or some type of identification card. These cards typically have the user's name, some type of identification number, and signature embossed on the card. Additionally, encoded information is often stored on the card as well. Card readers interpret this encoded information. There are two basic types:

- By far the most common is the **magnetic card reader.** The encoded information is stored on a thin magnetic strip located on the back of the card. When the card is swiped through the magnetic card reader, the information is read.

Figure 7-13 Radio frequency card reader

Figure 7-14 Bar code reader

- **Radio frequency card readers** are not as common but more convenient because they do not require the card to actually make contact with the reader. The card has a small **RFID (radio frequency identification)** microchip that contains the user's encoded information. Whenever the card is passed within a few inches of the card reader, the user's information is read. (See Figure 7-13.)

Bar Code Readers

You are probably familiar with **bar code readers** or **scanners** from grocery stores. (See Figure 7-14.) These devices are either handheld **wand readers** or **platform scanners.** They contain photoelectric cells that scan or read **bar codes,** or the vertical zebra-striped marks printed on product containers.

Almost all supermarkets use electronic cash registers and a bar code system called the **Universal Product Code (UPC).** At the checkout counter, electronic cash registers use a bar code reader to scan each product's UPC code. The codes are sent to the supermarket's computer, which has a description, the latest price, and an inventory level for each product. The computer processes this input to update the inventory level and to provide the electronic cash register with the description and price for each product. These devices are so easy to use that many supermarkets are offering customers self-checkout stations.

Character and Mark Recognition Devices

Character and mark recognition devices are scanners that are able to recognize special characters and marks. They are specialty devices that are essential tools for certain applications. Three types are

- **Magnetic-ink character recognition (MICR)**—used by banks to automatically read those unusual numbers on the bottom of checks and deposit slips. A special-purpose machine known as a reader/sorter reads these numbers and provides input that allows banks to efficiently maintain customer account balances.

- **Optical-character recognition (OCR)**—uses special preprinted characters that can be read by a light source and changed into machine-readable code. A common OCR device is the handheld wand reader. (See Figure 7-15.) These are used in department stores to read retail price tags by reflecting light on the printed characters.

- **Optical-mark recognition (OMR)**—senses the presence or absence of a mark, such as a pencil mark. OMR is often used to score standardized multiple-choice tests.

Figure 7-15 Wand reader

CONCEPT CHECK

How are pointing and scanning devices different?

Describe four types of scanners.

Describe three common character and mark recognition devices.

Image Capturing Devices

Optical scanners, like traditional copy machines, can make a copy from an original. For example, an optical scanner can make a digital copy of a photograph. Image capturing devices, on the other hand, create or capture original images. These devices include digital cameras and digital video cameras.

Digital Cameras

Digital cameras are similar to traditional cameras except that images are recorded digitally on a disk or in the camera's memory rather than on film and then downloaded, or transferred, to your computer. (See Figure 7-16.) You can take a picture, view it immediately, and even place it on your own Web page, within minutes.

To learn more about how digital photography works, visit us on the Web at www.computing2013.com and enter the keyword **photo.** Digital photographs can be shared easily with others over the Internet.

Digital Video Cameras

Unlike traditional video cameras, **digital video cameras** record motion digitally on a disk or in the camera's memory. Most have the capability to take still images as well. **WebCams** are specialized digital video cameras that cap-

tips

Are you having trouble getting the kind of photos you want with a digital camera? Would you like to make the most of digital technology in your photos? Here are some tips to help you get started:

1. **Buttons and Knobs.** Get to know the functions of your camera before you begin. Most cameras have an automatic mode, but be sure you know how to turn on the flash, zoom the lens, and set the image resolution.

2. **Photography Basics.** Digital cameras have an LCD screen on the back. You can use it to help frame your shots more accurately.

3. **Red-Eye Reduction.** Many digital cameras have a red-eye reduction feature. When photographing people in low light and using a flash, you can use this setting to eliminate glassy red eyes in photos. Consult your owner's manual to learn more about this feature.

4. **Blurry Photos.** Hold the camera still with your arms at your sides while snapping a photo. Many cameras also have built-in image-stabilization features.

To see additional tips, visit our Web site at www.computing2013.com and enter the keyword tips.

Figure 7-16 Digital camera

Built-in WebCam

Attached WebCam

Figure 7-17 Two types of WebCams

ture images and send them to a computer for broadcast over the Internet. Some WebCams are built-in while others are designed to be attached to the computer monitor. (See Figure 7-17.) To learn more about WebCams, visit our Web site at www.computing2013.com and enter the keyword **webcam.** To learn how you can videoconference, see Making IT Work for You: WebCams and Instant Messaging on pages 208 and 209.

Audio-Input Devices

Audio-input devices convert sounds into a form that can be processed by the system unit. By far the most widely used audio-input device is the microphone. Audio input can take many forms, including the human voice and music.

Voice Recognition Systems

Voice recognition systems use a microphone, a sound card, and special software. These systems allow users to operate computers and other devices as well as to create documents using voice commands. Examples include voice-controlled dialing features on mobile phones, navigation on GPS devices, and control of car audio systems such as Microsoft Sync. Specialized portable voice recognition systems are widely used by doctors, lawyers, and others to record dictation. (See Figure 7-18.) These devices are able to record for several hours before connecting to a computer system to edit, store, and print the dictated information. Some systems are even able to translate dictation from one language to another, such as from English to Japanese.

☑ CONCEPT CHECK

○ How are digital cameras different from traditional cameras?

○ What is a WebCam? Describe the two basic designs.

○ Discuss voice recognition systems.

Making IT work for you

WEBCAMS AND INSTANT MESSAGING

Do you enjoy chatting with your friends? Are you working on a project and need to collaborate with others in your group? What if you could see and hear your group online? Perhaps instant messaging is just what you're looking for. It's easy and free with an Internet connection and the right software.

Sending Messages   In instant messaging applications, your friends are added to a list of contacts that shows you when they are online and available to chat. For example, you could use Windows Live Messenger as follows:

1 ● **Add contacts by clicking the *Add a Contact* button and following the on-screen instructions.**

● **Double-click the name of a friend in the *Available* section.**

● **Enter your message in the window that appears.**

● **Select *Enter* on your keyboard to send.**

Your message appears on your friend's screen instantly. Your friend can then continue the conversation by following the steps above.

Add a contact button

Contact currently online

Transferring Files   While chatting, it is sometimes useful to share a file. For example, you might want to send a copy of a report you have been working on to a classmate to review. To send a file during an online chat:

1 ● Click the *Files* menu item and select *Send a file or photo . . .*

● Browse your computer for the file you want to share and click *Open*.

Your friend is given an option to accept your file. A notification appears in your conversation when your file upload is complete.

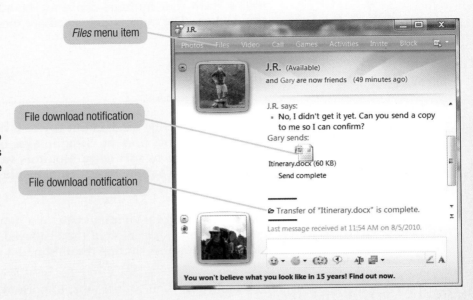

Files menu item

File download notification

File download notification

Using a WebCam   In addition to typing text messages, some instant messaging software allows you to have voice or video conversations over the Internet so you can see and hear the person you are collaborating with. To do this, both users must have a microphone and speakers, as well as WebCams for video conferencing. You could hold a video conference using Windows Live Messenger by following these steps.

1 ● Start a conversation with a contact as shown on the previous page.

● Click the *Video call* menu item.

Your friend is given the option to accept the video conference. Once he or she accepts, the video conference begins.

The Web is continually changing, and some of the specifics presented in this Making IT Work for You may have changed.

Video call menu item

Video image of your friend

Video image you are sending

To learn about other ways to make information technology work for you, visit our Web site at www.computing2013.com and enter the keyword miw.

What Is Output?

Output is processed data or information. Output typically takes the form of text, graphics, photos, audio, and/or video. For example, when you create a presentation using a presentation graphics program, you typically input text and graphics. You also could include photographs and even add voice narration. The output would be the completed presentation.

Output devices are any hardware used to provide or to create output. They translate information that has been processed by the system unit into a form that humans can understand. There are a wide range of output devices. The most widely used are monitors, printers, and audio-output devices.

Monitors

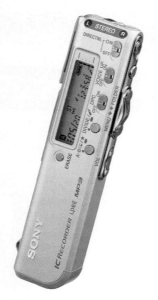

Figure 7-18 Portable voice recognition system

The most frequently used output device is the **monitor.** Also known as **display screens,** monitors present visual images of text and graphics. The output is often referred to as **soft copy.** Monitors vary in size, shape, and cost. Almost all, however, have some basic distinguishing features.

Features

The most important characteristic of a monitor is its clarity. **Clarity** refers to the quality and sharpness of the displayed images. It is a function of several monitor features, including resolution, dot pitch, refresh rate, size, and aspect ratio.

- **Resolution** is one of the most important features. Images are formed on a monitor by a series of dots or **pixels (picture elements).** (See Figure 7-19.) Resolution is expressed as a matrix of these dots or pixels. For example, many monitors today have a resolution of 1,600 pixel columns by 1,200 pixel rows for a total of 1,920,000 pixels. The higher a monitor's resolution (the more pixels), the clearer the image produced. See Figure 7-20 for the most common monitor resolutions.

- **Dot (pixel) pitch** is the distance between each pixel. Most newer monitors have a dot pitch of .31 mm (31/100th of a millimeter) or less. The lower the dot pitch (the shorter the distance between pixels), the clearer the images produced.

Pixel

Figure 7-19 Monitor resolution

- **Refresh rate** indicates how often a displayed image is updated or refreshed. Most monitors operate at a rate of 75 hertz, which means that the monitor is refreshed 75 times each second. Images displayed on monitors with refresh rates lower than 75 hertz appear to flicker and can cause eye strain. The faster the refresh rate (the more frequently images are redrawn), the better the quality of images displayed.

- Size, or **active display area,** is measured by the diagonal length of a monitor's viewing area. Common sizes are 15, 17, 19, 21, and 24 inches.

- **Aspect ratio** is determined by the width of a monitor divided by its height. Common aspect ratios for monitors are 4:3 (standard, similar to traditional television pictures) and 16:10 (wide screen).

Flat-Panel Monitors

Flat-panel monitors are the most widely used type of monitor today. Compared to other types, they are thinner, are more portable, and require less power to operate. (See Figure 7-21.)

Many of today's flat-panel monitors are **LCD (liquid crystal display).** There are two basic types: passive-matrix and active-matrix. **Passive-matrix** or **dual-scan monitors** create images by scanning the entire screen. This type requires very little power, but the clarity of the images is not as sharp. **Active-matrix** or **thin film transistor (TFT) monitors** do not scan down the screen; instead, each pixel is independently activated. They can display more colors with better clarity. Active-matrix monitors are more expensive and require more power.

OLED (organic light-emitting diode) is a newer technology and is becoming widely used. Unlike LCD, OLED technology has the benefits of lower power consumption and longer battery life, as well as possibilities for much thinner displays.

Standard	Pixels
SVGA	800 × 600
XGA	1,024 × 768
SXGA	1,280 × 1,024
UXGA	1,600 × 1,200
QXGA	2,048 × 1,536
QXSGA	2,560 × 2,048

Figure 7-20 Resolution standards

Cathode-Ray Tubes

Just a few years ago, the most common type of monitor for the office and the home was the **cathode-ray tube (CRT).** (See Figure 7-22.) These monitors are typically placed directly on the system unit or on the desktop. CRTs are similar in size and technology to older televisions. Compared to other types of monitors, their primary advantages are low cost and excellent resolution. Their primary disadvantages are that they are bulky, are less energy efficient, and occupy a considerable amount of space on the desktop.

Discarded CRTs are a serious threat to our environment. Each color CRT contains approximately four pounds of lead and numerous other hazardous materials. Don't just throw out an obsolete CRT. Dispose of it in a responsible manner through an EPA-certified recycling program. Most large cities and manufacturers including IBM, Microsoft, and Dell have certified programs.

Other Monitors

There are several other types of monitors. These monitors are used for more specialized applications, such as reading books, making presentations, and watching television. Three of these specialized devices are book readers, digital whiteboards, and high-definition television.

Explorations

Flat-panel monitors have become the standard for personal computers.

To learn more about a leading manufacturer in this industry, visit our Web site at www.computing2013.com and enter the keyword flatpanel.

Figure 7-21 Flat-panel monitor

Figure 7-22 CRT monitor

Figure 7-23 E-book reader

Figure 7-24 Digital whiteboard

- **E-book readers,** such as the Kindle or Nook, also known simply as **e-books,** are dedicated, handheld, book-sized devices that display text and graphics. To learn more about one of the most widely used e-book readers, see Making IT Work for You: Using an E-Book on page 213. Using content downloaded from the Web or from special cartridges, these devices are used to read newspapers, magazines, and entire books. (See Figure 7-23.) These devices use a special type of screen called **electronic paper** or **e-paper** that requires power only when changing pages, and not the entire time a page is displayed on the screen. The biggest challenge for e-book readers is tablet PCs like the iPad. In addition to operating like an e-book, tablet PCs can perform a wide variety of other functions.

- **Digital** or **interactive whiteboards** are specialized devices with a large display connected to a computer or projector. The computer's desktop is displayed on the digital whiteboard and controlled using a special pen, a finger, or some other type of device. Digital whiteboards are widely used in classrooms and corporate board rooms. (See Figure 7-24.)

- **High-definition television (HDTV)** delivers a much clearer and more detailed wide-screen picture than regular television. Because the output is digital, users can readily freeze video sequences to create high-quality still images. The video and still images can then be digitized, edited, and stored on disk for later use. This technology is very useful to graphic artists, designers, and publishers. One the most recent and dramatic advances is 3D HDTV. (See Figure 7-25.) Using special viewing glasses, 3D HDTV provides theater-quality three-dimensional viewing.

Figure 7-25 3D HDTV

CONCEPT CHECK

 What is output? What are output devices?

 Define these monitor features: resolution, dot pitch, refresh rate, size, and aspect ratio.

 Describe flat-panel, CRT, and other more specialized monitors.

Making IT work for you

USING E-BOOKS

E-book readers are a great way to enjoy reading on the go. Did you know they also can help you stay current in your profession? Many e-book readers feature subscriptions to newspapers and magazines, including publications that will keep you up-to-date on topics important to your career. Some devices, such as the Amazon Kindle, can even download subscriptions automatically wherever you are without the need for a computer connection.

Subscribing   To subscribe to a magazine using the Kindle:

1 Press the *Menu* button and select *Shop in Kindle Store.*

> Turn Wireless Off
>
> Shop in Kindle Store
>
> View Archived Items
>
> Search
>
> Settings
>
> Experimental
>
> Sync & Check for Items

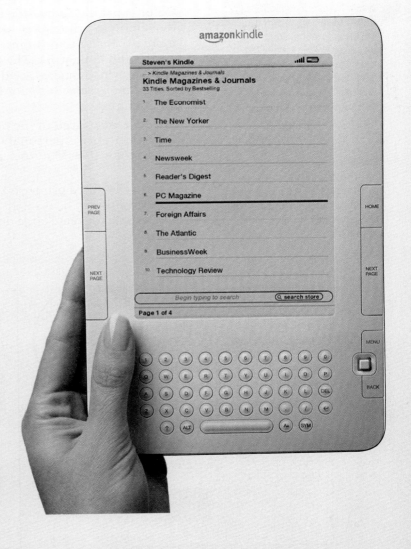

2 Select *Magazines* from the *Browse* menu.

> **Browse:**
> Books - *Over 300,000 titles available*
> Newspapers
> Magazines
> Blogs

3 Select a publication of interest and follow the on-screen instructions to complete your subscription.

The Web is continually changing, and some of the specifics presented in Making IT Work for You may have changed.

To learn about other ways to make information technology work for you, visit our Web site at www.computing2013.com and enter the keyword miw.

Printers

You probably use a printer with some frequency to print homework assignments, photographs, and Web pages. **Printers** translate information that has been processed by the system unit and present the information on paper. Printer output is often called **hard copy.**

Features

There are many different types of printers. Almost all, however, have some basic distinguishing features, including resolution, color capability, speed, memory, and duplex printing.

- **Resolution** for a printer is similar to monitor resolution. It is a measure of the clarity of images produced. Printer resolution, however, is measured in **dpi (dots per inch).** (See Figure 7-26.) Most printers designed for personal use average 1,200 dpi. The higher the dpi, the better the quality of images produced.

- **Color** capability is provided by most printers today. Users typically have the option to print either with just black ink or with color. Because it is more expensive to print in color, most users select black ink for letters, drafts, and homework. The most common black ink selection is **grayscale** in which images are displayed using many shades of gray. Color is used more selectively for final reports containing graphics and for photographs.

- **Speed** is measured in the number of pages printed per minute. Typically, printers for personal use average 15 to 19 pages per minute for single-color (black) output and 13 to 15 pages per minute for color output.

- **Memory** within a printer is used to store printing instructions and documents waiting to be printed. The more memory in a printer, the faster it will be able to create large documents.

300 dpi

1,200 dpi

Figure 7-26 Dpi comparison

- **Duplex printing** allows automatic printing on both sides of a sheet of paper. Although not currently a standard feature for all printers, it will likely become standard in the future as a way to reduce paper waste and to protect the environment.

Ink-Jet Printers

Ink-jet printers spray ink at high speed onto the surface of paper. This process not only produces a letter-quality image but also permits printing to be done in a variety of colors, making them ideal for select special applications. (See Figure 7-27.) Ink-jet printers are the most widely used printers. They are reliable, quiet, and relatively inexpensive. The most costly aspect of ink-jet printers is replacing the ink cartridges. For this reason, most users specify black ink for the majority of print jobs and use the more expensive color printing for select applications. Typical ink-jet printers produce 17 to 19 pages per minute of black-only output and 13 to 15 pages of color output.

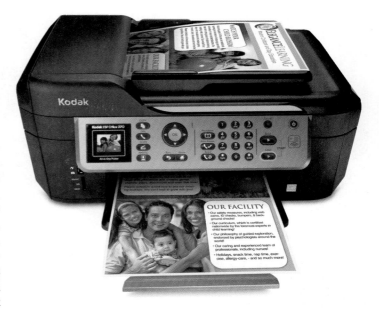

Figure 7-27 A special-application ink-jet printer

Laser Printers

The **laser printer** uses a technology similar to that used in a photocopying machine. Laser printers use a laser light beam to produce images with excellent letter and graphics quality. More expensive than ink-jet printers, laser printers are faster and are used in applications requiring high-quality output. (See Figure 7-28.)

There are two categories of laser printers. **Personal laser printers** are less expensive and are used by many single users. They typically can print 15 to 17 pages a minute. **Shared laser printers** typically support color, are more expensive, and are used (shared) by a group of users. Shared laser printers typically print over 50 pages a minute.

Explorations

For fast high-quality printouts, laser printers are the standard.

To learn more about a company that makes laser printers, visit our Web site at www.computing2013.com and enter the keyword printer.

Other Printers

There are several other types of printers. These printers include cloud printers, dot-matrix printers, thermal printers, plotters, photo printers, and portable printers:

- **Cloud printers** are printers connected to the Internet that provide printing services to others on the Internet. **Google Cloud Print** is a service that supports cloud printing. Once a user activates a printer using the Google Chrome OS, the user can access that printer anywhere with an Internet connection.
- **Thermal printers** use heat elements to produce images on heat-sensitive paper. These printers are widely used with ATMs and gasoline pumps to print receipts.
- **Plotters** are special-purpose printers for producing a wide range of specialized output. Using output from graphics tablets and other graphical input devices, plotters create maps, images, and architectural and engineering drawings. Plotters are typically used by graphic artists, engineers, and architects to print out designs, sketches, and drawings.

Figure 7-28 Laser printer

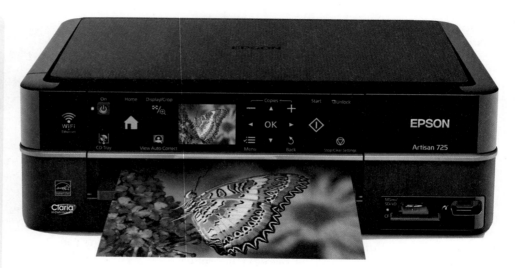

Figure 7-29 Photo printer

- **Photo printers** are special-purpose printers designed to print photo-quality images from digital cameras. (See Figure 7-29.) Most photo printers print 3 × 5″ or 4 × 6″ images on glossy, photo-quality paper.
- **Portable printers** are usually small and lightweight printers designed to work with a notebook computer. Portable printers may be ink-jet or laser printers, print in black and white or color, and connect with USB.

tips

Do you find extra pages in the printer when you try to print from the Web? Would you like to print your favorite articles without all the ads and hyperlinks? There are several ways to get what you want in a printout. Here are a few suggestions you can use with Internet Explorer:

 Preview. To see what will be printed, choose *Print Preview* from the *File* menu. You can scroll through the pages and make sure the items you want will be printed.

 Choose Printer Friendly. Many Web pages have a **Printer Friendly** button that removes all the ads and sidebars. Look for the button at the conclusion of most Web articles.

 Print Selection. You can highlight and print only the text you would like to print. Highlight the text and graphics you would like to print and choose *File/Print* and check the *Selection* option under the *Page range* box.

 Be selective. Print only the pages you need. The common print default is to print *all* pages. Unless you really need all the pages, specify the *Page range* as *selection*, *current* page, or *specific* pages.

To see other tips, visit our Web site at www.computing2013.com and enter the keyword tips.

☑ CONCEPT CHECK

- Discuss these printer features: resolution, color capability, speed, memory, and duplex printing.
- Compare ink-jet printers and laser printers.
- Discuss cloud, thermal, plotter, photo, and portable printers.

Audio and Video Devices

Audio-output devices translate audio information from the computer into sounds that people can understand. The most widely used audio-output devices are **speakers** and **headsets**. (See Figure 7-30.) These devices are connected to a sound card in the system unit. The sound card is used to capture as well as play back recorded sounds. Audio-output devices are used to play music, vocalize translations from one language to another, and communicate information from the computer system to users.

Creating voice output is not anywhere near as difficult as recognizing and interpreting voice input. In fact, voice output is quite common. It is used with many soft-drink machines, telephones, and cars. It is used as a reinforcement tool for learning, such as to help students study a foreign language. It also is used in many supermarkets at the checkout counter to confirm purchases. One of its most powerful capabilities is to assist the physically challenged.

Figure 7-30 **Headset**

Portable Media Players

Portable media players, also known as digital media players, are electronic devices for storing and playing digital media. Some of the best-known specialized audio and video players are the Apple iPod, Creative Zen, and Microsoft Zune. (See Figure 7-31.)

One of the most recent applications for portable media players is to watch live TV. This is possible through **Mobile Digital Television (Mobile DTV)** technology, which allows television stations to broadcast their programming directly to smartphones, computers, and **digital media players.**

Combination Input and Output Devices

Many devices combine input and output capabilities. Sometimes this is done to save space. Other times it is done for very specialized applications. Common combination devices include fax machines, multifunctional devices, and Internet telephones.

Fax Machines

A **fax machine** is a standard tool in nearly every office. At one time, all fax machines were separate stand-alone devices for sending and receiving images over telephone lines. Now, most computer systems have that capability with the simple addition of a fax/modem board. To send a fax, these devices scan the image of a document converting the light and dark areas into a format that can be sent electronically over standard telephone lines. To receive a fax, these devices reverse the process and print the document (or display the document on your monitor) using signals received from the telephone line.

Multifunctional Devices

Multifunctional devices (MFD) typically combine the capabilities of a scanner, printer, fax, and copy machine.

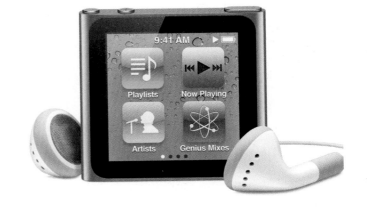

Figure 7-31 **Digital media player**

These multifunctional devices offer a cost and space advantage. They cost about the same as a good printer or copy machine but require much less space than the single-function devices they replace. Their disadvantage is that the quality and functionality are not quite as good as those of the separate single-purpose devices. Even so, multifunctional devices are widely used in home and small business offices.

Internet Telephones

Internet telephones are specialized input and output devices for receiving and sending voice communication. (See Figure 7-32.)

Voice over IP (VoIP) is the transmission of telephone calls over computer networks. Also known as **telephony, Internet telephony,** and **IP telephony,** VoIP uses the Internet rather than traditional communication lines to support voice communication. To place telephone calls using Internet telephony requires a high-speed Internet connection and a service provider. Many cable service providers offer bundles including Internet, telephone, and television. While these bundles offer a price break, there are other lower-cost options for VoIP from a variety of providers including Ooma, Vonage, MagicJack, and Skype.

- *Ooma* and *Vonage* offer similar services in which you directly insert your telephone or cordless telephone base unit directly into their unit. (See Figure 7-33). This unit connects to your modem or network and provides traditional telephone service. Both Ooma and Vonage provide free or very-low-cost domestic and international service with high-quality voice and service reliability.

- *MagicJack* requires a smaller adapter that connects directly to your computer's USB port. (See Figure 7-34.) Then you can connect any telephone to the MagicJack adapter and make very-low-cost calls. Advantages compared to Ooma and Vonage are lower cost and the ability to make calls anywhere your computer (including your smartphone) has an Internet connection. The disadvantages are that your computer has to be on to send or receive calls, voice quality is typically lower, and reliability is not as good.

- *Skype* provides audio and video service that does not require any dedicated hardware. Once you subscribe to this free service, you can use your computer's existing audio and video devices to connect to any other Skype subscribers. The advantages compared to the other providers are that Skype is free for domestic calls (as well as for international calls), supports video as well as audio, and does not require any special equipment. The disadvantages include that both parties must have their computers on to make or receive calls; calls can only be made between Skype subscribers, although, for an additional fee, you can place calls to non-Skype subscribers; and voice quality and reliability are not as good as for Ooma and Vonage.

Explorations

Multifunctional devices save space and money, making them a favorite in home offices and small businesses.

To learn more about MFDs, visit our Web site at www.computing2013.com and enter the keyword mfd.

Figure 7-32 Internet telephone

Figure 7-33 Vontage adapter

Figure 7-34 MagicJack adapter

CONCEPT CHECK

 What are the two most widely used audio-output devices? What is a portable media player? What is Mobile Digital Television?

 Describe the following combination devices: fax machine, MFD, and Internet telephone.

 Define VoIP and discuss four service providers.

Careers in IT

Technical writers prepare instruction manuals, technical reports, and other scientific or technical documents. Most technical writers work for computer software firms, government agencies, or research institutions. They translate technical information into easily understandable instructions or summaries. As new technology continues to develop and expand, the need for technical writers who can communicate technical expertise to others is expected to increase.

Technical writing positions typically require an associate or a college degree in communications, journalism, or English and a specialization in, or familiarity with, a technical field. However, individuals with strong writing skills sometimes transfer from jobs in the sciences to positions in technical writing.

Technical writers can expect to earn an annual salary in the range of $46,500 to $76,500. Advancement opportunities can be limited within a firm or company, but there are additional opportunities in consulting. To learn about other careers in information technology, visit us at www.computing2013.com and enter the keyword **careers.**

Now that you've learned about input and output devices, I'd like to tell you about my career as a technical writer.

A LOOK TO THE FUTURE

Crashing through the Foreign Language Barrier

Have you ever wished you could speak more than one language fluently? What if you could speak hundreds of languages instantly? Would you like to have your own personal interpreter to accompany you whenever you traveled to a foreign country? What if you could take a picture of a foreign road sign or restaurant menu and have it immediately translated for you? Technology called machine translation (MT) may soon exist to do all of these things. The military and private sector are funding a variety of research projects on electronic interpreters, and the commercial opportunities are enormous. The worldwide translation services market is an over $8 billion-a-year industry and is expected to grow even more.

Prototype portable handheld electronic interpreters are currently in a testing phase at the U.S. Office of Naval Research. In fact, it is expected that these devices will be widely used in the near future. The company SpeechGear has developed software called Compadre that takes verbal statements in one language, converts the statements to text, translates that text to another language, and then vocalizes the translated text. And it does all this in two seconds! The military is particularly interested in instant electronic interpreters as they focus on peacekeeping objectives. More than ever before, U.S. soldiers find themselves needing to communicate with non-English-speaking civilians to settle disputes and maintain order.

Despite advances in translation software, several challenges remain. Current translation techniques are labor intensive; they require linguists and programmers to create large lists of words and their corresponding meanings. Unfortunately, computers have a difficult time understanding idioms, such as "It is raining cats and dogs." They also may have difficulty correctly identifying words by their context. For example, the sentences "The stove is hot" and "The latest tech gadget is hot" use the same word, *hot,* but it has a very different meaning in each sentence. Researchers have been working on a solution to these problems. One is the EliMT project. Instead of translating from word to word, EliMT compares books that have been translated in different languages, looking for sentence fragment patterns. By comparing sentence fragments, it is hoped that translation programs will be able to identify word groupings and translate them into another language's comparable word groupings, essentially translating concepts instead of individual words. Other systems are supplementing machine translation with expert human translators for verification of unusual phrases.

What are the uses for such software and devices? Will the average person want or need an electronic translator? What type of professions and professionals will use them? What industries would benefit most from electronic translators? How could you use this technology?

INPUT

Input is any data or instructions used by a computer. **Input devices** translate words, images, and actions into a form a computer can process.

Keyboards

Keyboards are the most common way to input data.

- Common types are **traditional, ergonomic, wireless, PDA,** and **virtual.**
- Features include **numeric keypads, toggle keys,** and **combination keys.**

Pointing Devices

Pointing devices accept pointing gestures and convert them to machine-readable input.

- **Mouse** controls a **mouse pointer. A wheel button** rotates to scroll through information. Three basic mouse designs are **optical, mechanical,** and **cordless (wireless).** Similar devices include **trackball (roller ball), touch pad,** and **pointing stick.**

INPUT

- **Touch screen** operations are controlled by fingers touching the screen. **Multitouch screens** can be touched with more than one finger; commonly used on mobile devices such as the Apple iPhone.
- **Joystick** operations are controlled by varying pressure, speed, and direction.
- **Stylus** is a penlike device used with tablet PCs and PDAs. **Handwriting recognition software** translates handwritten notes.

Scanning Devices

Scanners move across text and graphics. Scanning devices convert scanned text and images into a form that can be processed by the system unit.

- **Optical scanners** record light, dark, and colored areas of scanned text or images. There are three types: **flatbed, document,** and **portable.**
- **Card readers** interpret encoded information. Two types: **magnetic** (reads **magnetic strip**) and **radio frequency** (reads **RFID** microchip) card readers.

To be a competent end user, you need to be aware of the most commonly used input and output devices. These devices are translators for information into and out of the system unit. Input devices translate words, sounds, and actions into symbols the system unit can process. Output devices translate symbols from the system unit into words, images, and sounds that people can understand.

INPUT

- **Bar code readers** are used with electronic cash registers in supermarkets. **Wand readers** or **platform scanners** read **UPC** codes that are used to determine product descriptions and prices and to update inventory levels.
- Character and mark recognition devices recognize special characters and marks. Three types: **MICR (magnetic ink character recognition**, read by readers/sorters), **OCR (optical-character recognition)**, and **OMR (optical-mark recognition)**.

Image Capturing Devices

Image capturing devices create or capture original images. These devices include **digital cameras** (images downloaded to system unit for further processing and/or printing) and **digital video cameras. WebCams** capture and send images over the Internet; one design is built-in and the other is attached.

Audio-Input Devices

Audio-input devices convert sounds into a form that can be processed by the system unit. Audio input takes many forms, including the human voice and music. **Voice recognition systems** use a combination of a microphone, a sound card, and special software.

OUTPUT

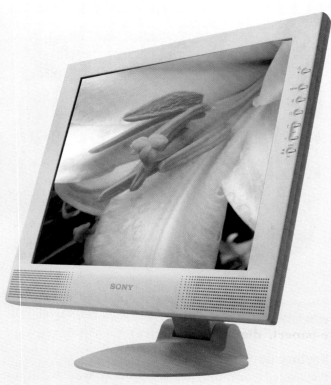

Output is data or information processed by a computer. **Output devices** translate processed text, graphics, audio, and video into a form humans can understand.

Monitors

Monitors **(display screens)** present visual images of text and graphics. Monitor output is described as **soft copy**.

Clarity is a function of several monitor features including **resolution** (expressed as matrix of **pixels** or **picture elements**), **dot (pixel) pitch, refresh rate**, size (active display area), and **aspect ratio**.

- **Flat-panel monitors** have become the standard for computer systems. Many are **LCD (liquid crystal display).** Two basic types are **passive-matrix (dual-scan)** and **active-matrix (thin film transistor, TFT). OLED (organic light-emitting diode)** is newer technology requiring lower power consumption, longer battery life, and potential for thinner displays.

OUTPUT

- **Cathode-ray tubes (CRTs)** use technology similar to older televisions. Compared to flat-panels, CRTs are bulky, require more electricity to run, and occupy considerable space on the desktop.

Three specialized types of monitors are **e-book readers** (screen known as **electronic paper** or **e-paper**), **digital (interactive) whiteboards**, and **high-definition television (HDTV)**.

Printers

Printers translate information processed by the system unit and present the information on paper. Output from printers is described as **hard copy**. Some distinguishing features of printers include **resolution** (measured in **dpi** or **dots per inch**), color and **gray-scale** capability, speed, memory, and **duplex printing**.

- **Ink-jet printers** spray ink to produce high-quality output. These printers are inexpensive and the most widely used type of printer.
- **Laser printers** use technology similar to photo-copying machines. Two categories are **personal** and **shared**.

Other printers include **cloud printing (Google Cloud Print)**, **thermal printers**, **plotters**, **photo printers**, and **portable printers**.

Audio and Video Devices

Audio-output devices translate audio information from the computer into sounds that people can understand. **Speakers** and **headsets** are the most widely used audio-output devices.

COMBINATION DEVICES

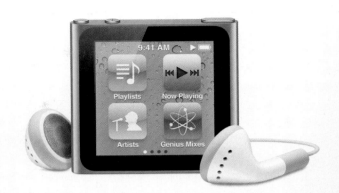

Portable media players (digital media players) store and play digital media. **Mobile Digital Television (Mobile DTV)** technology supports television broadcasting directly to smartphones, computers, and digital media players. Combination devices combine input and output capabilities.

Fax Machines

Fax machines send and receive images via standard telephone lines.

Multifunctional Devices

Multifunctional devices (MFD) typically combine the capabilities of a scanner, printer, fax, and copy machine.

Internet Telephones

Internet telephones receive and send voice communication. **Voice over IP (VoIP)**, also known as **telephony**, **Internet telephony**, and **IP telephony**, uses the Internet to transmit telephone calls. Four providers are Ooma, Vonage, MagicJack, and Skype.

CAREERS IN IT

Technical writers prepare instruction manuals, technical reports, and other documents. An associate or a college degree in communication, journalism, or English and a specialization in, or familiarity with, a technical field is required. Salary range is $46,500 to $76,500.

KEY TERMS

active display area   (210)
active-matrix
    monitor   (211)
aspect ratio   (210)
bar code   (205)
bar code reader   (205)
bar code scanner   (205)
cathode-ray tube
    (CRT)   (211)
clarity   (210)
cloud printer   (215)
combination key   (200)
cordless mouse   (201)
digital camera   (206)
digital media player   (217)
digital video
    camera   (206)
digital whiteboard   (212)
display screen   (210)
document scanner   (203)
dot pitch   (210)
dots per inch (dpi)   (214)
dual-scan monitor   (211)
duplex printing   (215)
e-book   (212)
e-book reader   (212)
e-paper   (212)
electronic paper   (212)
ergonomic
    keyboard   (199)
fax machine   (217)
flat-panel monitor   (211)
flatbed scanner   (203)
Google Cloud Print   (215)
grayscale   (214)
handwriting recognition
    software   (203)
hard copy   (214)
headsets   (217)
high-definition television
    (HDTV)   (212)
ink-jet printer   (215)
input   (198)
input device   (198)
interactive
    whiteboard   (212)

Internet telephone   (218)
Internet telephony   (218)
IP telephony   (218)
joystick   (202)
keyboard   (198)
laser printer   (215)
liquid crystal display
    (LCD)   (211)
magnetic card
    reader   (204)
magnetic-ink character
    recognition
    (MICR)   (205)
mechanical mouse   (201)
Mobile Digital
    Television   (217)
Mobile DTV   (217)
monitor   (210)
mouse   (200)
mouse pointer   (200)
multifunctional device
    (MFD)   (217)
multitouch screen   (202)
numeric keypad   (199)
optical-character
    recognition
    (OCR)   (205)
optical-mark recognition
    (OMR)   (205)
optical mouse   (201)
optical scanner   (203)
organic light-emitting
    diode (OLED)   (211)
output   (210)
output device   (210)
passive-matrix
    monitor   (211)
PDA keyboard   (199)
personal laser
    printer   (215)
photo printer   (216)
picture element   (210)
pixel   (210)
pixel pitch   (210)
platform scanner   (205)
plotter   (216)

pointing stick   (201)
portable media
    player   (217)
portable printer   (216)
portable scanner   (204)
printer   (214)
radio frequency card
    reader   (205)
radio frequency
    identification
    (RFID)   (205)
refresh rate   (210)
resolution   (210, 214)
roller ball   (201)
scanner   (203)
shared laser
    printer   (215)
soft copy   (210)
speakers   (217)
stylus   (202)
technical writer   (219)
telephony   (218)
thermal printer   (215)
thin film transistor (TFT)
    monitor   (211)
toggle key   (199)
touch pad   (201)
touch screen   (202)
trackball   (201)
traditional
    keyboard   (199)
Universal Product Code
    (UPC)   (205)
virtual keyboard   (199)
Voice over IP
    (VoIP)   (218)
voice recognition
    system   (207)
wand reader   (205)
WebCam   (206)
wheel button   (201)
wireless
    keyboard   (199)
wireless mouse   (201)

To test your knowledge of these key terms with animated flash cards, visit our Web site at www.computing2013.com and enter the keyword terms7.

MULTIPLE CHOICE

Circle the correct answer.

1. Most keyboards use an arrangement of keys known as:
   - **a.** Alpha
   - **b.** Daisy
   - **c.** OptiKey
   - **d.** QWERTY

2. The device that controls a pointer displayed on the monitor.
   - **a.** cord
   - **b.** mouse
   - **c.** printer
   - **d.** scanner

3. Also known as a roller ball, this device controls the pointer by rotating a ball with your thumb.
   - **a.** trackball
   - **b.** joystick
   - **c.** cordless mouse
   - **d.** stylus

4. The type of screen that can be touched with more than one finger and supports zooming in and out by pinching and stretching your fingers.
   - **a.** digital
   - **b.** dynamic
   - **c.** multitouch
   - **d.** OLED

5. Flatbed and document are types of:
   - **a.** headsets
   - **b.** HDTVs
   - **c.** monitors
   - **d.** scanners

6. Device used by banks to automatically read those unusual numbers on the bottom of checks and deposit slips.
   - **a.** MICR
   - **b.** FDIC
   - **c.** OMR
   - **d.** UPC

7. The most widely used audio-input device.
   - **a.** mouse
   - **b.** VR
   - **c.** microphone
   - **d.** TFT

8. The monitor feature that specifies how often a displayed image is updated.
   - **a.** aspect ratio
   - **b.** dot pitch
   - **c.** refresh rate
   - **d.** resolution rate

9. Handheld, book-sized devices that display text and graphics.
   - **a.** e-book readers
   - **b.** HDTV
   - **c.** lasers
   - **d.** whiteboards

10. This technology allows television stations to broadcast their programming directly to smartphones, computers, and digital media players.
    - **a.** CRT
    - **b.** HDTV
    - **c.** LED
    - **d.** Mobile DTV

For an interactive multiple-choice practice test, visit our Web site at www.computing2013.com and enter the keyword multiple7.

MATCHING

Match each numbered item with the most closely related lettered item. Write your answers in the spaces provided.

a. active-matrix

b. digital camera

c. dot pitch

d. MagicJack

e. mechanical

f. plotters

g. scanners

h. stylus

i. caps lock

j. UPC

_____ 1. Pressing this key turns this feature on or off.

_____ 2. This type of mouse has a ball on the bottom and is attached with a cord to the system unit.

_____ 3. A penlike device commonly used with tablet PCs and PDAs.

_____ 4. Bar code readers use either handheld wand readers or platform _____.

_____ 5. Bar code system used by many electronic cash registers.

_____ 6. Records images digitally on a disk or in its memory.

_____ 7. The distance between each pixel.

_____ 8. A type of monitor that activates each pixel independently.

_____ 9. Special-purpose printers for creating maps, images, and architectural and engineering drawings.

_____10. A type of Internet telephone service that requires a small adapter that connects directly to your computer's USB port.

For an interactive matching practice test, visit our Web site at www.computing2013 .com and enter the keyword matching7.

OPEN-ENDED

On a separate sheet of paper, respond to each question or statement.

1. Define input and input devices.

2. Describe the different types of keyboard, pointing, scanning, image capturing, and audio-input devices.

3. Define output and output devices.

4. Describe the featrues and different types of monitors and printers.

5. Describe audio and video devices including portable media devices and Mobile DTV.

6. What are combination input and output devices? Discuss some examples.

7. What are Internet telephones? List and discuss four Internet telephone service providers.

MAKING IT WORK FOR YOU

The following questions are designed to demonstrate ways that you can effectively use technology today.

1 WEBCAMS AND INSTANT MESSAGING

Do you enjoy chatting with friends? Are you working on a project and need to collaborate with others in your group? What if you could see and hear your group online? Perhaps instant messaging and WebCams are just what you're looking for. It's easy and free with an Internet connection and the right software. To learn more about WebCams and instant messaging, review Making IT Work for You: WebCams and Instant Messaging on pages 208 and 209. Then answer the following questions: (a) How do you add a new friend to Windows Live Messenger? (b) What hardware is necessary to videoconference with Windows Live Messenger? (c) Describe the steps for sharing a file using Windows Live Messenger. Be sure to include both the steps you take and those your friend must take to receive the file.

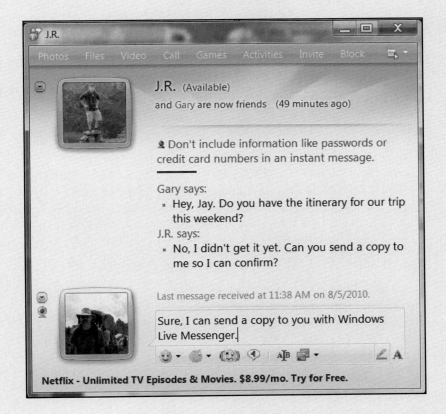

② E-BOOK READERS

Do you like to read? Wouldn't it be convenient to have access to thousands of books, magazines, and newspapers anytime you wanted? Perhaps an e-book reader is for you. They are easy to use. To learn more about e-book readers, review the Making IT Work for You: Using E-Book Readers on page 213. Then answer the following questions: (a) What is the Kindle Store? (b) How is the store accessed? (c) Have you ever used an e-book reader? If so, describe what reader you used and what you used it for. If you have not used an e-book reader, do you think that you ever would use one? Is so, please describe how you would likely use one. (d) Do you think e-book readers will be popular for years to come? Or do you think that tablet PCs like the iPad will replace them? Defend your answer.

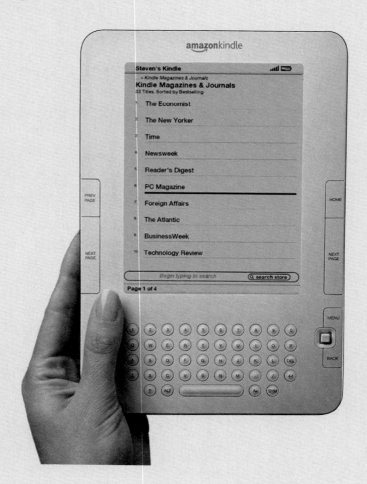

EXPLORATIONS

The following questions are designed to add depth and detail to your understanding of specific topics presented within this chapter. The questions direct you to sources other than the textbook to obtain this knowledge.

1 HOW DIGITAL CAMERAS WORK

While traditional cameras capture images on film, digital cameras capture images, then convert them into a digital form. These images can be viewed immediately and saved to a disk or into the camera's memory. To learn more about how digital cameras work, visit our Web site at www.computing2013.com and enter the keyword photo. Then answer the following questions: (a) What is a CCD and what is its function? (b) What is an ADC and what is its function? (c) How are images transported from a digital camera to a computer?

2 HOW INTERNET TELEPHONES WORK

Internet telephones offer a low-cost alternative to making long-distance calls. Using an Internet telephone (or other appropriate audio-input and audio-output devices), the Internet, a special service provider, a sound card, and special software, you can place long-distance calls to almost anywhere in the world. To learn more about how Internet telephony works, visit our Web site at www.computing2013.com and enter the keyword phone. Then answer the following questions: (a) What input and output devices are used? (b) What advantages and disadvantages would these devices have compared to traditional telephone? (c) If Chris were to place a call to Steve, would she incur traditional long-distance charges? Why or why not? (d) Create a drawing similar to the animation that would represent computer-to-computer telephony. Be sure to include and number the appropriate steps.

3 HANDWRITING RECOGNITION

Handwriting recognition is a developing technology for direct input. Conduct a Web search with the keywords "handwriting recognition" to learn more about this technology. Then answer the following questions: (a) What types of devices and applications use handwriting recognition now? (b) What are some applications where handwriting recognition is the best choice for input? Why is this the case? (c) What are current limitations of handwriting recognition?

ETHICS

The following questions are designed to explore ethical issues related to technology and to develop the ability to think critically and communicate effectively. Respond to the questions by either creating a one-page paper or preparing for an in-depth classroom discussion.

1 WEBCAMS

WebCams can be set up almost anywhere by anyone. Once in place, these WebCams can continuously broadcast images on the Internet. For example, many cities use WebCams to provide live traffic updates. (a) Do you think there are any ethical or privacy issues related to broadcasting these images? Some cities use WebCams to monitor traffic behavior and speed of individual cars and to record images of those individuals who are violating traffic laws. Traffic tickets are mailed to those violating the law. (b) Do you think that are any ethical or privacy issues related to capturing and using images in this way? Sometimes WebCams capture embarrassing or incriminating images of individuals without their knowledge. There are many instances where these images are broadcast over the Internet. (c) If you think that under certain circumstances that it is unethical to capture and distribute images of individuals, discuss those circumstances and create some general guidelines for capturing and using images of individuals. If you do not think capturing and distributing images of individuals is unethical under any circumstances, defend your position.

ENVIRONMENT

The following questions are designed to explore environmental issues related to technology and to develop the ability to think critically and communicate effectively. Respond to the questions by either creating a one-page paper or preparing for an in-depth classroom discussion.

1 PRINTING

Did you know that printing your e-mail instead of reading it on the screen contributes to global warming and clogs our landfills? (a) Do you think this is a serious problem? Why or why not? According to the EPA nearly 40 percent of the waste in American landfills is paper waste, much of it from business printing. (b) Identify several other specific computer-related situations leading to paper waste. (c) What can be done to avoid each of the situations identified in (b)? (d) Develop general guidelines to control paper waste in computer-related situations and in general.

2 PRINTER CARTRIDGES

Did you know that the ingredients in most printer cartridges contain hazardous chemicals? In fact, much of the production of new printer ink and toner has moved to third-world nations as a result of pollution concerns. One approach to minimizing the impact is to recycle printer cartridges. (a) Have you ever recycled printer cartridges? Why or why not? (b) Do you think there is an economical incentive to recycling printer cartridges? Why or why not? One manufacture is addressing the problem by developing a printer that replaces printer ink with coffee grounds to print text and images. (c) Do you think technological change like this will ultimately solve the hazardous chemical problem? Why or why not? (d) What can you do starting today to help?

Secondary Storage

▲ Download the free *Computing Essentials 2013* app for videos, key term flashcards, quizzes, and the game, *Over the Edge!*

Competencies

After you have read this chapter, you should be able to:

1 Distinguish between primary and secondary storage.

2 Discuss the important characteristics of secondary storage including media, capacity, storage devices, and access speed.

3 Describe hard-disk platters, tracks, sectors, and head crashes.

4 Compare internal and external hard drives.

5 Discuss performance enhancements including disk caching, RAIDs, file compression, and file decompression.

6 Define optical storage including compact, digital versatile, and high-definition discs.

7 Define solid-state storage including solid-state drives, flash memory, and USB drives.

8 Define cloud storage and cloud storage services.

9 Discuss mass storage devices, enterprise storage systems, and storage area networks.

Why should I read this chapter?

At one time, floppy disks were the only way to distribute software and the only way to share files between microcomputers. That was then and this is now. Now, we can store data and information using a variety of different types of media including hard disks, optical discs, and solid-state devices like flash memory and USB drives.

This chapter discusses a variety of different types of secondary storage including internal

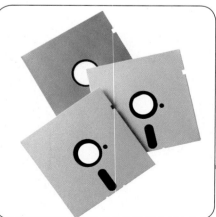

and external hard disks and a variety of optical discs including CDs, DVDs, and Blu-ray discs. Additionally, you'll learn about the advantages and disadvantages of cloud storage. Also, you'll learn about very large capacity storage devices including file servers, network application servers, and RAID systems. To be competent and to be competitive in today's professional workplace, you need to know and to understand these things.

chapter 8

Hi, I'm James, and I'm a software engineer. I'd like to talk with you about secondary storage, one of the most critical parts of any computer system. I'd also like to talk about cloud storage and solid-state storage used in portable media players, tablet PCs, and smartphones.

Introduction

Secondary storage devices are used to save, to back up, and even to transport files consisting of data or programs from one location or computer to another. At one time, almost all files contained only numbers and letters. The demands for saving these files were easily met with low-capacity storage devices.

Data storage has expanded from text and numeric files to include digital music files, photographic files, video files, and much more. These new types of files require secondary storage devices that have much greater capacity.

Secondary storage devices have always been an indispensable element in any computer system. They have similarities to output and input devices. Like output devices, secondary storage devices receive information from the system unit in the form of the machine language of 0s and 1s. Rather than translating the information, however, secondary storage devices save the information in machine language for later use. Like input devices, secondary storage devices send information to the system unit for processing. However, the information, since it is already in machine form, does not need to be translated. It is sent directly to memory (RAM), where it can be accessed and processed by the CPU.

Competent end users need to be aware of the different types of secondary storage. They need to know the capabilities, limitations, and uses of hard disks, solid-state drives, optical discs, cloud storage, and other types of secondary storage. Additionally, they need to be aware of specialty storage devices for portable computers and to be knowledgeable about how large organizations manage their extensive data resources.

Storage

An essential feature of every computer is the ability to save, or store, information. As discussed in Chapter 6, random-access memory (RAM) holds or stores data and programs that the CPU is presently processing. Before data can be processed or a program can be run, it must be in RAM. For this reason, RAM is sometimes referred to as **primary storage.**

Unfortunately, most RAM provides only temporary or volatile storage. That is, it loses all of its contents as soon as the computer is turned off. Its contents also are lost if there is a power failure that disrupts the electric current going into the system unit. This volatility results in a need for more permanent or nonvolatile storage for data and programs. We also need external storage because users need much more storage capacity than is typically available in a computer's primary or RAM memory.

Secondary storage provides permanent or nonvolatile storage. Using **secondary storage devices** such as a hard-disk drive, data and programs can be retained after the computer has been shut off. This is accomplished by *writing* files to and *reading* files from secondary storage devices. Writing is the process of saving information *to* the secondary storage device. Reading is the process of accessing information *from* secondary storage. This chapter focuses on secondary storage devices.

Some important characteristics of secondary storage include

- **Media** are the actual physical material that holds the data and programs. (See Figure 8-1.)
- **Capacity** measures how much a particular storage medium can hold.
- **Storage devices** are hardware that reads data and programs from storage media. Most also write to storage media.
- **Access speed** measures the amount of time required by the storage device to retrieve data and programs.

Most desktop microcomputer systems have hard-disk and optical disc drives, as well as ports where additional storage devices can be connected.

Hard Disks

Hard disks save files by altering the magnetic charges of the disk's surface to represent 1s and 0s. Hard disks retrieve data and programs by reading these charges from the magnetic disk. Characters are represented by positive (+) and negative (−) charges using the ASCII, EBCDIC, or Unicode binary codes. For example, the letter A would require a series of 8 charges. (See Figure 8-2.) **Density** refers to how tightly these charges can be packed next to one another on the disk.

Hard disks use rigid metallic **platters** that are stacked one on top of another. Hard disks store and organize files using tracks, sectors, and cylinders. **Tracks** are rings of concentric circles without visible grooves. Each track is divided into invisible wedge-shaped sections called **sectors.** (See Figure 8-3.) A **cylinder** runs through each track of a stack of platters. Cylinders are necessary to differentiate files stored on the same track and sector of different platters. When a hard disk is formatted, tracks, sectors, and cylinders are assigned.

Hard disks are sensitive instruments. Their read/write heads ride on a cushion of air about 0.000001 inch thick. It is so thin that a smoke particle, fingerprint, dust, or human hair could cause what is known as a head crash. (See Figure 8-4.)

Figure 8-1 Secondary storage media

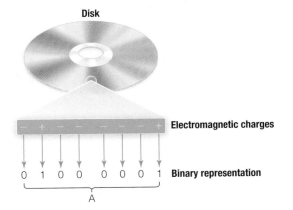

Figure 8-2 How charges on a disk surface store the letter A

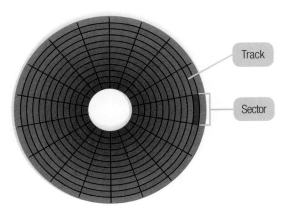

Figure 8-3 Tracks and sectors

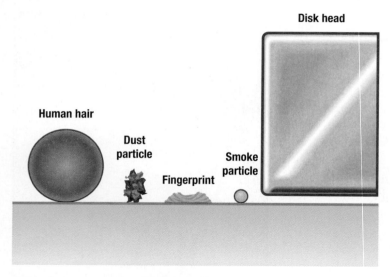

Disk head

Human hair

Dust particle

Fingerprint

Smoke particle

Figure 8-4 Materials that can cause a head crash

A **head crash** occurs when a read/write head makes contact with the hard disk's surface or with particles on its surface. A head crash is a disaster for a hard disk. The disk surface is scratched and some or all of the data is destroyed. At one time, head crashes were commonplace. Now, fortunately, they are rare.

There are two basic types of hard disks: internal and external.

Internal Hard Disk

An **internal hard disk** is located inside the system unit. These hard disks are able to store and retrieve large quantities of information quickly. They are used to store programs and data files. For example, nearly every microcomputer uses its internal hard disk to store its operating system and major applications such as Word and Excel.

To see how a hard disk works, visit our Web site at www.computing2013.com and enter the keyword **disk.**

To ensure adequate performance of your internal hard disk and the safety of your data, you should perform routine maintenance and periodically make backup copies of all important files. For hard-disk maintenance and backup procedures, refer to Chapter 5's coverage of the Windows utilities Backup and Restore, Disk Cleanup, and Disk Defragmenter.

External Hard Drives

While internal hard disks provide fast access, they have a fixed amount of storage and cannot be easily removed from the system cabinet. External hard disks typically connect to a USB or FireWire port on the system unit, are easily removed, and effectively provide an unlimited amount of storage. (See Figure 8-5.)

tips

Does your internal hard disk run a lot and seem slow? The problem could be with fragmented files—files that when saved were broken into pieces (fragments) and stored in different locations on your hard disk, which take longer for the hard disk to access. Defragging rearranges the file parts so they are stored in adjacent locations. To clean up the disk and speed up access times, consider defragmenting. If you are using Windows 7:

1 **Start Disk Defragmenter.** Type *defrag* into the Start menu search box and select *Disk Defragmenter* to open the Disk Defragmenter utility. Click *Defragment disk* to begin defragmenting your disk.

2 **Keep working.** You can continue running other applications while your disk is being defragmented. Unfortunately, your computer operates more slowly, and Disk Defragmenter takes longer to finish.

3 **Automate.** Windows 7 will defragment your disk for you automatically. Click *Configure schedule* in the Disk Defragmenter utility to set this to a time that is convenient for you.

To see additional tips, visit our Web site at www.computing2013.com and enter the keyword tips.

Figure 8-5 External hard drive

External hard drives use the same basic technology as internal hard disks and are used primarily to complement an internal hard disk. Because they are easily removed, they are particularly useful to protect or secure sensitive information. Other uses for external drives include backing up the contents of the internal hard disk and providing additional hard-disk capacity.

Performance Enhancements

Three ways to improve the performance of hard disks are disk caching, redundant arrays of inexpensive disks, and file compression/decompression.

Disk caching improves hard-disk performance by anticipating data needs. It performs a function similar to cache memory discussed in Chapter 6. While cache memory improves processing by acting as a temporary high-speed holding area between memory and the CPU, disk caching improves processing by acting as a temporary high-speed holding area between a secondary storage device and the CPU. Disk caching requires a combination of hardware and software. During idle processing time, frequently used data is automatically identified and read from the hard disk into memory (cache). When needed, the data is then accessed directly from memory. The transfer rate from memory is much faster than from the hard disk. As a result, overall system performance is often increased by as much as 30 percent.

Figure 8-6 RAID storage device

Redundant arrays of inexpensive disks (RAID) improve performance by expanding external storage, improving access speed, and providing reliable storage. Several inexpensive hard-disk drives are connected to one another. These connections can be by a network or within specialized RAID devices. (See Figure 8-6.) The connected hard-disk drives are related or grouped together, and the computer system interacts with the RAID system as though it were a single large-capacity hard-disk drive. The result is expanded storage capability, fast access speed, and high reliability. For these reasons, RAID is often used by Internet servers and large organizations.

File compression and **file decompression** increase storage capacity by reducing the amount of space required to store data and programs. File compression is not limited to hard-disk systems. It is frequently used to compress files on DVDs, CDs, and flash drives as well. File compression also helps to speed up transmission of files from one computer system to another. Sending and receiving compressed files across the Internet is a common activity.

File compression programs scan files for ways to reduce the amount of required storage. One way is to search for repeating patterns. The repeating patterns are replaced with a token, leaving enough tokens so that the original can be rebuilt or decompressed. These programs often shrink files to a quarter of their original size. To learn more about file compression, visit our Web site at www.computing2013.com and enter the keyword **compression.**

You can compress and decompress files using specialized utilities such as WinZip. Or, if a specialized utility is not available, you can use utility programs in Windows. For a summary of performance enhancement techniques, see Figure 8-7.

Explorations

A computer can be a library, a jukebox, even a home entertainment system, but to do any of these tasks requires large amounts of hard-disk space.

To learn more about the leaders in high-capacity hard disks, visit our Web site at www.computing2013.com and enter the keyword capacity.

Technique	Description
Disk caching	Uses cache and anticipates data needs
RAID	Linked, inexpensive hard-disk drives
File compression	Reduces file size
File decompression	Expands compressed files

Figure 8-7 Performance enhancement techniques

CONCEPT CHECK

Discuss four important characteristics of secondary storage.

What are the two types of hard disks? Briefly describe each.

What is density? What are tracks, sectors, cylinders, and head crashes?

List and describe three ways to improve the performance of hard disks.

Optical Discs

Today's **optical discs** can hold over 100 gigabytes of data. (See Figure 8-8.) That is the equivalent of millions of typewritten pages or a medium-sized library all on a single disc. Optical discs are having a great impact on storage today, but we are probably only beginning to see their effects.

In optical disc technology, a laser beam alters the surface of a plastic or metallic disc to represent data. Unlike hard disks, which use magnetic charges to represent 1s and 0s, optical discs use reflected light. The 1s and 0s are represented by flat areas called **lands** and bumpy areas called **pits** on the disc surface. The disc is read by an **optical disc drive** using a laser that projects a tiny beam of light on these areas. The amount of reflected light determines whether the area represents a 1 or a 0. To see how an optical disc drive works, visit our Web site at www.computing2013.com and enter the keyword **optical.**

Like hard disks, optical discs use tracks and sectors to organize and store files. Unlike the concentric tracks and wedge-shaped sectors used for hard disks, however, optical discs typically use a single track that spirals toward the center of the disc. This single track is divided into equally sized sectors.

The most widely used optical discs are CD, DVD, and Blu-ray discs.

Compact Disc

Compact disc, or as it is better known, **CD,** was the most widely used optical format. CD drives were standard on many microcomputer systems. Typically, CD drives can store from 650 MB (megabytes) to 1 GB (gigabyte) of data on one side of a CD.

There are three basic types of CDs: read only, write once, and rewritable:

- **Read only—CD-ROM,** which stands for **compact disc–read-only memory,** is similar to a commercial music CD. *Read only* means it cannot be written on or erased by the user. Thus, you as a user have access only to the data imprinted by the publisher. CD-ROMs are used to distribute large databases and references. They also are used to distribute large software application packages.

- **Write once—CD-R,** which stands for **CD-recordable,** can be written to once. After that they can be read many times without deterioration but cannot be written on or erased. CD-R drives often are used to archive data and to record music downloaded from the Internet.

- **Rewritable—CD-RW** stands for **compact disc rewritable.** Also known as **erasable optical discs,** these discs are very similar to CD-Rs except that the disc surface is not permanently altered when data is recorded. Because they can be changed, CD-RWs are often used to create and edit multimedia presentations.

Figure 8-8 Optical disc

Digital Versatile Disc

DVD stands for **digital versatile disc** or **digital video disc.** This disc has replaced CDs as the standard optical disc. DVDs are very similar to CDs except that more data can be packed into the same amount of space. (See Figure 8-9.) DVD discs can store 4.7 GB to 17 GB on a single DVD disc—17 times the capacity of CDs. There are three basic types of DVDs, similar to CDs: read only, write once, and rewritable.

Figure 8-9 **DVD disc drive**

- **Read only—DVD-ROM** stands for **digital versatile disc–read-only memory.** DVD-ROM drives are also known as **DVD players.** DVD-ROMs are having a major impact on the video market. While CD-ROMs are effective for distributing music, they can only contain just over an hour of fair-quality video. DVD-ROMs can provide over two hours of high-quality video and sound comparable to that found in motion picture theaters. The motion picture industry has rapidly shifted video distribution from video cassettes to DVD-ROMs.

- **Write once—DVD+R** and **DVD−R** are two competing write-once formats. Both stand for **DVD recordable.** Each has a slightly different way in which it formats its discs. Fortunately, most new DVD players can use either format. These drives are typically used to create permanent archives for large amounts of data and to record videos. DVD recordable drives are rapidly replacing CD-R drives due to their massive capacity.

- **Rewritable—DVD+RW, DVD−RW,** and **DVD-RAM** are the three most widely used formats. DVD+RW and DVD−RW stand for **DVD rewritable. DVD-RAM** stands for **DVD random-access memory.** Each format has a unique way of storing data. Unfortunately, older DVD players typically can read only one type of format. Newer DVD players, however, are able to read and use any of the formats. Rewritable DVD disc drives have rapidly replaced CD rewritable drives. Applications range from recording video from camcorders to developing multimedia presentations that include extensive graphics and video.

Blu-ray Disc

While CDs and DVDs represent the past and the present for optical disc storage, the future belongs to discs of even greater capacity. While DVD discs have sufficient capacity to record standard-definition movies and music, they are insufficient for recording high-definition video, which requires about four times as much storage. This next generation of optical disc is called **hi def (high definition),** with a far greater capacity than DVDs. The hi-def standard is **Blu-ray Disc (BD).** The name comes from the blue-colored laser that is used to read the disc.

Blu-ray Discs have a capacity of 25 to 128 gigabytes, more than 20 times the capacity of a standard single-layer DVD. Although Blu-ray media are the same size as other optical media, the discs require special drives. Most of these drives are capable of reading standard DVDs and CDs in addition to Blu-ray.

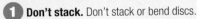

tips

Are you concerned about damaging your optical discs? Actually, they are quite durable, and taking care of them boils down to just a few basic rules.

1 **Don't stack.** Don't stack or bend discs.

2 **Don't touch.** Don't touch the recording surfaces. Hold only by their edges.

3 **Don't remove.** Never attempt to remove a disc when it is rotating and in use.

4 **Avoid extreme conditions.** Keep discs from extreme heat and direct sunlight.

5 **Use storage boxes or binders.** Store discs in plastic storage boxes or binders with plastic slips for discs.

Of course, the best protection is to make a backup or duplicate copy of your disc.

To see additional tips, visit our Web site at www.computing2013.com and enter the keyword tips.

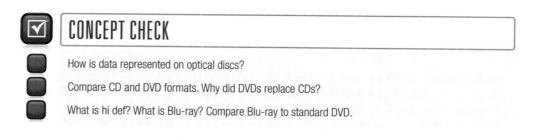

Format	Typical Capacity	Description
CD	650 MB to 1 GB	Once the standard optical disc
DVD	4.7 GB to 17 GB	Current standard
Blu-ray	25 GB to 128 GB	Hi-def format, large capacity

Figure 8-10 Types of optical discs

Like CDs and DVDs, Blu-ray has three basic types: read only, write once, and rewritable. As with any optical disc, a device with recording capabilities is required for writing data.

For a summary of the different types of optical discs, see Figure 8-10.

CONCEPT CHECK

How is data represented on optical discs?

Compare CD and DVD formats. Why did DVDs replace CDs?

What is hi def? What is Blu-ray? Compare Blu-ray to standard DVD.

Solid-State Storage

Unlike hard disks, which rotate and have read/write heads that move in and out, **solid-state storage** devices have no moving parts. Data and information are stored and retrieved electronically directly from these devices much as they would be from conventional computer memory.

Solid-State Drives

Solid-state drives (SSDs) are designed to be connected inside a microcomputer system the same way an internal hard disk would be but contain solid-state memory instead of magnetic disks to store data. (See Figure 8-11.) SSDs are faster and more durable than hard disks. SSDs also require less power, which can lead to increased battery life for laptops and mobile devices. SSDs are more expensive and generally have a lower capacity than hard disks, but this is changing as the popularity of SSDs continues to increase. SDDs are widely used for tablet PCs, such as the iPad.

Flash Memory

Flash memory cards are small solid-state storage devices widely used in portable devices such as mobile phones and GPS navigation systems. (See Figure 8-12.) Flash memory also is used in a variety of specialized input devices to capture and transfer data to desktop computers.

For example, flash memory is used to store images captured from digital cameras and then to transfer the images to desktop and other computers. Flash memory is used in digital media players like the iPod to store and play music and video files. To learn more about digital video players, see Making IT Work for You: iPods and Video from the Internet on page 34.

Figure 8-11 Solid-state drive

Figure 8-12 **Flash memory card**

Figure 8-13 **USB drive**

USB Drives

USB drives, or **flash drives,** are so compact that they can be transported on a key ring. (See Figure 8-13.) These drives conveniently connect directly to a computer's USB port to transfer files and can have capacities ranging from 1 GB to 256 GB, with a broad price range to match. Due to their convenient size and large capacities, USB drives have become a very popular option for transporting data and information between computers, specialty devices, and the Internet. To learn more about using flash drives to transport data, see Making IT Work for You: USB Storage Devices on page 254.

☑ CONCEPT CHECK

What is solid-state storage?

Compare solid-state technology to that used in hard disks.

What are solid-state storage devices?

What are flash memory cards? What are they used for?

What are USB drives? What are they used for?

Cloud Storage

Recently, many applications that would have required installation on your computer to run have moved to the Web. Numerous Web sites now exist to provide application services. As we have discussed, this is known as **cloud computing,** where the Internet acts as a "cloud" of servers that supply applications as a *service* rather than a *product*. Additionally, these servers provide **cloud storage,** also known as **online storage.**

If you have used Google Docs to create a word processing document or a spreadsheet, used Mint.com to manage your financial information, or stored

Making IT work for you

CLOUD STORAGE

Do you ever need to share large files with others? Perhaps you have found many video and other types of files can be too large to effectively send as an e-mail attachment. You could distribute large files on a CD or DVD, or by using an FTP site. A simpler alternative is to use a cloud storage service. Using a cloud storage service makes it easy to upload and share files with anyone quickly.

Create a Custom Address   The first step is to choose a custom URL where your files will be located and upload your files to that address. To do this using the sendspace file-sharing service:

1 ● **Visit http://www.sendspace.com**

   ● **Click the *Browse* button to locate the file to share.**

   ● **Optionally, enter the recipient's e-mail and your e-mail to automatically receive a message with your custom address.**

   ● **Click the *Upload* button to upload your selected file.**

   ● **After the file has finished uploading, you will be given a custom address for it.**

242

Sharing Your Address Once your files are uploaded, you can share your custom address with anyone you want to have access to your files, just as you would share any other link. For example, you might choose to send your address to others using e-mail.

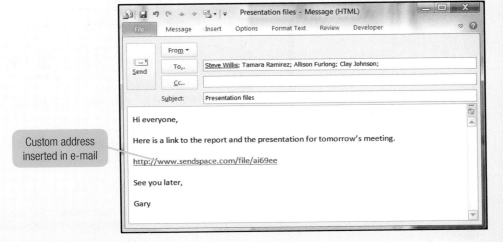

Custom address inserted in e-mail

Updating Your Files You can visit the site at any time from a Web browser to add, delete, or update files. For example, to add additional files:

1 ● **Visit the site in any Web browser (*http://www. sendspace.com/*).**

 ● **Click the *Signup* link and register the account to your e-mail address.**

 ● **Click the *My Files* link to select files to share or delete.**

My Files link

Shared Files

Note you may also choose to copy and paste the HTML link provided for your file if you would like to share it via a personal Web site, blog, or social networking site. File sharing services are continually changing and some of the specifics presented in this Making IT Work for You may have changed.

To learn about other ways to make information technology work for you, visit our Web site at www.computing2013.com and enter the keyword miw.

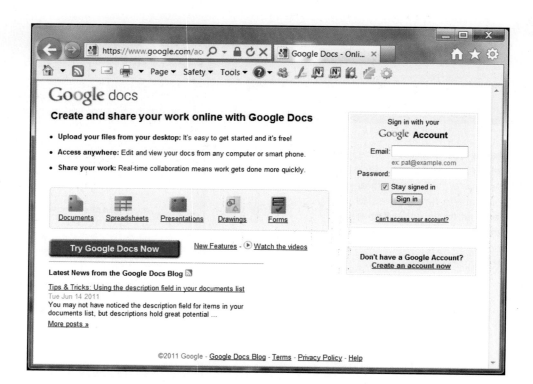

Figure 8-14 Google Docs

Focus	Company	Location
Individual	Dropbox	www.dropbox.com
Individual	iBackup	www.ibackup.com
Individual	Microsoft	www.skydrive.com
Business	Amerivault	www.amerivault.com
Business	Box.net	www.box.net
Business	Mozy	www.mozy.com

Figure 8-15 Cloud storage services

data using Amazon S3, you have already used cloud computing. (See Figure 8-14.) The processing power of the service provider's server is used to run the applications, and your local computer is responsible only for displaying the results. The applications and data can be accessed from any Internet-ready device. This means that even devices with little storage, memory, or processing power, such as mobile phones, can run the same powerful applications as a desktop computer.

The benefits to this arrangement are numerous. Imagine how much easier it would be to install or upgrade software in a large company. In the past, a software technician would need to visit every computer the company owned to install the software from disk and manage licensing for the number of computers the software was purchased for. With software delivered from the cloud as a service, the company can simply purchase the appropriate number of accounts from the service provider and direct employees to use the provider's Web site.

There are numerous Web sites that provide cloud storage services. (See Figure 8-15.) To learn more about how you could use cloud storage, see Making IT Work for You: Cloud Storage on pages 242 and 243.

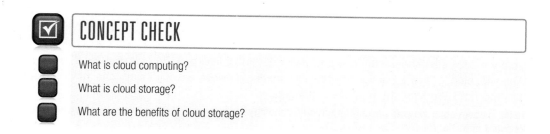

CONCEPT CHECK

What is cloud computing?

What is cloud storage?

What are the benefits of cloud storage?

Mass Storage Devices

It is natural to think of secondary storage media and devices as they relate to us as individuals. It may not be as obvious how important these matters are to organizations. **Mass storage** refers to the tremendous amount of secondary storage required by large organizations. **Mass storage devices** are specialized high-capacity secondary storage devices designed to meet organizational demands for data.

Enterprise Storage System

Most large organizations have established a strategy called an **enterprise storage system** to promote efficient and safe use of data across the networks within their organizations. (See Figure 8-16.) Some of the mass storage devices that support this strategy are

- **File servers**—dedicated computers with very large storage capacities that provide users access to fast storage and retrieval of data.
- **Network attached storage (NAS)**—similar to a file server except simpler and less expensive; widely used for home and small business storage needs.

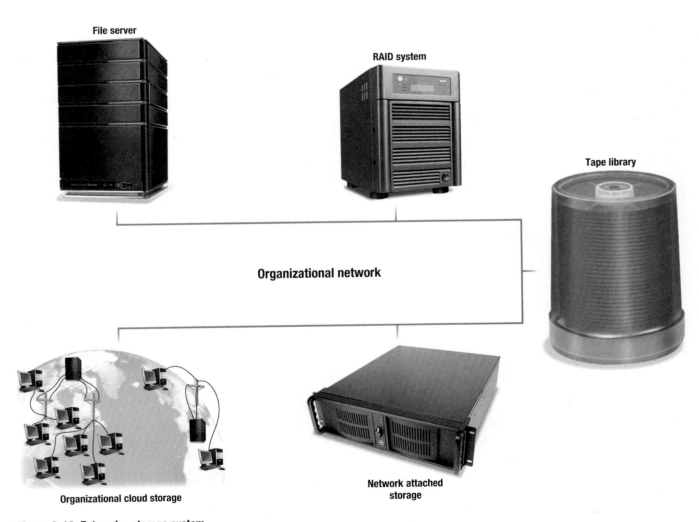

Figure 8-16 Enterprise storage system

- **RAID systems**—larger versions of the specialized devices discussed earlier in this chapter that enhance organizational security by constantly making backup copies of files moving across the organization's networks.
- **Tape library**—device that provides automatic access to data archived on a library of tapes.
- **Organizational cloud storage**—high-speed Internet connection to a dedicated remote organizational cloud storage server.

Storage Area Network

A recent mass storage development is **storage area network (SAN)** systems. SAN is an architecture to link remote computer storage devices, such as enterprise storage systems, to computers such that the devices are as available as locally attached drives. In a SAN system, the user's computer provides the file system for storing data, but the SAN provides the disk space for data.

The key to a SAN is a high-speed network, connecting individual computers to mass storage devices. Special file systems prevent simultaneous users from interfering with each other. SANs provide the ability to house data in remote locations and still allow efficient and secure access.

CONCEPT CHECK

Define mass storage and list five mass storage devices.

What is an enterprise storage system?

What is a storage area network system?

Now that you've learned about secondary storage, let me tell you a little bit about my career as a software engineer.

Careers in IT

Software engineers analyze users' needs and create application software. Software engineers typically have experience in programming but focus on the design and development of programs using the principles of mathematics and engineering.

A bachelor's or an advanced specialized associate's degree in computer science or information systems and an extensive knowledge of computers and technology are required by most employers. Internships may provide students with the kinds of experience employers look for in a software engineer. Those with specific experience with networking, the Internet, and Web applications may have an advantage over other applicants. Employers typically look for software engineers with good communication and analytical skills.

Software engineers can expect to earn an annual salary in the range of $63,000 to $98,500. Advancement opportunities are usually tied to experience. Experienced software engineers may be promoted to project manager or have opportunities in systems design. To learn about other careers in information technology, visit us at www.computing2013.com and enter the keyword **careers**.

A LOOK TO THE FUTURE

Your Entire Life Recorded on a Single Disk

Imagine if you could store every conversation you ever had on a single disk. What if you could capture your entire life on video stored on just a few discs? What if you could hold in your pocket the contents of the Library of Congress? Innovations in secondary storage capacity using molecular storage promise all of this and more.

Currently, information is stored on magnetic or optical discs. In the future, the electron state of atoms in a molecule will hold information at a much greater density. Currently, experiments have yielded densities of 200 gigabytes per square inch. If successfully brought to market, such a product would yield two terabytes on one disk, enough to hold every conversation a person has throughout his or her entire lifetime. Experiments with three-dimensional storing (where information is stored in height as well as area) and optical holography (where

information is stored by light photons on specially treated crystals) promise to yield even greater storage in smaller packages.

The capability to store vast amounts of data offers a future both tantalizing and problematic. Although having a video of your life would be a wonderful memory tool, how could you sort and use so much information? Imagine having to search through hours of video just to verify the time of a lunch date or to remember where you parked your car. Fortunately, computer scientists are developing computer programs that can rapidly sort through and understand audio and visual material. Great strides have been made in creating programs that can scan photos and videos searching for a particular person's face. This technology is currently being used in airports to identify suspected terrorists. In the future, you may use this technology to search for photos of a loved one or video of the family vacation.

Is there a downside to recording every event in a person's life? Could your personal video log be used to incriminate you in a court of law? Could someone else's video log be an invasion of your right to privacy? The technology will soon be here. Are you ready for it? Would you use it to record your every move?

STORAGE

RAM is **primary storage**. Most RAM is volatile, meaning that it loses its contents whenever power is disrupted. **Secondary storage** provides nonvolatile storage. Secondary storage retains data and information after the computer system is turned off.

Writing is the process of saving information to **secondary storage devices**. Reading is the process of accessing information from secondary storage devices.

Important characteristics of secondary storage include

- **Media**—actual physical material that retains data and programs.
- **Capacity**—how much a particular storage medium can hold.
- **Storage devices**—hardware that reads and writes to storage media.
- **Access speed**—time required to retrieve data from a secondary storage device.

HARD DISKS

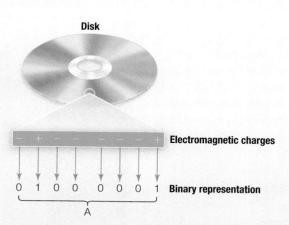

Hard disks use rigid metallic **platters** that provide a large amount of capacity. They store data and programs by altering the electromagnetic charges on the platter's surface. Files are organized according to

- **Tracks**—concentric rings without visible grooves.
- **Sectors**—wedge-shaped sections.
- **Cylinders**—run through each track of a stack of platters.

Density refers to how tightly electromagnetic charges can be packed next to one another on the disk.

A **head crash** occurs when the hard disk makes contact with the drive's read/write heads.

Two types of hard disks are internal and external hard disks.

Internal Hard Disk
Internal hard disks are located within the system unit. Used to store programs and data files.

External Hard Drives
Unlike internal hard disks, **external hard drives** are removable. External drives use the same basic technology as internal disks.

To be a competent end user, you need to be aware of the different types of secondary storage. You need to know their capabilities, limitations, and uses. There are three widely used storage media: hard disk, optical disc, and solid-state storage.

HARD DISKS

Performance Enhancements

Three ways to improve hard-disk performance are disk caching, RAID, and file compression and decompression.

- **Disk caching**—provides a temporary high-speed holding area between a secondary storage device and the CPU; improves performance by anticipating data needs and reducing time to access data from secondary storage.
- **RAID (redundant array of inexpensive disks)**—several inexpensive hard-disk drives are connected together; improves performance by providing expanded storage, fast access, and high reliability.
- **File compression** and **decompression**—files compressed before storing and then decompressed before being used again; improves performance through efficient storage.

OPTICAL DISCS

Optical discs use laser technology. 1s and 0s are represented by **pits** and **lands**. Optical disc drives project light and measure the reflected light.

Compact Disc

Compact discs (CDs) have typical capacity of 650 MB to 1 GB. Three types are **CD-ROM (compact disc–read-only memory)**, **CD-R (CD-recordable;** CD-R drives are also known as CD burners), and **CD-RW (compact disc rewritable, erasable optical discs).**

Digital Versatile Disc

DVDs (digital versatile discs, digital video discs) have far greater capacity than CDs (4.7 GB to 17 GB). Three types are **DVD-ROM (digital versatile disc–read-only memory; DVD players** are drives), write once **(DVD+R, DVD−R)**, and rewritable **(DVD+RW, DVD−RW, DVD−RAM)**.

Blu-ray Disc

Hi-def (high-definition) Blu-ray Discs are the next standard optical disc. **Blu-ray Discs (BDs)** have a capacity of 25 GB to 128 GB. Same size as other optical media, but much greater capacity and requires special drives. Three basic types: read only, write once, and rewritable.

SOLID-STATE STORAGE

Solid-state storage devices have no moving parts and are more reliable and require less power than hard disks.

Solid-State Drives

Solid-state drives are similar to internal hard-disk drives except they use solid-state memory; are faster, more durable, and more expensive; and generally provide less capacity.

Flash Memory

Flash memory cards are small solid-state storage devices that are widely used with notebook computers. They are used with a variety of specialized input devices including digital cameras to store and transfer images and digital media players like the iPod to store and transfer music and video files.

USB Drives

USB drives (flash drives) are so small that they fit onto a key ring. These drives connect to a computer's USB port and are widely used to transfer data and information between computers, specialty devices, and the Internet.

CLOUD STORAGE

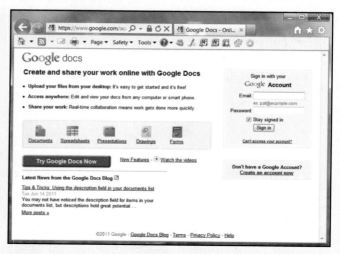

With **cloud computing**, the Internet acts as a "cloud" of servers that supply applications as a service rather than a product. **Cloud storage (online storage)** is supplied by servers.

- Examples include Google Docs for word processing and spreadsheets, Mint.com for financial management, and Amazon S3 for storing data.
- Cloud servers provide storage, processing, and memory.
- With cloud computing software installation and upgrade are avoided.

MASS STORAGE DEVICES

Mass storage refers to the tremendous amount of secondary storage required by large organizations. **Mass storage devices** are specialized high-capacity secondary storage devices.

Most large organizations have established a strategy called an **enterprise storage system** to promote efficient and safe use of data across the networks within their organizations.

Mass storage devices that support this strategy are **file servers, network attached storage (NAS), RAID systems, tape libraries,** and **organizational cloud storage.** A **storage area network (SAN)** is a method of using enterprise-level remote storage systems as if they were local to your computer.

CAREERS IN IT

Software engineers analyze users' needs and create application software. Bachelor's or advanced specialized accociate's degree in computer science or information systems and extensive knowledge of computers and technology required. Salary range is $63,000 to $98,500.

KEY TERMS

access speed (235)
Blu-ray Disc (BD) (239)
capacity (235)
CD (compact disc) (238)
CD-R (CD-recordable) (238)
CD-ROM (compact disc–read-only
   memory) (238)
CD-RW (compact disc
   rewritable) (238)
cloud computing (241)
cloud storage (241)
cylinder (235)
density (235)
disk caching (237)
DVD (digital versatile disc or digital
   video disc) (239)
DVD player (239)
DVD−R (DVD recordable) (239)
DVD+R (DVD recordable) (239)
DVD-RAM (DVD random-access
   memory) (239)
DVD-ROM (DVD–read-only
   memory) (239)
DVD−RW (DVD rewritable) (239)
DVD+RW (DVD rewritable) (239)
enterprise storage system (245)
erasable optical disc (238)
external hard drive (237)
file compression (237)
file decompression (237)
file server (245)

flash drive (241)
flash memory card (240)
hard disk (235)
head crash (236)
hi def (high definition) (239)
internal hard disk (236)
land (238)
mass storage (245)
mass storage devices (245)
media (235)
network attached storage (NAS) (245)
online storage (241)
optical disc (238)
organizational cloud storage (246)
pit (238)
platter (235)
primary storage (234)
RAID system (246)
redundant array of inexpensive disks
   (RAID) (237)
secondary storage (234)
secondary storage device (234)
sector (235)
software engineer (246)
solid-state drive (SSD) (240)
solid-state storage (240)
storage area network (SAN) (246)
storage device (235)
tape library (246)
track (235)
USB drive (241)

To test your knowledge of these key terms with animated flash cards, visit our Web
site at www.computing2013.com and enter the keyword terms8.

MULTIPLE CHOICE

Circle the letter of the correct answer.

1. RAM is sometimes referred to as:
   a. primary storage
   b. ratio active memory
   c. read-only memory
   d. secondary storage

2. The actual physical material that holds the data and programs.
   a. primary storage
   b. media
   c. capacity
   d. access

3. Measures how tightly the magnetic charges can be packed next to one another on the disk.
   a. density
   b. cylinders
   c. tracks
   d. sectors

4. When a read/write head makes contact with the hard disk's surface, it causes a head:
   a. crash
   b. land
   c. pit
   d. scratch

5. This hard-disk performance enhancement anticipates data needs.
   a. disk caching
   b. file compression
   c. file decompression
   d. RAID

6. This type of storage uses pits and lands to represent 1s and 0s.
   a. cloud
   b. hard disk
   c. optical
   d. solid state

7. DVD stands for:
   a. digital versatile disc
   b. digital video data
   c. dynamic versatile disc
   d. dynamic video disc

8. USB drives are also known as:
   a. flash drives
   b. optical drives
   c. ports
   d. universal state bus

9. An organizational strategy to promote efficient and safe use of data across the networks.
   a. cloud dynamic
   b. data mission statement
   c. enterprise storage system
   d. RAID

10. A mass storage device that provides access to data archived on tapes.
    a. file system
    b. NAS
    c. RAID system
    d. tape library

For an interactive multiple-choice practice test, visit our Web site at www.computing2013.com and enter the keyword multiple8.

MATCHING

Match each numbered item with the most closely related lettered item. Write your answers in the spaces provided.

a. CD-R
b. file compression
c. formats
d. network attached storage
e. secondary storage
f. sectors
g. solid-state drives
h. storage area network
i. storage devices
j. tracks

_____ 1. Provides permanent or nonvolatile storage.

_____ 2. Hardware that reads data and programs from storage media.

_____ 3. Rings of concentric circles without visible grooves on a hard-disk platter.

_____ 4. Each track is divided into invisible wedge-shaped sections called:

_____ 5. Increases storage capacity by reducing the amount of space required to store data and programs.

_____ 6. Discs that can be written only one time.

_____ 7. DVD+R and DVD–R are two competing write-once_____

_____ 8. Designed to be connected inside a microcomputer system the same way an internal hard disk would be but contains solid-state memory instead of magnetic disks to store data.

_____ 9. Mass storage device that is similar to a file server and widely used for home and small business storage.

_____10. An architecture to link remote computer storage devices, such as enterprise storage systems, to computers such that the devices are as available as locally attached drives.

For an interactive matching practice test, visit our Web site at www.computing2013 .com and enter the keyword matching8.

OPEN-ENDED

On a separate sheet of paper, respond to each question or statement.

1. Compare primary storage and secondary storage, and discuss the most important characteristics of secondary storage.

2. Discuss hard disks including density, platters, tracks, sectors, cylinders, head crashes, internal, external, and performance enhancements.

3. Discuss optical discs including pits, lands, CDs, DVDs, Blu-ray, and hi def.

4. Discuss solid-state storage including solid-state drives, flash memory, and USB drives.

5. Discuss cloud computing and cloud storage.

6. Describe mass storage devices including enterprise storage systems, file servers, network attached storage, RAID systems, tape libraries, organizational cloud storage, and storage area network systems.

MAKING IT WORK FOR YOU

The following questions are designed to demonstrate ways that you can effectively use technology today.

① CLOUD STORAGE

Do you ever need to share large files with others? Perhaps you have found that many video and other types of files can be too large to effectively send as an e-mail attachment. To learn how to share large files using cloud storage, review Making IT Work for You: Cloud Storage on pages 242 and 243. Then respond to the following: (a) Describe how the sendspace file-sharing service works. (b) What is a custom address and how is it used? (c) Describe how and why you might use cloud storage.

② USB STORAGE DEVICES

Do you need to carry more data than will fit on a single floppy disk or CD? A USB storage device might be for you. These devices store large amounts of data in a package small enough to travel with your car keys. Connect to our Web site at www.computing2013.com and enter the keyword keychain to link to a site that features USB storage devices. Explore the site and then answer the following questions: (a) What type of secondary storage do USB storage devices use? (b) How is data transferred to and from computer systems? (c) What system software are the USB storage devices compatible with? (d) What are typical capacities of the USB storage devices?

EXPLORATIONS

The following questions are designed to add depth and detail to your understanding of specific topics presented within this chapter. The questions direct you to sources other than the textbook to obtain this knowledge.

1 IPOD

Apple's iPod is a personal portable music player that stores a large number of digital music files. Connect to our Web site at www.computing2013.com and enter the keyword ipod to link to the iPod Web site. Once connected, read about the features and capabilities of iPod, and then answer the following questions: (a) How are music files transferred to iPod? (b) What type of secondary storage does iPod use? (c) What is iPod's storage capacity?

2 FILE COMPRESSION

A common problem for computer users is that they run out of hard-disk space. File compression software can open up space on a full hard drive, improve system performance, and make files easier to find and organize. To learn more about file compression, visit our Web site at www.computing2013.com and enter the keyword compression. Then answer the following questions: (a) What are the two types of file compression? How do they differ? (b) What type of file compression is used for home movies? Why? (c) What type of file compression is used for a résumé? Why? (d) Research a compression/decompression utility on the Web. What types of files does your utility create? Is this a lossy or lossyless file compression?

3 CLOUD STORAGE SERVICES

Cloud storage services offer remote file storage or backup. Research a cloud storage service on the Web and then answer the following questions: (a) What cloud storage service did you research? (b) What is the cost for using the service, and what features do you get for that price? (c) How are files accessed from and uploaded to the service? (d) What assurances does the service provider offer concerning availability of your data? What about security?

ETHICS

The following questions are designed to explore ethical issues related to technology and to develop the ability to think critically and communicate effectively. Respond to the questions by either creating a one-page paper or preparing for an in-depth classroom discussion.

1 CD-R AND MUSIC FILES

Creating a custom CD of your favorite music is a popular use of secondary storage. Many sites on the Web offer free music that you can download. However, not all music files that are available on the Internet are freely distributable. Review the Ethics box on page 238 and then respond to the following: (a) Is it fair to make a copy on your computer of a CD you have purchased? (b) Would it be fair to give a burned copy of a CD to a friend? What if the friend would not have otherwise purchased that CD? (c) Why is using the Internet to make and distribute copies of music receiving so much attention?

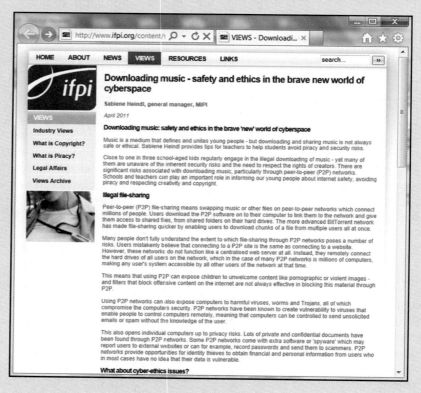

ENVIRONMENT

The following questions is designed to explore environmental issues related to technology and to develop the ability to think critically and communicate effectively. Respond to the questions by either creating a one-page paper or preparing for an in-depth classroom discussion.

1 SOLID-STATE STORAGE

Did you know that hard-disk storage requires more energy than solid-state storage? Unlike solid-state storage, which has no moving parts, hard disks have to be rotating in order to save or to retrieve data. Review the Environment box on page 241 and then respond to the following: (a) Why do you suppose that less energy is required for solid-state drives? (b) Why are not all hard drives being replaced? (c) Do you think hard drives will become obsolete in the near future? Why or why not? (d) Would you be willing to pay more for a solid-state hard drive? If so, how much? If not, why not?

Communications and Networks

▲ Download the free *Computing Essentials 2013* app for videos, key term flashcards, quizzes, and the game, *Over the Edge!*

Competencies

After you have read this chapter, you should be able to:

1 Discuss connectivity, the wireless revolution, and communication systems.

2 Describe physical and wireless communications channels.

3 Discuss connection devices and services including dial-up, DSL, cable, satellite, and cellular.

4 Describe data transmission factors, including bandwidth and protocols.

5 Discuss networks and key network terminology including network interface cards and network operating systems.

6 Describe different types of networks, including local, home, wireless, personal, metropolitan, and wide area networks.

7 Describe network architectures, including topologies and strategies.

8 Discuss the organization issues related to Internet technologies and network security.

Why should I read this chapter?

At one time, the wiring for computers was incredibly complicated with wires seemingly going everywhere. That was then and this is now. Do you know what is driving today's mobile computing? The iPhone, iPad, and other mobile computing devices use today's communication and network technologies. Specifically, it is the wireless revolution that is driving mobile computing.

This chapter discusses the wireless revolution, wireless connections including Wi-Fi, Bluetooth, and satellite connections. You'll also learn about hotspots, GPS, 4G networks, and protocols or rules that control the Internet. Additionally, you'll learn about home wireless networks and about firewalls to protect the privacy and security of networks. To be competent and to be competitive in today's professional workplace, you need to know and to understand these things.

chapter 9

Introduction

Hi, I'm Michael, and I'm a network administrator. I'd like to talk with you about computer communications and networks. I'd also like to talk about technologies that support mobile computing including global positioning systems, Wi-Fi, and 3G and 4G networks.

We live in a truly connected society. We can communicate almost instantaneously with others worldwide; changing events from the smallest of countries and places are immediately broadcast to the world; our e-mail messages are delivered to handheld devices; cars access the Internet to provide driving instructions and solve mechanical problems. Even household appliances can connect to the Internet and be remotely controlled. The communications and information options we have at our fingertips have changed how we react and relate to the world around us.

As the power and flexibility of our communication systems have expanded, the sophistication of the networks that support these systems has become increasingly critical and complex. The network technologies that handle our cellular, business, and Internet communications come in many different forms. Satellites, broadcast towers, telephone lines, even buried cables and fiber optics carry our telephone messages, e-mail, and text messages. These different networks must be able to efficiently and effectively integrate with one another.

Competent end users need to understand the concept of connectivity, wireless networking, and the elements that make up network and communications systems. Additionally, they need to understand the basics of communications channels, connection devices, data transmission, network types, network architectures, and organizational networks.

Communications

Computer communications is the process of sharing data, programs, and information between two or more computers. We have discussed numerous applications that depend on communication systems, including

- **E-mail**—provides a fast, efficient alternative to traditional mail by sending and receiving electronic documents.
- **Instant messaging**—supports direct, "live" electronic communication between two or more friends or buddies.
- **Internet telephone**—provides a very low-cost alternative to long-distance telephone calls using electronic voice and video delivery.
- **Electronic commerce**—buying and selling goods electronically.

In this chapter, we will focus on the communication systems that support these and many other applications. Connectivity, the wireless revolution, and communication systems are key concepts and technologies for the 21st century.

Connectivity

Connectivity is a concept related to using computer networks to link people and resources. For example, connectivity means that you can connect your microcomputer to other computers and information sources almost anywhere. With this connection, you are linked to the world of larger computers and the Internet. This includes hundreds of thousands of Web servers and their extensive information resources. Thus, becoming computer competent and knowledgeable becomes a matter of knowing not only about connectivity through networks to microcomputers, but also about larger computer systems and their information resources.

The Wireless Revolution

The single most dramatic change in connectivity and communications in the past few years has been the widespread use of mobile devices like smartphones and tablet PCs with wireless Internet connectivity. Students, parents, teachers, businesspeople, and others routinely talk and communicate with these devices. It is estimated that over 1.5 billion smartphones are in use worldwide. This wireless technology allows individuals to stay connected with one another from almost anywhere at any time.

Figure 9-1 Wireless revolution

So what's the revolution? While wireless technology was originally used primarily for voice communications, today's mobile computers support e-mail, Web access, and a variety of Internet applications. In addition, wireless technology allows a wide variety of nearby devices to communicate with one another without any physical connection. You can share a high-speed printer, share data files, and collaborate on working documents with a nearby co-worker without having your computers connected by cables or telephone—wireless communication. High-speed Internet wireless technology allows individuals to connect to the Internet and share information from almost anywhere in the world. (See Figure 9-1.) But is it a revolution? Most experts say yes and that the revolution is just beginning.

Communication Systems

Communication systems are electronic systems that transmit data from one location to another. Whether wired or wireless, every communication system has four basic elements. (See Figure 9-2.)

- **Sending and receiving devices.** These are often a computer or specialized communication device. They originate (send) as well as accept (receive) messages in the form of data, information, and/or instructions.
- **Communication channel.** This is the actual connecting or transmission medium that carries the message. This medium can be a physical wire or cable, or it can be wireless.

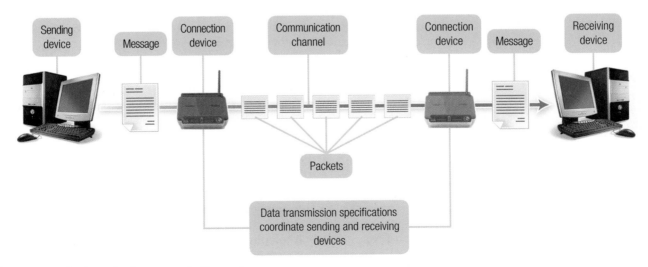

Figure 9-2 Basic elements of a communication system

- **Connection devices.** These devices act as an interface between the sending and receiving devices and the communication channel. They convert outgoing messages into packets that can travel across the communication channel. They also reverse the process for incoming messages.

- **Data transmission specifications.** These are rules and procedures that coordinate the sending and receiving devices by precisely defining how the message will be sent across the communication channel.

For example, if you wanted to send an e-mail to a friend, you could create and send the message using your computer, the *sending device.* Your modem, a *connection device,* would modify and format the message so that it could travel efficiently across *communication channels,* such as telephone lines. The specifics describing how the message is modified, reformatted, and sent would be described in the *data transmission specifications.* After your message traveled across the channel, the receiver's modem, a connection device, would reform it so that it could be displayed on your friend's computer, the *receiving device.* (Note: This example presents the basic communication system elements involved in sending e-mail. It does not and is not intended to demonstrate all the specific steps and equipment involved in an e-mail delivery system.)

CONCEPT CHECK

 Define computer communications and connectivity.

 What is the wireless revolution?

Describe the four elements of every communication system.

Communication Channels

Communication channels are an essential element of every communication system. These channels actually carry the data from one computer to another. There are two categories of communication channels. One category connects sending and receiving devices by providing a physical connection, such as a wire or cable. The other category is wireless.

Physical Connections

Physical connections use a solid medium to connect sending and receiving devices. These connections include telephone lines (twisted pair), coaxial cable, and fiber-optic cable.

- **Twisted-pair cable** consists of pairs of copper wire that are twisted together. Both standard **telephone lines** and **Ethernet cables** use twisted pair. (See Figure 9-3.) Ethernet cables are often used in networks and to connect a variety of components to the system unit.

- **Coaxial cable,** a high-frequency transmission cable, replaces the multiple wires of telephone lines with a single solid-copper core. (See Figure 9-4.) In terms of the number of telephone connections, a coaxial cable has over 80 times the transmission capacity of twisted pair. Coaxial cable is used to deliver television signals as well as to connect computers in a network.

Figure 9-3 Twisted-pair cable

Figure 9-4 Coaxial cable

- **Fiber-optic cable** transmits data as pulses of light through tiny tubes of glass. (See Figure 9-5.) In terms of the number of telephone connections, fiber-optic cable has over 26,000 times the transmission capacity of twisted-pair cable. Compared to coaxial cable, it is lighter, faster, and more reliable at transmitting data. Fiber-optic cable is rapidly replacing twisted-pair cable telephone lines.

Figure 9-5 Fiber-optic cable

Wireless Connections

Wireless connections do not use a solid substance to connect sending and receiving devices. Rather, they move data through the air. Primary technologies used for wireless connections are radio frequency, microwave, satellite, and infrared.

- **Radio frequency (RF)** uses radio signals to communicate between wireless devices. For example, smartphones and many Internet-enabled devices use RF to place telephone calls and/or to connect to the Internet. Most home or business wireless networks are based on a technology called **Wi-Fi (wireless fidelity)** to communicate over short distances. A number of standards for Wi-Fi exist, and each can send and receive data at a different speed. (See Figure 9-6.) **Bluetooth** is a short-range radio communication standard that transmits data over short distances of up to approximately 33 feet. Bluetooth is widely used for wireless headsets, printer connections, and hand-held devices. The range of Wi-Fi networks is being extended over greater distances using a new technology known as **WiMax (Worldwide Interoperability for Microwave Access).** WiMax is commonly used by universities and others to extend the capability of existing Wi-Fi networks.

Standard	Maximum speed
802.11b	11 Mbps
802.11a	54 Mbps
802.11g	54 Mbps
802.11n	600 Mbps

Figure 9-6 Wi-Fi standards

- **Microwave** communication uses high-frequency radio waves. Like infrared, microwave communication provides line-of-sight communication because microwaves travel in a straight line. Because the waves cannot bend with the curvature of the earth, they can be transmitted only over relatively short distances. Thus, microwave is a good medium for sending data between buildings in a city or on a large college campus. For longer distances, the waves must be relayed by means of microwave stations with microwave dishes or antennas. (See Figure 9-7.)

Figure 9-7 Microwave dish

- **Satellite** communication uses satellites orbiting about 22,000 miles above the earth as microwave relay stations. Many of these are offered by Intelsat, the International Telecommunications Satellite Consortium, which is owned by 114 governments and forms a worldwide communication system. Satellites rotate at a precise point and speed above the earth. They can amplify and relay microwave signals from one transmitter on the ground to another. Satellites can be used to send and receive large volumes of data. Uplink is a term relating to sending data to a satellite. Downlink refers to receiving data from a satellite. The major drawback to satellite communication is that bad weather can sometimes interrupt the flow of data.

One of the most interesting applications of satellite communications is for global positioning. A network of satellites owned and managed by the Department of Defense continuously sends location information to earth. **Global positioning system (GPS)** devices use that information to uniquely determine the geographical location of the device. Available

environment

Did you know that GPS devices in cars might help protect the environment? GPS devices are now common in many cars and they can help save fuel by providing drivers with the shortest route to a destination. But newer devices also provide traffic avoidance data, which can really save on carbon emissions. Cars trapped idling in traffic get zero miles to the gallon and pollution from gridlock can affect the air quality for miles around freeways. Networked GPS devices now make it possible to find the cheapest fuel and maximize your fuel economy with the most direct route and least congestion. For additional discussion of this issue, see GPS on page 290. To see more environmental facts, visit our Web site at www. computing2013.com and enter the keyword environment.

Figure 9-8 GPS navigation

in many automobiles to provide navigational support, these systems are often mounted into the dash with a monitor to display maps and speakers to provide spoken directions. (See Figure 9-8.) Many of today's cell phones, including the Apple iPhone, use GPS technology for handheld navigation.

• **Infrared** uses infrared light waves to communicate over short distances. It is sometimes referred to as line-of-sight communication because the light waves can only travel in a straight line. This requires that sending and receiving devices must be in clear view of one another without any obstructions blocking that view. One of the most common applications is to transfer data and information from a portable device such as a notebook computer or PDA to a desktop computer.

For a summary of communication channels, see Figure 9-9.

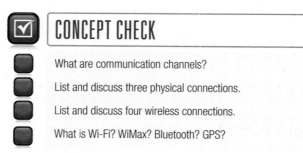

CONCEPT CHECK

What are communication channels?

List and discuss three physical connections.

List and discuss four wireless connections.

What is Wi-Fi? WiMax? Bluetooth? GPS?

Channel	Description
Twisted pair	Twisted copper wire, used for standard telephone lines and Ethernet cables
Coaxial cable	Solid copper core, more than 80 times the capacity of twisted pair
Fiber-optic cable	Light carries data, more than 26,000 times the capacity of twisted pair
Radio frequency	Radio waves connect wireless devices including cell phones and computer components
Microwave	High-frequency radio waves, travels in straight line through the air
Satellite	Microwave relay station in the sky, used by GPS devices
Infrared	Infrared light travels in a straight line

Figure 9-9 Communication channels

Connection Devices

At one time nearly all computer communication used telephone lines. However, because the telephone was originally designed for voice transmission, telephones typically send and receive **analog signals,** which are continuous electronic waves. Computers, in contrast, send and receive **digital signals.** (See Figure 9-10.) These represent the presence or absence of an electronic pulse—the on/off binary signals we mentioned in Chapter 6. To convert the digital signals to analog signals and vice versa, you need a modem.

Modems

The word **modem** is short for *modulator-demodulator.* **Modulation** is the name of the process of converting from digital to analog. **Demodulation** is the process of converting from analog to digital. The modem enables digital microcomputers to communicate across different media, including telephone wires, cable lines, and radio waves.

The speed with which modems transmit data varies. This speed, called **transfer rate,** is typically measured in thousands of bits **(kilobits) per second (Kbps).** (See Figure 9-11.) The higher the speed, the faster you can send and receive information. For example, transferring an image like Figure 9-10 might take 5 seconds with a 500 Kbps modem and less than 3 seconds with an 850 Kbps modem. To learn more about transfer rates, visit our Web site at www.computing2013.com and enter the keyword **rate.**

There are four commonly used types of modems: telephone, DSL, cable, and wireless. (See Figure 9-12.)

- A **telephone modem** is used to connect a computer directly to a telephone line. These modems can be either internal or external. Internal modems are on an expansion card that plugs into a slot on the system board. An external modem is typically connected to the system unit through a serial or USB port.
- A **DSL (digital subscriber line)** modem uses standard phone lines to create a high-speed connection directly to your phone company's offices. These devices are usually external and connect to the system unit using either USB or Ethernet ports.

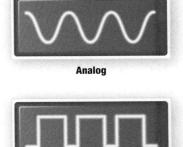

Analog

Digital

Figure 9-10 Analog and digital signals

Unit	Speed
Kbps	thousand bits per second
Mbps	million bits per second
Gbps	billion bits per second

Figure 9-11 Typical transfer rates

Telephone

DSL

Cable

Wireless

Figure 9-12 Basic types of modems

- A **cable modem** uses the same coaxial cable as your television. Like a DSL modem, a cable modem creates high-speed connections using the system unit's USB or Ethernet port.
- A **wireless modem** is also known as a **WWAN (wireless wide area network) modem.** It is usually a small plug-in USB or ExpressCard device that provides very portable high-speed connectivity from virtually anywhere.

Connection Service

For years, large corporations have been leasing special high-speed lines from telephone companies. Originally, these were copper lines, known as **T1** lines, that could be combined to form higher-capacity options known as **T3** or **DS3** lines. These lines have largely been replaced by **optical carrier (OC)** lines, which are substantially much faster.

While the special high-speed lines are too costly for most individuals, Internet service providers (as discussed in Chapter 2) do provide affordable connections. For years, individuals relied on **dial-up services** using existing telephones and telephone modems to connect to the Internet. This type of service has been replaced by higher-speed connection services including DSL, cable, satellite, and cellular services.

- **Digital subscriber line (DSL) service** is provided by telephone companies using existing telephone lines to provide high-speed connections. **ADSL (asymmetric digital subscriber line)** is one of the most widely used types of DSL. DSL is much faster than dial-up.
- **Cable service** is provided by cable television companies using their existing television cables. These connections are faster than DSL.
- **Satellite connection services** use satellites to provide wireless connections. While slower than DSL and cable modem, satellite connections are available almost anywhere using a satellite-receiving disk.

- **Cellular services** use **3G** and **4G cellular networks** to provide wireless connectivity to the Internet. Although not as fast as the other services, cellular services are rapidly growing in popularity for mobile devices such as cell phones and other portable devices.

CONCEPT CHECK

- What is the function of a modem?
- Compare four types of modems.
- What is a connection service?
- Compare four affordable higher-speed connection services.

Data Transmission

Several factors affect how data is transmitted. These factors include bandwidth and protocols.

Bandwidth

Bandwidth is a measurement of the width or capacity of the communication channel. Effectively, it means how much information can move across the communication channel in a given amount of time. For example, to transmit text documents, a slow bandwidth would be acceptable. However, to effectively transmit video and audio, a wider bandwidth is required. There are four categories of bandwidth.

- **Voiceband,** also known as **low bandwidth,** is used for standard telephone communication. Microcomputers with telephone modems and dial-up service use this bandwidth. While effective for transmitting text documents, it is too slow for many types of transmission, including high-quality audio and video.
- **Medium band** is used in special leased lines to connect minicomputers and mainframes as well as to transmit data over long distances. This bandwidth is capable of very high-speed data transfer.
- **Broadband** is widely used for DSL, cable, and satellite connections to the Internet. Several users can simultaneously use a single broadband connection for high-speed data transfer.
- **Baseband** is widely used to connect individual computers that are located close to one another. Like broadband, it is able to support high-speed transmission. Unlike broadband, however, baseband can only carry a single signal at one time.

Protocols

For data transmission to be successful, sending and receiving devices must follow a set of communication rules for the exchange of information. These rules for exchanging data between computers are known as **protocols.**

The standard protocol for the Internet is **TCP/IP (transmission control protocol/Internet protocol).** The essential features of this protocol involve (1) identifying sending and receiving devices and (2) breaking information into small parts for transmission across the Internet.

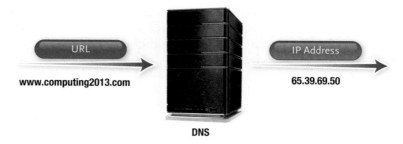

Figure 9-13 DNS converts text-based addresses to numeric IP addresses

- **Identification:** Every computer on the Internet has a unique numeric address called an **IP address (Internet protocol address).** Similar to the way a postal service uses addresses to deliver mail, the Internet uses IP addresses to deliver e-mail and to locate Web sites. Because these numeric addresses are difficult for people to remember and use, a system was developed to automatically convert text-based addresses to numeric IP addresses. This system uses a **domain name server (DNS)** that converts text-based addresses to IP addresses. For example, whenever you enter a URL, say www.computing2013.com, a DNS converts this to an IP address before a connection can be made. (See Figure 9-13.)

- **Packetization:** Information sent or transmitted across the Internet usually travels through numerous interconnected networks. Before the message is sent, it is reformatted or broken down into small parts called **packets.** Each packet is then sent separately over the Internet, possibly traveling different routes to one common destination. At the receiving end, the packets are reassembled into the correct order.

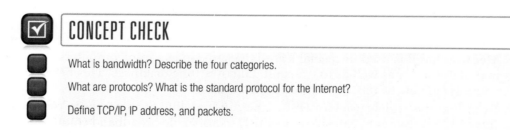

CONCEPT CHECK

What is bandwidth? Describe the four categories.

What are protocols? What is the standard protocol for the Internet?

Define TCP/IP, IP address, and packets.

Networks

A **computer network** is a communication system that connects two or more computers so that they can exchange information and share resources. Networks can be set up in different arrangements to suit users' needs. (See Figure 9-14.)

Terms

There are a number of specialized terms that describe computer networks. These terms include

- **Node**—any device that is connected to a network. It could be a computer, printer, or data storage device.

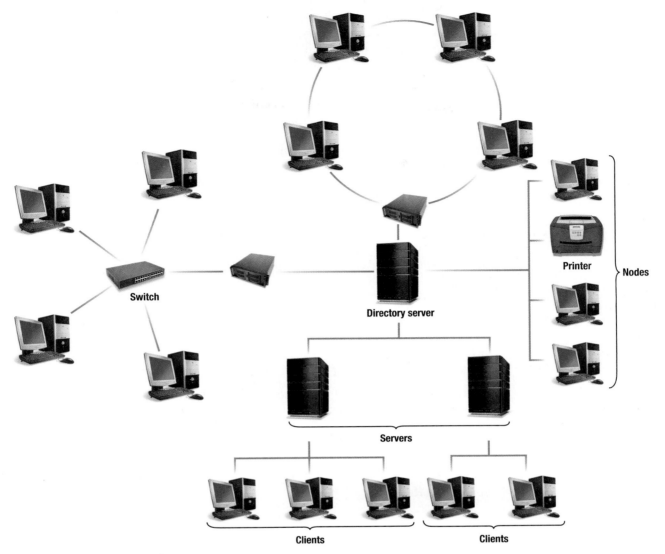

Figure 9-14 Computer network

- **Client**—a node that requests and uses resources available from other nodes. Typically, a client is a user's microcomputer.
- **Server**—a node that shares resources with other nodes. Dedicated servers specialize in performing specific tasks. Depending on the specific task, they may be called an application server, communication server, database server, file server, printer server, or Web server.
- **Directory server**—a specialized server that manages resources, such as user accounts, for an entire network.
- **Host**—any computer system that can be accessed over a network.
- **Switch**—central node that coordinates the flow of data by sending messages directly between sender and receiver nodes. A **hub** previously filled this purpose by sending a received message to all connected nodes, rather than just the intended node.
- **Network interface cards (NIC)**—as discussed in Chapter 6, these are expansion cards located within the system unit that connect the computer to a network. Sometimes referred to as a LAN adapter.
- **Network operating systems (NOS)**—control and coordinate the activities of all computers and other devices on a network. These activities

include electronic communication and the sharing of information and resources.

- **Network administrator**—a computer specialist responsible for efficient network operations and implementation of new networks.

A network may consist only of microcomputers, or it may integrate microcomputers or other devices with larger computers. Networks can be controlled by all nodes working together equally or by specialized nodes coordinating and supplying all resources. Networks may be simple or complex, self-contained or dispersed over a large geographical area.

CONCEPT CHECK

 What is a computer network? What are nodes, clients, servers, directory servers, hosts, and switches?

 What is the function of an NIC and an NOS?

What is a network administrator?

Network Types

Clearly, different types of channels—wired or wireless—allow different kinds of networks to be formed. Telephone lines, for instance, may connect communications equipment within the same building or within a home. Networks also may be citywide and even international, using both cable and wireless connections. Local area, metropolitan area, and wide area networks are distinguished by the geographical area they serve.

Local Area Networks

Networks with nodes that are in close physical proximity—within the same building, for instance—are called **local area networks (LANs).** Typically, LANs span distances less than a mile and are owned and operated by individual organizations. LANs are widely used by colleges, universities, and other types of organizations to link microcomputers and to share printers and other resources. For a simple LAN, see Figure 9-15.

The LAN represented in Figure 9-15 is a typical arrangement and provides two benefits: economy and flexibility. People can share costly equipment. For instance, the four microcomputers share the laser printer and the file server, which are expensive pieces of hardware. Other equipment or nodes also may be added to the LAN—for instance, more microcomputers, a mainframe computer, or optical disc storage devices. Additionally, the **network gateway** is a device that allows one LAN to be linked to other LANs or to larger networks. For example, the LAN of one office group may be connected to the LAN of another office group.

There are a variety of different standards or ways in which nodes can be connected to one another and ways in which their communications are controlled in a LAN. The most common standard is known as **Ethernet.** LANs using this standard are sometimes referred to as Ethernet LANs.

Home Networks

While LANs have been widely used within organizations for years, they are now being commonly used by individuals in their homes and apartments. These LANs, called **home networks,** allow different computers to share resources, including a common Internet connection. Computers can be connected in

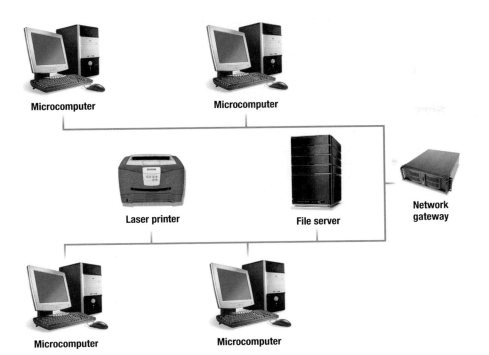

Microcomputer   Microcomputer

Laser printer   File server   Network gateway

Microcomputer   Microcomputer

Figure 9-15 Local area network

a variety of ways, including electrical wiring, telephone wiring, and special cables. One of the simplest ways, however, is without cables, or wireless.

Wireless LAN

A wireless local area network is typically referred to as a **wireless LAN (WLAN).** It uses radio frequencies to connect computers and other devices. All communications pass through the network's centrally located **wireless access point** or **base station.** This access point interprets incoming radio frequencies and routes communications to the appropriate devices. To see how wireless home networks work, visit our Web site at www.computing2013.com and enter the keyword **network.** To learn more about how to set up and use a wireless home network, see Making IT Work for You: Home Networking on pages 272 and 273.

Wireless access points that provide Internet access are widely available in public places such as coffee shops, libraries, bookstores, colleges, and universities. These access points are known as **hotspots** and typically use Wi-Fi technology. Many of these services are free and easy to find using free locator sites such as www.hotspot-locations.com. Most mobile computing devices have an internal wireless network card to connect to hotspots. If your mobile device does not have an internal wireless network card, you can use an external wireless adapter (see Figure 9-16) that plugs into your computer's USB port or PC card slot.

Do you use your laptop to connect to wireless networks at school or in public places such as coffee shops, airports, or hotels? If so, it is important to use caution to protect your computer and your privacy. Here are a few suggestions:

1 **Use a firewall.** A personal firewall is essential when connecting your computer directly to public networks. Some firewalls, such as the one built into Windows 7, can be set to use more restrictive rules for public networks.

2 **Turn off file sharing.** Turning off file-sharing features in your operating system will ensure that no one can read or delete your files, or add infected files to your computer.

3 **Avoid typing sensitive information.** When possible, avoid sites that require personal information such as passwords or credit card numbers to log in.

4 **Turn it off.** Turn off your laptop's wireless connection when you are not using it. This prevents automatic connections to wireless networks you do not authorize and limits your exposure to public networks.

To see additional tips, visit our Web site at www.computing2013.com and enter the keyword tips.

Making IT work for you

HOME NETWORKING

Computer networks are not just for corporations and schools anymore. If you have more than one computer, you can use a home network to share files and printers, to allow multiple users access to the Internet at the same time, and to play multiplayer computer games.

Installing the Access Point A wireless access point is a device that broadcasts wireless signals for the network and is the gateway to the Internet for the wireless network. To set up a wireless access point using Windows Vista:

1 ● Click *Start/ControlPanel/Network and Internet/Network and Sharing Center.*

● Click *Set up a connection or network.*

● Choose *Set up a wireless router or access point.*

2 ● Follow the on-screen instructions, which might include opening a special Web page to configure your access point.

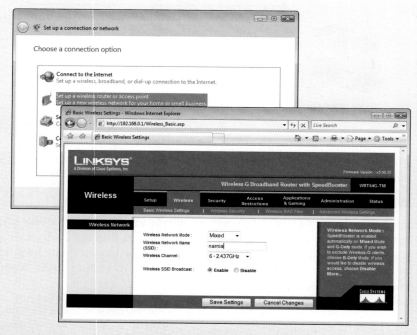

Connecting Computers Each computer on a wireless network requires a wireless network card. Many laptops and some desktops come equipped with a wireless network card built-in. Add-on cards also can be purchased. Once a computer is equipped with a wireless network card, it is simple to connect it to the wireless network. For example, to connect to a wireless network using Windows Vista:

1 ● Click *Start/Connect To.*

● Select the name of the network you configured in the previous step.

● Enter the password you chose in the previous step to connect to the wireless network.

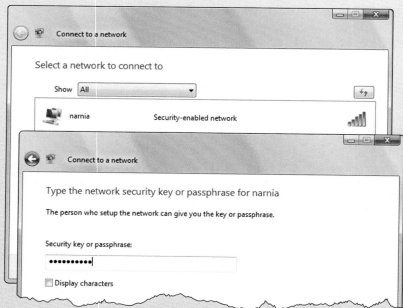

Using the Network Now your wireless devices are ready to share their resources. Some common uses are file and printer sharing, online gaming, Internet phone, and streaming music and video.

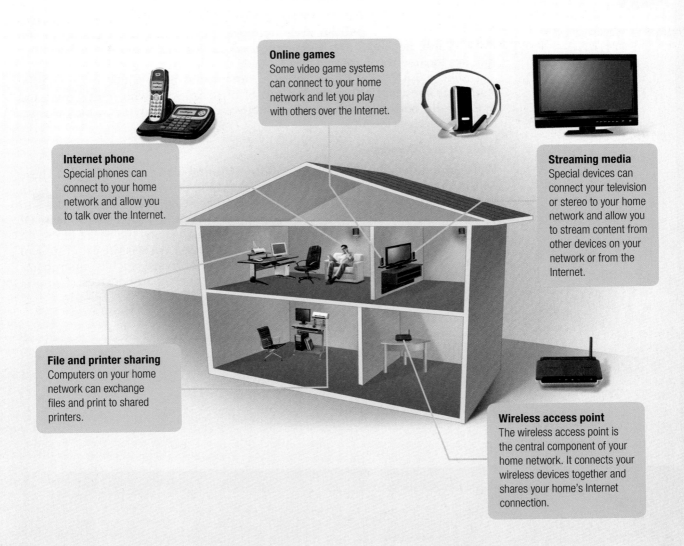

Online games
Some video game systems can connect to your home network and let you play with others over the Internet.

Internet phone
Special phones can connect to your home network and allow you to talk over the Internet.

Streaming media
Special devices can connect your television or stereo to your home network and allow you to stream content from other devices on your network or from the Internet.

File and printer sharing
Computers on your home network can exchange files and print to shared printers.

Wireless access point
The wireless access point is the central component of your home network. It connects your wireless devices together and shares your home's Internet connection.

Home networks are continually changing, and some of the specifics presented in this Making IT Work for You may have changed.

To learn about other ways to make information technology work for you, visit our Web site at www.computing2013.com and enter the keyword miw.

Figure 9-16 Wireless adapter

Personal Area Network

A **personal area network (PAN)** is a type of wireless network that works within a very small area—your immediate surroundings. PANs connect cell phones to headsets, PDAs to other PDAs, keyboards to cell phones, and so on. These tiny, self-configuring networks make it possible for all of our gadgets to interact wirelessly with each other. The most popular PAN technology is Bluetooth, with a maximum range of around 30 feet. Virtually all wireless peripheral devices available today use Bluetooth, including the controllers on popular game systems like the PlayStation and Wii.

Metropolitan Area Networks

The next step up from the LAN is the **MAN**—the **metropolitan area network.** MANs span distances up to 100 miles. These networks are frequently used as links between office buildings that are located throughout a city.

Unlike a LAN, a MAN is typically not owned by a single organization. Rather, it is owned either by a group of organizations who jointly own and operate the network or by a single network service provider who provides network services for a fee.

Wide Area Networks

Wide area networks (WANs) are countrywide and worldwide networks. These networks provide access to regional service (MAN) providers and typically span distances greater than 100 miles. They use microwave relays and satellites to reach users over long distances—for example, from Los Angeles to Paris. Of course, the widest of all WANs is the Internet, which spans the entire globe.

The primary difference between a LAN, MAN, and WAN is the geographical range. Each may have various combinations of hardware, such as microcomputers, minicomputers, mainframes, and various peripheral devices.

For a summary of network types, see Figure 9-17.

 CONCEPT CHECK

 Describe LANs, home networks, wireless LAN, and PAN.

What is a MAN? What is a WAN?

Type	Description
LAN	Local area network; located within close proximity
Home	Local area network for home and apartment use; typically wireless
WLAN	Wireless local area network; all communication passes through access point
PAN	Personal area network; connects digital devices, such as PDAs
MAN	Metropolitan area network; typically spans cities with coverage up to 100 miles
WAN	Wide area network for countrywide or worldwide coverage; the Internet is the largest WAN

Figure 9-17 Types of networks

Network Architecture

Network architecture describes how a network is arranged and how resources are coordinated and shared. It encompasses a variety of different network specifics, including network topologies and strategies. Network topology describes the physical arrangement of the network. Network strategies define how information and resources are shared.

Topologies

A network can be arranged or configured in several different ways. This arrangement is called the network's **topology.** Three of the most common topologies are star, tree, and mesh.

- **Star network**—each device is connected directly to a central network switch. (See Figure 9-18.) Whenever a node sends a message, it is routed to the switch, which then passes the message along to the intended recipient. The star network is the most widely used network topology today. It is applied to a broad range of applications from small networks in the home to very large networks in major corporations.

- **Tree network**—each device is connected to a central node, either directly or through one or more other devices. The central node is connected to two or more subordinate nodes that in turn are connected to other subordinate nodes, and so forth, forming a treelike structure. This network, also known as a **hierarchical network,** is often used to share corporatewide data.

- **Mesh network**—this topology is the newest type and does not use a specific physical layout (such as a star or a tree). Rather, the mesh network requires that each node have more than one connection to the other nodes. The resulting pattern forms the appearance of a mesh. If a path between two nodes is somehow disrupted, data can be automatically rerouted around the failure using another path. Wireless technologies are frequently used to build mesh networks.

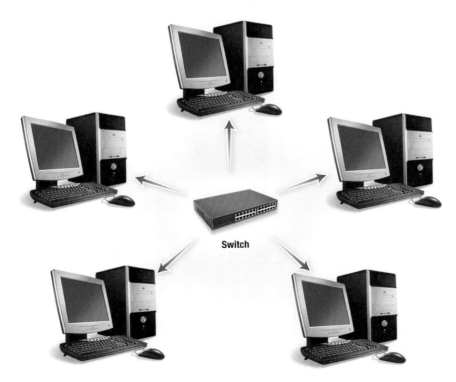

Switch

Figure 9-18 Star network

Strategies

Every network has a **strategy,** or way of coordinating the sharing of information and resources. Two of the most common network strategies are client/server and peer-to-peer.

Client/server networks use central computers to coordinate and supply services to other nodes on the network. The server provides access to resources such as Web pages, databases, application software, and hardware. (See Figure 9-19.) This strategy is based on specialization. Server nodes coordinate and supply specialized services, and client nodes request the services. Commonly used server operating systems are Windows Server, Mac OS X Server, Linux, and Solaris.

Client/server networks are widely used on the Internet. For example, each time you open a Web browser, your computer (the client) sends out a request for a specific Web page. This request is routed over the Internet to a server. This server locates and sends the requested material back to your computer.

One advantage of the client/server network strategy is the ability to handle very large networks efficiently. Another advantage is the availability of powerful network management software to monitor and control network activities. The major disadvantages are the cost of installation and maintenance.

In a **peer-to-peer (P2P) network,** nodes have equal authority and can act as both clients and servers. The most common way to share games, movies, and music over the Internet is to use a P2P network. For example, special file-sharing software such as eDonkey or BitTorrent can be used to obtain files located on another microcomputer and also can provide files to other microcomputers.

P2P networks are rapidly growing in popularity as people continue to share information with others around the world. The primary advantage is that they are easy and inexpensive (often free) to set up and use. One disadvantage of P2P networks is the lack of security controls or other common management functions. For this reason, few businesses use this type of network to communicate sensitive information.

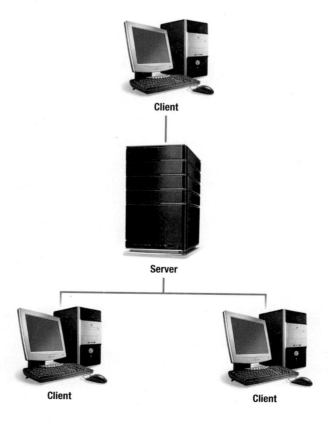

Client

Server

Client

Client

Figure 9-19 Client/server network

Organizational Networks

Computer networks in organizations have evolved over time. Most large organizations have a complex and wide range of different network configurations, operating systems, and strategies. These organizations face the challenge of making these networks work together effectively and securely.

Internet Technologies

Many organizations today employ Internet technologies to support effective communication within and between organizations using intranets and extranets.

• An **intranet** is a *private* network within an organization that resembles the Internet. Like the *public* Internet, intranets use browsers, Web sites, and Web pages. Typical applications include electronic telephone directories, e-mail addresses, employee benefit information, internal job openings, and much more. Employees find surfing their organizational intranets to be as easy and as intuitive as surfing the Internet.

• An **extranet** is a *private* network that connects *more than one* organization. Many organizations use Internet technologies to allow suppliers and others limited access to their networks. The purpose is to increase efficiency and reduce costs. For example, an automobile manufacturer has hundreds of suppliers for the parts that go into making a car. By having access to the car production schedules, suppliers can schedule and deliver parts as they are needed at the assembly plants. In this way, operational efficiency is maintained by both the manufacturer and the suppliers.

Network Security

Large organizations face the challenge of ensuring that only authorized users have access to network resources, sometimes from multiple geographic locations or across the Internet. Securing large computer networks requires specialized technology. Three technologies commonly used to ensure network security are firewalls, intrusion detection systems, and virtual private networks.

• A **firewall** consists of hardware and software that control access to a company's intranet and other internal networks. Most use software or a special computer called a **proxy server.** All communications between the company's internal networks and the outside world pass through this server. By evaluating the source and the content of each communication, the proxy server decides whether it is safe to let a particular message or file pass into or out of the organization's network. (See Figure 9-20.)

• **Intrusion detection systems (IDS)** work with firewalls to protect an organization's network. These systems use sophisticated statistical techniques to analyze all incoming and outgoing network traffic. Using advanced pattern matching and heuristics, an IDS system can recognize signs of a network attack and disable access before an intruder can do damage.

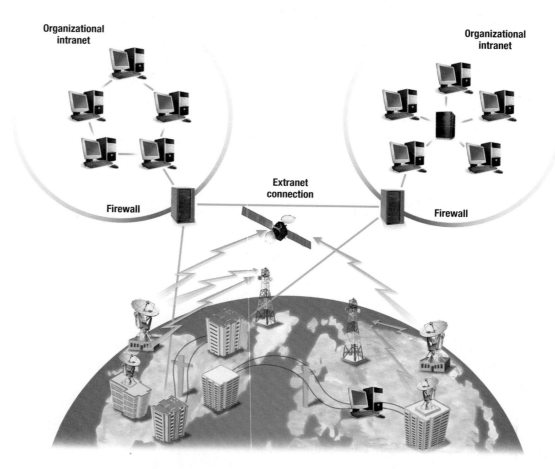

Figure 9-20 Intranets, extranets, firewalls, and proxy servers

- **Virtual private networks (VPN)** create a secure private connection between a remote user and an organization's internal network. Special VPN protocols create the equivalent of a dedicated line between a user's home or laptop computer and a company server. The connection is heavily encrypted and, from the perspective of the user, it appears that their workstation is actually located on the corporate network.

Like organizations, end users have security challenges and concerns. We need to be concerned about the privacy of our personal information. In the next chapter, we will discuss personal firewalls and other ways to protect personal privacy and security.

☑ CONCEPT CHECK

What are Internet technologies? Compare intranets and extranets.

What is a firewall? What is a proxy server?

What are intrusion detection systems?

What are virtual private networks?

Careers in IT

Network administrators manage a company's LAN and WAN networks. They may be responsible for design, implementation, and maintenance of networks. Responsibilities usually include maintenance of both hardware and software related to a company's intranet and Internet networks. Network administrators are typically responsible for diagnosing and repairing problems with these networks. Some network administrators are responsible for planning and implementation of network security as well.

Employers typically look for candidates with a bachelor's or an advanced specialized associate's degree in computer science, computer technology, or information systems as well as practical networking experience. Experience with network security and maintenance is preferred. Technical certification also may be helpful in obtaining this position. Because network administrators are involved directly with people in many departments, good communication skills are essential.

Network administrators can expect to earn an annual salary of $48,500 to $79,000. Opportunities for advancement typically include upper management positions. This position is expected to be among the fastest-growing jobs in the near future. To learn about other careers in information technology, visit us at www.computing2013.com and enter the keyword **careers**.

Now that you have learned about computer communications and networks, let me tell you about my career as a network administrator.

A LOOK TO THE FUTURE

Telepresence Lets You Be There without Actually Being There

How would you like to speak with distant friends or family as though they were in the same room at the touch of a button? Can you imagine receiving a physical examination from a doctor thousands of miles away? All this and more could be possible in the future thanks to the emerging technology known as *telepresence.*

Telepresence seeks to create the illusion that you are actually at a remote location, seeing, hearing, and someday maybe even feeling as though you were really there. Today's early telepresence implementations mainly focus on an extension of videoconferencing, allowing rooms of people in different locations to conduct meetings as though they are sitting across a table from one another, an illusion created with very high definition video, acoustically tuned audio systems, and high-speed networks. However, telepresence could someday go beyond the simple

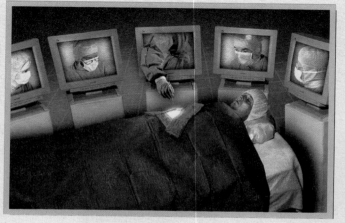

voice and video conferencing available today, and the applications seem endless.

Telepresence might be used to allow people to work in hazardous areas from a safe remote location. Doctors and medical specialists might be able to perform surgeries on people unable to travel. You might use telepresence as a vacation. Imagine touring remote cities or going on a deep sea diving expedition without hassle or risk.

Cisco is already marketing one video-based telepresence solution, known as Cisco TelePresence. At schools like MIT, developments are being made in the areas of holography, which is technology that creates 3-dimensional images called holograms, and sophisticated sensors that might pave the way to advanced telepresence. In the coming decade, you might be able to virtually interact with others with no video screen at all.

How would you use telepresence? What benefits do you see from this technology? How might telepresence impact travel in the future? Do you see any disadvantages?

VISUAL SUMMARY | Communications and Networks

COMMUNICATIONS

Communications is the process of sharing data, programs, and information between two or more computers. Applications include e-mail, instant messaging, Internet telephones, and electronic commerce.

Connectivity

Connectivity is a concept related to using computer networks to link people and resources. You can link or connect to large computers and the Internet, providing access to extensive information resources.

The Wireless Revolution

Mobile devices like smartphones and tablet PCs have brought dramatic changes in connectivity and communications. These wireless devices are becoming widely used for computer communication.

Communication Systems

Communication systems transmit data from one location to another. Four basic elements are

- Sending and receiving devices
- Communication channel (transmission medium)
- Connection (communication) devices
- Data transmission specifications

COMMUNICATION CHANNELS

Communication channels carry data from one computer to another.

Physical Connections

Physical connections use a solid medium to connect sending and receiving devices. Connections include **twisted pair (telephone lines and Ethernet cables), coaxial cable,** and **fiber-optic cable.**

Wireless Connections

Wireless connections do not use a solid substance to connect devices.

- **Radio frequency (RF)**—uses radio signals; **Wi-Fi (wireless fidelity)** is a widely used standard; **Bluetooth** is a short-range RF-based wireless standard. **WiMax (Worldwide Interoperability for Microwave Access)** extends Wi-Fi networks.
- **Microwave**—uses high-frequency radio waves; line-of-sight communication; uses microwave stations and dishes.
- **Satellite**—uses microwave relay stations in the sky; **GPS (global positioning system)** tracks geographical locations.
- **Infrared**—uses light waves over a short distance; line-of-sight communication.

To be a competent end user you need to understand the concepts of connectivity, the wireless revolution, and communication systems. Additionally, you need to know the essential parts of communication technology, including channels, connection devices, data transmission, networks, network architectures, and network types.

CONNECTION DEVICES

Many communication systems use standard telephone lines and **analog signals**. Computers use **digital signals**.

Modems

Modems modulate and **demodulate. Transfer rate** is measured in **kilobits per second**. Four types are telephone, DSL, cable, and **wireless (wireless wide area network, WWAN)**.

Connection Service

T1, T3 (DS3), and **OC (optical carrier)** lines provide support for very high-speed, all-digital transmission for large corporations. More affordable technologies include **dial-up, DSL (digital subscriber line), ADSL** (widely used), **cable, satellite** and **cellular services (3G** and **4G cellular networks)**.

DATA TRANSMISSION

Bandwidth measures a communication channel's width or capacity. Four bandwidths are **voiceband (low bandwidth), medium band, broadband** (high-capacity transmissions), and **baseband. Protocols** are rules for exchanging data. **TCP/IP (transmission control protocol/Internet protocol)** is the standard Internet protocol. **IP addresses (Internet protocol addresses)** are unique numeric Internet addresses. **DNS (domain name server)** converts text-based addresses to and from numeric IP addresses. **Packets** are small parts of messages.

NETWORKS

Computer networks connect two or more computers. Some specialized network terms include

- **Node**—any device connected to a network.
- **Client**—node requesting resources.
- **Server**—node providing resources.
- **Directory server**—specialized node that manages resources.
- **Host**—any computer system that can be accessed over a network.
- **Switch**—node that coordinates direct flow of data between other nodes. **Hub** is an older device that directed flow to all nodes.
- **NIC (network interface card)**—LAN adapter card for connecting to a network.
- **NOS (network operating system)**—controls and coordinates network operations.
- **Network administrator**—network specialist responsible for network operations.

NETWORK TYPES

Networks can be citywide or even international, using both wired and wireless connections.

- **Local area networks (LANs)** connect nearby devices. **Network gateways** connect networks to one another. **Ethernet** is a LAN standard. These LANs are called Ethernet LANs.
- **Home networks** are LANs used in homes.
- **Hotspots** provide Internet access typically using Wi-Fi technology.
- **Wireless LANs (WLANs)** use a **wireless access point (base station)** as a hub.
- **Personal area networks (PANs)** are wireless networks for PDAs, cell phones, and other small gadgets.
- **Metropolitan area networks (MANs)** link office buildings within a city, spanning up to 100 miles.
- **Wide area networks** or **WANs** are the largest type. They span states and countries or form worldwide networks. The Internet is the largest wide area network in the world.

NETWORK ARCHITECTURE

Switch

Network architecture describes how a computer network is arranged and how resources are coordinated and shared.

Topologies

A network's **topology** describes the physical arrangement of a network. Three common topologies are star, tree, and mesh.

- **Star network**—each device connected directly to a central network switch; most common type today.
- **Tree (hierarchical) network**—a central node connected to subordinate nodes and so forth, forming a treelike structure; often used to share corporatewide data.
- **Mesh network**—newest; each node has two or more connecting nodes; data can be routed around disrupted paths.

Strategies

Every network has a **strategy**, or way of sharing information and resources. Common network strategies include client/server and peer-to-peer.

- **Client/server (hierarchical) network**—central computers coordinate and supply services to other nodes; based on specialization of nodes; widely used on the Internet; able to handle very large networks efficiently; powerful network management software available.
- **Peer-to-peer network**—nodes have equal authority and act as both clients and servers; widely used to share games, movies, and music over the Internet; easy to set up and use; lacks security controls.

ORGANIZATIONAL NETWORKS

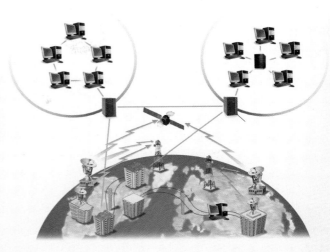

Internet Technologies

Internet technologies support effective communication using intranets and extranets.

- **Intranet**—private network within an organization; uses browsers, Web sites, and Web pages. Typical applications include electronic telephone directories, e-mail addresses, employee benefit information, internal job openings, and much more.
- **Extranet**—like intranet except connects *more than one* organization; typically allows suppliers and others limited access to their networks.

Network Security

Three technologies commonly used to ensure network security are firewalls, intrusion detection systems, and virtual private networks.

- **Firewall**—controls access; all communications pass through **proxy server.**
- **Intrusion detection systems (IDS)**—work with firewalls; use sophisticated statistical techniques to recognize and disable network attacks.
- **Virtual private network (VPN)**—creates secure private connection between remote user and organization's internal network.

CAREERS IN IT

Network administrators manage a company's LAN and WAN networks. Bachelor's or specialized advanced associate's degree in computer science, computer technology, or information systems and practical networking experience required. Salary range is $48,500 to $79,000.

KEY TERMS

3G cellular network   (267)
4G cellular network   (267)
analog signal   (265)
asymmetric digital
    subscriber line
    (ADSL)   (266)
bandwidth   (267)
base station   (271)
baseband   (267)
Bluetooth   (263)
broadband   (267)
cable modem   (266)
cable service   (266)
cellular service   (267)
client   (269)
client/server
    network   (276)
coaxial cable   (262)
communication
    channel   (262)
communication
    system   (261)
computer network   (268)
connectivity   (260)
demodulation   (265)
dial-up service   (266)
digital signal   (265)
digital subscriber line
    (DSL)   (265)
digital subscriber line
    (DSL) service   (266)
directory server   (269)
domain name server
    (DNS)   (268)
DS3   (266)
Ethernet   (270)
Ethernet cable   (262)
extranet   (277)
fiber-optic cable   (263)
firewall   (277)
global positioning system
    (GPS)   (263)

hierarchical
    network   (275)
home network   (270)
host   (269)
hotspot   (271)
hub   (269)
infrared   (264)
intranet   (277)
intrusion detection
    system (IDS)   (277)
IP address (Internet
    protocol address)   (268)
kilobits per second
    (Kbps)   (265)
local area network
    (LAN)   (270)
low bandwidth   (267)
medium band   (267)
mesh network   (275)
metropolitan area
    network (MAN)   (274)
microwave   (263)
modem   (265)
modulation   (265)
network
    administrator   (270, 279)
network
    architecture   (275)
network gateway   (270)
network interface card
    (NIC)   (269)
network operating system
    (NOS)   (269)
node   (268)
optical carrier (OC)   (266)
packet   (268)
peer-to-peer (P2P)
    network   (276)
personal area network
    (PAN)   (274)
protocol   (267)
proxy server   (277)

radio frequency
    (RF)   (263)
satellite   (263)
satellite connection
    service   (266)
server   (269)
star network   (275)
strategy   (276)
switch   (269)
T1   (266)
T3   (266)
telephone line   (262)
telephone modem   (265)
topology   (275)
transfer rate   (265)
transmission control
    protocol/Internet
    protocol (TCP/
    IP)   (267)
tree network   (275)
twisted-pair cable   (262)
virtual private network
    (VPN)   (278)
voiceband   (267)
wide area network
    (WAN)   (274)
Wi-Fi (wireless
    fidelity)   (263)
WiMax (Worldwide
    Interoperability for
    Microwave
    Access)   (263)
wireless access
    point   (271)
wireless LAN
    (WLAN)   (271)
wireless modem   (266)
wireless wide area
    network (WWAN)
    modem   (266)

To test your knowledge of these key terms with animated flash cards, visit our Web site at www.computing2013.com and enter the keyword terms9.

MULTIPLE CHOICE

Circle the letter of the correct answer.

1. The concept related to using computer networks to link people and resources.
   a. connectivity
   b. GPS
   c. TCP/IP
   d. Wi-Fi

2. A high-frequency transmission cable that delivers television signals as well as connects computers in a network.
   a. coaxial
   b. hi def
   c. 3-D
   d. twisted pair

3. A short-range radio communication standard that transmits data over short distances of up to approximately 30 feet.
   a. Bluetooth
   b. broadband
   c. DSL
   d. TCP/IP

4. The speed with which a modem transmits data is called its:
   a. digital velocity
   b. dynamic rate
   c. modular rating
   d. transfer rate

5. The bandwidth typically used for DSL, cable, and satellite connections to the Internet.
   a. baseband
   b. broadband
   c. medium band
   d. voiceband

6. Every computer on the Internet has a unique numeric address called a(n):
   a. IP address
   b. DNS
   c. broadcast
   d. packet

7. Sometimes referred to as a LAN adapter, these expansion cards connect a computer to a network.
   a. PCMCIA
   b. NIC
   c. server
   d. VPN

8. A device that allows one LAN to be linked to other LANs or to larger networks.
   a. IDS
   b. network gateway
   c. PAN
   d. switch

9. Typically using Wi-Fi technology, these wireless access points are typically available from public places such as coffee shops, libraries, bookstores, colleges, and universities.
   a. hotspots
   b. extranets
   c. PANs
   d. LANs

10. Star, tree, and mesh are three types of network:
    a. topologies
    b. protocols
    c. strategies
    d. devices

For an interactive multiple-choice practice test, visit our Web site at www.computing 2013.com and enter the keyword multiple9.

MATCHING

Match each numbered item with the most closely related lettered item. Write your answers in the spaces provided.

a. analog
b. instant messaging
c. intrusion detection systems
d. microwave
e. network administrator
f. node
g. peer-to-peer
h. protocols
i. RF
j. tree

_____ 1. Supports direct, "live" electronic communication between two or more friends or buddies.
_____ 2. Uses radio signals to communicate between wireless devices.
_____ 3. Uses high-frequency radio waves.
_____ 4. Signals that are continuous electronic waves.
_____ 5. Rules for exchanging data between computers.
_____ 6. Any device that is connected to a network.
_____ 7. A computer specialist responsible for efficient network operations and implementation of new networks.
_____ 8. This network, also known as a hierarchical network, is often used to share corporatewide data.
_____ 9. In this network, nodes have equal authority and can act as both clients and servers.
_____ 10. Work with firewalls to protect an organization's network.

For an interactive matching practice test, visit our Web site at www.computing2013.com and enter the keyword matching9.

OPEN-ENDED

On a separate sheet of paper, respond to each question or statement.

1. Define communications including connectivity, the wireless revolution, and communication systems.
2. Discuss communication channels including physical connections (twisted-pair, coaxial, and fiber-optic cable) and wireless connections (radio frequency, microwave, satellite, and infrared).
3. Discuss connection devices including modems (telephone, DSL, cable, and wireless modems) and connection services (DSL, ADSL, cable, and satellite connection services).
4. Discuss data transmission including bandwidths (voiceband, medium band, broadband, and baseband) as well as protocols (IP addresses, domain name servers, and packetization).
5. Discuss networks by identifying and defining specialized terms that describe computer networks.
6. Discuss network types including local area, home, wireless, personal, metropolitan, and wide area networks.
7. Define network architecture including topologies (star, tree, and mesh) and strategies (client/server and peer-to-peer).
8. Discuss organization networks including Internet technologies (intranets and extranets) and network security (firewalls, proxy servers, intrusion detection systems, and virtual private networks).

MAKING IT WORK FOR YOU

The following questions are designed to demonstrate ways that you can effectively use technology today.

1 HOME NETWORKING

Computer networks are not just for corporations and schools anymore. If you have more than one computer, you can use a home network to share files and printers, to allow multiple users access to the Internet at the same time, and to play multiplayer computer games. To learn more about this technology, review Making IT Work for You: Home Networking on pages 272 and 273. Then answer the following: (a) Describe the window shown for the setup of the wireless access point. What brand of access point is demonstrated? (b) What name is used for the wireless home network? (c) What are four common uses for a wireless home network?

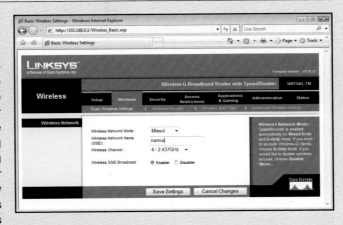

2 DISTRIBUTED COMPUTING

When networked computers are not in use, their processing power can be combined with other networked computers to perform a common task. In some cases, the problems that can be solved by many individual computers are far too large to be solved by any single computer. Connect to our site at www.computing2013.com and enter the keyword distributed for a link to a site that features distributed computing. Explore the site and answer the following questions: (a) What type of problem does this site solve with distributed computing? (b) How do users donate unused computer time to this project? (c) Would you donate your extra computer time to a distributed computing project? Why or why not?

3 WIRELESS MOBILE DEVICES

Recent advances in technology allow mobile devices to communicate on the go faster than ever before. Visit our Web site at www.computing2013.com and enter the keyword mobile to link to a Web site featuring connected mobile devices. Once connected, review the latest products and then answer the following questions: (a) What support for Internet connection is available? How fast is the connection? (b) Are the connection options you researched in part (a) available where you live? Is there any place they are not available? (c) What is required to connect a mobile device to the Internet? (d) What type of Internet information is accessible? Is there any type that is not accessible?

EXPLORATIONS

The following questions are designed to add depth and detail to your understanding of specific topics presented within this chapter. The questions direct you to sources other than the textbook to obtain this knowledge.

1 HOW WIRELESS HOME NETWORKS WORK

Wireless home networks are becoming very popular. These LANs are easy to set up and use. They allow different computers to share resources including a common Internet connection and printer. To learn how home networks work, visit our Web site at www.computing2013.com and enter the keyword network. Then answer the following questions: (a) What is a node? (b) What is a base station (access point) and what is its function? (c) What is a wireless card and what is its function? (d) If one or more requests to print a document are made at exactly the same time, what node determines which document is printed first? (e) Can the nodes TIM, LINDA, and STEVE access and use the Internet at the same time? If yes, how can this be done with a single Internet connection?

2 BITTORRENT

BitTorrent is a file-sharing protocol used to distribute large files across the Internet. Connect to our Web site at www.computing2013.com and enter the keyword torrent to learn more about how BitTorrent works, and then answer the following: (a) What is a "torrent"? How is a torrent created and published? (b) What network strategy does BitTorrent use? Review the network strategies presented on pages 276 through 277 and justify your answer. (c) What are the advantages to downloading files using BitTorrent rather than traditional client-server methods? How does BitTorrent reduce bandwidth usage for content providers?

3 HOTSPOTS

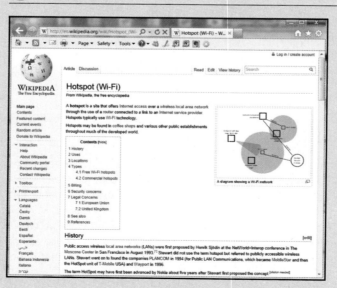

Hotspots are areas set up to provide public access to wireless Internet service. You will find them in coffee shops, airports, or hotels. Connect to our Web site at www.computing2013 .com and enter the keyword hotspots to link to a directory of hotspots. Locate one near you. Where is the hotspot? What equipment is necessary to use the hotspot? What does it cost to use the hotspot?

ETHICS

The following questions are designed to explore ethical issues related to technology and to develop the ability to think critically and communicate effectively. Respond to the questions by either creating a one-page paper or preparing for an in-depth classroom discussion.

1 ELECTRONIC MONITORING

Programs known as "sniffers" are sometimes used to monitor communications on corporate networks. Recently, the FBI unveiled a technology known as Carnivore that can monitor an individual's Internet activity and eavesdrop on e-mail messages. Review the Ethics box on page 262 and respond to the following: (a) Is it a violation of an employee's privacy for an organization or corporation to use sniffer programs to monitor communications on their network? (b) Is it a violation of privacy for a government agency such as the FBI to use programs like Carnivore to monitor communications on the Internet? (c) Under what conditions are the types of monitoring discussed in parts (a) and (b) acceptable and ethical? (d) How can these conditions be enforced?

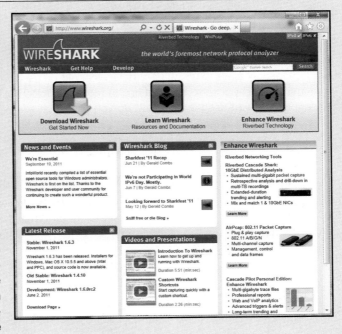

2 DIGITAL RIGHTS MANAGEMENT

In response to the issue of sharing copyrighted material over computer networks, many different forms of digital rights management, or DRM, have been proposed. However, DRM is controversial and hotly debated by industry groups and consumer advocates. Use the Web to research DRM, and then respond to the following: (a) Define "digital rights management." (b) What systems have been proposed for DRM? (c) Why are some consumers opposed to these systems? (d) Do you think DRM is an ethical and fair solution to online piracy? Justify your answer.

ENVIRONMENT

The following questions are designed to explore environmental issues related to technology and to develop the ability to think critically and communicate effectively. Respond to the questions by either creating a one-page paper or preparing for an in-depth classroom discussion.

 GPS

Did you know that some believe that GPS devices in cars can actually help protect the environment? These devices can be used to direct motorists to the most direct routes, to monitor and avoid traffic jams. Review the Environmental box on page 263 and then respond to the following: (a) Do you think that GPS devices can significantly help protect the environment? Why or why not? (b) Identify ways in which GPS devices could be used for environmental protection. You need not limit your response to applications in motor vehicles. (c) Have you used a GPS device? If so, describe what you used it for. If not, do you think that you will in the near future? (d) Do you think that GPS devices should be standard equipment for every new car? Why or why not? (e) Do you think that they should be required by law? Why or why not.

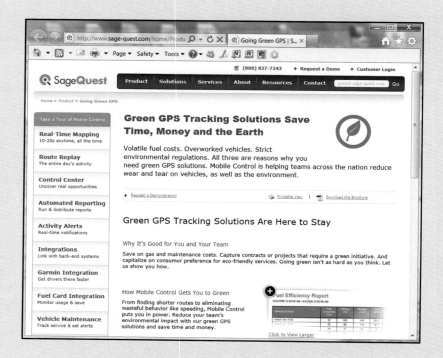

2 IPHONE

Did you know that tablet PCs including the iPhone can use network connections to the Internet to help protect the environment? They can be used to reduce CO_2 by providing the shortest distances to locations and by using online shopping. (a) Have you ever used a tablet PC in a way that helped protect the environment? If so, describe what you did and how it helped the environment. There are numerous apps that are focused specifically on environmental protection. (b) Have you ever used an environmental app? If so, describe the app and its effectiveness. If not, use the Internet to research at least one environment app and then describe it and its potential effectiveness. (c) Identify ways in which a tablet PC might effectively be used for environmental protection. (d) Do you think that tablet PCs or other types of computers can be effectively used for environmental protection? Why or why not. Be specific.

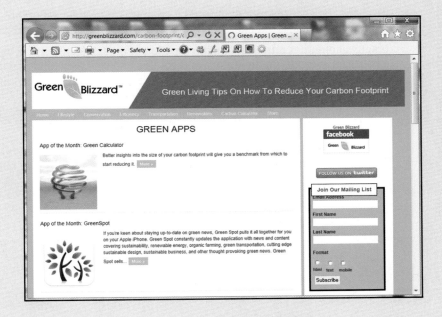

Privacy, Security, and Ethics

Competencies

▲ Download the free *Computing Essentials 2013* app for videos, key term flashcards, quizzes, and the game, *Over the Edge!*

After you have read this chapter, you should be able to:

1   Identify the most significant concerns for effective implementation of computer technology.

2   Discuss the primary privacy issues of accuracy, property, and access.

3   Describe the impact of large databases, private networks, the Internet, and the Web on privacy.

4   Discuss online identity and the major laws on privacy.

5   Describe the security threats posed by computer criminals including employees, hackers, crackers, carders, organized crime, and terrorists.

6   Discuss computer crimes including creation of malicious programs such as viruses, worms, Trojan horses, and zombies as well as denial of service attacks, Internet scams, social networking risks, cyber-bullying, rogue Wi-Fi hotspots, theft, data manipulation, and other hazards.

7   Detail ways to protect computer security including restricting access, encrypting data, anticipating disasters, and preventing data loss.

8   Discuss computer ethics including copyright law, software piracy, and digital rights management as well as plagiarism and ways to identify plagiarism.

Why should I read this chapter?

In the past, protecting your privacy and security was pretty simple. You needed a paper shredder and perhaps an unlisted phone number. That was then and this is now. Now, in the digital age, personal security and privacy are much more complicated and difficult. Every minute there are thousands of malicious programs that are being spread across the Internet.

This chapter discusses privacy including identity theft, cookies, Web bugs, and keystroke loggers. Additionally, you'll learn about viruses, worms, rogue Wi-Fi hotspots, and the risks associated with Facebook and other social networking sites. You will also learn how to protect your computer security using a variety of techniques including biometric scanners and encryption. To be competent and to be competitive in today's professional workplace, you need to know and to understand these things.

chapter 10

Introduction

The tools and products of the information age do not exist in a world by themselves. As we said in Chapter 1, a computer system consists not only of software, hardware, data, and procedures, but also of people. Because of people, computer systems may be used for both good and bad purposes.

There are more than one billion microcomputers in use today. What are the consequences of the widespread presence of this technology? Does technology make it easy for others to invade our personal privacy? When we apply for a loan or for a driver's license, or when we check out at the supermarket, is that information about us being distributed and used without our permission? When we use the Web, is information about us being collected and shared with others?

This technology prompts lots of questions—very important questions. Perhaps these are some of the most important questions for the 21st century. Competent end users need to be aware of the potential impact of technology on people and how to protect themselves on the Web. They need to be sensitive to and knowledgeable about personal privacy, organizational security, ergonomics, and the environmental impact of technology.

Hi, I'm Anthony, and I'm a specialist in protecting privacy and securing information. I'd like to talk with you about privacy, security, and ethics, three critical topics for anyone who uses computers today. I would also like to talk about how you can protect your privacy, ensure your security, and act ethically.

People

As we have discussed, information systems consist of people, procedures, software, hardware, and data. This chapter focuses on people. (See Figure 10-1.) While most everyone agrees that technology has had a very positive impact on people, it is important to recognize the negative, or potentially negative, impacts as well.

Effective implementation of computer technology involves maximizing its positive effects while minimizing its negative effects. The most significant concerns are

- **Privacy:** What are the threats to personal privacy and how can we protect ourselves?
- **Security:** How can access to sensitive information be controlled and how can we secure hardware and software?
- **Ethics:** How do the actions of individual users and companies affect society?

Let us begin by examining privacy.

Figure 10-1 People are part of an information system

Privacy

As you have seen, computing technology makes it possible to collect and use data of all kinds, including information about people. The Web sites you visit, the stores where you shop, and the television shows you watch are all examples of information about you. How would you feel if you learned such information was being collected or shared? Would it matter who was collecting it, or how it was being used, or whether it was even correct?

Privacy concerns the collection and use of data about individuals. There are three primary privacy issues:

- **Accuracy** relates to the responsibility of those who collect data to ensure that the data is correct.
- **Property** relates to who owns data and rights to software.
- **Access** relates to the responsibility of those who have data to control who is able to use that data.

Large Databases

Large organizations are constantly compiling information about us. The federal government alone has over 2,000 databases. Every day, data is gathered about us and stored in large databases. For example, telephone companies compile lists of the calls we make, the numbers called, and so on. A special telephone directory (called a **reverse directory**) lists telephone numbers sequentially. (See Figure 10-2.) Using it, government authorities and others can easily get the names, addresses, and other details about the persons we call.

Credit card companies keep similar records. Supermarket scanners in grocery checkout counters record what we buy, when we buy it, how much we buy, and

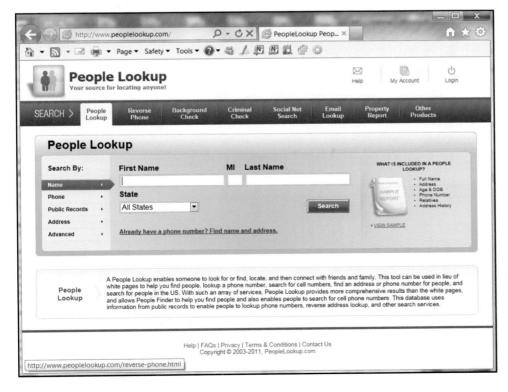

Figure 10-2 Reverse directory Web site

the price. Financial institutions, including banks and credit unions, record how much money we have, what we use it for, and how much we owe. Publishers of magazines, newspapers, and mail-order catalogues have our names, addresses, phone numbers, and what we order.

A vast industry of data gatherers known as **information resellers** or **information brokers** now exists that collects and sells such personal data. Using publicly available databases and in many cases nonpublic databases, information resellers create **electronic profiles** or highly detailed and personalized descriptions of individuals. Very likely, you have an electronic profile that includes your name, address, telephone number, Social Security number, driver's license number, bank account numbers, credit card numbers, telephone records, and shopping and purchasing patterns. Information resellers sell these electronic profiles to direct marketers, fundraisers, and others. Many provide these services on the Web for free or for a nominal cost. (See Figure 10-3.)

Your personal information, including preferences, habits, and financial data, has become a marketable commodity. This raises many issues, including

- **Collecting public, but personally identifying information:** What if people anywhere in the world could view detailed images of you, your home, or your car? Using detailed images captured with a specially equipped van, Google's Street View project allows just that. Street View makes it possible to take a virtual tour of many cities and neighborhoods from any computer with a connection to the Internet. (See Figure 10-4.) Although the images available on Street View are all taken in public locations, some have objected to the project as being an intrusion on their privacy.

As digital cameras and WebCams become cheaper and software becomes more sophisticated, it is likely that many more issues involving personal privacy in public spaces will need to be addressed. Such a combination of computing technologies could, for example, make real-time tracking of individuals in public places possible.

Figure 10-3 Information reseller's Web site

Figure 10-4 Google Street View

- **Spreading information without personal consent:**
How would you feel if an employer were using your
medical records to make decisions about hiring, placement, promotion, and firing? A survey of Fortune 500
companies found that over one-third were using medical records for just these purposes.

    How would you feel if someone obtained a driver's
license and credit cards in your name? What if that
person then assumed your identity to buy clothes,
cars, and a house? It happens every day. Every year,
nearly 10 million people are victimized in this way.
It is called **identity theft.** Identity theft is the illegal
assumption of someone's identity for the purposes of
economic gain. It is one of the fastest-growing crimes
in the country. To learn more about identity theft and
how to minimize your risk, visit our Web site at www.
computing2013.com and enter the keyword **theft.**

- **Spreading inaccurate information:** How would you
like to be turned down for a home loan because of an
error in your credit history? This is much more common than you might expect. What if you could not
find a job or were fired from a job because of an error
giving you a serious criminal history? This can and has happened due to
simple clerical errors. In one case, an arresting officer while completing an
arrest warrant incorrectly recorded the Social Security number of a criminal. From that time forward, this arrest and the subsequent conviction
became part of another person's electronic profile. This is an example of

mistaken identity in which the electronic profile of one person is switched with another.

It's important to know that you have some recourse. The law allows you to gain access to those records about you that are held by credit bureaus. Under the **Freedom of Information Act,** you are also entitled to look at your records held by government agencies. (Portions may be deleted for national security reasons.)

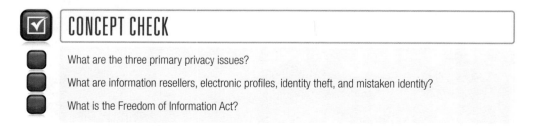

CONCEPT CHECK

What are the three primary privacy issues?

What are information resellers, electronic profiles, identity theft, and mistaken identity?

What is the Freedom of Information Act?

Private Networks

Suppose you use your company's electronic mail system to send a co-worker an unflattering message about your supervisor or to send a highly personal message to a friend. Later you find the boss has been spying on your exchange. This is legal, and a recent survey revealed that nearly 75 percent of all businesses search employees' electronic mail and computer files using so-called **snoopware.** (See Figure 10-5.) These programs record virtually everything you do on your computer. One proposed law would not prohibit this type of electronic monitoring but would require employers to provide prior written notice. Employers also would have to alert employees during the monitoring

Figure 10-5 Snoopware

with some sort of audible or visual signal. If you are employed and would like to know your company's current policy on monitoring electronic communication, contact your human relations department.

The Internet and the Web

When you send e-mail on the Internet or browse the Web, do you have any concerns about privacy? Most people do not. They think that as long as they are using their own computer and are selective about disclosing their names or other personal information, then little can be done to invade their personal privacy. Experts call this the **illusion of anonymity** that the Internet brings.

As we discussed in Chapter 9, every computer on the Internet is identified by a unique number known as an IP address. IP addresses can be used to trace Internet activities to their origin, allowing computer security experts and law enforcement officers to investigate computer crimes such as unauthorized access to networks or sharing of copyrighted files without permission.

When you browse the Web, your browser stores critical information onto your hard disk, typically without your explicit permission or knowledge. For example, your browser creates a **history file** that includes the locations of sites visited by your computer system. This history file can be displayed by your browser. To view the history file using Internet Explorer version 9.0, follow the steps in Figure 10-6.

Explorations

Several organizations monitor the legislation on privacy issues.

To learn more about one such organization, visit our Web site at www.computing2013.com and enter the keyword privacy.

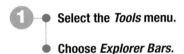

1 ● Select the *Tools* menu.

● Choose *Explorer Bars.*

2 ● Select *History.*

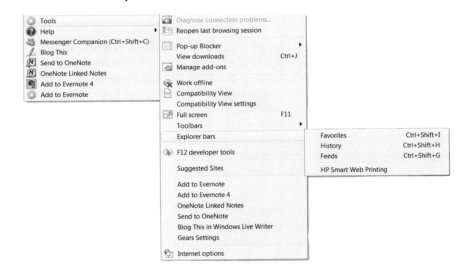

Figure 10-6 Viewing history files

1 ● Select *Tools* from the menu bar.

● Choose *Internet Options*.

2 ● Select *Settings* in the *Browsing history* section of the *General* tab.

● Click *View files*.

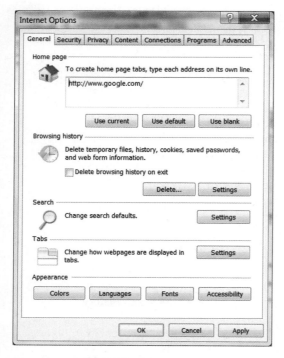

Figure 10-7 Viewing cookies

Another way your Web activity can be monitored is with **cookies,** or small pieces of information that are deposited on your hard disk from Web sites you have visited. Typically, cookies are deposited without your explicit knowledge or consent. While cookies are harmless in and of themselves, what makes them potentially dangerous is that they can store information about you without your knowledge. Using them, a record of what sites you visit, what you do at the sites, and other information you provide can be created. To view the cookies on a hard drive using Internet Explorer version 9.0, follow the steps in Figure 10-7.

There are two basic types of cookies: traditional and ad network. Most cookies can be displayed by your browser.

- **Traditional cookies** provide information to a single site. When you first visit a site, a cookie is deposited with information that identifies you specifically (such as information you provided on a form). Any further pages you visit on the site will have access to the cookie and be able to read its contents. When you leave the site, the cookie is usually saved. When you revisit, the cookie is reactivated and the information accessed. Most cookies are intended to provide customized service. For example, when you revisit an electronic commerce site, you can be greeted by name, presented with customized advertising banners, and directed to Web pages promoting items you have previously purchased.

- **Ad network** or **adware cookies** record your activities across different sites. Once deposited onto your hard drive, they can be activated and accessed from many of the Web sites that you visit. These cookies are deposited on your hard disk by organizations that compile and market the information. Two such organizations are DoubleClick and Avenue A.

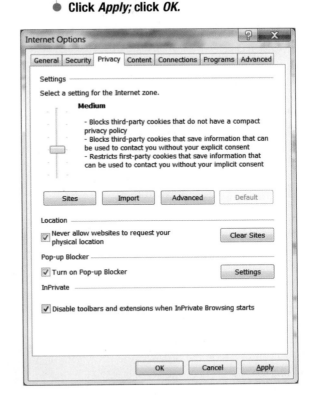

1 ● Select *Tools* from the menu bar.

● Choose *Internet Options.*

2 ● Select the *Privacy* tab.

● Move the slide to desired level of protection.

● Click *Apply;* click *OK.*

Figure 10-8 Blocking cookies

Most browsers are able to control many types of cookies. For example, Internet Explorer version 9.0 provides settings to selectively block cookies from being deposited onto a system's hard disk. (See Figure 10-8.) Additionally, most browsers offer a **privacy mode** that eliminates history files as well as blocks most cookies. For example, Internet Explorer provides **InPrivate Browsing** accessible from the Tools option on the main menu and Safari provides **Private Browsing** from the Safari option on the main menu.

The term **spyware** is used to describe a wide range of programs that are designed to secretly record and report an individual's activities on the Internet. Ad network cookies are just one type of spyware. Two other types are Web bugs and computer monitoring software.

- **Web bugs** are small images or HTML code hidden within an e-mail message. When a user opens an e-mail containing a Web bug, information is sent back to the source of the bug. One of the most common Web bugs is used by companies that sell active mailing lists to spammers. This bug is simply an invisible graphic embedded into an e-mail message. When the e-mail is opened, a request is sent to display the graphic without the reader's knowledge. The request is sent to a remote server that then knows that this e-mail address is active. Although this Web bug does no serious harm, others are more dangerous. To see how Web bugs can work, visit our Web site at www.computing2013.com and enter the keyword **bugs.**

- **Computer monitoring software** is the most invasive and dangerous type of spyware. These programs record every activity and keystroke made on your computer system, including credit card numbers, bank account numbers, and e-mail messages. Also known as **keystroke loggers,** computer monitoring software can be deposited onto your hard drive without your knowledge either from the Web or by someone installing the programs directly onto your computer. The previously mentioned snoopware is a type of computer monitoring software used by businesses to monitor their employees. Computer monitoring software also has been used by the FBI and the CIA to collect incriminating evidence on suspected terrorists and organized crime members. These programs are also widely used by private investigators, criminals, and spouses.

Unfortunately, it is more difficult to remove Web bugs and computer monitoring software than ad network cookies because they are more difficult to detect. There are over 90,000 active spyware programs, and chances are you have one or more of them on your computer. A recent study reported finding an average of 28 active spyware programs on microcomputers it had evaluated.

A category of programs known as **antispyware** or **spy removal programs,** which are designed to detect and remove cookies, Web bugs, and monitoring software, has evolved to battle the threat. (See Figure 10-9.) For a list of some of these programs, see Figure 10-10. To learn more about protecting yourself

Figure 10-9 Antispyware

from spyware, see Making IT Work for You: Spyware Removal on pages 304 and 305.

Online Identity

Another aspect of Internet privacy comes from **online identity,** the information that people voluntarily post about themselves online. With the popularity of social networking, blogging, and photo- and video-sharing sites, many people post intimate details of their lives without considering the consequences. Although it is easy to think of online identity as something shared between friends, the archiving and search features of the Web make it available indefinitely to anyone who cares to look. How would you feel if information you posted about yourself on the Web kept you from getting a job?

Major Laws on Privacy

Some federal laws governing privacy matters have been created. For example, the **Gramm-Leach-Bliley Act** protects personal financial information, the **Health Insurance Portability and Accountability Act (HIPAA)** protects medical records, and the **Family Educational Rights and Privacy Act (FERPA)** restricts disclosure of educational records. To learn more about existing privacy laws, visit our Web site at www. computing2013.com and enter the keyword **law.**

Most of the information collected by private organizations is not covered by existing laws. However, as more and more individuals become concerned about controlling who has the right to personal information and how that information is used, companies and law makers will respond.

Program	Web Site
Ad-Aware	www.lavasoft.com
CounterSpy	www.counterspy.com
Spy Doctor	www.spydoctor.com
Windows Defender	www.microsoft.com
Zone Alarm	www.zonealarm.com

Figure 10-10 Antispyware programs

tips

What can you do to protect your privacy while on the Web? Here are a few suggestions.

1 **Encrypt sensitive e-mail.** Encrypt or code sensitive e-mail using special encryption programs.

2 **Shield your identity.** Use an anonymous remailer or special Web site that forwards your e-mail without disclosing your identity.

3 **Block cookies.** Use your browser or a cookie-cutter program to block unwanted cookies.

4 **Check for Web bugs and computer monitoring software.** Use spy removal programs to check for Web bugs and computer monitoring software.

5 **Notify providers.** Instruct your service provider or whomever you use to link to the Internet not to sell your name or any other personal information.

6 **Be careful.** Never disclose your telephone number, passwords, or other private information to strangers.

To see more tips, visit our Web site at www.computing2013.com and enter the keyword tips.

CONCEPT CHECK

What is snoopware? Describe the illusion of anonymity.

What is a history file? Compare traditional and ad network cookies. What is privacy mode?

What are spyware, Web bugs, keystroke loggers, antispyware programs, and online identity?

Describe three federal laws to protect privacy.

Making IT work for you

SPYWARE REMOVAL

Have you installed any free software from the Internet? Did you know seemingly harmless software might actually be spying on you, even sending personal information to advertisers or worse? Fortunately, spyware removal software is available to help keep your personal information private.

Finding and Removing Spyware   Once spyware removal software is installed on your system, you can scan your system for known spyware and remove it. Follow the steps below to find and remove spyware using Ad-Aware.

1 ● Connect to www.lavasoft.com and follow the on-screen instructions to download and install the Ad-Aware software.

2 ● Launch the Ad-Aware application.

● Click the *Scan Now* button.

● Click the *Scan* button to begin scanning for spyware.

● Review the results of the scan, and place a check mark next to any detected items you would like to remove.

● Click the *Remove* button to remove the detected spyware from your system.

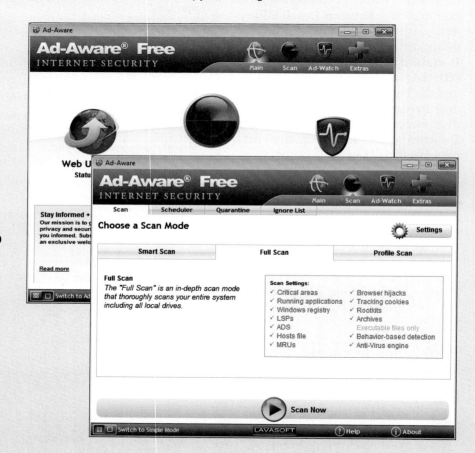

Automating Spyware Removal   To protect your system from spyware, it is recommended that you run your spyware removal software automatically. Follow the steps below to set Ad-Aware to run automatically on a regular schedule.

1 ● Click the *Scan* button.

● Click the *Schedule* button.

2 ● Choose how frequently you would like your system scanned for spyware.

● Click the *Add* button to add your selection to the scheduler.

Ad-Aware will now run automatically on the days and times you selected.

Staying Up to Date   Now that your system is protected from spyware, you'll want to keep it that way. Spyware removal programs keep a profile of known spyware, which must be updated from time to time. Follow the steps below to update the spyware profile in Ad-Aware.

1 ● Click the *Web Update* button.

2 ● Click the *Update* button.

Ad-Aware connects to the Internet and updates its spyware profile. The newest Ad-Aware reference file is installed automatically. You can now follow the steps in the "Finding and Removing Spyware" section to rid your system of the latest known spyware.

The Web is continually changing, and some of the specifics presented in this Making IT Work for You may have changed.

To learn about other ways to make information technology work for you, visit our Web site at www.computing2013.com and enter the keyword miw.

Security

We are all concerned with having a safe and secure environment to live in. We are careful to lock our car doors and our homes. We are careful about where we walk at night and whom we talk to. This is personal security. What about computer security? What if someone gains unauthorized access to our computer or other computers that contain information about us? What if someone steals our computer or other computers that contain information about us? What are the major threats to computer security, and how can we be protected?

Computer Criminals

A **computer crime** is an illegal action in which the perpetrator uses special knowledge of computer technology. Typically, computer criminals are either employees, outside users, hackers, crackers, carders, organized crime members, or terrorists.

- **Employees:** The largest category of computer criminals consists of those with the easiest access to computers—namely, employees. Sometimes the employee is simply trying to steal something from the employer— equipment, software, electronic funds, proprietary information, or computer time. Sometimes the employee is acting out of resentment and is trying to get back at the company.

- **Outside users:** Not only employees but also some suppliers or clients may have access to a company's computer system. Examples are bank customers who use an automated teller machine. Like employees, these authorized users may be able to obtain confidential passwords or find other ways of committing computer crimes.

- **Hackers and crackers:** Some people think of these two groups as being the same, but they are not. **Hackers** are people who create or improve programs and share those programs with fellow hackers. Typically, they are not criminals. **Crackers,** on the other hand, create and share programs designed to gain unauthorized access to computer systems or disrupt networks. Their motives are malicious and can be very destructive and costly. Typically, they are criminals.

- **Carders:** As discussed in Chapter 2, carders are criminals who specialize in stealing, trading, and using stolen credit cards over the Internet. Some carders use sophisticated electronic devices to copy data from your credit or debit card including account numbers and PINs. One of these devices is a magnetic-strip reading device that fits over existing ATM readers that automatically relays information wirelessly to the carder. Other devices are able to eavesdrop on communications from hotspots.

- **Organized crime:** Members of organized crime groups have discovered that they can use computers just as people in legitimate businesses do, but for illegal purposes. For example, computers are useful for keeping track of stolen goods or illegal gambling debts. In addition, counterfeiters and forgers use microcomputers and printers to produce sophisticated-looking documents such as checks and driver's licenses.

- **Terrorists:** Knowledgeable terrorist groups and hostile governments could potentially crash satellites and wage economic warfare by disrupting navigation and communication systems. The Department of Defense reports that its computer systems are probed approximately 250,000 times a year by unknown sources.

Computer Crime

The FBI estimates that businesses lose trillions of dollars a year from computer crimes. The number of these crimes has tripled in the past two years. Computer crime can take various forms including the creation of malicious programs, denial of service attacks, Internet scams, theft, and data manipulation.

Malicious Programs Crackers are notorious for creating and distributing malicious programs. These programs are called **malware,** which is short for **mal**icious soft**ware.** They are specifically designed to damage or disrupt a computer system. The three most common types of malware are viruses, worms, and Trojan horses.

- **Viruses** are programs that migrate through networks and operating systems, and most attach themselves to different programs and databases. While some viruses are relatively harmless, many can be quite destructive. Once activated, these destructive viruses can alter and/or delete files. Some delete all files on the hard disk and can damage system components. Creating and knowingly spreading a virus is a very serious crime and a federal offense punishable under the **Computer Fraud and Abuse Act.**

    Unfortunately, new computer viruses are appearing all the time. The best way to stay current is through services that keep track of viruses on a daily basis. For example, the Virus Radar On-line project tracks the most serious virus threats. See Figure 10-11.
- **Worms** are a special type of virus that does not attach itself to programs and databases. Rather it fills a computer system with self-replicating information, clogging the system so that its operations are slowed or stopped.

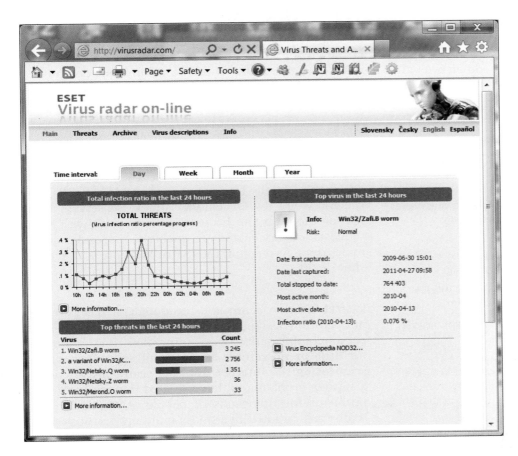

Figure 10-11 Tracking viruses

A recent worm traveled across the world within hours, stopping tens of thousands of computers along its way. Internet worms also can be carriers of more traditional viruses. Once the traditional virus has been deposited by a worm onto an unsuspecting computer system, the virus will either activate immediately or lie dormant until some future time.

Viruses and worms typically find their way into microcomputers through e-mail attachments and programs downloaded from the Internet. Because viruses can be so damaging, computer users are advised to never open an e-mail attachment from an unknown source and to exercise great care in accepting new programs and data from any source.

As we discussed in Chapter 5, antivirus programs alert users when certain kinds of viruses and worms enter their system. Some of the most widely used are Dr. Solomon's Anti-Virus, McAfee VirusScan, eSafe, and Norton AntiVirus. Unfortunately, new viruses are being developed all the time, and not all viruses can be detected. (See Making IT Work for You: Virus Protection on pages 150 and 151 in Chapter 5.)

- **Trojan horses** are programs that come into a computer system disguised as something else. Trojan horses are not viruses. Like worms, however, they can be carriers of viruses. The most common types of Trojan horses appear as free computer games and free screen saver programs that can be downloaded from the Internet. Once the Trojan horse is downloaded onto a computer system, the viruses are deposited and ready to activate. One of the most dangerous types of Trojan horse claims to provide free antivirus programs. They begin by locating and disabling any existing virus protection programs before depositing a virus.

- **Zombies** are computers infected by a virus, worm, or Trojan horse that allows them to be remotely controlled for malicious purposes. A collection of zombie computers is known as a **botnet,** or **robot network.** Botnets harness the combined power of many zombies for malicious activities like password cracking or sending junk e-mail. Because they are formed by many computers distributed across the Internet, botnets are hard to shut down even after they are detected. Unfortunately for individual computer owners, it also can be difficult to detect when a personal computer has been compromised.

Denial of Service A **denial of service (DoS) attack** attempts to slow down or stop a computer system or network by flooding a computer or network with requests for information and data. The targets of these attacks are usually Internet service providers (ISPs) and specific Web sites. Once under attack, the servers at the ISP or the Web site become overwhelmed with these requests for service and are unable to respond to legitimate users. As a result, the ISP or Web site is effectively shut down.

Internet Scams A **scam** is a fraudulent or deceptive act or operation designed to trick individuals into providing personal information or spending their time and money for little or no return. An **Internet scam** is simply a scam using the Internet. Internet scams are becoming a serious problem and have created financial and legal problems for thousands of people. Almost all of the scams are initiated by a mass mailing to unsuspecting individuals.

Type	Description
Identity theft	Individual(s) pose as ISPs, bank representatives, or government agencies requesting personal information. Once obtained, criminal(s) assume a person's identity for a variety of financial transactions.
Chain letter	Classic chain letter instructing recipient to send a nominal amount of money to each of five people on a list. The recipient removes the first name on the list, adds his or her name at the bottom, and mails the chain letter to five friends. This is also known as a pyramid scheme. Almost all chain letters are fraudulent and illegal.
Auction fraud	Merchandise is selected and payment is sent. Merchandise is never delivered.
Vacation prize	"Free" vacation has been awarded. Upon arrival at vacation destination, the accommodations are dreadful but can be upgraded for a fee.
Advance fee loans	Guaranteed low-rate loans available to almost anyone. After applicant provides personal loan-related information, the loan is granted subject to payment of an "insurance fee."

Figure 10-12 **Common Internet scams**

A technique often employed by scammers is **phishing** (pronounced "fishing"). Phishing attempts to trick Internet users into thinking a fake but official-looking Web site or e-mail is legitimate. Phishing has grown in sophistication, replicating entire Web sites like PayPal to try to lure users into divulging their financial information.

See Figure 10-12 for a list of common types of Internet scams.

Social Networking Risks As we have discussed in Chapter 2, social networking is designed for open sharing of information among individuals that share a common interest. Unfortunately, this openness can put individuals using social networking sites at risk. Some have lost their jobs after posting unflattering remarks about their supervisor or after discussing their dislike of their current job. Others post detailed personal information such as their birth dates, family member names, home addresses, and photos of their children. This information can be used by others to steal personal identities and commit other types of crimes. Always exercise caution when providing information on Facebook, Twitter, MySpace, and other social networking sites. Always use the privacy settings and controls that are provided at the social networking sites you use. (See Figure 10-13.)

Cyber-bullying A fairly recent and all-too-common phenomenon, **cyber-bullying** is the use of the Internet, cell phones, or other devices to send or post content intended to hurt or embarrass another person. Although not always a crime, it can lead to criminal prosecution. Cyber-bullying includes sending repeated unwanted e-mails to an individual who has stated that he or she wants no further contact with the sender, ganging up on victims in electronic forums, posting false statements designed to injure the reputation of another, maliciously disclosing personal data about a person that could lead to harm to that person, and sending any type of communication that is threatening or harassing. Never participate in cyber-bullying, and discourage others from participating in this dangerous and hateful activity.

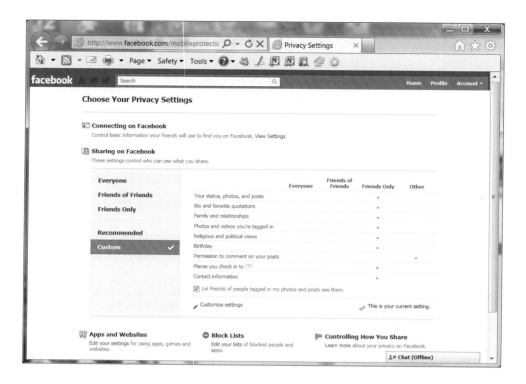

Figure 10-13 Facebook privacy controls

Rogue Wi-Fi Hotspots Free Wi-Fi networks are available almost everywhere from libraries to fast food restaurants and coffee shops. **Rogue Wi-Fi hotspots** imitate these free networks. These rogue networks operate close to the legitimate free hotspots and typically provide stronger signals that many users unsuspectingly connect to. Once connected, the rogue networks capture any and all information sent by the users to legitimate sites including user names and passwords.

Theft Theft can take many forms—of hardware, of software, of data, of computer time. Thieves steal equipment and programs, of course, but there are also white-collar crimes. These crimes include the theft of data in the form of confidential information such as preferred-client lists. Another common crime is the use (theft) of a company's computer time by an employee to run another business.

Data Manipulation Finding entry into someone's computer network and leaving a prankster's message may seem like fun, which is why hackers do it. It is still against the law. Moreover, even if the manipulation seems harmless, it may cause a great deal of anxiety and wasted time among network users.

The **Computer Fraud and Abuse Act** makes it a crime for unauthorized persons even to view—let alone copy or damage—data using any computer across state lines. It also prohibits unauthorized use of any government computer or a computer used by any federally insured financial institution. Offenders can be sentenced to up to 20 years in prison and fined up to $100,000.

For a summary of computer crimes, see Figure 10-14. For a brief history of computer crimes, visit our Web site at www.computing2013.com and enter the keyword **crime.**

Other Hazards

There are plenty of other hazards to computer systems and data besides criminals. They include the following:

- **Natural hazards:** Natural forces include fires, floods, wind, hurricanes, tornadoes, and earthquakes. Even home computer users should store

Computer Crime	Description
Malicious programs	Include viruses, worms, and Trojan horses
DoS	Causes computer systems to slow down or stop
Internet scams	Are scams over the Internet usually initiated by e-mail and involving phishing
Social networking risks	Includes posting work-related criticisms and disclosure of personal information
Cyber-bullying	Using the Internet, cell phones, or other devices to send or post content intended to hurt or embarrass another person
Rogue Wi-Fi hotspots	Imitate legitimate Wi-Fi hotspot in order to capture personal information
Theft	Includes hardware, software, and computer time
Data manipulation	Involves changing data or leaving prank messages

Figure 10-14 Computer crimes

backup disks of programs and data in safe locations in case of fire or storm damage.

- **Civil strife and terrorism:** Wars, riots, and terrorist activities are real risks in all parts of the world. Even people in developed countries must be mindful of these acts.
- **Technological failures:** Hardware and software don't always do what they are supposed to do. For instance, too little electricity, caused by a brownout or blackout, may cause the loss of data in primary storage. Too much electricity, as when lightning or some other electrical disturbance affects a power line, may cause a **voltage surge,** or **spike.** This excess of electricity may destroy chips or other electronic components of a computer.

  Microcomputer users should use a **surge protector,** a device that separates the computer from the power source of the wall outlet. When a voltage surge occurs, it activates a circuit breaker in the surge protector, protecting the computer system.

  Another technological catastrophe occurs when a hard-disk drive suddenly crashes, or fails (as discussed in Chapter 8), perhaps because it has been bumped inadvertently. If the user has forgotten to make backup copies of data on the hard disk, data may be lost. (See Figure 10-15.)

- **Human errors:** Human mistakes are inevitable. Data-entry errors are probably the most commonplace and, as we have discussed, can lead to mistaken identity. Programmer errors also occur frequently. Some mistakes may result from faulty design, as when a software manufacturer makes a deletion command closely resembling another command. Some errors may be the result of sloppy procedures. One such example occurs when office workers save important documents under file names that are not descriptive and not recognizable by others.

Figure 10-15 Crashes can result in lost data

CONCEPT CHECK

 Describe computer criminals including employees, outside users, hackers, crackers, carders, organized crime, and terrorists.

 Describe computer crimes including malicious programs, denial of service, Internet scams, social networking risks, rogue Wi-Fi spots, cyber-bullying, and theft.

 Define other hazards.

Measures to Protect Computer Security

Security is concerned with protecting information, hardware, and software from unauthorized use as well as from damage from intrusions, sabotage, and natural disasters. Considering the numerous ways in which computer systems and data can be compromised, we can see why security is a growing field. Some of the principal measures to protect computer security are restricting access, encrypting messages, anticipating disasters, and preventing data loss.

Restricting Access Security experts are constantly devising ways to protect computer systems from access by unauthorized persons. Sometimes security is a matter of putting guards on company computer rooms and checking the identification of everyone admitted. Other times it is using **biometric scanning** devices such as fingerprint and iris (eye) scanners. (See Figure 10-16.)

Oftentimes it is a matter of being careful about assigning passwords to people and of changing the passwords when people leave a company. **Passwords** are secret words or phrases (including numbers) that must be keyed into a computer system to gain access. For many applications on the Web, users assign their own passwords.

The strength of a password depends on how easily it can be guessed. A **dictionary attack** uses software to try thousands of common words sequentially in an attempt to gain unauthorized access to a user's account. For this reason, words, names, and simple numeric patterns make poor passwords. It is also important not to reuse passwords for different accounts. If one account is compromised, that password might be tried for access to other systems as well. For example, if a low-security account such as an online Web forum is compromised, that password could also be tried on higher-security accounts such as banking Web sites.

Explorations

Encryption is the only thing between criminals and private information on the Internet, such as bank accounts, passwords, and even tax returns.

To learn more about how encryption works, visit our Web site at www.computing2013.com and enter the keyword encryption.

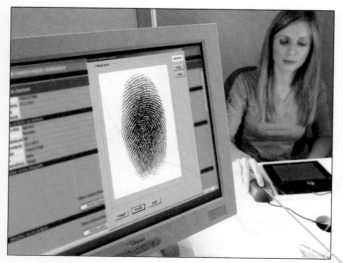

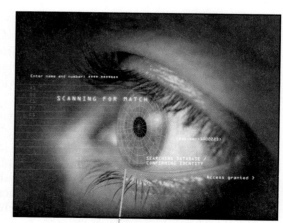

Fingerprint scanner   Iris scanner

Figure 10-16 Biometric scanning devices

As mentioned in previous chapters, major corporations today use special firewalls to control access to their internal computer networks. **Firewalls** act as a security buffer between the corporation's private network and all external networks, including the Internet. All electronic communications coming into and leaving the corporation must be evaluated by the firewall. Security is maintained by denying access to unauthorized communications.

Encrypting Data Whenever information is sent over a network or stored on a computer system, the possibility of unauthorized access exists. The solution is **encryption,** the process of coding information to make it unreadable except to those who have a special piece of information known as an **encryption key,** or, simply, **key.** Some common uses for encryption include

- **E-mail encryption:** Protects e-mail messages as they move across the Internet. One of the most widely used personal e-mail encryption programs is Pretty Good Privacy. (See Figure 10-17.)

- **File encryption:** Protects sensitive files by encrypting them before they are stored on a hard drive. Files can be encrypted individually, or specialized

Figure 10-17 Encrypted e-mail

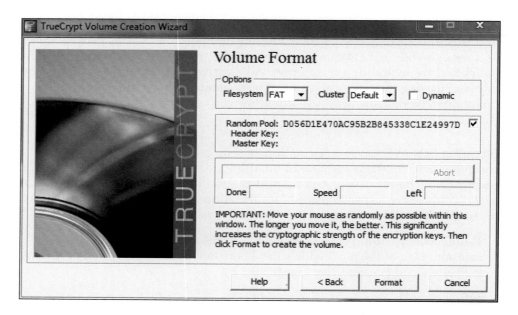

Figure 10-18 File encryption

software can be used to encrypt all files automatically each time they are saved to a certain hard drive location. (See Figure 10-18.)

- **Web site encryption:** Secures Web transactions, especially financial transactions. Web pages that accept passwords or confidential information like a credit card number are often encrypted.
- **Virtual Private Networks: Virtual private networks (VPNs)** encrypt connections between company networks and remote users such as workers connecting from home. This connection creates a secure virtual connection to a company LAN across the Internet.
- **Wireless network encryption:** Restricts access to authorized users on wireless networks. **WEP (Wired Equivalent Privacy)** is one of the best-known wireless encryption protocols. It is being replaced by more secure encryption protocols such as **WPA** and **WPA2 (Wi-Fi Protected Access)**.

Anticipating Disasters Companies (and even individuals) should prepare themselves for disasters. **Physical security** is concerned with protecting hardware from possible human and natural disasters. **Data security** is concerned with protecting software and data from unauthorized tampering or damage. Most large organizations have a **disaster recovery plan** describing ways to continue operating until normal computer operations can be restored.

Preventing Data Loss Equipment can always be replaced. A company's *data,* however, may be irreplaceable. Most companies have ways of trying to keep software and data from being tampered with in the first place. They include careful screening of job applicants, guarding of passwords, and auditing of data and

Explorations

How strong is your password?

To test password strength, visit our Web site a www.computing2013.com and enter the keyword password.

tips

What can you do to protect the security of your microcomputer system? Here are a few suggestions.

1 **Avoid viruses, spyware, and spam:** Install, use, and periodically update virus protection, antispyware, and antispam programs. All incoming files should be checked for viruses before they are executed or saved.

2 **Avoid attachments:** Never run an e-mail attachment with an .exe extension unless you are sure of its source.

3 **Update software:** Occasionally programs (especially operating systems) have security weaknesses. Software manufacturers often provide corrective code to eliminate the security holes. This code is often referred to as a patch.

4 **Guard the computer:** If you are concerned that your computer may be stolen, put a cable lock on it. If you subscribe or belong to an online information service, do not leave passwords nearby in a place accessible to others. Etch your driver's license number into your equipment. That way it can be identified in the event it is recovered after theft.

To see more tips, visit our Web site at www.computing2013.com and enter the keyword tips.

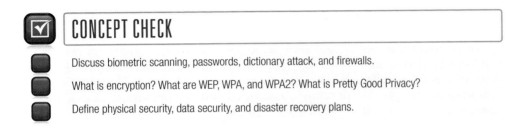

Measure	Description
Restricting access	Limit access to authorized persons using such measures as passwords and firewalls.
Encrypting data	Code all messages sent over a network.
Anticipating disasters	Prepare for disasters by ensuring physical security and data security through a disaster recovery plan.
Preventing data loss	Routinely copy data and store it at a remote location.

Figure 10-19 Measures to protect computer security

programs from time to time. Some systems use redundant storage to prevent loss of data even when a hard drive fails. We discussed RAID in Chapter 8, which is a commonly used type of redundant storage. Backup batteries protect against data loss due to file corruption during unexpected power outages.

Making frequent backups of data is essential to prevent data loss. Backups are often stored at an off-site location to protect data in case of theft, fires, floods, or other disasters. Incremental backups store multiple versions of data at different points in time to prevent data loss due to unwanted changes or accidental deletion.

See Figure 10-19 for a summary of the different measures to protect computer security.

☑ CONCEPT CHECK

- Discuss biometric scanning, passwords, dictionary attack, and firewalls.

- What is encryption? What are WEP, WPA, and WPA2? What is Pretty Good Privacy?

- Define physical security, data security, and disaster recovery plans.

Ethics

What do you suppose controls how computers can be used? You probably think first of laws. Of course, that is right, but technology is moving so fast that it is very difficult for our legal system to keep up. The essential element that controls how computers are used today is *ethics*.

Ethics, as you may know, are standards of moral conduct. **Computer ethics** are guidelines for the morally acceptable use of computers in our society. Ethical treatment is critically important to us all, and we are all entitled to ethical treatment. This includes the right to keep personal information, such as credit ratings and medical histories, from getting into unauthorized hands. These issues, largely under the control of corporations and government agencies, were covered earlier in this chapter. These issues and many more have been addressed in the Ethics boxes throughout this book. Now we'll examine two important issues in computer ethics where average users have a role to play.

Copyright and Digital Rights Management

Copyright is a legal concept that gives content creators the right to control use and distribution of their work. Materials that can be copyrighted include paintings, books, music, films, and even video games. Some users choose to make unauthorized copies of digital media, which violates copyright. For

ethics

Do you know anyone who has copied a term paper off the Internet? Or perhaps you know someone who has copied parts of Web page content from a variety of sites and combined the parts to form a term paper. Of course, this is unethical and most likely illegal. How widespread do you think these activities are? Not long ago, a professor at the University of Virginia developed a program to compare term paper content to published material on the Web. He found widespread indications of plagiarism. This program is now used at many schools and universities. Where do you fall on this one? Do you think it is ethical for instructors to employ a program that checks for plagiarism? Do you think it is ethical for students or other individuals to copy all or part of Internet content and then present the information as their original work? For additional discussion of this issue, see PLAGIARISM on page 327. To see more ethical issues, visit our Web site at www.computing2013.com and enter the keyword ethics.

Figure 10-20 iTunes Music Store Web site

example, making an unauthorized copy of a digital music file for a friend might be a copyright violation.

Software piracy is the unauthorized copying and distribution of software. According to a recent study, software piracy costs the software industry over $30 billion annually. The **Digital Millennium Copyright Act** establishes the right of a program owner to make a backup copy of any program. The act also establishes that none of these copies may be legally resold or given away. This may come as a surprise to those who copy software from a friend, but that's the law. It is also illegal to download copyright-protected music and videos from the Internet.

To prevent copyright violations, corporations often use **digital rights management (DRM).** DRM encompasses various technologies that control access to electronic media and files. Typically, DRM is used to (1) control the number of devices that can access a given file as well as (2) limit the kinds of devices that can access a file. Although some companies see DRM as a necessity to protect their rights, some users feel they should have the right to use the media they buy—including movies, music, software, and video games—as they choose.

Today, there are many legal sources for digital media. Television programs can be watched online, often for free, on television-network-sponsored sites. Sites like Pandora allow listeners to enjoy music at no cost. There are several online stores for purchasing music and video content. A pioneer in this area is Apple's iTunes Music Store. (See Figure 10-20.)

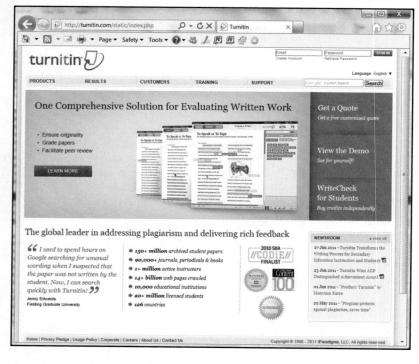

Figure 10-21 Turnitin Web site

Plagiarism

Another ethical issue is **plagiarism,** which means representing some other person's work and ideas as your own without giving credit to the original source. Although plagiarism was a problem long before the invention of computers, computer technology has made plagiarism easier. For example, simply cutting and pasting content from a Web page into a report or paper may seem tempting to an overworked student or employee.

Correspondingly, computer technology has made it easier than ever to recognize and catch **plagiarists.** For example, services such as Turnitin are dedicated to preventing Internet plagiarism. This service will examine the content of a paper and compare it to a wide range of known public electronic documents including Web page content. In this way, Turnitin can identify an undocumented paper or even parts of an undocumented paper. (See Figure 10-21.)

What is the distinction between ethics and computer ethics?

 Define copyright, software privacy, the Digital Millennium Copyright Act, and digital rights management.

 What is plagiarism? What is Turnitin and what does it do?

Careers in IT

Cryptography is the science of disguising and revealing encrypted information; in terms of information technology, cryptography usually refers to keeping any intercepted information private. For example, such information may be financial data, like banking and credit card information used in online shopping, or private e-mail and correspondence. **Cryptographers** design systems, break systems, and do research on encryption. Responsibilities typically do not include building and maintaining the computer networks that use cryptography; these are the duties of security engineers and network administrators. In general, cryptographers are mathematicians who specialize in making and breaking codes.

Many cryptographers work as consultants or professors of cryptography, yet there are full-time positions available at some large corporations or for the government. A PhD in cryptography is usually an essential prerequisite for a position as a cryptographer. However, all cryptographers must have broad experience in both mathematics and computer science or information systems.

Cryptographers can expect to earn an annual salary of $60,000 to over $100,000. Opportunities for advancement typically depend on experience; the most competitive field will be research positions in the military and at universities. Those with experience in computer science and information technology should be among the most employable mathematicians and increasingly in demand. To learn more about becoming a cryptographer, visit us at www.computing2013 .com and enter the keyword **careers.**

Now that you have learned about privacy, security, and ethics, let me tell you about my career as a cryptographer.

A LOOK TO THE FUTURE

A WebCam on Every Corner

Wireless Internet connections are becoming widely available in public places. At the same time, digital video and still camera technology is becoming more sophisticated and cheaper. As a result, images of public places are more accessible than ever before. Mobile phones are now equipped with cameras and Internet connectivity, and such devices are likely to improve in quality and speed in the future.

In 2007, Google launched Google Street View, a Web site that collected digital photographs from a car that drove around the streets of major cities and associated them with physical addresses. Since that time, many more cities have been added. This allowed users to take "virtual sight-seeing tours" from the comfort of their homes. A person could explore the streets of Manhattan or San Francisco, for example, or catch a glimpse of a destination before booking a hotel. However, this service stirred controversy when some of the images captured inadvertently showed people in embarrassing situations or engaged in illegal activities. The U.S. Department of Defense even banned this service from displaying images of military bases.

In the future, you might be able to see live video of a vacation spot, or even check in on your house while you are traveling. Public WebCams continue to grow in popularity, and new technology will enhance the images produced so very fine details can be observed. However, others might be able to observe your activities with a simple Web search. What do you think about public WebCams? Can you think of some benefits of seeing the world live on your computer? What concerns do you have about your privacy?

VISUAL SUMMARY | Privacy, Security, and Ethics

PRIVACY

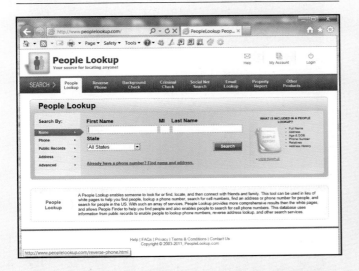

Effective implementation of computer technology involves maximizing positive effects while minimizing negative effects. The most significant concerns are **privacy, security,** and **ethics.**

Large Databases

Large organizations are constantly compiling information about us. **Reverse directories** list telephone numbers followed by subscriber names. **Information resellers (information brokers)** collect and sell personal data. **Electronic profiles** are compiled from databases to provide highly detailed and personalized descriptions of individuals.

Identity theft is the illegal assumption of someone's identity for the purposes of economic gain. **Mistaken identity** occurs when an electronic profile of one person is switched with another. The **Freedom of Information Act** entitles individuals access to governmental records relating to them.

Private Networks

Many organizations monitor employee e-mail and computer files using special software called **snoopware.**

The Internet and the Web

Many people believe that, while using the Web, little can be done to invade their privacy. This is called the **illusion of anonymity.**

PRIVACY

History files record locations of visited sites. **Cookies** store and track information. Two basic types are **traditional cookies** and **ad network cookies (adware cookies).** **Privacy mode (InPrivate Browsing; Private Browsing)** eliminates history files and blocks cookies.

Spyware secretly records and reports Internet activities. **Computer monitoring (keystroke loggers)** watches what you do. **Web bugs** provide information back to spammers about activity on your e-mail account. **Antispyware (spy removal programs)** detects Web bugs and monitoring software.

Online Identity

Many people post personal information and sometimes intimate details of their lives without considering the consequences. This creates an **online identity.** With the archiving and search features of the Web, this identity is indefinitely available to anyone who cares to look for it.

Major Laws on Privacy

The **Gramm-Leach-Bliley Act** protects personal financial information; the **Health Insurance Portability and Accountability Act (HIPAA)** protects medical records; and the **Family Educational Rights and Privacy Act (FERPA)** restricts disclosure of educational records.

To be a competent end user, you need to be aware of the potential impact of technology on people. You need to be sensitive to and knowledgeable about personal privacy, organizational security, and ethics.

SECURITY

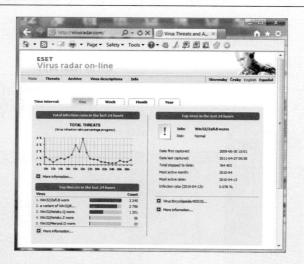

Computer Criminals

Computer criminals include employees, outside users, hackers and crackers, carders, organized crime, and terrorists.

- **Hackers**—create or improve programs and share those programs with fellow hackers. Typically are not criminals.
- **Crackers**—share programs designed to gain unauthorized access to computer systems or disrupt networks. Typically are criminals.
- **Carders**—specialize in stealing, trading, and using stolen credit cards over the Internet.

Computer Crime

Computer crime is an illegal action involving special knowledge of computer technology.

- Malicious programs (**malware**) include **viruses** (the **Computer Fraud and Abuse Act** makes spreading a virus a federal offense), **worms**, and **Trojan horses**. **Zombies** are remotely controlled infected computers used for malicious purposes. A collection of zombie computers is known as a **botnet**, or **robot network**.
- **Denial of service attack (DoS)** is an attempt to shut down or stop a computer system or network. It floods a computer or network with requests for information and data.
- **Scams** are designed to trick individuals into spending their time and money with little or no return. Common **Internet scams** include identity theft, chain letters, auction fraud, vacation prizes, and advance fee loans. These are frequently coupled with **phishing** Web sites or e-mails.

SECURITY

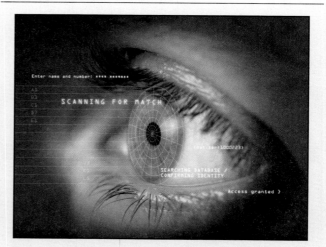

- Social networking risks include posting work-related criticisms and disclosure of personal information.
- **Cyber-bullying** is the use of the Internet, cell phones, or other devices to send or post content intended to hurt or embarrass another person.
- **Rogue Wi-Fi hotspots** imitate legitimate hotspots to capture personal information.
- Theft takes many forms including stealing hardware, software, data, and computer time.
- Data manipulation involves changing data or leaving prank messages. The **Computer Fraud and Abuse Act** helps protect against data manipulation.
- Other hazards include natural disasters, civil strife, terrorism, technological failures (**surge protectors** protect against **voltage surges** or **spikes**), and human error.

Measures to Protect Computer Security

Security is concerned with keeping hardware, software, data, and programs safe. Some measures are restricting access by using **biometric scanning** devices, **passwords**, and **firewalls**; encrypting data using **encryption keys** for e-mail, Web site access, **VPN**, and **wireless network encryption** (**WEP, WPA,** and **WPA2** protocols); anticipating disasters (**physical** and **data security, disaster recovery plans**); and preventing data loss.

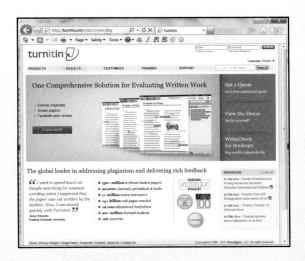

What do you suppose controls how computers can be used? You probably think first of laws. Of course, that is right, but technology is moving so fast that it is very difficult for our legal system to keep up. The essential element that controls how computers are used today is *ethics*.

Ethics are standards of moral conduct. **Computer ethics** are guidelines for the morally acceptable use of computers in our society. We are all entitled to ethical treatment. This includes the right to keep personal information, such as credit ratings and medical histories, from getting into unauthorized hands.

Copyright and Digital Rights Management

Copyright is a legal concept that gives content creators the right to control use and distribution of their work. Materials that can be copyrighted include paintings, books, music, films, and even video games.

Software piracy is the unauthorized copying and distribution of software. The software industry loses over $30 billion annually to software piracy. Two related topics are the Digital Millennium Copyright Act and digital rights management.

- **Digital Millennium Copyright Act** establishes the right of a program owner to make a backup copy of any program and disallows the creation of copies to be sold or given away. It is also illegal to download copyright-protected music and videos from the Internet.
- **Digital rights management (DRM)** is a collection of technologies designed to prevent copyright violations. Typically, DRM is used to (1) control the number of devices that can access a given file as well as (2) limit the kinds of devices that can access a file.

Today, many legal sources for digital media exist, including:

- Television programs that can be watched online, often for free, on television-network-sponsored sites.
- Sites like Pandora that allow listeners to enjoy music at no cost.
- Online stores that legally sell music and video content. A pioneer in this area is Apple's iTunes Music Store.

Plagiarism

Plagiarism is the illegal and unethical representation of some other person's work and ideas as your own without giving credit to the original source. Examples of plagiarism include cutting and pasting Web content into a report or paper.

Recognizing and catching **plagiarists** is relatively easy. For example, services such as *Turnitin* are dedicated to preventing Internet plagiarism. This service examines a paper's content and compares it to a wide range of known public electronic documents including Web page content. Exact duplication or paraphrasing is readily identified.

CAREERS IN IT

Cryptographers design encryption algorithms, break codes, and provide support to national security efforts. PhD in mathematics and broad experience in computer science are required. Salary range is $60,000 to over $100,000.

KEY TERMS

access (295)
accuracy (295)
ad network cookie (300)
adware cookie (300)
antispyware (302)
biometric scanning (312)
botnet (308)
carders (306)
computer crime (306)
computer ethics (315)
Computer Fraud and Abuse
  Act (307, 310)
computer monitoring software (302)
cookies (300)
copyright (315)
cracker (306)
cryptographer (317)
cryptography (317)
cyber-bullying (309)
data security (314)
denial of service (DoS) attack (308)
dictionary attack (312)
Digital Millennium Copyright Act (316)
digital rights management
  (DRM) (316)
disaster recovery plan (314)
electronic profile (296)
encryption (313)
encryption key (313)
ethics (315)
Family Educational Rights and Privacy
  Act (FERPA) (303)
firewall (313)
Freedom of Information Act (298)
Gramm-Leach-Bliley Act (303)
hacker (306)
Health Insurance Portability and
  Accountability Act (HIPAA) (303)
history file (299)
identity theft (297)
illusion of anonymity (299)

information broker (296)
information reseller (296)
InPrivate Browsing (301)
Internet scam (308)
key (313)
keystroke logger (302)
malware (307)
mistaken identity (298)
online identity (303)
password (312)
phishing (309)
physical security (314)
plagiarism (316)
plagiarist (316)
privacy (295)
privacy mode (301)
Private Browsing (301)
property (295)
reverse directory (295)
robot network (308)
rogue Wi-Fi hotspot (310)
scam (308)
security (312)
snoopware (298)
software piracy (316)
spike (311)
spy removal program (302
spyware (301)
surge protector (311)
traditional cookies (300)
Trojan horse (308)
virtual private network (VPN) (314)
virus (307)
voltage surge (311)
Web bug (301)
WEP (Wired Equivalent Privacy) (314)
wireless network encryption (314)
worm (307)
WPA (Wi-Fi Protected Access) (314)
WPA2 (Wi-Fi Protected Access 2) (314)
zombie (308)

To test your knowledge of these key terms with animated flash cards, visit us at
www.computing2013.com and enter the keyword terms10.

MULTIPLE CHOICE

Circle the letter of the correct answer.

1. The three primary privacy issues are accuracy, property, and:
   a. access
   b. ethics
   c. ownership
   d. security

2. To easily get names, addresses, and other details about a person using only his or her telephone number, government authorities and others use a(n):
   a. adware cookie
   b. keystroke logger
   c. reverse directory
   d. worm

3. Browsers store the locations of sites visited in a:
   a. history file
   b. menu
   c. tool bar
   d. firewall

4. The browser mode that eliminates history files and blocks most cookies.
   a. detect
   b. insert
   c. privacy
   d. sleep

5. The information that people voluntarily post in social networking sites, blogs, and photo- and video-sharing sites is used to create their:
   a. access approval
   b. firewall
   c. online identity
   d. phish

6. Computer criminals who specialize in stealing, trading, and using stolen credit cards over the Internet are known as:
   a. carders
   b. card scammers
   c. cyber traders
   d. identity thieves

7. Programs that come into a computer system disguised as something else are called:
   a. Trojan horses
   b. viruses
   c. Web bugs
   d. zombies

8. The use of the Internet, cell phones, or other devices to send or post content intended to hurt or embarrass another person is known as:
   a. cyber-bullying
   b. online harassment
   c. social media discrimination
   d. unethical communication

9. Special hardware and software used to control access to a corporation's private network is known as a(n):
   a. antivirus program
   b. communication gate
   c. firewall
   d. spyware removal program

10. To prevent copyright violations, corporations often use:
    a. ACT
    b. DRM
    c. VPN
    d. WPA

For an interactive multiple-choice practice test, visit us at www.computing2013 .com and enter the keyword multiple10.

MATCHING

Match each numbered item with the most closely related lettered item. Write your answers in the spaces provided.

a. accuracy
b. biometric
c. cookies
d. encryption
e. information brokers
f. malware
g. phishing
h. plagiarism
i. spyware
j. zombies

_____ 1. Privacy concern that relates to the responsibility to ensure correct data collection.

_____ 2. Individuals who collect and sell personal data.

_____ 3. Small pieces of information deposited on your hard disk from Web sites you have visited.

_____ 4. Wide range of programs that secretly record and report an individual's activities on the Internet.

_____ 5. Malicious programs that damage or disrupt a computer system.

_____ 6. Infected computers that can be remotely controlled.

_____ 7. Used by scammers to trick Internet users with official-looking Web sites.

_____ 8. A type of scanning device such as fingerprint and iris (eye) scanner.

_____ 9. Process of coding information to make it unreadable except to those who have a key.

_____ 10. An ethical issue relating to using another person's work and ideas as your own without giving credit to the original source.

For an interactive matching practice test, visit our Web site at www.computing2013 .com and enter the keyword matching10.

OPEN-ENDED

On a separate sheet of paper, respond to each question or statement.

1. Define privacy, and discuss the impact of large databases, private networks, the Internet, and the Web.
2. Define and discuss online identity and the major privacy laws.
3. Define security and discuss computer criminals including employees, hackers, crackers, carders, and organized crime.
4. Define computer crime, and the impact of malicious programs, including viruses, worms, and Trojan horses, and zombies as well as cyber-bullying, denial of service, Internet scams, social networking risks, rogue Wi-Fi hotspots, theft, data manipulation, and other hazards.
5. Discuss ways to protect computer security including restricting access, encrypting data, anticipating disasters, and preventing data loss.
6. Define ethics, and describe copyright law and plagiarism.

MAKING IT WORK FOR YOU

The following questions are designed to demonstrate ways that you can effectively use technology today.

1 SPYWARE

Have you installed any free software from the Internet? Did you know that seemingly harmless software might actually be spying on you, even sending personal information to advertisers or worse? Fortunately, spyware removal programs can help. After reviewing Making IT Work for You: Spyware Removal on pages 304 and 305, answer the following: (a) Define spyware and discuss how it works. (b) Describe the process for downloading and installing Lavasoft's Ad-Aware. (c) Describe the capabilities of Ad-Aware. (d) Do you think that spyware might be on your computer? If yes, how do you suppose the spyware was deposited onto your system? If no, why are you so confident?

2 PERSONAL FIREWALLS

At one time, firewalls were used only for large servers. Today firewalls are available for almost any device that connects to the Internet and are essential to ensure security. Connect to our Web site at www.computing2013.com and enter the keyword security to link to a personal firewall product for home users. Once connected, read about the firewall and then answer the following: (a) Is this firewall a hardware or software solution? (b) Describe the procedure for installing the firewall. (c) What types of security risks does this firewall protect against? (d) Are there any security risks the firewall does not cover? If so, how can those risks be reduced?

3 PERSONAL BACKUPS

Do you make backups of your files? If your computer crashed or was lost or stolen today, would you be able to recover all your important data? Backup systems used to be just for large companies and organizations, but today personal backup software makes it simple to keep your information safe. Visit our Web site at www.computing2013.com and enter the keyword backup to link to a site about personal backup software. Once connected, explore the site, and briefly answer the following: (a) Where does the backup software store the backups it makes? (b) Describe the steps necessary to back up a computer using the software. (c) Describe the steps necessary to restore files to a computer from a previous backup using the software.

EXPLORATIONS

The following questions are designed to add depth and detail to your understanding of specific topics presented within this chapter. The questions direct you to sources other than the textbook to obtain this knowledge.

1 HOW WEB BUGS WORK

The Internet is popular because it is fast, cheap, and open to everyone. These qualities also make it an ideal tool for criminals. Unscrupulous people can use programs called Web bugs to spy on you when you use the Internet. To learn more about how Web bugs work, visit our Web site at www.computing2013.com and enter the keyword bugs. Then answer the following questions: (a) How can a Web bug infect your computer? (b) When a Web bug is delivered by e-mail, it typically sends a copy of that e-mail back to the server. What is the significance or purpose of this activity? (c) Do you think Web bugs are really a privacy concern? Do you think your computer may have one? How could you find out?

2 MISTAKEN IDENTITY

A simple typo can result in mistaken identity. Such mistakes can have a tremendous impact on a person's career, family, and future. To learn more about mistaken identity, visit our Web site at www.computing2013.com and enter the keyword id. Then answer the following questions: (a) Have you been a victim of mistaken identity? If so, please discuss. (b) If your response was "yes," how would you verify that mistaken identity has occurred? (c) Perhaps you have been a victim without knowing it. List the questions that should be considered.

3 AIR TRAVEL DATABASE

To curb possible terrorist threats, the government has implemented a controversial database, known as the Computer Assisted Passenger Prescreening System (CAPPS). This database determines a "possible threat score" for each individual to determine whether he or she can fly. Research CAPPS on the Internet and then answer the following questions: (a) How does CAPPS determine who is a security risk? (b) What personal information is gathered by CAPPS? (c) How might CAPPS infringe on personal privacy?

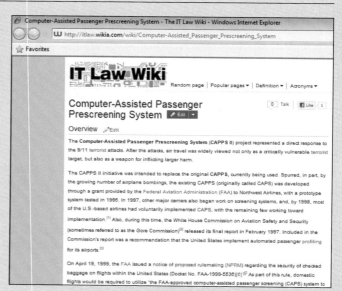

ETHICS

The following questions are designed to explore ethical issues related to technology and to develop the ability to think critically and communicate effectively. Respond to the questions by either creating a one-page paper or preparing for an in-depth classroom discussion.

1 PLAGIARISM

Some argue that when writing a paper using research from the Internet, it is difficult to draw a distinction between using information found on a Web site and plagiarizing its content. They also contend that no one is injured from this activity. Others argue that it is easy to distinguish between researching information and plagiarism. They further claim that the students who do not plagiarize bear the burden or cost when one of their classmates plagiarizes. Review the Ethics box on page 315 and then respond to the following: (a) Do you think it is ethical for instructors to employ a program that checks for plagiarism? Why or why not? (b) Do you think it is ethical for students or any individual to copy all or part of a Web page's content and then present the information as his or her original work? Why or why not? (c) How would you distinguish between using the Web for research and plagiarizing Web content? Be as specific as possible. (d) Does your school have a policy specifically regarding plagiarism of Web content? If yes, what is the policy? If not, what would you suggest would be an appropriate policy?

ENVIRONMENT

The following questions are designed to explore environmental issues related to technology and to develop the ability to think critically and communicate effectively. Respond to the questions by either creating a one-page paper or preparing for an in-depth classroom discussion.

1 ENVIRONMENTAL SCAMS

With all the interest in environmental protection and renewable energy sources, almost everyone is open to new ideas and products. Unfortunately, con artists and scammers are actively at work promoting fake products and investment opportunities. Review the Environment box on page 308 and research energy scams. Then respond to the following: (a) What is an energy scam? (b) List and briefly describe three such scams. (c) Have you ever received an e-mail promoting environmentally related products? If so, describe the product and discuss whether it appeared legitimate. (d) Have you ever been a victim of an environmentally related scam? If so, describe the scam. If not, do you think that you could be a target in the future? Why or why not?

Your Future and Information Technology

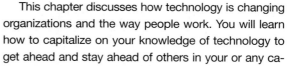

Competencies

After you have read this chapter, you should be able to:

1 Explain why it's important to have an individual strategy to be a "winner" in the information age.

2 Describe how technology is changing the nature of competition.

3 Discuss four ways people may react to new technology.

4 Describe how you can stay current with your career.

5 Describe different careers in information technology.

▲ Download the free *Computing Essentials 2013* app for videos, key term flashcards, quizzes, and the game, *Over the Edge!*

Why should I read this chapter?

Not long ago, for professionals to know one another and to work together, they had to be in the same location. That was then, and this is now. Now, many professionals can work and live almost anywhere they choose. Today's professionals use their tablet PCs, smartphones, and other types of mobile computers to communicate, work together, network, and even find new career opportunities.

This chapter discusses how technology is changing organizations and the way people work. You will learn how to capitalize on your knowledge of technology to get ahead and stay ahead of others in your or any career path. Additionally, you'll learn how to use technology to discover new career opportunities. To be competent and to be competitive in today's professional workplace, you need to know and to understand these things.

chapter 11

Hi, I'm Alan. We talked all the way back in Chapter 1. Since then, you've talked with several computer specialists and learned a lot about computers and information technology. I'd like to conclude this book by talking with you about your future and how to use information technology to your advantage in your personal life and in your professional career.

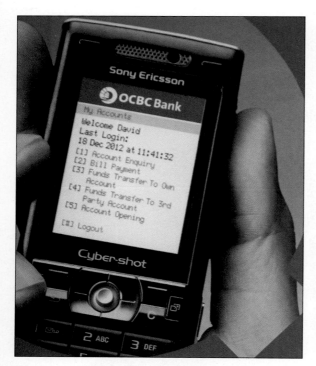

Figure 11-1 Online banking is an example of technology used in business strategy

Introduction

Throughout this book, we have emphasized practical subjects that are useful to you now or will be very soon. Accordingly, this final chapter is not about the far future, say, 10 years from now. Rather, it is about today and the near future—about developments whose outlines we can already see. It is about how organizations adapt to technological change. It is also about what you as an individual can do to keep your computer competency up to date.

Are the times changing any faster now than they ever have? It's hard to say. People who were alive when radios, cars, and airplanes were being introduced certainly lived through some dramatic changes. Has technology made our own times even more dynamic? Whatever the answer, it is clear we live in a fast-paced age. The challenge for you as an individual is to devise ways to stay current and to use technology to your advantage.

To stay competent, end users need to recognize the impact of technological change on organizations and people. They need to know how to use change to their advantage and how to be winners. Although end users do not need to be specialists in information technology, they should be aware of career opportunities in the area.

Changing Times

Almost all businesses have become aware that they must adapt to changing technology or be left behind. Almost all organizations have formal plans to keep track of technology and implement it in their competitive strategies. For example, almost every major bank now provides online banking using smartphones. Users can keep track of their spending, pay bills, and make deposits all from their smartphones from almost anywhere. (See Figure 11-1.) Not only do they require fewer human tellers, but also they are available 24 hours a day. More and more banks also are trying to go electronic, doing away with paper transactions wherever possible.

What's next for the banking industry? Some banks, known as Internet banks, have even done away with physical bank buildings and conduct all business over the Web. (See Figure 11-2.) In addition, banks are exploring the use of some very sophisticated application programs. These programs will accept cursive writing (the handwriting on checks) directly as input, verify check signatures, and process the check without human intervention.

Clearly, such changes do away with some jobs—those of many bank tellers and cashiers, for example. However, they create opportunities for other people. New technology requires people who are truly capable of working with it. These are not the people who think every piece of equipment is so simple they can just turn it on and use it. Nor

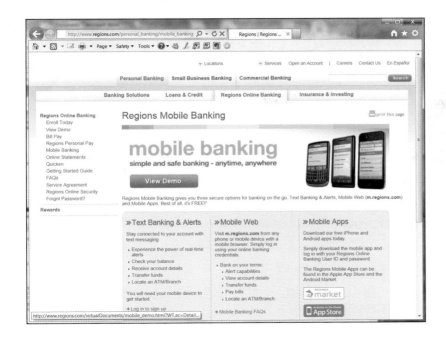

Figure 11-2 **Internet banks conduct business over the Web**

are they those who think each new machine is a potential disaster. In other words, new technology needs people who are not afraid to learn about it and are able to manage it. The real issue, then, is not how to make technology better. Rather, it is how to integrate the technology with people.

You are in a very favorable position compared with many other people in industry today. After reading the previous chapters, you have learned more than just the basics of hardware, software, connectivity, and the Internet. You have learned about the most current technology. You are therefore able to use these tools to your advantage—to be a winner.

How do you become and stay a winner? In brief, the answer is: You must form your own individual strategy for dealing with change. First let us look at how businesses are handling technological change. Then let's look at how people are reacting to these changes. Finally, we will offer a few suggestions that will enable you to keep up with and profit from the information revolution.

CONCEPT CHECK

Cite examples of ways computers are changing the business world.

What are the human requirements of new technology?

Technology and Organizations

Technology can introduce new ways for businesses to compete with each other. Some of the principal changes are as follows.

New Products

Technology creates products that operate faster, are priced cheaper, are often of better quality, or are wholly new. Indeed, new products can be individually tailored to a particular customer's needs. For example, the Chase Bank accepts remote deposits from mobile computers. (See Figure 11-3.) Using the Internet, the

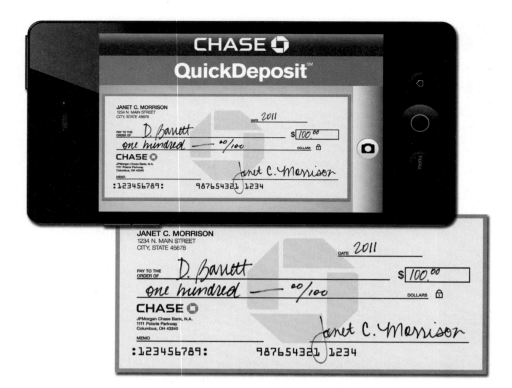

Figure 11-3 Remote deposit via mobile computer

customer simply connects to Chase, sends images of the front and back of a check to be deposited, and requests that Chase deposit the amount of the check into his or her account. Upon receiving the images, Chase completes the transaction.

New Enterprises

Information technology can build entirely new businesses. Two examples are Internet service providers and Web site development companies.

- Years ago, the only computer connectivity options available to individuals were through online service providers like America Online and through colleges and universities. Now, connectivity is available through hundreds of national service providers, thousands of local service providers, and locations that offer WiFi access.
- Thousands of small companies specializing in Web site development have sprung up in the past few years. These companies help small- to medium-sized organizations by providing assistance in evaluating, creating, and maintaining Web sites.

New Customer and Supplier Relationships

Businesses that make their information systems easily available may make their customers less likely to take their business elsewhere. For instance, Federal Express, the overnight package delivery service, does everything possible to make its customers dependent on it. Upon request, customers receive airbills with their name, address, and account number preprinted on them, making shipping and billing easier. Package numbers are scanned into the company's information system so that they can be tracked from pickup point to destination. (See Figure 11-4.) Thus, apprehensive customers can be informed very quickly of the exact location of their package as it travels toward its destination.

Figure 11-4 New technology helps FedEx maintain customer loyalty

CONCEPT CHECK

- What is the role of technology in creating new products?

- Describe two new enterprises built by information technology.

- Discuss how technology can create new customers and affect supplier relationships.

Technology and People

Clearly, recent technological changes, and those sure to come in the near future, will produce significant changes and opportunities in the years ahead. How should we be prepared for them?

People have different coping styles when it comes to technology. It has been suggested, for instance, that people react to changing technology in one of four ways: cynicism, naivete, frustration, and proactivity.

Cynicism

The **cynic** feels that, for a manager at least, the idea of using a microcomputer is overrated. (See Figure 11-5.) Learning and using it take too much time, time that could be delegated to someone else. Doing spreadsheets and word processing, according to the cynic, are tasks that managers should understand. However, the cynic feels that such tasks take time away from a manager's real job of developing plans and setting goals for the people being supervised.

Cynics may express their doubts openly, especially if they are top managers. Or they may only pretend to be interested in microcomputers, when actually they are not interested at all.

Naivete

Many **naive** people are unfamiliar with computers. They may think computers are magic boxes capable of solving all kinds of problems that computers really can't handle. On the other hand, some naive persons are actually quite familiar with computers but underestimate the difficulty of changing computer systems or of generating certain information.

Frustration

The **frustrated** person may already be quite busy and may hate having to take time to learn about microcomputers. Such a person feels it is an imposition to have to learn something new or is too impatient to try to understand the manuals explaining what hardware and software are supposed to do. The result is continual frustration. (See Figure 11-6.) Some people are frustrated because they try to do too much. Or they're frustrated because they find manuals difficult to understand. In some cases poorly written manuals are at fault.

Proactivity

Webster's Collegiate Dictionary defines **proactive,** in part, as "acting in anticipation of future problems, needs, or changes." A proactive person looks at technology in a positive realistic way. (See Figure 11-7.) They are not cynics, underestimating the likely impact of technology on their

Figure 11-5 The cynic: "These gadgets are overrated."

Figure 11-6 The frustrated person: "This stuff doesn't make sense half the time."

Figure 11-7 The proactive person: "How can I use this new tool?"

lives. They are not naive, overestimating the ability of technology to solve the world's or their problems. They do not become frustrated easily and give up using technology. Proactive people are positive in their outlook and look at new technology as providing new tools that, when correctly applied, can positively impact their lives.

Most of us fall into one of the four categories. Cynicism, naivete, frustration, and proactivity are common human responses to change. Do you see yourself or others around you responding to technology in any of these ways? For those who respond negatively, just being aware of their reaction can help them become more positive and proactive to tomorrow's exciting new changes in technology.

CONCEPT CHECK

 Describe three negative ways people cope with technological changes in the workplace.

 Describe one positive way people cope with technological change in the workplace.

 Define proactive.

How You Can Be a Winner

So far we have described how progressive organizations are using technology in the information age. Now let's concentrate on you as an individual. (See Making IT Work for You: Locating Job Opportunities Online on pages 336 and 337.) How can you stay ahead? Here are some ideas.

Stay Current

Whatever their particular line of work, successful professionals keep up both with their own fields and with the times. We don't mean you should try to become a computer expert and read a lot of technical magazines. Rather, you should concentrate on your profession and learn how computer technology is being used within it.

Every field has trade journals, whether the field is interior design, personnel management, or advertising. Most such journals regularly present articles about the uses of computers. It's important that you also belong to a trade or industry association and go to its meetings. Many associations sponsor seminars and conferences that describe the latest information and techniques.

Another way to stay current is by participating electronically with special-interest newsgroups on the Internet.

Maintain Your Computer Competency

Actually, you should try to stay ahead of the technology. Books, journals, and trade associations are the best sources of information about new technology that applies to your field. The general business press—*Bloomberg Businessweek, Fortune, Inc., The Wall Street Journal*, and the business section of your local newspaper—also carries computer-related articles.

However, if you wish, you can subscribe to a magazine that covers micro-computers and information technology more specifically. Examples are *Info-*

Figure 11-8 **Professional organizations and contacts help you keep up in your field**

World, PC World, and *MacWorld*. You also may find it useful to look at newspapers and magazines that cover the computer industry as a whole. An example of such a periodical is *ComputerWorld*. Most of these magazines also have online versions available on the Web.

Develop Professional Contacts

Besides being members of professional associations, successful people make it a point to maintain contact with others in their field. They stay in touch by telephone, e-mail, and social networking sites like Facebook, MySpace, LinkedIn, and Google+. Whevever possible, they go to lunch with others in their line of work. Doing this lets them learn what other people are doing in their jobs. It tells them what other firms are doing and what tasks are being automated. Developing professional contacts can keep you abreast not only of new information but also of new job possibilities. (See Figure 11-8.) It also offers social benefits. An example of a professional organization found in many areas is the local association of Realtors.

Develop Specialties

Develop specific as well as general skills. You want to be well-rounded *within* your field, but certainly not a "jack of all trades, master of none." Master a trade or two within your profession. At the same time, don't become identified with a specific technological skill that might very well become obsolete.

The best advice is to specialize to some extent. However, don't make your specialty so tied to technology that you'll be in trouble if the technology shifts. For example, if your career is in marketing or graphic design, it makes sense to learn about desktop publishing and Web page design. (See Figure 11-9.) In this way, you can learn to make high-quality, inexpensive graphics layouts. It would not make as much sense for you to become an expert on, say, the various types of monitors used to display the graphics layouts because such monitors are continually changing.

Expect to take classes during your working life to keep up with developments in your field. Some professions require more keeping up than others—a

Figure 11-9 **Desktop publishing: A good specialty to develop for certain careers**

Making IT work for you

LOCATING JOB OPPORTUNITIES ONLINE

Did you know that you can use the Internet to find a job? You can locate and browse through job listings. You can even electronically post your résumé for prospective employers to review.

Browsing Job Listings Four of the top job search sites on the Web are LinkedIn (linkedin.com), Monster (monster.com), Career-Cast (careercast.com), and Indeed (indeed.com). You can connect to these sites and browse through job opportunities. For example, after connecting to indeed.com, you can search for a job by following steps similar to those shown below.

1
- Visit www.indeed.com.
- Enter a job title, keyword, or company name.
- Enter location to search.
- Click the *Find Jobs* button, or click the *Advanced Job Search* link underneath to enter keywords for refining your search.

2
- Select a job title from the table of results to learn more about that job posting.

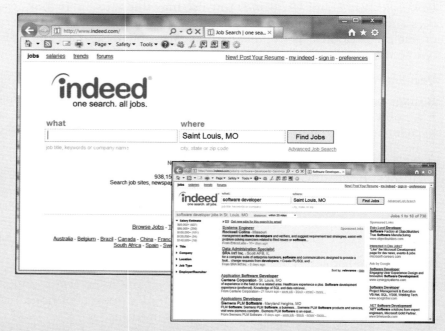

Posting Your Résumé To make your qualifications known to prospective employers, you can post your résumé at the job search site.

1 ● Click *Post Your Resume* on the home page.

● Enter an e-mail address and password to create a free account.

● Select *Browse* and *Upload Resume.* If you do not have a résumé to upload, select *create a blank resume* to create one.

2 ● Fill in the blanks to create a professional résumé.

Your résumé is posted and searchable by potential employers.

Automated Alerts To help you find a job faster, you can set up automatic searches. When new jobs are posted that match your search, you can be alerted instantly by e-mail or mobile phone.

1 ● Click *Tools* on the home page.

● Select the appropriate link to *Download a Mobile Job Search* app, save searches with *my.indeed,* or *E-mail Job.*

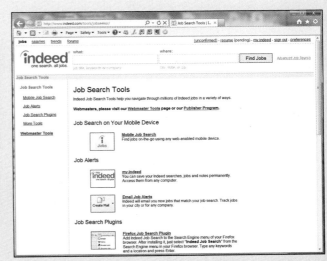

The Web is continually changing, and some of the specifics presented in this Making IT Work for You may have changed.

To learn about other ways to make information technology work for you, visit our Web site at www.computing2013.com and enter the keyword miw.

computer specialist, for example, compared to a human resources manager. Whatever the training required, always look for ways to adapt and improve your skills to become more productive and marketable. There may be times when you are tempted to start all over again and learn completely new skills. However, a better course of action may be to use emerging technology to improve your present base of skills. This way you can build on your current strong points and then branch out to other fields from a position of strength.

Be Alert for Organizational Change

Every organization has formal lines of communication—for example, supervisor to middle manager to top manager. However, there is also the *grapevine*—informal lines of communication. (See Figure 11-10.) Some service departments will serve many layers of management and be abreast of the news on all levels. For instance, the art director for advertising may be aware of several aspects of a companywide marketing campaign. Secretaries and administrative assistants know what is going on in more than one area.

Being part of the office grapevine can alert you to important changes—for instance, new job openings—that can benefit you. However, you always have to assess the validity of what you hear on the grapevine. Moreover, it's not advisable to be a contributor to office gossip. Behind-the-back criticisms of other people have a way of getting back to the person criticized.

Be especially alert for new trends within the organization—future hiring, layoffs, automation, mergers with other companies, and the like. Notice which areas are receiving the greatest attention from top management. One tip-off is to see what kind of outside consultants are being brought in. Independent consultants are usually invited in because a company believes it needs advice in an area with which it has insufficient experience.

Look for Innovative Opportunities

You may understand your job better than anyone—even if you've only been there a few months. Look for ways to make it more efficient. How can present procedures be automated? How can new technology make your tasks easier? Discuss your ideas with your supervisor, the training director, or the head of the information systems department. Or discuss them with someone else who can see that you get the recognition you deserve. (Co-workers may or may not be receptive and may or may not try to take credit themselves.)

A good approach is to present your ideas in terms of saving money rather than "improving information." Managers are generally more impressed with

Figure 11-10 Informal communication can alert you to important organizational changes

ideas that can save dollars than with ideas that seem like potential break-throughs in the quality of decisions.

In general, it's best to concentrate on the business and organizational problems that need solving. Then look for a technological way of solving them. That is, avoid becoming too enthusiastic about a particular technology and then trying to make it fit the work situation.

CONCEPT CHECK

 Outline the strategies you can use to stay ahead and be successful in your career.

 Discuss the advantages and disadvantages of specialization.

Describe how you would stay alert for organizational changes.

Careers in IT

Being a winner does not necessarily mean having a career in information systems. There are, however, several jobs within information technology that you might like to consider. We have discussed many of these careers in the preceding chapters (see Figure 11-11).

To learn more about these careers, visit our Web site at www.computing2013.com and enter the keyword **careers**.

If you are considering a career in information technology, here is a list of some of the most-interesting, best-paid careers. Best of luck to you in whatever career you choose.

Career	Responsibilities
Computer support specialist	Provides technical support to customers and other users
Computer technician	Repairs and installs computer components and systems
Computer trainer	Instructs users on the latest software or hardware
Cryptographer	Designs, tests, and researches encryption procedures
Data entry worker	Inputs customer information, lists, and other types of data
Database administrator	Uses database management software to determine the most efficient ways to organize and access data
Desktop publisher	Creates and formats publication-ready material
Information systems manager	Oversees the work of programmers, computer specialists, systems analysts, and other computer professionals
Network administrator	Creates and maintains networks
Programmer	Creates, tests, and troubleshoots computer programs
Software engineer	Analyzes users' needs and creates application software
Systems analyst	Plans and designs information systems
Technical writer	Prepares instruction manuals, technical reports, and other scientific or technical documents
Webmaster	Develops and maintains Web sites and Web resources

Figure 11-11 Careers in information systems

A LOOK TO THE FUTURE

Maintaining Computer Competency and Becoming Proactive

This is not the end; it is the beginning. Being a skilled computer end user and having computer competency are not a matter of thinking, "Someday I'll have to learn all about that." They are a matter of living in the present and keeping an eye on the future. Computer competency also demands the discipline to keep up with emerging technology. Yet it is important not to focus on the "what ifs" of technology. Computer competency demands concentration on your goals and dedication to learning how the computer can aid you in obtaining these goals. Being an end user, in short, is not about trying to avoid failure. Rather, it is about always moving toward success—about taking control of the exciting new tools available to you.

CHANGING TIMES

Individuals, businesses, and organizations must adapt to changing technology or be left behind.

Banking Industry

The banking industry provides online banking using smartphones to provide 24-hour service without incurring additional employee costs. Internet banks conduct all business over the Web.

Many changes do away with jobs. Technology, however, creates opportunities. New technology requires people who are truly capable of working with it. To become and stay a winner, you must form your own individual strategy for dealing with changes.

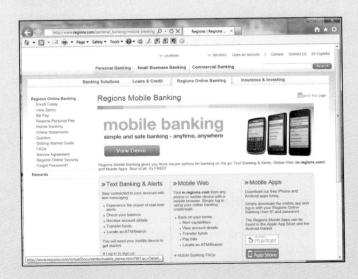

TECHNOLOGY AND ORGANIZATIONS

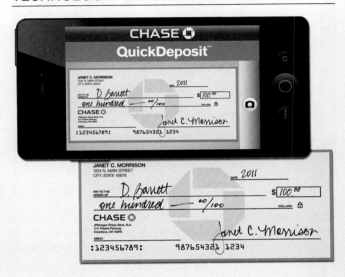

Technology can introduce new ways for businesses to compete with each other. They can compete by *creating new products, establishing new enterprises,* and *developing new customer and supplier relationships.*

New Products

Technology creates products that operate faster, are priced more cheaply, are often better quality, or are wholly new. New products can be individually tailored to a particular customer's needs.

New Enterprises

Technology can build entirely new businesses. Two examples:

- Internet service providers—years ago, only a few Internet service providers were available. Now, thousands of national and local providers are available.
- Web site development companies—thousands of small companies specializing in developing Web sites have sprung up in just the past few years.

New Customer and Supplier Relationships

Businesses that make their information systems easily available may make their customers less likely to take their business elsewhere (e.g., overnight delivery services closely track packages and bills).

To stay competent, you need to recognize the impact of technological change on organizations and people. You need to know how to use change to your advantage and how to become a winner. Although you do not need to be a specialist in information technology, you should be aware of career opportunities in the area.

TECHNOLOGY AND PEOPLE

People have different coping styles when it comes to technology. Four common reactions to new technology are cynicism, naivete, frustration, and proactivity.

Cynicism

The **cynics** feel that new technology is overrated and too troublesome to learn. Some cynics openly express their doubts. Others pretend to be interested.

Naivete

Naive people may be unfamiliar or quite familiar with computers. People who are unfamiliar tend to think of computers as magic boxes. Even those familiar with technology often underestimate the time and difficulty of using technology to generate information.

Frustration

Frustrated users are impatient and irritated about taking time to learn new technology. Often these people have too much to do, find manuals difficult to understand, and/or feel stupid.

Proactivity

A **proactive** person looks at technology in a positive and realistic way. He or she is not cynical, naive, or frustrated regarding new technology. Proactive people are positive and look at new technology as providing new tools that can positively impact their lives.

HOW YOU CAN BE A WINNER

There are six ongoing activities that can help you be successful.

Stay Current

Read trade journals and the general business press, join professional associations, and participate in special-interest groups on the Internet.

Maintain Your Computer Competency

Stay current by reading computer-related articles in the general press and trade journals, as well as online.

Develop Professional Contacts

Stay active in your profession and meet people in your field. This provides information about other people, firms, job opportunities, and social contacts.

Develop Specialties

Develop specific as well as general skills. Expect to take classes periodically to stay current with your field and technology.

Be Alert for Organizational Change

Use formal and informal lines of communication. Be alert for new trends within the organization.

Look for Innovative Opportunities

Look for ways to increase efficiency. Present ideas in terms of saving money rather than "improving information."

Computer Support Specialist

Computer support specialists provide technical support to customers and other users.

Computer Technician

Computer technicians repair and install computer components and systems.

Computer Trainer

Computer trainers instruct users on the latest software or hardware.

Cryptographer

Cryptographers design, test, and research encryption procedures.

Data Entry Worker

Data entry workers input customer information, lists, and other types of data.

Database Administrator

Database administrators use database management software to determine the most efficient ways to organize and access data.

Desktop Publisher

Desktop publishers create and format publication-ready material.

Information Systems Manager

Information systems managers oversee the work of programmers, computer specialists, systems analysts, and other computer professionals.

Network Administrator

Network administrators create and maintain networks.

Programmer

Programmers create, test, and troubleshoot computer programs.

Software Engineer

Software engineers analyze users' needs and create application software.

Systems Analyst

Systems analysts plan and design information systems.

Technical Writer

Technical writers prepare instruction manuals, technical reports, and other scientific or technical documents.

Webmaster

Webmasters develop and maintain Web sites and Web resources.

KEY TERMS

computer support specialist (339)
computer technician (339)
computer trainer (339)
cryptographer (339)
cynic (333)
data entry worker (339)
database administrator (339)
desktop publisher (339)
frustrated (333)

information systems manager (339)
naive (333)
network administrator (339)
proactive (333)
programmer (339)
software engineer (339)
systems analyst (339)
technical writer (339)
Webmaster (339)

To test your knowledge of these key terms with animated flash cards, visit our Web site at www.computing2013.com and enter the keyword terms11.

MULTIPLE CHOICE

Circle the letter of the correct answer.

1. People who react to technology by thinking computers are magic boxes capable of solving all kinds of problems that computers really can't handle are:

   a. cynics
   b. frustrated
   c. naive
   d. proactive

2. The type of person that looks at technology in a positive realistic way is:

   a. cynical
   b. proactive
   c. naive
   d. frustrated

3. Books, journals, and trade associations are the best sources to help you:

   a. develop personal contacts
   b. develop specialties
   c. look for innovative opportunities
   d. maintain your computer competency

4. If your career is in marketing, it makes sense to develop a specialty in:

   a. database
   b. desktop publishing
   c. programming
   d. systems analysis and design

5. What computer professional repairs and installs computer components and systems?

   a. computer technician
   b. data entry worker
   c. desktop publisher
   d. software engineer

6. What computer professional designs, tests, and researches encryption procedures?

   a. cryptographer
   b. network administrator
   c. programmer
   d. software engineer

7. What computer professional uses database management software to determine the most efficient ways to organize and access data?

   a. cryptographer
   b. database administrator
   c. programmer
   d. software engineer

8. What computer professional oversees the work of programmers, computer specialists, systems analysts, and other computer professionals?

   a. information systems manager
   b. network manager
   c. software engineer
   d. technical writer

9. What computer professional creates, tests, and troubleshoots computer programs?

   a. network manager
   b. programmer
   c. software engineer
   d. technical writer

10. What computer professional plans and designs information systems?

    a. network manager
    b. programmer
    c. software engineer
    d. systems analyst

For an interactive multiple-choice practice test, visit our Web site at www.computing2013.com and enter the keyword multiple11.

MATCHING

Match each numbered item with the most closely related lettered item. Write your answers in the spaces provided.

a. administrators
b. contacts
c. current
d. cynic
e. engineers
f. frustrated
g. publishers
h. specialists
i. trainers
j. writers

_____ 1. Type of person who may feel it is an imposition to have to learn something new or is too impatient to try to understand the manuals explaining what hardware and software are supposed to do.

_____ 2. Type of person who thinks the idea of using a microcomputer is overrated.

_____ 3. Individuals should keep abreast with new information and job possibilities by developing professional _____.

_____ 4. Reading trade journals, joining industry associations, and participating in special-interest newsgroups are ways to stay _____.

_____ 5. Computer professionals who provide technical support to customers and other users are computer support _____.

_____ 6. Computer professionals who create and maintain networks are network _____.

_____ 7. Computer professionals who instruct users on the latest software and hardware are computer _____.

_____ 8. Computer professionals who create and format publication-ready materials are desktop _____.

_____ 9. Computer professionals who prepare instruction manuals, technical reports, and other documents are technical _____.

_____ 10. Computer professionals who analyze users' needs and create application software are software _____.

For an interactive matching practice test, visit our Web site at www.computing2013.com and enter the keyword matching11.

346

OPEN-ENDED

On a separate sheet of paper, respond to each question or statement.

1. Why is strategy important to individual success in the information age? What is your strategy?
2. Describe how technology changes the nature of competition.
3. How can your computer competencies and knowledge help you get ahead in today's market?
4. What does proactive mean? What is a proactive computer user? What advantages does this type of user have over the other types?
5. Discuss several different careers in information technology. Which are of interest to you?

MAKING IT WORK FOR YOU

The following questions are designed to demonstrate ways that you can effectively use technology today.

1 JOBS ONLINE

Did you know that you can use the Internet to find a job? You can browse through job listings, post résumés for prospective employers, and even use special agents to continually search for that job that's just right for you. To learn more about online job searches, review Making IT Work for You: Locating Job Opportunities Online on pages 336 and 337. Then visit our Web site at www.computing2013 .com and enter the keyword jobs. Once at that site, play the video and answer the following: (a) What locations and categories were selected for the job search? (b) Describe the process for posting a résumé. (c) What search criteria were used to set up the job search agent?

2 MAINTAIN COMPUTER COMPETENCE

There are several sources of information to help keep you up-to-date on current computing trends. Visit our Web site at www. computing2013.com and enter the keyword competence to link to a few computing sites. Explore the sites and then answer the following: (a) List the sites you visited and describe the focus of each. (b) Which of these sites was most useful? Why? (c) Which of these sites was least useful? Why? (d) What are other ways you can stay in step with current computing issues?

EXPLORATIONS

The following questions are designed to add depth and detail to your understanding of specific topics presented within this chapter. The questions direct you to sources other than the textbook to obtain this knowledge.

1 YOUR CAREER

Have you thought about what your career might be? Perhaps it is in marketing, education, or information technology. If you have a career in mind, conduct a Web search to learn more about your chosen career. If you don't have a career in mind, select one of the information systems careers presented in this chapter and conduct a Web search to learn more about that career. After reviewing at least five sites, answer the following: (a) Describe your career of choice. (b) Why did you choose that career? (c) How is information technology used in this career? (d) How will changing technology impact your chosen career?

2 RÉSUMÉ ADVICE

There are several excellent resources available online to help you write a winning résumé. Conduct a Web search using the keywords "resume help" to learn more. Review at least five sites and then compose a sample résumé for yourself, applying the information from the sites.

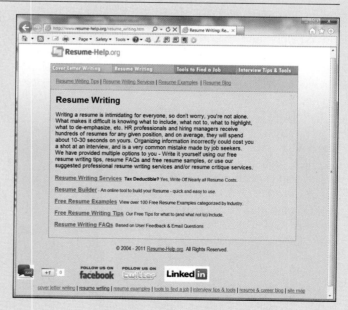

ETHICS

The following questions are designed to explore ethical issues related to technology and to develop the ability to think critically and communicate effectively. Respond to the questions by either creating a one-page paper or preparing for an in-depth classroom discussion.

1 ETHICAL ISSUES

Numerous ethical issues have been discussed throughout this book. Review the ethics boxes and the end-of-chapter ethics questions. Select five that you believe are the most important ethical topics. Then respond to the following: (a) Rank the five topics from the most important to the least important. (b) What criteria did you use to determine which topic is the most important? (c) Defend your choice for the most important topic. (d) Describe an additional ethical topic or issue that has not been discussed in this book.

ENVIRONMENT

The following questions are designed to explore environmental issues related to technology and to develop the ability to think critically and communicate effectively. Respond to the questions by either creating a one-page paper or preparing for an in-depth classroom discussion.

1 ENVIRONMENTAL ISSUES

Numerous environmental issues have been discussed throughout this book. Review the environment boxes and the end-of-chapter environment questions. Select five that you believe are the most important environmental topics. Then respond to the following: (a) Rank the five topics from the most important to the least important. (b) What criteria did you use to determine which topic is the most important? (c) Defend your choice for the most important topic. (d) Describe an additional environmental topic or issue that has not been discussed in this book.

The Evolution of the Computer Age

Many of you probably can't remember a world without computers, but for some of us, computers were virtually unknown when we were born and have rapidly come of age during our lifetime.

Although there are many predecessors to what we think of as the modern computer—reaching as far back as the 18th century, when Joseph Marie Jacquard created a loom programmed to weave cloth and Charles Babbage created the first fully modern computer design (which he could never get to work)—the computer age did not really begin until the first computer was made available to the public in 1951.

The modern age of computers thus spans slightly more than 60 years (so far), which is typically broken down into five generations. Each generation has been marked by a significant advance in technology.

- **First Generation (1951–57):** During the first generation, computers were built with vacuum tubes—electronic tubes that were made of glass and were about the size of lightbulbs.

- **Second Generation (1958–63):** This generation began with the first computers built with transistors—small devices that transfer electronic signals across a resistor. Because transistors are much smaller, use less power, and create less heat than vacuum tubes, the new computers were faster, smaller, and more reliable than the first-generation machines.

- **Third Generation (1964–69):** In 1964, computer manufacturers began replacing transistors with integrated circuits. An integrated circuit (IC) is a complete electronic circuit on a small chip made of silicon (one of the most abundant elements in the earth's crust). These computers were more reliable and compact than computers made with transistors, and they cost less to manufacture.

- **Fourth Generation (1970–90):** Many key advances were made during this generation, the most significant being the microprocessor—a specialized chip developed for computer memory and logic. Use of a single chip to create a smaller "personal" computer (as well as digital watches, pocket calculators, copy machines, and so on) revolutionized the computer industry.

- **Fifth Generation (1991–2012 and beyond):** Our current generation has been referred to as the "Connected Generation" because of the industry's massive effort to increase the connectivity of computers. The rapidly expanding Internet, World Wide Web, and intranets have created an information superhighway that has enabled both computer professionals and home computer users to communicate with others across the globe.

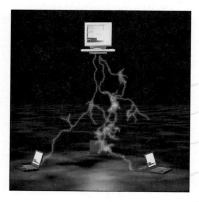

This appendix provides you with a timeline that describes in more detail some of the most significant events in each generation of the computer age.

First Generation: The Vacuum Tube Age

1951 Dr. John W. Mauchly and J. Presper Eckert Jr. introduce the first commercially available electronic digital computer—the UNIVAC—built with vacuum tubes. This computer was based on their earlier ENIAC (Electronic Numerical Integrator and Computer) design completed in 1946.

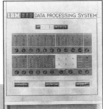

1951–53 IBM adds computers to its business equipment products and sells over 1,000 IBM 650 systems.

1951	1952	1953	1954	1955	1956	1957

1957 Introduction of first high-level programming language—FORTRAN (FORmula TRANslator).

1952 Development team led by Dr. Grace Hopper, former U.S. Navy programmer, introduces the A6 Compiler—the first example of software that converts high-level language symbols into instructions that a computer can execute.

Second Generation: The Transistor Age

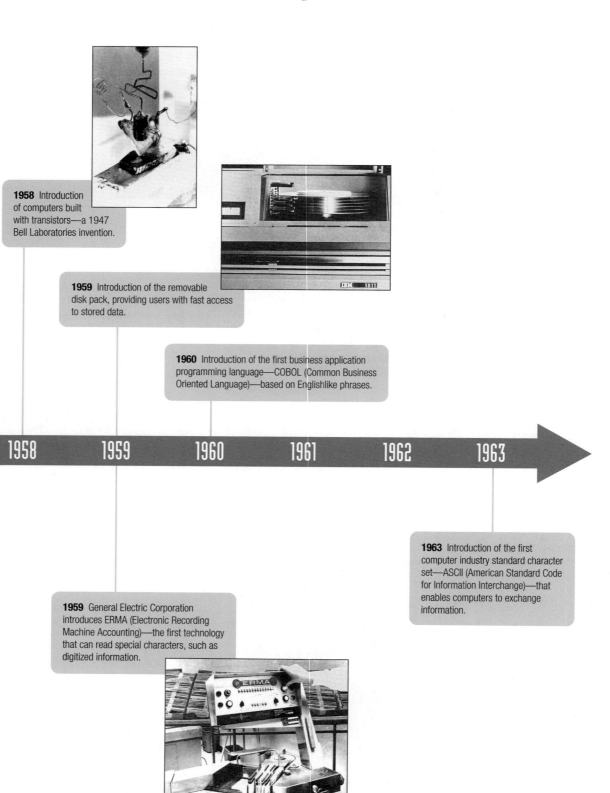

1958 Introduction of computers built with transistors—a 1947 Bell Laboratories invention.

1959 Introduction of the removable disk pack, providing users with fast access to stored data.

1960 Introduction of the first business application programming language—COBOL (Common Business Oriented Language)—based on Englishlike phrases.

1958 1959 1960 1961 1962 1963

1963 Introduction of the first computer industry standard character set—ASCII (American Standard Code for Information Interchange)—that enables computers to exchange information.

1959 General Electric Corporation introduces ERMA (Electronic Recording Machine Accounting)—the first technology that can read special characters, such as digitized information.

Third Generation: The Integrated Circuit Age

1964 Introduction of computers built with an integrated circuit (IC), which incorporates multiple transistors and electronic circuits on a single silicon chip.

1965 Digital Equipment Corporation (DEC) introduces the first minicomputer.

1969 Introduction of ARPANET and the beginning of the Internet.

1964   1965   1966   1967   1968   1969

1965 Introduction of the BASIC programming language.

1969 IBM announces its decision to offer unbundled software, priced and sold separately from the hardware.

1964 IBM introduces its System/360 line of compatible computers, which can all use the same programs and peripherals.

Fourth Generation: The Microprocessor Age

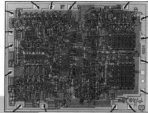

1970 Introduction of computers built with chips that used LSI (large-scale integration).

1975 First local area network (LAN)—Ethernet—developed at Xerox PARC (Palo Alto Research Center).

1977 Apple Computer, Inc., founded by Steve Wozniak and Steve Jobs, and Apple I introduced as an easy-to-use "hobbyist" computer.

1970   1971   1972   1973   1974   1975   1976   1977   1978   1979

1971 Dr. Ted Hoff of Intel Corporation develops a microprogrammable computer chip—the Intel 4004 microprocessor.

1975 The MITS, Inc., Altair becomes the first commercially successful microcomputer, selling for less than $400 a kit.

1979 Introduction of the first public information services—Compuserve and The Source.

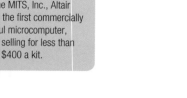

1980 IBM asks Microsoft founder, Bill Gates, to develop an operating system—MS-DOS—for the soon-to-be-released IBM personal computer.

1981 Introduction of the IBM PC, which contains an Intel microprocessor chip and Microsoft's MS-DOS operating system.

1989 Introduction of Intel 486—the first 1,000,000-transistor microprocessor.

| 1980 | 1981 | 1982 | 1983 | 1984 | 1985 | 1986 | 1987 | 1988 | 1989 | 1990 |

1984 Apple introduces the Macintosh Computer, with a unique, easy-to-use graphical user interface.

1985 Microsoft introduces its Windows graphical user interface.

1990 Microsoft releases Windows 3.0, with an enhanced graphical user interface and the ability to run multiple applications.

Fifth Generation: The Age of Connectivity

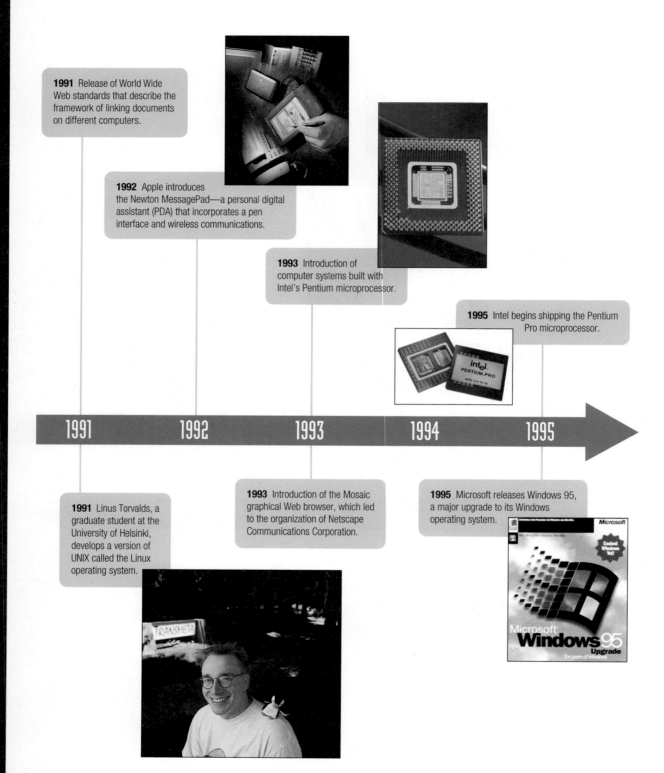

1991 Release of World Wide Web standards that describe the framework of linking documents on different computers.

1992 Apple introduces the Newton MessagePad—a personal digital assistant (PDA) that incorporates a pen interface and wireless communications.

1993 Introduction of computer systems built with Intel's Pentium microprocessor.

1995 Intel begins shipping the Pentium Pro microprocessor.

1991   1992   1993   1994   1995

1991 Linus Torvalds, a graduate student at the University of Helsinki, develops a version of UNIX called the Linux operating system.

1993 Introduction of the Mosaic graphical Web browser, which led to the organization of Netscape Communications Corporation.

1995 Microsoft releases Windows 95, a major upgrade to its Windows operating system.

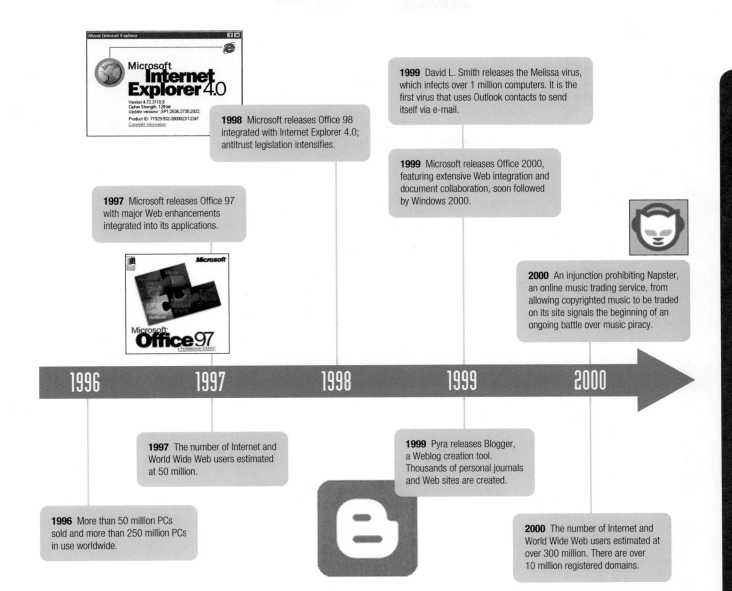

About Internet Explorer

Microsoft
Internet Explorer 4.0

Version 4.72.3110.8
Cipher Strength: 128-bit
Update versions: ;SP1;2636;2735;2922;
Product ID: 71929-932-2000023-12347
Copyright Information

1998 Microsoft releases Office 98 integrated with Internet Explorer 4.0; antitrust legislation intensifies.

1999 David L. Smith releases the Melissa virus, which infects over 1 million computers. It is the first virus that uses Outlook contacts to send itself via e-mail.

1999 Microsoft releases Office 2000, featuring extensive Web integration and document collaboration, soon followed by Windows 2000.

1997 Microsoft releases Office 97 with major Web enhancements integrated into its applications.

Microsoft
Office 97
Professional Edition

2000 An injunction prohibiting Napster, an online music trading service, from allowing copyrighted music to be traded on its site signals the beginning of an ongoing battle over music piracy.

1996   1997   1998   1999   2000

1997 The number of Internet and World Wide Web users estimated at 50 million.

1999 Pyra releases Blogger, a Weblog creation tool. Thousands of personal journals and Web sites are created.

1996 More than 50 million PCs sold and more than 250 million PCs in use worldwide.

2000 The number of Internet and World Wide Web users estimated at over 300 million. There are over 10 million registered domains.

2002 Amazon.com, the largest online retailer, announces its first profitable quarter nearly 10 years after the company was founded.

2004 CAN-SPAM Act enacted, requiring unsolicited e-mail to be labeled and making it illegal to use deceptive headers and anonymous return addresses. The law also requires unsolicited e-mail to allow recipients to opt out and authorizes the FTC to create a "do-not-e-mail" registry.

2002 Microsoft initiates its .NET platform that allows users to create a profile for use across platforms and allows developers to create Web services quickly.

Microsoft
.net

2005 Wireless connections (Wi-Fi) to the Internet, called hotspots, allow the public to access the Internet at airports, hotels, and many cafes. Many expect Wi-Fi connections to be available almost everywhere in the next few years—from doctors' offices to airplanes. By 2007 it is expected that nearly 20 million people will use Wi-Fi to access the Web.

2003 Apple opens the iTunes music store with a catalog of over 700,000 songs. Users can buy and then download songs for 99¢.

2001 Microsoft releases Windows XP and Office XP with enhanced user interfaces, better integration and collaboration tools, and increased stability.

2001   2002   2003   2004   2005

2002 Internet2, with over 200 university affiliates, regularly broadcasts live theater and HDTV transmissions.

2004 Google releases invitations to test Gmail, its e-mail service that includes a search function and 1 GB of storage.

2001 Apple releases Mac OS X with a UNIX backbone and new interface.

Mac OS
X

2007 Microsoft releases Windows Vista with enhanced Media Player and Instant Search features.

2009 Microsoft releases Windows 7 with multitouch support, a redesigned user interface, and a home networking system called HomeGroup.

2006 In August, MySpace.com announces the registration of its 100-millionth user.

2008 Netflix partners with Microsoft Xbox 360 to deliver streaming movies.

2010 Microsoft releases Office 2010 with online versions of Word, Excel, PowerPoint, and OneNote, which will work in the three most popular Web browsers.

2006   2007   2008   2009   2010

2008 Intel announces new low-power Atom microprocessor.

2009 Wireless devices move to 3G network with speeds up to 1.4 megabits per second.

2006 Google purchases YouTube.com for $1.65 billion.

2007 Apple announces the iPhone at its annual MacWorld Expo.

2010 Apple introduces the highly innovative iPad.

The Buyer's Guide How to Buy Your Own Microcomputer System

FOUR STEPS IN BUYING A MICROCOMPUTER SYSTEM

The following is not intended to make buying a microcomputer an exhausting experience. Rather, it is to help you clarify your thinking about what you need and can afford.

The four steps in buying a microcomputer system are presented on the following pages. We divide each step into two parts based on the assumptions that both your needs and the money you have to spend on a microcomputer may change.

STEP 1

What Needs Do I Want a Computer to Serve?

The trick is to distinguish between your needs and your wants. Sure, you *want* a cutting-edge system powerful enough to run every conceivable program you'll ever need. And you want a system fast enough to process them all at the speed of light. But do you *need* this? Your main concern is to address the following two questions:

- What do I need a computer system to do for me today?

- What will I need it to do for me in another year or two?

The questionnaire at the end of this guide will help you determine the answers to both questions.

Suggestions

Consider the type of computer most available on campus. Some schools favor Apple computers; others favor Windows-based computers. If you own a system that's incompatible with most computers on campus, you may be stuck if your computer breaks down.

Look ahead and determine whether your major requires a computer. Business and engineering students may find one a necessity; physical education and drama majors may not. Your major also may

determine the kind of computer that's best. A journalism major may want a Windows-based notebook. An architecture major may want a powerful desktop Macintosh with a laser printer that can produce elaborate drawings. Ask your academic advisor for some recommendations.

Example

Suppose you are a college student beginning your sophomore year, with no major declared. Looking at the courses you will likely take this year, you decide you will probably need a computer mainly for word processing. That is, you need a system that will help you write short (10- to 20-page) papers for a variety of courses.

By this time next year, however, you may be an accounting major. Having talked to some juniors and seniors, you find that courses in this major, such as financial accounting, will require you to use elaborate spreadsheets. Or maybe you will be a fine arts or architecture major. Then you may be required to submit projects for which drawing and painting desktop publishing software would be helpful.

STEP 2

How Much Money Do I Have to Spend on a Computer System?

When you buy your first computer, you are not necessarily buying your last. Thus, you can think about spending just the bare-bones amount for a system that meets your needs while in college. Then you might plan to get another system later on.

You know the amount of money you have to spend. Your main concern is to answer the following two questions:

- How much am I prepared to spend on a computer system today?

- How much am I prepared to spend in another year or two?

The questionnaire at the end of this guide asks you this.

Suggestions

You can probably buy a good used computer of some sort for under $300 and a printer for under $50. On the other hand, you might spend $1,000 to $2,500 on a new state-of-the-art system. When upgraded, this computer could meet your needs for the next five years.

There is nothing wrong with getting a used system if you have a way of checking it out. For a reasonable fee, a computer-repair shop can examine it prior to your purchase. Look at newspaper ads and notices on campus bulletin boards for good buys on used equipment. Also try the Internet. If you stay with recognized brands, such as Apple, Sony, HP, or Dell, you probably won't have any difficulties.

If you're buying new equipment, be sure to look for student discounts. Most college bookstores, for instance, offer special prices to students. Also check the Web. There are numerous sites specializing in discounted computer systems.

Example

Perhaps you have access to a microcomputer at the campus student computing center, the library, or the dormitory. Or you can borrow a friend's. However, this computer isn't always available when it's convenient for you. Moreover, you're not only going to college, but you're also working, so both time and money are tight. Having your own computer would enable you to write papers when it's convenient for you. Spending more than $350 might cause real hardship, so a new microcomputer system may be out of the question. You'll need to shop the newspaper classified ads or the campus bulletin boards to find a used but workable computer system.

Or maybe you can afford to spend more now—say, between $1,000 and $2,000—but probably only $500 next year. By this time next year, however, you'll know your major and how your computer needs have changed.

STEP 3

What Kind of Software Will Best Serve My Needs?

Most computer experts urge that you determine what software you need before you buy the hardware. The reasoning here is that some hardware simply won't run the software that is important to you. This is certainly true once you get into *sophisticated* software. Examples include specialized programs available for certain professions (such as certain agricultural or retail-management programs). However, if all you are interested in today are the basic software tools—word processing, spreadsheet, and communications programs—these are available for nearly all microcomputers. The main caution is that some more

recent versions of application software won't run on older hardware. Still, if someone offers you a free computer, don't say no because you feel you have to decide what software you need first. You will no doubt find it sufficient for many general purposes, especially during your early years in college.

That said, you are better served if you follow step 3 after step 2—namely, finding the answers to the following two questions:

- **What kind of software will best serve my needs today?**
- **What kind will best serve my needs in another year or two?**

The questionnaire at the end of this guide will help you determine your answers.

Suggestions

No doubt some kinds of application software are more available on your campus—and in certain departments on your campus—than others. Are freshman and sophomore students mainly writing their term papers in Word, Google Docs, or Apple Pages? Which spreadsheet is most often used by business students: Excel, Apple iWork's Numbers, or Quattro Pro? Which desktop publishing program is most favored by graphic arts majors: Quark or Adobe InDesign? Do engineering and architecture majors use their own machines for CAD/CAM applications? Start by asking other students and your academic advisor.

If you're looking to buy state-of-the-art software, you'll find plenty of advice in various computer magazines. Several of them rate the quality of newly issued programs. Such periodicals include *PC World* and *MacWorld*.

Example

Suppose you determine that all you need is software to help you write short papers. In that case, nearly any kind of word processing program would do. But will this software be sufficient a year or two from now? Looking ahead, you guess that you'll major in theater arts and minor in screenwriting, which you may pursue as a career. At that point, a simple word processing program might not do. You learn from juniors and seniors in that department that screenplays are written using special screenwriting programs. This is software that's not available for some computers. Or, as an advertising and marketing major, you're expected to turn word-processed promotional pieces into brochures. For this, you need desktop publishing software. Or, as a physics major, you discover you will need to write reports on a word processor that can handle equations. In short, you need to look at your software needs not just for today but also for the near future. You especially want to consider what programs will be useful to you in building your career.

STEP 4

What Kind of Hardware Will Best Serve My Needs?

A bare-bones hardware system might include a three-year-old desktop or notebook computer with a CD-ROM disc drive and a hard-disk drive. It also should include a monitor and a printer. On the one hand, as a student—unless you're involved in some very specialized activities—it's doubtful you'll really need such things as voice-input devices, touch screens, scanners, and the like. On the other hand, you will probably need speakers and a DVD-ROM drive. The choices of equipment are vast.

As with the other steps, the main task is to find the answers to the following two questions:

- **What kind of hardware will best serve my needs today?**
- **What kind will best serve my needs in another year or two?**

There are several questions on the questionnaire at the end of this guide to help you determine answers to these concerns.

Suggestions

Clearly, you should let the software be your guide in determining your choice of hardware. Perhaps you've found that the most popular software in your department runs on an Apple computer rather than a Windows-based computer. If so, that would seem to determine your general brand of hardware.

Whether you buy IBM or Macintosh, a desktop or a notebook, we suggest you get a hard-disk drive with at least 300 gigabytes of storage, a DVD drive, at least 3 gigabytes of memory, and an ink-jet printer.

As with software, several computer magazines not only describe new hardware but also issue ratings. See *PC World* and *MacWorld*, for example.

Example

Right now, let's say, you're mainly interested in using a computer to write papers, so almost anything would do. But you need to look ahead.

Suppose you find that Word seems to be the software of choice around your campus. You find that Word 2007 will run well on a Pentium machine with 256 megabytes of memory and a 1.5-gigabyte hard disk. Although this equipment is now outdated, you find from looking at classified ads that there are many such used machines around. Plus, they cost very little—well under $400 for a complete system.

Your choice then becomes: Should I buy an inexpensive system now that can't be upgraded, then sell it later and buy a better one? Or should I buy at least some of the components of a good system now and upgrade it over the next year or so?

As an advertising major, you see the value of learning desktop publishing. This will be a useful if not essential skill once you embark on a career. In exploring the software, you learn that Word includes some desktop publishing capabilities. However, the hardware you previously considered simply isn't sufficient. Moreover, you learn from reading about software and talking to people in your major that there are better desktop publishing programs. Specialized desktop publishing programs like Adobe InDesign are considered more versatile than Word. Probably the best software arrangement, in fact, is to have Word as a word processing program and Adobe InDesign for a desktop publishing program.

To be sure, the campus has computers that will run this software available to students. If you can afford it, however, you're better off having your own. Now, however, we're talking about a major expense. A computer running a multicore microprocessor, with 6 gigabytes of memory, a rewriteable DVD disc drive, and a 400-gigabyte hard disk, plus a modem, monitor, and laser printer, could cost in excess of $1,000.

DEVELOPING A PHILOSOPHY ABOUT COMPUTER PURCHASING

It's important not to develop a case of "computer envy." Even if you buy the latest, most expensive microcomputer system, in a matter of months something better will come along. Computer technology is still in a very dynamic state, with more powerful, versatile, and compact systems constantly hitting the marketplace. So what if your friends have the hottest new piece of software or hardware? The main question is: Do you need it to solve the tasks required of you or to keep up in your field? Or can you get along with something simpler but equally serviceable?

Visual Summary The Buyer's Guide: How to Buy Your Own Microcomputer System

To help clarify your thinking about buying a microcomputer system, complete the questionnaire by checking the appropriate boxes.

NEEDS

What do I need a computer system to do for me today? In another year or two?

I WISH TO USE THE COMPUTER FOR:

	Today	1–2 years
Word processing—writing papers, letters, memos, or reports	❑	❑
Business or financial applications—balance sheets, sales projections, expense budgets, or accounting problems	❑	❑
Record keeping and sorting—research bibliographies, scientific data, or address files	❑	❑
Graphic presentations of business, scientific, or social science data	❑	❑
Online information retrieval to campus networks, service providers, or the Internet	❑	❑
Publications, design, or drawing for printed newsletters, architectural drawing, or graphic arts	❑	❑
Multimedia for video games, viewing, creating, presenting, or research	❑	❑
Other (specify): _____	❑	❑

BUDGET

How much am I prepared to spend on a system today? In another year or two?

I CAN SPEND:

	Today	1–2 years
Under $500	❑	❑
Up to $1,000	❑	❑
Up to $1,500	❑	❑
Up to $2,000	❑	❑
Up to $2,500	❑	❑
Over $3,000	❑	❑
(specify): _____		

Buying a Microcomputer System	
Step	**Questions**
1	*My needs:* What do I need a computer system to do for me today? In another year or two?
2	*My budget:* How much am I prepared to spend on a system today? In another year or two?
3	*My software:* What kind of software will best serve my needs today? In another year or two?
4	*My hardware:* What kind of hardware will best serve my needs today? In another year or two?

SOFTWARE

What kinds of software will best serve my needs today? In another year or two?

The Application Software I Need Includes:

	Today	1–2 years
Word processing—Word, WordPerfect, or other (specify): _____	❏	❏
Spreadsheet—Excel, iWork's Numbers, or other (specify): _____	❏	❏
Database—Access, Paradox, or other (specify): _____	❏	❏
Presentation graphics— PowerPoint, CorelPresentations, or other (specify): _____	❏	❏
Browsers—Mozilla Firefox, Apple Safari, Microsoft Internet Explorer, or other (specify): _____	❏	❏
Other—integrated packages, software suites, graphics, multimedia, Web authoring, CAD/CAM, or other (specify): _____	❏	❏

The System Software I Need:

	Today	1–2 years
Windows 7	❏	❏
Windows Vista	❏	❏
Mac OS	❏	❏
Linux	❏	❏
Other (specify): _____	❏	❏

HARDWARE

What kinds of hardware will best serve my needs today? In another year or two?

The Hardware I Need Includes:

	Today	1–2 years
Microprocessor—Celeron, Apple, or other (specify): _____	❏	❏
Memory—(specify amount): _____	❏	❏
Monitor—size (specify): _____	❏	❏
Optical disc drive—CD-ROM, DVD-ROM (specify type, speed, and capacity): _____	❏	❏
Hard-disk drive—(specify capacity): _____	❏	❏
Portable computer—laptop, notebook, netbook, personal digital assistant (specify): _____	❏	❏
Printer—ink-jet, laser, or other (specify): _____	❏	❏
Other—modem, network card, speakers, fax, surge protector (specify): _____	❏	❏

The Upgrader's Guide How to Upgrade Your Microcomputer System

If you own a microcomputer, chances are that your machine is not the latest and greatest. Microcomputers are always getting better—more powerful and faster. While that is a good thing, it can be frustrating trying to keep up.

What can you do? If you have lots of money, you can simply buy a new one. Another alternative is to upgrade or add new components to increase the power and speed of your current microcomputer. You probably can increase your system's performance at a fraction of the cost of a new one.

THREE STEPS IN UPGRADING A MICROCOMPUTER SYSTEM

The following is not intended to detail specific hardware upgrades. Rather, it is intended to help you clarify your thinking about what you need and can afford.

The three steps in upgrading a microcomputer system are presented on the following pages. Each step begins by asking a key question and then provides some suggestions or factors to consider when responding to the question.

STEP 1

Is It Time to Upgrade?

Almost any upgrade you make will provide some benefit; the trick is determining if it is worth the monetary investment. It is rarely practical to rebuild an older computer system into a newer model piece by piece. The cost of a complete upgrade typically far exceeds the purchase price of a new system. But if your system is just a piece or two away from meeting your needs, an upgrade may be in order.

Clearly defining what you hope to gain with an upgrade of some of your system's hardware will enable you to make the most relevant and cost-effective selections. Before deciding what to buy, decide what goal you hope to accomplish. Do you want to speed up your computer's performance? Do you need more

space to save your files? Do you want to add a new component such as a DVD-RW drive?

Suggestions

A good place to start is to look at the documentation on the packaging of any software you use or plan to use. Software manufacturers clearly label the minimum requirements to use their products. These requirements are usually broken down into categories that relate to specific pieces of hardware. For instance, how much RAM (random-access memory) does a new program require? How much hard disk space is needed? Keep in mind these ratings are typically the bare minimum. If your system comes very close to the baseline in any particular category, you should still consider an upgrade.

Another thing to investigate is whether there is a software solution that will better serve your needs. For instance, if you are looking to enhance performance or make more room on your hard disk, there are diagnostic and disk optimization utility programs that may solve your problem. In Chapter 3, we discuss a variety of utility programs, such as Norton SystemWorks, that monitor, evaluate, and enhance system performance and storage capacity.

Typical objectives of an upgrade are to improve system performance, increase storage capacity, or add new technology.

STEP 2

What Should I Upgrade?

Once you have clearly defined your objectives, the focus shifts to identifying specific components to meet those objectives.

Suggestions

If your objective is to improve performance, three components to consider are RAM, the microprocessor, and expansion cards. If your objective is to increase storage capacity, two components to consider are hard-disk drive and optical disc drive. If you are adding new technology, consider the capability of your current system to support new devices.

Performance

If you want to increase the speed of your computer, consider increasing the amount of RAM. In most cases, this upgrade is relatively inexpensive and will yield the highest performance result per dollar invested. How much your system's performance will increase depends on how much RAM you start with, the size of programs you run, and how often you run large programs.

Another way to increase speed is to replace your system's microprocessor. Processor speed is measured in gigahertz (GHz). This rating is not a direct measurement of how fast the processor works, but rather it gives you a general idea of how it compares to other processors. (Computing magazines such as *PC World* often publish articles comparing the relative effectiveness of different processors.) The concept behind a microprocessor upgrade is simple: A faster processor will process faster. This is often an expensive upgrade and not as cost-effective as increasing RAM.

If you are looking at upgrading for a specific type of application, perhaps an expansion card is your answer. Expansion cards connect to slots on the system board, provide specialized support, and often free up resources and increase overall system performance. For example, if you run graphics-intensive programs, such as a drafting program or a video game, a video-card upgrade may be a good buy. An upgraded video card can be used to support higher-resolution displays, handle all video data, and speed up overall system performance.

Storage Capacity

It's not hard to know when it's time to upgrade your storage capacity. If you frequently have to delete old files to make way for new ones, then it is probably time for more space. A larger or an additional hard drive is usually the solution. Two things to consider when comparing new hard drives are (1) size, which is usually rated in gigabytes (GB) of data the drive can hold, and (2) seek time, which is a rating of the average time it takes the drive to access any particular piece of data.

If you are storing a lot of data that you no longer use, such as old term papers, you might consider a USB drive. This is usually cheaper and is a good way to archive and transport data.

New Technology

Perhaps you are not looking to modify existing hardware but would like to add a new device. Examples include large high-resolution monitors, DVD-RW drives, and high-speed printers.

The key consideration is whether the new device will work with your existing hardware. The requirements for these devices are typically printed on the outside packaging or available at the product's Web site. If not, then refer to the product's operating manuals. Obviously, if your current system cannot support the new technology, you need to evaluate the cost of the new device plus the necessary additional hardware upgrades.

STEP 3

Who Should Do the Upgrade?

Once you've decided that the cost of the upgrade is justified and you know what you want to upgrade, the final decision is who is going to do it. Basically, there are two choices. You can either do it yourself or pay for professional installation.

Suggestions

The easiest way, and many times the best way, is to have a professional perform the upgrade. If you select this option, be sure to include the cost of installation in your analysis. If you have had some prior hardware experience or are a bit adventurous, you may want to save some money and do it yourself.

Visit a few computer stores that carry the upgrades you have selected. Most stores that provide the parts will install them as well. Talk with their technical people, describe your system (better yet, bring your system unit to the store), and determine the cost of professional installation. If you are thinking of doing it yourself, ask for their advice. Ask if they will provide assistance if you need it.

If you decide to have the components professionally installed, get the total price in writing and inquire about any guarantees that might exist. Before leaving your system, be sure that it is carefully tagged with your name and address. After the service has been completed, pay by credit card and thoroughly test the upgrade. If it does not perform satisfactorily, contact the store and ask for assistance. If the store's service is not satisfactory, you may be able to have your credit card company help to mediate any disputes.

Visual Summary The Upgrader's Guide: How to Upgrade Your Microcomputer System

To help clarify your thinking about upgrading a microcomputer system, complete the questionnaire by checking the appropriate boxes.

Upgrading a Microcomputer System	
Step	Questions
1	*Needs:* Is it time to upgrade? What do I need that my current system is unable to deliver?
2	*Analysis:* What should I upgrade? Will the upgrade meet my needs and will it be cost-effective?
3	*Action:* Who should do the upgrade? Should I pay a professional or do it myself?

NEEDS

Is it time to upgrade? What do I need that my current system is unable to deliver?

I Am Considering an Upgrade to:

❏ **Improve performance because**
  ❏ My programs run too slowly
  ❏ I cannot run some programs I need

❏ **Increase storage capacity because**
  ❏ I don't have enough space to store all my files
  ❏ I don't have enough space to install new programs
  ❏ I need a secure place to back up important files
  ❏ I'd like to download large files from the Internet

❏ **Add new technology**
  ❏ DVD-RW
  ❏ High-performance monitor
  ❏ Printer
  ❏ TV tuner card
  ❏ Enhanced video card
  ❏ Enhanced sound card
  ❏ Other _____

ANALYSIS

What should I upgrade? Will the upgrade meet my needs, and will it be cost-effective?

I Will Improve:

❏ **Performance by**
  ❏ Adding random-access memory (RAM)
    Current RAM (MB) _____
    Upgrade to _____
    Cost $ _____
    Expected improvement _____
    Other factors _____
  ❏ Replacing the current microprocessor
    Current processor _____
    Upgrade processor _____
    Cost $ _____
    Expected improvement _____
    Other factors _____
  ❏ Adding an expansion card
    Type _____
    Purpose _____
    Cost $ _____
    Expected improvement _____
    Other factors _____

❏ **Storage capacity by**
  ❏ Adding a hard-disk drive
    Current size (GB) _____
    Upgrade size (GB) _____
    Cost $ _____
    Expected improvement _____
    Other factors _____

❑ Adding a USB drive

    Upgrade size (GB) _____

    Cost $ _____

    Type _____

    Expected improvement _____

    Other factors _____

❑ Functionality by adding

    New technology _____

    System requirements _____

    Cost $ _____

    Expected improvement _____

    Other factors _____

ACTION

Who should do the upgrade? Should I do it myself, or should I pay a professional?

The Two Choices are:

❑ **Professional installation**

The easiest way, and many times the best way, is to have a professional perform the upgrade. If you select this option, be sure to include the cost of installation in your analysis. Pay with a credit card, and make sure your system is tagged with your name and address before you part with it.

❑ **Do-it-yourself installation**

If you have had some prior hardware experience or are a bit adventurous, you may want to save some money and do it yourself. Avoid touching sensitive electronic parts, and be sure to ground yourself by touching an unpainted metal surface in your computer.

Glossary

3G and 4G cellular network: A network that allows portable devices such as cell phones and properly equipped laptop computers to download data from the Internet.

3GLs (third-generation languages): High-level procedural language. *See* Procedural language.

4GLs (fourth-generation languages): Very high-level or problem-oriented languages. *See* Task-oriented language.

5GLs (fifth-generation languages): *See* Fifth-generation language.

802.11: *See* Wi-Fi (wireless fidelity).

a

AC adapter: Notebook computers use AC adapters that are typically outside the system unit. They plug into a standard wall outlet, convert AC to DC, provide power to drive the system components, and can recharge batteries.

Access: Refers to the responsibility of those who have data to control who is able to use that data.

Access speed: Measures the amount of time required by the storage device to retrieve data and programs.

Accounting: The organizational department that records all financial activity from billing customers to paying employees.

Accounts payable: The activity that shows the money a company owes to its suppliers for the materials and services it has received.

Accounts receivable: The activity that shows what money has been received or is owed by customers.

Accuracy: Relates to the responsibility of those who collect data to ensure that the data is correct.

Active display area: The diagonal length of a monitor's viewing area.

Active-matrix monitor: Type of flat-panel monitor in which each pixel is independently activated. Displays more colors with better clarity; also known as thin film transistor (TFT) monitor.

Ad network cookies: Cookies that monitor your activities across all sites you visit and are continually active in collecting information on your Web activities.

Add a Device Wizard: A Windows wizard that provides step-by-step guidance for selecting and installing an appropriate printer driver for a new printer.

Address: Located in the header of an e-mail message; the e-mail address of the persons sending, receiving, and, optionally, anyone else who is to receive copies.

Advanced graphics card: Provides high-quality 3D graphics and animation for games and simulations.

Advanced Research Project Agency Network (ARPA-NET): A national computer network from which the Internet developed.

Adware cookie: *See* Ad network cookies.

Agile development: A development methodology that starts by getting core functionality of a program working, then expands on it until the customer is satisfied with the results.

AJAX: An advanced use of JavaScript found on many interactive sites. This technology is used to create interactive Web sites that respond quickly like traditional desktop application software.

Analog: Continuous signals that vary to represent different tones, pitches, and volume.

Analog signal: Signals that represent a range of frequencies, such as the human voice. They are a continuous electronic wave signal as opposed to a digital signal that is either on or off. To convert the digital signals of your computer to analog and vice versa, you need a modem. Another cable connects the modem to the telephone wall jack.

Analytical graphs or charts: Form of graphics used to put numeric data into objects that are easier to analyze, such as bar charts, line graphs, and pie charts.

Android: Mobile operating system originally developed by Android Inc. and later purchased by Google.

Animation: Feature involving special visual and sound effects like moving pictures, audio, and video clips that play automatically when selected.

Antispyware: *See* Spy removal programs.

Antivirus program: A utility program that guards a computer system from viruses or other damaging programs.

App: *See* Application software.

App store: A Web site that provides access to specific mobile apps that can be downloaded either for a nominal fee or free of charge.

Applets: Web pages contain links to programs called applets, which are written in a programming language called Java. These programs are used to add interest to a Web site by presenting animation, displaying graphics, providing interactive games, and so forth.

Application generation subsystem: Provides tools to create data entry forms and specialized programming languages that interface or work with common languages, such as C or Visual Basic.

Application generator: Also called program coder; provides modules of prewritten code to accomplish various tasks, such as calculation of overtime pay.

Application software: Also referred to as apps. Software that can perform useful work, such as word processing, cost estimating, or accounting tasks. The user primarily interacts with application software.

Arithmetic-logic unit (ALU): The part of the CPU that performs arithmetic and logical operations.

Arithmetic operation: Fundamental math operations: addition, subtraction, multiplication, and division.

Artificial intelligence (AI): A field of computer science that attempts to develop computer systems that can mimic or simulate human thought processes and actions.

Artificial reality: *See* Virtual reality.

ASCII (American Standard Code for Information Interchange): Binary coding scheme widely used on all computers, including microcomputers. Eight bits form each byte, and each byte represents one character.

Aspect ratio: The width of a monitor divided by its height. Common aspect ratios for monitors are 4:3 (standard) and 16:9 (wide screen).

Assembly language: A step up from machine language, using names instead of numbers. These languages use abbreviations or mnemonics, such as ADD, that are automatically converted to the appropriate sequence of 1s and 0s.

Asymmetric digital subscriber line (ADSL): One of the most widely used types of telephone high-speed connections (DSL).

Attachment: A file, such as a document or worksheet, that is attached to an e-mail message.

Attribute: A data field represents an attribute (description or characteristic) of some entity (person, place, thing, or object). For example, an employee is an entity with many attributes, including his or her last name, address, phone, etc.

Auction house sites: Web sites that operate like a traditional auction to sell merchandise to bidders.

Audio editing software: Allows you to create and edit audio clips like filtering out pops and scratches in an old recording.

Automated design tool: Software package that evaluates hardware and software alternatives according to requirements given by the systems analyst. Also called computer-aided software engineering (CASE) tools.

b

Backbone: *See* Bus.

Background: Other programs running simultaneously with the program being used in an operating system. *See* foreground.

Backup: A Windows utility program. *See* Backup program.

Backup and Restore: A utility program included with the many versions of Windows that makes a copy of all files or selected files that have been saved onto a disk.

Backup program: A utility program that helps protect you from the effects of a disk failure by making a copy of selected or all files that have been saved onto a disk.

Balance sheet: Lists the overall financial condition of an organization.

Bandwidth: Bandwidth determines how much information can be transmitted at one time. It is a measurement of the communication channel's capacity. There are three bandwidths: voice band, medium band, and broadband.

Bar code: Code consisting of vertical zebra-striped marks printed on product containers, read with a bar code reader.

Bar code reader: Photoelectric scanner that reads bar codes for processing.

Bar code scanner: *See* Bar code reader.

Base station: *See* Wireless access point.

Baseband: Bandwidth used to connect individual computers that are located close to one another. Though it supports high-speed transmission, it can only carry a single signal at a time.

Basic application: Applications used for doing common tasks, such as browsers and word processors, spreadsheets, databases, management systems, and presentation graphics. Also known as productivity applications.

Batch processing: Processing performed all at once on data that has been collected over time.

BD (Blu-ray Discs): A type of high-definition disc with a capacity of 25 to 50 gigabytes.

Beta testing: Testing by a select group of potential users in the final stage of testing a program.

Binary system: Numbering system in which all numbers consist of only two digits: 0 and 1.

Biometric scanning: Devices that check fingerprints or retinal scans.

Bit (binary digit): Each 1 or 0 is a bit; short for binary digit.

Bitmap image: Graphic file in which an image is made up of thousands of dots (pixels).

BitTorrent: A peer-to-peer file-sharing protocol used for distributing large amounts of data over the Internet.

BlackBerry OS: Mobile phone operating system originally designed for the BlackBerry handheld computer.

Blog: *See* Web log.

Bluetooth: A recent wireless technology that allows nearby devices to communicate without the connection of cables or telephone systems.

Boot Camp: Feature of Leopard, a version of Mac OS, that allows appropriately equipped Apple computers to run both Mac OS and Windows.

Booting: Starting or restarting your computer.

Botnet: A collection of zombie computers.

Broadband: Bandwidth that includes microwave, satellite, coaxial cable, and fiber-optic channels. It is used for very-high-speed computers.

Browser: Special Internet software connecting you to remote computers; opens and transfers files, displays text and images, and provides an uncomplicated interface to the Internet and Web documents. Examples of browsers are Internet Explorer, Mozilla Firefox, and Google Chrome.

Bulleted list: The sequence of topics arranged on a page and organized by bullets.

Bus: All communication travels along a common connecting cable called a bus or a backbone. As information passes along the bus, it is examined by each device on the system board to see if the information is intended for that device. *See* Bus line and Ethernet.

Bus line: Electronic data roadway, along which bits travel; connects the parts of the CPU to each other and links the CPU with other important hardware. The common connecting cable in a bus network.

Bus width: The number of bits traveling simultaneously down a bus is the bus width.

Business suite: *See* Productivity suites.

Business-to-business (B2B): A type of electronic commerce that involves the sale of a product or service from one business to another. This is typically a manufacturer–supplier relationship.

Business-to-consumer (B2C): A type of electronic commerce that involves the sale of a product or service to the general public or end users.

Button: A special area you can click to make links that "navigate" through a presentation.

Byte: Unit consisting of eight bits. There are 256 possible bit combinations in a byte and each byte represents one character.

C

Cable: Cords used to connect input and output devices to the system unit.

Cable modem: Allows all-digital communication, which is a speed of 27 million bps.

Cable service: Service provided by cable television companies using existing television cables.

Cache memory: Area of random-access memory (RAM) set aside to store the most frequently accessed information. Cache memory improves processing by acting as a temporary high-speed holding area between memory and the CPU, allowing the computer to detect which information in RAM is most frequently used.

Capacity: Capacity is how much data a particular storage medium can hold and is another characteristic of secondary storage.

Carder: Criminal who steals credit cards over the Internet.

Carrier package: The material that chips are mounted on which then plugs into sockets on the system board.

Cathode-ray tube (CRT) monitor: Desktop-type monitor built in the same way as a television set.

CD: *See* Compact disc.

CD-R: Stands for CD-recordable. This optical disc can be written to only once. After that it can be read many times without deterioration but cannot be written on or erased. Used to create custom music CDs and to archive data.

CD-ROM (compact disc–read only memory): Optical disc that allows data to be read but not recorded. Used to distribute large databases, references, and software application packages.

CD-RW (compact disc rewriteable): A reusable, optical disc that is not permanently altered when data is recorded. Used to create and edit large multimedia presentations.

Cell: The space created by the intersection of a vertical column and a horizontal row within a worksheet in a program like Microsoft Excel. A cell can contain text or numeric entries.

Cellular service: Links car phones and portable phones.

Center for European Nuclear Research (CERN): In Switzerland, where the Web was introduced in 1992.

Central processing unit (CPU): The part of the computer that holds data and program instructions for processing the data. The CPU consists of the control unit and the arithmetic-logic unit. In a microcomputer, the CPU is on a single electronic component called a microprocessor chip.

Character: A single letter, number, or special character, such as a punctuation mark or $.

Character effect: Changes the appearance of font characters by using bold, italic, shadow, and colors.

Character encoding standards: Assign unique sequence of bits to each character.

Chart: Displaying numerical data in a worksheet as a pie chart or a bar chart, making it easier to understand.

Checklist: In analyzing data, a list of questions helps guide the systems analyst and end user through key issues for the present system.

Child node: A node one level below the node being considered in a hierarchical database or network. *See* Parent node.

Chip: A tiny circuit board etched on a small square of sandlike material called silicon. A chip is also called a silicon chip, semiconductor, or integrated circuit.

Chrome OS: An operating system designed by Google for netbook computers and Internet connectivity through cloud computing.

Clarity: Indicated by the resolution, or number of pixels, on a monitor. The greater the resolution, the better the clarity.

Class: In an object-oriented database, classes are similar objects grouped together.

Client: A node that requests and uses resources available from other nodes. Typically, a client is a user's microcomputer.

Client-based e-mail account: An account that requires a special program known as an e-mail client to be installed on your computer.

Client/server network: Network in which one powerful computer coordinates and supplies services to all other nodes on the network. Server nodes coordinate and supply specialized services, and client nodes request the services.

Clip art: Graphic illustrations representing a wide variety of topics.

Clock speed: Also called clock rate. It is measured in gigahertz, or billions of beats per second. The faster the clock speed, the faster the computer can process information and execute instructions.

Cloud computing: Data stored at a server on the Internet and available anywhere the Internet can be accessed.

Cloud printer: A printer connected to the Internet that provides printing services to others on the Internet.

Cloud storage: Also known as online storage. An Internet-based space for storing data and files.

Cloud suite: Suite stored at a server on the Internet and available anywhere from the Internet.

Coaxial cable: High-frequency transmission cable that replaces the multiple wires of telephone lines with a single solid-copper core. It is used to deliver television signals as well as to connect computers in a network.

Code: Writing a program using the appropriate computer language.

Code review: *See* Desk checking.

Coding: Actual writing of a computer program, using a programming language.

Cold boot: Starting the computer after it has been turned off.

Column: Using Microsoft Excel, for example, a vertical block of cells one cell wide all the way down the worksheet.

Combination key: Keys such as the Ctrl key that perform an action when held down in combination with another key.

Commercial database: Enormous database an organization develops to cover certain particular subjects. Access to this type of database is usually offered for a fee or subscription. Also known as data bank and informational utility.

Common data item: In a relational database, all related tables must have a common data item or key field.

Communication channel: The actual connecting medium that carries the message between sending and receiving devices. This medium can be a physical wire, cable, or wireless connection.

Communication device: Computer systems that communicate with other computer systems using modems. For example, it modifies computer output into a form that can be transmitted across standard telephone lines.

Communication system: Electronic system that transmits data over communication lines from one location to another.

Compact disc (CD): Widely used optical disc format. It holds 650 MB (megabytes) to 1 GB (gigabyte) of data on one side of the CD.

Compact disc–read only memory: *See* CD-ROM.

Compact disc rewriteable: *See* CD-RW.

Company database: Also called shared database. Stored on a mainframe, users throughout the company have access to the database through their microcomputers linked by a network.

Compiler: Software that converts the programmer's procedural-language program (source code) into machine

language (object code). This object code can then be saved and run later.

Computer-aided design/computer-aided manufacturing (CAD/CAM) system: Knowledge work systems that run programs to integrate the design and manufacturing activities. CAD/CAM is widely used in manufacturing automobiles.

Computer-aided software engineering (CASE) tool: A type of software development tool that helps provide some automation and assistance in program design, coding, and testing. *See* Automated design tool.

Computer competency: Becoming proficient in computer-related skills.

Computer crime: Illegal action in which a perpetrator uses special knowledge of computer technology. Criminals may be employees, outside users, hackers and crackers, and organized crime members.

Computer ethics: Guidelines for the morally acceptable use of computers in our society.

Computer Fraud and Abuse Act: Law allowing prosecution of unauthorized access to computers and databases.

Computer monitoring software: The most invasive and dangerous type of spyware. These programs record every activity made on your computer, including credit card numbers, bank account numbers, and e-mail messages.

Computer network: Communications system connecting two or more computers and their peripheral devices to exchange information and share resources.

Computer support specialist: Specialists include technical writers, computer trainers, computer technicians, and help-desk specialists who provide technical support to customers and other users.

Computer technician: Specialist who installs hardware and software and troubleshoots problems for users.

Computer trainer: Computer professional who provides classes to instruct users.

Concatenation structure: Logic structure in which one program statement follows another.

Connectivity: Capability of the microcomputer to use information from the world beyond one's desk. Data and information can be sent over telephone or cable lines and through the air so that computers can talk to each other and share information.

Consumer-to-consumer (C2C): A type of electronic commerce that involves individuals selling to individuals.

Content-markup language: Also known as markup language. Uses symbols, words, and phrases that instruct a computer on how to display information to the user. For example, HTML is a content-markup language used to display Web pages.

Content template: Includes suggested content for each slide in a PowerPoint presentation.

Contextual tab: A type of tab found in Microsoft Word that only appears when needed and anticipates the next operations to be performed by the user.

Control unit: Section of the CPU that tells the rest of the computer how to carry out program instructions.

Conversion: Also known as systems implementation; four approaches to conversion: direct, parallel, pilot, and phased. *See* Systems implementation.

Cookies: Programs that record information on Web site visitors.

Coprocessor: Specialized processing chip designed to improve specific computer operations, such as the graphics coprocessor.

Copyright: A legal concept that gives content creators the right to control use and distribution of their work.

Cordless mouse: A battery-powered mouse that typically uses radio waves or infrared light waves to communicate with the system unit. Also known as wireless mouse.

Cracker: One who gains unauthorized access to a computer system for malicious purposes.

Cryptographer: Designs, tests, and researches encryption procedures.

Cryptography: The science of disguising and revealing encrypted information.

Cyber-bullying: The use of the Internet, a cell phone, or other device to deliver content intended to hurt or embarrass another person.

Cybercash: *See* Digital cash.

Cylinder: Hard disks store and organize files using tracks, sectors, and cylinders. A cylinder runs through each track of a stack of platters. Cylinders differentiate files stored on the same track and sector of different platters.

Cynic: Individual who feels that the idea of using a microcomputer is overrated and too troublesome to learn.

d

Dashboard Widgets: A collection of specialized programs on the Mac OS X operating system that constantly updates and displays information such as stock prices and weather information.

Data: Raw, unprocessed facts that are input to a computer system that will give compiled information when the computer processes those facts. Data is also defined as facts or observations about people, places, things, and events.

Data administration subsystem: Helps manage the overall database, including maintaining security, providing disaster recovery support, and monitoring the overall performance of database operations.

Data bank: *See* Commercial database.

Data cube: A multidimensional data model. *Also see* Multidimensional database.

Data definition subsystem: This system defines the logical structure of the database by using a data dictionary.

Data dictionary: Dictionary containing a description of the structure of data in a database.

Data entry worker: Inputs customer information, lists, and other types of data.

Data flow diagram: Diagram showing data or information flow within an information system.

Data integrity: Database characteristics relating to the consistency and accuracy of data.

Data maintenance: Maintaining data includes adding new data, deleting old data, and editing existing data.

Data manipulation subsystem: Provides tools to maintain and analyze data.

Data mining: Technique of searching data warehouses for related information and patterns.

Data processing system (DPS): Transaction processing system that keeps track of routine operations and records these events in a database. Also called transaction processing system (TPS).

Data redundancy: A common database problem in which data is duplicated and stored in different files.

Data security: Protection of software and data from unauthorized tampering or damage.

Data warehouse: Data collected from a variety of internal and external databases and stored in a database called a data warehouse. Data mining is then used to search these databases.

Data worker: Person involved with the distribution and communication of information, such as secretaries and clerks.

Database: A collection of related information, like employee names, addresses, and phone numbers. It is organized so that a computer program can quickly select the desired pieces of information and display them for you.

Database administrator (DBA): Uses database management software to determine the most efficient way to organize and access data.

Database file: File containing highly structured and organized data created by database management programs.

Database management system (DBMS): To organize, manage, and retrieve data. DBMS programs have five subsystems: DBMS engine, data definition, data manipulation, applications generation, and data administration. An example of a database management system is Microsoft Access. *See* Database manager.

Database manager: Software package used to set up, or structure, a database such as an inventory list of supplies. It also provides tools to edit, enter, and retrieve data from the database.

Database model: Defines rules and standards for all data in a database. There are five database models: hierarchical, network, relational, multidimensional, and object-oriented. For example, Access uses the relational data model.

DBMS engine: Provides a bridge between the logical view of data and the physical view of data.

Debugging: Programmer's word for testing and then eliminating errors in a program. Programming errors are of two types: syntax and logic errors.

Decision model: The decision model gives the decision support system its analytical capabilities. There are three types of models included in the decision model: tactical, operational, and strategic.

Decision support system (DSS): Flexible analysis tool that helps managers make decisions about unstructured problems, such as effects of events and trends outside the organization.

Decision table: Table showing decision rules that apply when certain conditions occur and what action should take place as a result.

Demand report: A demand report is produced on request. An example is a report on the numbers and types of jobs held by women and minorities done at the request of the government.

Demodulation: Process performed by a modem in converting analog signals to digital signals.

Denial of service (DoS) attack: A variant virus in which Web sites are overwhelmed with data and users are unable to access the Web site. Unlike a worm that self-replicates, a DoS attack floods a computer or network with requests for information and data.

Density: Refers to how tightly the bits (electromagnetic charges) can be packed next to one another on a disk.

Design template: Provides professionally selected combinations of color schemes, slide layouts, and special effects for presentation graphics.

Desk checking: Process of checking out a computer program by studying a printout of the program line by line, looking for syntax and logic errors.

Desktop: The screen that is displayed on the monitor when the computer starts up. All items and icons on the screen are considered to be on your desktop and are used to interact with the computer.

Desktop computer: Computer small enough to fit on top of or along the side of a desk and yet too big to carry around.

Desktop operating systems: *See* Stand-alone operating system.

Desktop publisher: One who creates and formats publication-ready material.

Desktop publishing program: Program that allows you to mix text and graphics to create publications of professional quality.

Desktop system unit: A system unit that typically contains the system's electronic components and selected secondary storage devices. Input and output devices, such as the mouse, keyboard, and monitor, are located outside the system unit.

Device driver: Every device that is connected to the computer has a special program associated with it called a device driver that allows communication between the operating system and the device.

Diagnostic program: *See* Troubleshooting program.

Dialog box: Provides additional information and requests user input.

Dictionary attack: Uses software to try thousands of common words sequentially in an attempt to gain unauthorized access to a user's account.

Digital: Computers are digital machines because they can only understand 1s and 0s. It is either on or off. For example, a digital watch states the exact time on the face, whereas an analog watch has the second hand moving in constant motion as it tells the time.

Digital camera: Similar to a traditional camera except that images are recorded digitally in the camera's memory rather than on film.

Digital cash: Currency for Internet purchases. Buyers purchase digital cash from a third party (a bank that specializes in electronic currency) by transferring funds from their banks.

Digital media player: *See* Portable media player.

Digital Millennium Copyright Act: Law that makes it legal for a program owner to make only his or her own backup copies of a software program. However, it is illegal for those copies to be resold or given away.

Digital rights management (DRM): Encompasses various technologies that control access to electronic media and files.

Digital signal: Computers can only understand digital signals. Before processing can occur within the system unit, a conversion must occur from what we understand (analog) to what the system unit can electronically process (digital). *See* Analog signal.

Digital subscriber line (DSL): Provides high-speed connection using existing telephone lines.

Digital subscriber line (DSL) service: Service provided by telephone companies using existing telephone lines to provide high-speed connections.

Digital versatile disc (DVD): A type of optical disc similar to CD-ROMs except that more data can be packed into the same amount of space. *Also see* DVD (digital versatile disc).

Digital video camera: Input device that records motion digitally.

Digital video disc: *See* DVD (digital versatile disc).

Digital whiteboard: A specialized device with a large display connected to a computer or projector.

DIMM (dual in-line memory module): An expansion module used to add memory to the system board.

Direct approach: Approach for systems implementation whereby the old system is simply abandoned for the new system.

Directory server: A specialized server that manages resources such as user accounts for an entire network.

Disaster recovery plan: Plan used by large organizations describing ways to continue operations following a disaster until normal computer operations can be restored.

Disk caching: Method of improving hard-disk performance by anticipating data needs. Frequently used data is read from the hard disk into memory (cache). When needed, data is then accessed directly from memory, which has a much faster transfer rate than from the hard disk. Increases performance by as much as 30 percent.

Disk Cleanup: A Windows troubleshooting utility that eliminates nonessential files.

Disk Defragmenter: A Windows utility that optimizes disk performance by eliminating unnecessary fragments and rearranging files.

Display screen: *See* Monitor.

Distributed database: Database that can be made accessible through a variety of communications networks, which allow portions of the database to be located in different places.

DO UNTIL structure: Loop structure in programming that appears at the end of a loop. The DO UNTIL loop means that the loop statements will be executed at least once. In other words, this program tells you to DO option one UNTIL it is no longer true.

DO WHILE structure: Loop structure in programming that appears at the beginning of a loop. The DO WHILE loop will keep executing as long as there is information to be processed. For example, DO option one WHILE (or as long as) option one remains true.

Document: Any kind of text material.

Document file: File created by a word processor to save documents such as letters, research papers, and memos.

Document scanner: Similar to a flatbed scanner except that it can quickly scan multipage documents. It automatically feeds one page of a document at a time through a scanning surface.

Documentation: Written descriptions and procedures about a program and how to use it. *See* Program documentation.

Domain name: The second part of the URL; it is the name of the server where the resource is located. For example, www.mtv.com.

Domain name server (DNS): Internet addressing method that assigns names and numbers to people and computers. Because the numeric IP addresses are difficult to remember, the DNS server was developed to automatically convert text-based addresses to numeric IP addresses.

Dot-matrix printer: A type of printer that forms characters and images using a series of small pins on a print head. Used where high-quality output is not required.

Dot pitch: Distance between each pixel. The lower the dot pitch, the shorter the distance between pixels, and the higher the clarity of images produced.

Dots-per-inch (dpi): Printer resolution is measured in dpi. The higher the dpi, the better the quality of images produced.

Downloading: Process of transferring information from a remote computer to the computer one is using.

Drawing program: Program used to help create artwork for publications. *See* Illustration program.

Driver: *See* Device driver.

DS3: Provides support for very high-speed, all-digital transmission for large corporations.

DSL: *See* Digital subscriber line.

Dual-scan monitor: *See* Passive-matrix monitor.

Duplex printing: Allows automatic printing on both sides of a sheet of paper.

DVD (digital versatile disc or digital video disc): Similar to CD-ROMs except that more data can be packed into the same amount of space. DVD drives can store 4.7 GB to 17 GB on a single DVD disc or 17 times the capacity of CDs.

DVD player: Also known as DVD-ROM drives. *See* DVD.

DVD–R (DVD recordable): A DVD with a write-once format that differs slightly from the format of DVD+R. Typically used to create permanent archives for large amounts of data and to record videos.

DVD+R (DVD recordable): A DVD with a write-once format that differs slightly from the format of DVD–R. Typically used to create permanent archives for large amounts of data and to record videos.

DVD-RAM (DVD random-access memory): A high-capacity, maximum-performance disc that allows the user to read the information, write over it, and erase the data if necessary. Used like a floppy disk to copy, delete files, and run programs. It has up to 8 times the storage capacity of a CD and also can be used to read CD and DVD formats.

DVD–ROM (DVD–read-only memory): Used to distribute full-length feature films with theater-quality video and sound. Also known as DVD players. Are read-only.

DVD–RW (DVD rewriteable): A type of reusable DVD disc that is more flexible than the DVD-RAM. DVD–RW is able to create and read CD discs along with creating and editing large-scale multimedia presentations.

DVD+RW (DVD rewriteable): Another DVD format to record and erase repeatedly. Able to create and read CD discs along with creating and editing large-scale multimedia presentations.

DVI (Digital Video Interface) port: A type of port that provides a connection to a digital monitor.

e

EBCDIC (Extended Binary Coded Decimal Interchange Code): Binary coding scheme that is a standard for minicomputers and mainframe computers.

E-book: *See* E-book reader.

E-book reader: Handheld, book-sized device that displays text and graphics. Using content downloaded from the Web or special cartridges, these devices are used to read newspapers, magazines, and books.

E-commerce: Buying and selling goods over the Internet.

E-learning: A Web application that allows one to take educational courses online.

E-mail: Communicate with anyone in the world who has an Internet address or e-mail account with a system connected to the Internet. You can include a text message, graphics, photos, and file attachments.

E-mail client: A special program that communicates with the e-mail service provider and must be installed on the computer first.

E-paper: Requires power only when changing pages, and not the entire time a page is displayed on the screen.

Economic feasibility: Comparing the costs of a new system to the benefits it promises.

Editing: Features that modify a document such as using a thesaurus, find and replace, or spell check.

Electronic commerce (e-commerce): Buying and selling goods over the Internet.

Electronic mail: Transmission of electronic messages over the Internet. Also known as e-mail.

Electronic paper: *See* E-paper.

Electronic profile: Using publicly and privately available databases, information resellers create electronic profiles, which are highly detailed and personalized descriptions of individuals.

Embedded operating system: An operating system that is completely stored within the ROM (read-only memory) of the device that it is in; used for handheld computers and smaller devices like PDAs.

Encryption: Coding information so that only the user can read or otherwise use it.

Encryption key: A binary number used to gain access to encrypted information.

End user: Person who uses microcomputers or has access to larger computers.

Enterprise storage system: Using mass storage devices, a strategy designed for organizations to promote efficient and safe use of data across the networks within their organizations.

Entity: In an object-oriented database, a person, place, thing, or event that is to be described.

Erasable optical disc: Optical disc on which the disk drive can write information and also erase and rewrite information. Also known as CD-RW or compact disc rewriteable.

Ergonomic keyboard: Keyboard arrangement that is not rectangular and has a palm rest, which is designed to alleviate wrist strain.

Ethernet: Otherwise known as Ethernet bus or Ethernet LAN. The Ethernet bus is the pathway or arterial to which all nodes (PCs, file servers, print servers, Web servers, etc.) are connected. All of this is connected to a local area network (LAN) or a wide area network (WAN). *See* Bus network.

Ethernet cable: Twisted-pair cable commonly used in networks and to connect a variety of components to the system unit.

Ethernet port: A high-speed networking port that allows multiple computers to be connected for sharing files or for high-speed Internet access.

Ethics: Standards of moral conduct.

Exception report: Report that calls attention to unusual events.

Executive information system (EIS): Sophisticated software that can draw together data from an organization's databases in meaningful patterns and highly summarized forms.

Executive support system (ESS): *See* Executive information system.

Expansion bus: Connects the CPU to slots on the system board. There are different types of expansion buses such as industry standard architecture (ISA), peripheral component interconnect (PCI), accelerated graphics port (AGP), universal serial bus (USB), and FireWire buses. *See* System bus.

Expansion card: Optional device that plugs into a slot inside the system unit to expand the computer's abilities. Ports on the system board allow cables to be connected from the expansion board to devices outside the system unit.

Expansion slots: Openings on a system board. Users can insert optional devices, known as expansion cards, into these slots, allowing users to expand their systems. *See* Expansion card.

Expert system: Computer program that provides advice to decision makers who would otherwise rely on human experts. It's a type of artificial intelligence that uses a database to provide assistance to users.

ExpressCard: Technology replacing the PC Card to provide a direct connection to the system bus. *Also see* PC Card slots.

External data: Data gathered from outside an organization. Examples are data provided by market research firms.

External hard drive: Uses the same technology as an internal hard disk but is used primarily to complement an internal hard disk by providing additional storage. They are typically connected to a USB or FireWire port on the system unit and are easily removed.

Extranet: Private network that connects more than one organization.

f

Facebook: The most widely used social networking site, as of 2008.

Facebook groups: Communities of individuals who share common interest on Facebook.

Facebook Pages: Often used by businesses and public figures to promote ideas, products, and services.

Facebook Profile: An individual's Facebook page, which may include photos, lists of personal interests, contact information, and other personal information.

Family Educational Rights and Privacy Act (FERPA): A federal law that restricts disclosure of educational records.

Fax machine: A device for sending and receiving images over telephone lines.

Fiber-optic cable: Special transmission cable made of glass tubes that are immune to electronic interference. Data is transmitted through fiber-optic cables in the form of pulses of light.

Field: Each column of information within a record is called a field. A field contains related information on a specific item like employee names within a company department.

Fifth-generation language (5GL):   Computer language that incorporates the concept of artificial intelligence to allow direct human communication.

File: A collection of related records that can store data and programs. For example, the payroll file would include payroll information (records) for all of the employees (entities).

File compression: Process of reducing the storage requirements for a file.

File compression program: Utility programs that reduce the size of files so they require less storage on the computer and can be sent more efficiently over the Internet. Examples of such programs are WinZip and Wizard.

File decompression: Process of expanding a compressed file.

File server: Dedicated computer with large storage capacity providing users access to shared folders or fast storage and retrieval of information used in that business.

File transfer protocol (FTP):   Internet service for uploading and downloading files.

Filter: (1) A filter blocks access to selected Web sites. (2) A filter will locate or display records from a table that fit a set of conditions or criteria when using programs like Excel.

Find and replace: An editing tool that finds a selected word or phrase and replaces it with another. Click *edit, find.*

Firewall: Security hardware and software. All communications into and out of an organization pass through a special security computer, called a proxy server, to protect all systems against external threats.

FireWire bus: Operates much like USB buses on the system board but at higher speeds.

FireWire port: Used to connect high-speed printers, and even video cameras, to system unit.

Flash: An interactive animation program from Adobe that is usually full screen and highly dynamic, displaying moving text or complicated interactive features.

Flash drive: *See* USB drive.

Flash memory: RAM chips that retain data even when power is disrupted. Flash memory is an example of solid-state storage and is typically used to store digitized images and record MP3 files.

Flash memory card: A solid-state storage device widely used in notebook computers. Flash memory also is used in a variety of specialized input devices to capture and transfer data to desktop computers.

Flat-panel monitor: Or liquid crystal display (LCD) monitor. These monitors are much thinner than CRTs and can be used for desktop systems as well.

Flatbed scanner: An input device similar to a copying machine.

Folder: A named area on a disk that is used to store related subfolders and files.

Font: Also known as typeface, is a set of characters with a specific design.

Font size: The height of a character measured in points, with each point being 1/72 inch.

Foreground: The current program when multitasking or running multiple programs at once.

Form: Electronic forms reflecting the contents of one record or table. Primarily used to enter new records or make changes to existing records.

Format: Features that change the appearance of a document like font, font sizes, character effects, alignment, and bulleted and numbered lists.

Formula: Instructions for calculations in a spreadsheet. It is an equation that performs calculations on the data contained within the cells in a worksheet or spreadsheet.

Fourth-generation language (4GL):   Task-oriented language designed to solve a specific problem and requiring little special training on the part of the end user.

Fragmented: Storage technique that breaks up large files and stores the parts wherever space is available in adjacent sectors and clusters.

Freedom of Information Act of 1970:   Law giving citizens the right to examine data about them in federal government files, except for information restricted for national security reasons.

Friend: An individual on a list of contacts for an instant messaging server.

Frustrated: Person who feels it is an imposition to have to learn something new like computer technology.

Function: A built-in formula in a spreadsheet that performs calculations automatically.

Fuzzy logic: Used by expert systems to allow users to respond by using qualitative terms, such as *great* and *OK*.

g

Galleries: Feature of Microsoft Office 2007 and 2010 that simplifies the process of making selections from a list of alternatives by replacing dialog boxes with visual presentations of results.

Game port: Were used to connect video game controllers and joysticks.

General ledger: Activity that produces income statements and balance sheets based on all transactions of a company.

Generations (of programming languages):   The five generations are machine languages, assembly languages, procedural languages, problem-oriented languages, and natural languages. *See* Levels.

Gestures: A feature of Mac OS 10.7 that allows the use of fingers to run programs and to control the content of a display screen.

Global positioning system (GPS):   Devices that use location information to determine the geographic location of your car, for example.

Google Cloud Print: A Google service that supports cloud printing.

GPU (graphics processing unit): *See* Graphics coprocessor.

Gramm-Leach-Bliley Act: A law that protects personal financial information.

Grammar checker: In word processing, a tool that identifies poorly worded sentences and incorrect grammar.

Graphical map: Diagram of a Web site's overall design.

Graphical user interface (Gui): Special screen that allows software commands to be issued through the use of graphic symbols (icons) or pull-down menus.

Graphics coprocessor: Designed to handle requirements related to displaying and manipulating 2-D and 3-D graphic images.

Graphics suite: Group of graphics programs offered at a lower cost than if purchased separately, like CorelDraw.

Grayscale: The most common black ink selection in which images are displayed using many shades of gray.

Grid chart: Chart that shows the relationship between input and output documents.

Group decision support system (GDSS): System used to support the collective work of a team addressing large problems.

Groups: In Microsoft Word, each tab is organized into groups that contain related items.

Guest operating system: Operating system that operates on virtual machines.

h

Hacker: Person who gains unauthorized access to a computer system for the fun and challenge of it.

Handheld computer: *See* Personal digital assistant (PDA).

Handheld computer system unit: Smallest type of system unit, designed to fit into the palm of one hand.

Handwriting recognition software: Translates handwritten notes into a form that the system unit can process.

Hard copy: Information presented on paper; also referred to as printer output.

Hard disk: Enclosed disk drive containing one or more metallic disks. Hard disks use magnetic charges to record data and have large storage capacities and fast retrieval times.

Hardware: Equipment that includes a keyboard, monitor, printer, the computer itself, and other devices that are controlled by software programming.

Head crash: When a read-write head makes contact with the hard disk's surface or particles on its surface, the disk surface becomes scratched and some or all data is destroyed.

Header: A typical e-mail has three elements: header, message, and signature. The header appears first and includes addresses, subject, and attachments.

Headsets: Audio-output devices connected to a sound card in the system unit. The sound card is used to capture as well as play back recorded sound.

Health Insurance Portability and Accountability Act (HIPAA): A federal law that protects medical records.

Help: A feature in most application software providing options that typically include an index, a glossary, and a search feature to locate reference information about specific commands.

Hexadecimal system (hex): Uses 16 digits to represent binary numbers.

Hi def (high-definition) disc: The next generation of optical disc, which offers increased storage capacities.

Hierarchical database: Database in which fields or records are structured in nodes. Organized in the shape of a pyramid, and each node is linked directly to the nodes beneath it. Also called one-to-many relationship.

Hierarchical network: *See* Tree network.

High Definition Multimedia Interface (HDMI): Port that provides high-definition video and audio, making it possible to use a computer as a video jukebox or an HD video recorder.

High-definition television (HDTV): All-digital television that delivers a much clearer and more detailed widescreen picture.

Higher level: Programming languages that are closer to the language humans use.

History file: Created by the browser to store information on Web sites visited by your computer system.

Hits: The sites that a search engine returns after running a keyword search, ordered from most likely to least likely to contain the information requested.

Home network: LAN network for homes allowing different computers to share resources, including a common Internet connection.

Home software: *See* Integrated package.

Host: Also called a server or provider, is a large centralized computer.

Host operating system: Operating system that runs on the physical machine.

Hotspot: Wireless access points that provide Internet access and are often available in public places such as coffee shops, libraries, bookstores, colleges, and universities.

Household robot: Robot designed to vacuum or scrub floors, mow lawns, patrol the house, or simply provide entertainment.

HTML: *See* Hypertext Markup Language.

HTML editor: *See* Web authoring program.

Hub: The center or central node for other nodes. This device can be a server or a connection point for cables from other nodes.

Human resources: The organizational department that focuses on the hiring, training, and promoting of people, as well as any number of human-centered activities within the organization.

Hyperlink: Connection or link to other documents or Web pages that contain related information.

Hypertext Markup Language (HTML): Programming language that creates document files used to display Web pages.

i

Icons: Graphic objects on the desktop used to represent programs and other files.

Identity theft: The illegal assumption of someone's identity for the purpose of economic gain.

IF-THEN-ELSE structure: Logical selection structure whereby one of two paths is followed according to IF, THEN, and ELSE statements in a program. *See* Selection structure.

IFPS (interactive financial planning system): A 4GL language used for developing financial models.

Illusion of anonymity: The misconception that being selective about disclosing personal information on the Internet can prevent an invasion of personal privacy.

Illustration program: Also known as drawing programs; used to create digital illustrations and modify vector images and thus create line art, 3-D models, and virtual reality.

Image editor: An application for modifying bitmap images.

Image gallery: Libraries of electronic images.

Immersive experience: Allows the user to walk into a virtual reality room or view simulations on a virtual reality wall.

Income statement: A statement that shows a company's financial performance, income, expenses, and the difference between them for a specific time period.

Individual database: Collection of integrated records used mainly by just one person. Also called microcomputer database.

Industrial robot: Robot used in factories to perform a variety of tasks. For example, machines used in automobile plants to do painting and polishing.

Information: Data that has been processed by a computer system.

Information broker: *See* Information reseller.

Information reseller: Also known as information broker. It gathers personal data on people and sells it to direct marketers, fund-raisers, and others, usually for a fee.

Information system: Collection of hardware, software, people, data, and procedures that work together to provide information essential to running an organization.

Information systems manager: Oversees the work of programmers, computer specialists, systems analysts, and other computer professionals.

Information technology (IT): Computer and communication technologies, such as communication links to the Internet, that provide help and understanding to the end user.

Information utility: *See* Commercial database.

Information worker: Employee who creates, distributes, and communicates information.

Infrared: Uses infrared light waves to communicate over short distances. Sometimes referred to as line-of-sight communication because light waves can only travel in a straight line.

Infrared Data Association (IrDA) port: A wireless mechanism for transferring data between devices using infrared light waves.

Ink-jet printer: Printer that sprays small droplets of ink at high speed onto the surface of the paper, producing letter-quality images, and can print in color.

InPrivate Browsing: A privacy mode provided by Internet Explorer that eliminates history files as well as blocks most cookies.

Input: Any data or instructions used by a computer.

Input device: Piece of equipment that translates data into a form a computer can process. The most common input devices are the keyboard and the mouse.

Instant messaging (IM): A program allowing communication and collaboration for direct, "live" connections over the Internet between two or more people.

Integrated circuit: *See* Silicon chip.

Integrated package: A single program providing functionality of a collection of programs but not as extensive as a specialized program like Microsoft Word. Popular with home users who are willing to sacrifice some advanced features for lower cost and simplicity.

Interactive whiteboard: *See* digital whiteboard.

Interactivity: User participation in a multimedia presentation.

Internal data: Data from within an organization consisting principally of transactions from the transaction processing system.

Internal hard disk: Storage device consisting of one or more metallic platters sealed inside a container. Internal hard disks are installed inside the system cabinet of a microcomputer. It stores the operating system and major applications like Word.

Internet: A huge computer network available to everyone with a microcomputer and a means to connect to it. It is the actual physical network made up of wires, cables, and satellites as opposed to the Web, which is the multimedia interface to resources available on the Internet.

Internet scam: Using the Internet, a fraudulent act or operation designed to trick individuals into spending their time and money for little or no return.

Internet security suite: Collection of utility programs designed to make using the Internet easier and safer.

Internet service provider (ISP): Provides access to the Internet.

Internet telephone: Low-cost alternative to long-distance telephone calls using electronic voice delivery.

Internet telephony: *See* Telephony.

Interpreter: Software that converts a procedural language one statement at a time into machine language just before the statement is executed. No object code is saved.

Intranet: Like the Internet, it typically provides e-mail, mailing lists, newsgroups, and FTP services, but it is accessible only to those within the organization. Organizations use intranets to provide information to their employees.

Intrusion detection system (IDS): Using sophisticated statistical techniques to analyze all incoming and outgoing network traffic, this system works with firewalls to protect an organization's network.

Inventory: Material or products that a company has in stock.

Inventory control system: A system that keeps records of the number of each kind of part or finished good in the warehouse.

iOS: Previously known as iPhone, mobile operating system developed for Apple's iPhone, iPod Touch, and iPad.

IP address (Internet Protocol address): The unique numeric address of a computer on the Internet that facilitates the delivery of e-mail.

IP telephony: *See* Telephony.

iPhone OS: *See* iOS.

j

Java: Programming language for creating special programs like applets. *See* Applets.

JavaScript: A scripting language that adds basic interactivity to Web pages.

Joystick: Popular input device for computer games. You control game actions by varying the pressure, speed, and direction of the joystick.

k

Key: Another term for encryption key.

Key field: The common field by which tables in a database are related to each other. This field uniquely identifies the record. For example, in university databases, a key field is the Social Security number. Also known as primary key.

Keyboard: Input device that looks like a typewriter keyboard but has additional keys.

Keyboard port: Were used to connect keyboards to the system unit.

Keystroke logger: Also known as computer monitoring software and sniffer programs. They can be loaded onto your computer without your knowledge.

Kilobits per second (Kbps): Speed at which data is transferred.

Knowledge base: A system that uses a database containing specific facts, rules to relate these facts, and user input to formulate recommendations and decisions.

Knowledge-based systems: Programs duplicating human knowledge. It's like capturing the knowledge of a human expert and making it accessible through a computer program.

Knowledge work system (KWS): Specialized information system used to create information in a specific area of expertise.

Knowledge worker: Person involved in the creation of information, such as an engineer or a scientist.

l

Label: Provides structure to a worksheet by describing the contents of the rows and columns. *See* Text entry.

Land: *See* Lands and pits.

Lands and pits: Flat and bumpy areas, respectively, that represent 1s and 0s on the optical disc surface to be read by a laser.

Language translator: Converts programming instructions into a machine language that can be processed by a computer.

Laptop computer: *See* Notebook computer and Notebook system unit.

Laser printer: Printer that creates dotlike images on a drum, using a laser beam light source.

Launchpad: A feature of Mac OS 10.7 that displays and provides direct access to all apps installed on your computer.

Legacy port: Was common on microcomputer systems to connect specific types of devices. They have largely been replaced by faster, more flexible ports such as the universal serial bus (USB).

Levels: Generations or levels of programming languages ranging from "low" to "high." *See* Generations (of programming languages).

Link: A connection to related information.

LinkedIn: The premier business-oriented social networking site.

Linux: Type of UNIX operating system initially developed by Linus Torvalds, it is one of the most popular and powerful alternatives to the Windows operating system.

Lion: Also known as Mac OS 10.7, this operating system introduced launchpad, Mission Control, and gesture support.

Liquid crystal display (LCD): A technology used for flat-panel monitors.

Local area network (LAN): Network consisting of computers and other devices that are physically near each other, such as within the same building.

Location: For browsers to connect to resources, locations or addresses must be specified. Also known as uniform resource locators or URLs.

Logic error: Error that occurs when a programmer has used an incorrect calculation or left out a programming procedure.

Logic structure: Programming statements or structures called sequence, selection, or loop that control the logical sequence in which computer program instructions are executed.

Logical operation: Comparing two pieces of data to see whether one is equal to ($=$), less than ($<$), or greater than ($>$) the other.

Logical view: Focuses on the meaning and content of the data. End users and computer professionals are concerned with this view as opposed to the physical view, with which only specialized computer professionals are concerned.

Loop structure: Logic structure in which a process may be repeated as long as a certain condition remains true. This structure is called a "loop" because the program loops around or repeats again and again. There are two variations: DO UNTIL and DO WHILE.

Low bandwidth: *See* Voiceband.

Lower level: Programming language closer to the language the computer itself uses. The computer understands the 0s and 1s that make up bits and bytes.

m

Mac OS: Operating system designed for Macintosh computers.

Mac OS 10.7: one of the newest versions of Mac OS.

Mac OS X: Macintosh operating system featuring a user interface called Aqua.

Machine language: Language in which data is represented in 1s and 0s. Most languages have to be translated into machine language for the computer to process the data. Either a compiler or an interpreter performs this translation.

Magnetic card reader: A card reader that reads encoded information from a magnetic strip on the back of a card.

Magnetic-ink character recognition (MICR): Direct-entry scanning devices used in banks. This technology is used to automatically read the numbers on the bottom of checks.

Main board: See Motherboard or System board.

Mainframe computer: This computer can process several million program instructions per second. Sizeable organizations rely on these room-size systems to handle large programs and a great deal of data.

Maintenance programmer: Programmers who maintain software by updating programs to protect them from errors, improve usability, standardize, and adjust to organizational changes.

Malware: Short for malicious software.

MAN: *See* Metropolitan area network.

Management information system (MIS): Computer-based information system that produces standardized reports in a summarized and structured form. Generally used to support middle managers.

Many-to-many relationship: In a network database, each child node may have more than one parent node and vice versa.

Marketing: The organizational department that plans, prices, promotes, sells, and distributes an organization's goods and services.

Markup language: *See* Content-markup language.

Mass storage: Refers to the tremendous amount of secondary storage required by large organizations.

Mass storage devices: Devices such as file servers, RAID systems, tape libraries, optical jukeboxes, and more.

Mechanical mouse: Traditional and most widely used type of mouse. It has a ball on the bottom and is attached with a cord to the system unit.

Media: Media are the actual physical material that holds the data, such as a floppy disk, which is one of the important characteristics of secondary storage. Singular of media is medium.

Media center: Type of microcomputer that blurs the line between desktop computers and dedicated entertainment devices.

Media center system unit: Uses powerful desktop system hardware with specialized graphics cards for interfacing with televisions and other home entertainment devices.

Medium: *See* Media.

Medium band: Bandwidth of special leased lines, used mainly with minicomputers and mainframe computers.

Memory: Memory is contained on chips connected to the system board and is a holding area for data instructions and information (processed data waiting to be output to secondary storage). RAM, ROM, and CMOS are three types of memory chips.

Menu: List of commands.

Menu bar: Menus are displayed in a menu bar at the top of the screen.

Mesh network: A topology requiring each node to have more than one connection to the other nodes so that if a path between two nodes is disrupted, data can be automatically rerouted around the failure using another path.

Message: The content portion of e-mail correspondence.

Metasearch engine: Program that automatically submits your search request to several indices and search engines and then creates an index from received information. One of the best known is Dogpile.

Method: In an object-oriented database, description of how the data is to be manipulated.

Metropolitan area network (MAN): These networks are used as links between office buildings in a city.

Microblog: Publishes short sentences that only take a few seconds to write, rather than long stories or posts like a traditional blog.

Microcomputer: Small, low-cost computer designed for individual users. These include desktop, notebook, and personal digital assistant computers.

Microcomputer database: *See* Individual database.

Microprocessor: The central processing unit (CPU) of a microcomputer controls and manipulates data to produce information. The microprocessor is contained on a single integrated circuit chip and is the brains of the system.

Microwave: Communication using high-frequency radio waves that travel in straight lines through the air.

Middle management: Middle-level managers deal with control and planning. They implement the long-term goals of the organization.

MIDI: *See* Musical instrument digital interface.

Midrange computer: Also known as a minicomputer.

Minicomputer: Refrigerator-sized machines falling in between microcomputers and mainframes in processing speed and data-storing capacity. Medium-sized companies or departments of large companies use minicomputers.

Mission Control: A feature of Mac OS 10.7 that displays all running programs at one time.

Mistaken identity: When the electronic profile of one person is switched with another.

Mobile applications: Add-on features for a variety of mobile devices, including smartphones, netbooks, and tablets.

Mobile apps: *See* Mobile applications.

Mobile browser: Special browsers designed to run on portable devices.

Mobile Digital Television: A technology that allows television stations to broadcast their programming directly to smartphones, computers, and digital media players.

Mobile DTV: *See* Mobile Digital Television.

Mobile operating system: Embedded operating system that controls a smartphone.

Mobile OS: *See* Mobile operating system.

Mobile robots: Robots that act as transports and are used for a variety of different tasks.

Modem: Short for modulator-demodulator. It is a communication device that translates the electronic signals from a computer into electronic signals that can travel over telephone lines.

Modulation: Process of converting digital signals to analog signals.

Module: *See* Program module.

Monitor: Output device like a television screen that displays data processed by the computer.

Motherboard: Also called a system board; the communications medium for the entire system.

Mouse: Device that typically rolls on the desktop and directs the cursor on the display screen.

Mouse pointer: Typically in the shape of an arrow.

Mouse port: Was used to connect a mouse to the system unit.

Multicore chip: A new type of chip that provides two independent CPUs, allowing two programs to run simultaneously. *Also see* Central processing unit.

Multidimensional database: Data can be viewed as a cube having three or more sides consisting of cells. Each side of the cube is considered a dimension of the data; thus, complex relationships between data can be represented and efficiently analyzed. Sometimes called a data cube and designed for analyzing large groups of records.

Multifunctional devices (MFD):   Devices that typically combine the capabilities of a scanner, printer, fax, and copying machine.

Multimedia: Technology that can link all sorts of media into one form of presentation, such as video, music, voice, graphics, and text.

Multimedia authoring programs: Programs used to create multimedia presentations bringing together video, audio, graphics, and text elements into an interactive framework. Macromedia Director, Authorware, and Toolbook are examples of multimedia authoring programs.

Multitasking: Operating system that allows a single user to run several application programs at the same time.

Multitouch screen: Can be touched with more than one finger, which allows for interactions such as rotating graphical objects on the screen with your hand or zooming in and out by pinching and stretching your fingers.

Musical instrument digital interface (MIDI):   A standard that allows musical instruments to connect to the system using MIDI ports.

MySpace: One of the first large-scale social networking sites.

N

Naive: People who underestimate the difficulty of changing computer systems or generating information.

Natural language: Language designed to give people a more human connection with computers.

Netbook: A type of microcomputer that is smaller, lighter, and less expensive than a notebook computer.

Netbook system unit: Similar to notebook system units but smaller, less powerful, and less expensive.

Network: The arrangement in which various communications channels are connected through two or more computers. The largest network in the world is the Internet.

Network adapter card: Connects the system unit to a cable that connects to other devices on the network.

Network administrator: Also known as network manager. Computer professional who ensures that existing information and communication systems are operating effectively and that new ones are implemented as needed. Also responsible for meeting security and privacy requirements.

Network architecture: Describes how networks are configured and how the resources are shared.

Network attached storage (NAS):   Similar to a file server except simpler and less expensive. Widely used for home and small business storage needs.

Network database: Database with a hierarchical arrangement of nodes, except that each child node may have more than one parent node. Also called many-to-many relationship.

Network gateway: Connection by which a local area network may be linked to other local area networks or to larger networks.

Network interface card (NIC):   Also known as a network adapter card. Used to connect a computer to one or more computers forming a communication network whereby users can share data, programs, and hardware.

Network operating system (NOS):   Interactive software between applications and computers coordinating and directing activities between computers on a network. This operating system is located on one of the connected computers' hard disks, making that system the network server.

Network server: *See* Network operating system. This computer coordinates all communication between the other computers. Popular network operating systems include NetWare and Windows NT Server.

Node: Any device connected to a network. For example, a node is a computer, printer, or data storage device and each device has its own address on the network. Also, within hierarchical databases, fields or records are structured in nodes.

Notebook computer: Portable computer, also known as a laptop computer, weighing between 4 and 10 pounds.

Notebook system unit: A small, portable system unit that contains electronic components, selected secondary storage devices, and input devices.

Numbered list: Sequence of steps or topics on a page organized by numbers.

Numeric entry: In a worksheet or spreadsheet, typically used to identify numbers or formulas.

Numeric keypad: Enters numbers and arithmetic symbols and is included on all computer keyboards.

O

Object: An element, such as a text box, that can be added to a workbook can be selected, sized, and moved. For example, if a chart (object) in an Excel workbook file (source file) is linked to a Word document (destination file), the chart appears in the Word document. In this manner, the object contains both data and instructions to manipulate the data.

Object code: Machine language code converted by a compiler from source code. Object code can be saved and run later.

Object-oriented database: A more flexible type of database that stores data as well as instructions to manipulate data and is able to handle unstructured data such as photographs, audio, and video. Object-oriented databases organize data using objects, classes, entities, attributes, and methods.

Object-oriented programming (OOP):   Methodology in which a program is organized into self-contained, reusable modules called objects. Each object contains both the data and processing operations necessary to perform a task.

Object-oriented software development: Software development approach that focuses less on the tasks and more on defining the relationships between previously defined procedures or objects.

Objectives: In programming, it is necessary to make clear the problems you are trying to solve to create a functional program.

Office automation system (OAS):   System designed primarily to support data workers. It focuses on managing documents, communicating, and scheduling.

Office software suites: *See* Productivity suites.

Office suites: *See* Productivity suites.

One-to-many relationship: In a hierarchical database, each entry has one parent node, and a parent may have several child nodes.

Online: Being connected to the Internet is described as being online.

Online banking: A feature provided by banking institutions that allows customers to perform banking operations using a Web browser.

Online identity: The information that people voluntarily post about themselves online.

Online office suite: Office suite stored online and available anywhere the Internet can be accessed.

Online processing: *See* Real-time processing.

Online shopping: The buying and selling of a wide range of consumer goods over the Internet.

Online stock trading: Allows investors to research, buy, and sell stocks and bonds over the Internet.

Online storage: Provides users with storage space that can be accessed from a Web site.

Open source: A free and openly distributed software program intended to allow users to improve upon and further develop the program.

Operating system: Software that interacts between application software and the computer, handling such details as running programs, storing and processing data, and coordinating all computer resources, including attached peripheral devices. It is the most important program on the computer. Windows 7, Windows Vista, and Mac OS X are examples of operating systems.

Operational feasibility: Making sure the design of a new system will be able to function within the existing framework of an organization.

Operational model: A decision model that helps lower-level managers accomplish the organization's day-to-day activities, such as evaluating and maintaining quality control.

Operators: Operators handle correcting operational errors in any programs. To do that, they need documentation, which lets them understand the program, thus enabling them to fix any errors.

Optical audio connection: Port used to integrate computers into high-end audio and home theatre systems.

Optical carrier (OC):   Provides support for very high-speed, all-digital transmission for large corporations.

Optical-character recognition (OCR):   Scanning device that uses special preprinted characters, such as those printed on utility bills, that can be read by a light source and changed into machine-readable code.

Optical disc: Storage device that can hold over 17 gigabytes of data, which is the equivalent of several million typewritten pages. Lasers are used to record and read data on the disc. The two basic types of optical discs are compact discs (CDs) and digital versatile or video discs (DVDs).

Optical disc drive: A disc is read by an optical disc drive using a laser that projects a tiny beam of light. The amount of reflected light determines whether the area represents a 1 or a 0.

Optical-mark recognition (OMR):   Device that senses the presence or absence of a mark, such as a pencil mark. As an example, an OMR device is used to score multiple-choice tests.

Optical mouse: A type of mouse that emits and senses light to detect mouse movement.

Optical scanner: Device that identifies images or text on a page and automatically converts it to electronic signals that can be stored in a computer to copy or reproduce.

Organic light-emitting diode (OLED): Has the benefits of lower power consumption and longer battery life, as well as possibilities for much thinner displays.

Organization chart: Chart showing the levels of management and formal lines of authority in an organization.

Organizational cloud storage: High-speed Internet connection to a dedicated remote organizational Internet drive site.

Output: Processed data or information.

Output device: Equipment that translates processed information from the central processing unit into a form that can be understood by humans. The most common output devices are monitors and printers.

P

Packet: Before a message is sent on the Internet, it is broken down into small parts called packets. Each packet is then sent separately over the Internet. At the receiving end, the packets are reassembled into the correct order.

Page layout program: *See* Desktop publishing program.

Pages: In Microsoft PowerPoint, another name for slides.

Parallel approach: Systems implementation in which old and new systems are operated side by side until the new one has shown it is reliable.

Parallel port: Used to connect external devices that send or receive data over a short distance. Mostly used to connect printers to the system unit.

Parallel processing: Used by supercomputers to run large and complex programs.

Parent node: Node one level above the node being considered in a hierarchical database or network. Each entry has one parent node, although a parent may have several child nodes. Also called one-to-many relationship.

Passive-matrix monitor: Monitor that creates images by scanning the entire screen. This type requires little energy but clarity of images is not sharp. Also known as dual-scan monitor.

Password: Special sequence of numbers or letters that limits access to information, such as electronic mail.

Payroll: Activity concerned with calculating employee paychecks.

PC Card slot: Also known as Personal Computer Memory Card International Association (PCMCIA) card slot. Credit card–sized expansion cards developed for portable computers.

PCI Express (PCIe): New type of bus that is 30 times faster than PCI bus.

PCMCIA slot: *See* PC Card slot.

PDA keyboard: Miniature keyboard for PDAs used to send e-mail, create documents, and more.

Peer-to-peer (P2P) network: Network in which nodes can act as both servers and clients. For example, one microcomputer can obtain files located on another microcomputer and also can provide files to other microcomputers.

People: End users who use computers to make themselves more productive.

Perception system robot: Robot that imitates some of the human senses.

Periodic report: Reports for a specific time period as to the health of the company or a particular department of the company.

Person-to-person auction site: A type of Web auction site where the owner provides a forum for numerous buyers and sellers to gather.

Personal area network (PAN): A type of wireless network that works within a very small area—your immediate surroundings.

Personal digital assistant (PDA): A device that typically combines pen input, writing recognition, personal organizational tools, and communication capabilities in a very small package. Also called handheld PC or palm computer.

Personal laser printer: Inexpensive laser printer widely used by single users to produce black-and-white documents.

Personal software: *See* Integrated package.

Phased approach: Systems implementation whereby a new system is implemented gradually over a period of time.

Phishing: An attempt to trick Internet users into thinking a fake but official-looking Web site or e-mail is legitimate.

Photo editor: *See* Image editor.

Photo printer: A special-purpose ink-jet printer designed to print photo-quality images from digital cameras.

Physical security: Activity concerned with protecting hardware from possible human and natural disasters.

Physical view: This focuses on the actual format and location of the data. *See* Logical view.

Picture element: *See* Pixel.

Pilot approach: Systems implementation in which a new system is tried out in only one part of the organization. Later it is implemented throughout the rest of the organization.

Pit: *See* Lands and pits.

Pixel (picture element): Smallest unit on the screen that can be turned on and off or made different shades. Pixels are individual dots that form images on a monitor. The greater the resolution, the more pixels and the better the clarity.

Pixel pitch: The distance between each pixel on a monitor.

Plagiarism: Representing some other person's work and ideas as your own without giving credit to the original source.

Plagiarist: Someone who engages in plagiarism.

Platform: The operating system. Application programs are designed to run with a specific platform. *See* Operating system.

Platform scanner: Handheld direct-entry device used to read special characters on price tags. Also known as wand reader.

Platter: Rigid metallic disk; multiple platters are stacked one on top of another within a hard disk drive.

Plotter: Special-purpose output device for producing bar charts, maps, architectural drawings, and three-dimensional illustrations.

Plug and Play: Set of hardware and software standards developed to create operating systems, processing units, expansion cards, and other devices that are able to configure themselves. When the computer starts up, it will search for the Plug and Play device and automatically configure it to the system.

Plug-in: Program that is automatically loaded and operates as part of a browser.

Podcast: An Internet-based medium for delivering music and movie files from the Internet to a computer.

Pointer: For a monitor, a pointer is typically displayed as an arrow and controlled by a mouse. For a database, a pointer is a connection between a parent node and a child node in a hierarchical database.

Pointers: Within a network database, pointers are additional connections between parent nodes and child nodes. Thus, a node may be reached through more than one path and can be traced down through different branches.

Pointing stick: Device used to control the pointer by directing the stick with your finger.

Port: Connecting socket on the outside of the system unit. Used to connect input and output devices to the system unit.

Portable language: Language that can be run on more than one type of computer.

Portable media player: Also known as digital media player; a specialized device for storing, transferring, and playing audio files.

Portable printer: Small and lightweight printers designed to work with notebook computers.

Portable scanner: A handheld device that slides across an image to be scanned, making direct contact.

Power supply unit: Desktop computers have a power supply unit located within the system unit that plugs into a standard wall outlet, converting AC to DC, which becomes the power to drive all of the system unit components.

Preliminary investigation: First phase of the systems life cycle. It involves defining the problem, suggesting alternative systems, and preparing a short report.

Presentation file: A file created by presentation graphics programs to save presentation materials. For example, a file might contain audience handouts, speaker notes, and electronic slides.

Presentation graphics: Graphics used to combine a variety of visual objects to create attractive and interesting presentations.

Primary key: *See* Key field.

Primary storage: Holds data and program instructions for processing data. It also holds processed information before it is output. *See* Memory.

Printer: Device that produces printed paper output.

Privacy: Computer ethics issue concerning the collection and use of data about individuals.

Privacy mode: A browser feature that eliminates history files and blocks most cookies.

Private Browsing: A privacy mode provided by Safari. *See* Privacy mode.

Proactive: Person who looks at technology in a positive, realistic way.

Procedural language: Programming language designed to focus on procedures and how a program will accomplish a specific task. Also known as 3GL or third-generation language.

Procedures: Rules or guidelines to follow when using hardware, software, and data.

Processing rights: Refers to which people have access to what kind of data.

Processor: *See* Central processing unit.

Production: The organizational department that actually creates finished goods and services using raw materials and personnel.

Productivity suites: Also known as office suites; contain professional-grade application programs, including word processing, spreadsheets, and more. A good example is Microsoft Office.

Program: Instructions for the computer to follow to process data. *See* Software.

Program analysis: *See* Program specification.

Program coder: *See* Application generator.

Program definition: *See* Program specification.

Program design: Creating a solution using programming techniques, such as top-down program design, pseudocode, flowcharts, logic structures, object-oriented programming, and CASE tools.

Program documentation: Written description of the purpose and process of a program. Documentation is written within the program itself and in printed documents. Programmers will find themselves frustrated without adequate documentation, especially when it comes time to update or modify the program.

Program flowchart: Flowchart graphically presents a detailed sequence of steps needed to solve a programming problem.

Program maintenance: Activity of updating software to correct errors, improve usability, standardize, and adjust to organizational changes.

Program module: Each module is made up of logically related program statements. The program must pass in sequence from one module to the next until the computer has processed all modules.

Program specification: Programming step in which objectives, output, input, and processing requirements are determined.

Programmer: Computer professional who creates new software or revises existing software.

Programming: A program is a list of instructions a computer will follow to process data. Programming, also known as software development, is a six-step procedure for creating that list of instructions. The six steps are program specification, program design, program code (or coding), program test, program documentation, and program maintenance.

Programming language: A collection of symbols, words, and phrases that instruct a computer to perform a specific task.

Project manager: Software that enables users to plan, schedule, and control the people, resources, and costs needed to complete a project on time.

Property: Computer ethics issue relating to who owns data and rights to software.

Protocol: Rules for exchanging data between computers. The protocol http:// is the most common.

Prototyping: Building a model or prototype that can be modified before the actual system is installed.

Proxy server: Computer that acts as a gateway or checkpoint in an organization's firewall. *See* Firewall.

Pseudocode: An outline of the logic of the program to be written. It is the steps or the summary of the program before you actually write the program for the computer. Consequently, you can see beforehand what the program is to accomplish.

Purchase order: A form that shows the name of the company supplying the material or service and what is being purchased.

Purchasing: Buying of raw materials and services.

q

Query: A question or request for specific data contained in a database. Used to analyze data.

Query-by-example: A specific tool in database management that shows a blank record and lets you specify the information needed, like the fields and values of the topic you are looking to obtain.

Query language: Easy-to-use language and understandable to most users. It is used to search and generate reports from a database. An example is the language used on an airline reservation system.

r

Radio frequency (RF): Uses radio signals to communicate between wireless devices.

Radio frequency card reader: A device that reads cards having embedded radio frequency identification (RFID) information.

Radio frequency identification (RFID): A system that uses radio waves to read encoded information from a microchip.

RAID system: Several inexpensive hard-disk drives connected to improve performance and provide reliable storage.

RAM: *See* Random access memory.

Random access memory (RAM): Volatile, temporary storage that holds the program and data the CPU is presently processing. It is called temporary storage because its contents will be lost if electrical power to the computer is disrupted or the computer is turned off.

Range: A series of continuous cells in a worksheet.

Rapid applications development (RAD): Involves the use of powerful development software and specialized teams as an alternative to the systems development life cycle approach. Time for development is shorter and quality of the completed systems development is better, although cost is greater.

Raster image: *See* Bitmap image.

Read-only memory (ROM): Refers to chips that have programs built into them at the factory. The user cannot change the contents of such chips. The CPU can read or retrieve the programs on the chips but cannot write or change information. ROM stores programs that boot the computer, for example. Also called firmware.

Real-time processing: Or online processing. Occurs when data is processed at the same time a transaction occurs.

Recalculation: If you change one or more numbers in your spreadsheet, all related formulas will automatically recalculate and charts will be recreated.

Record: Each row of information in a database is a record. Each record contains fields of data about some specific item, like employee name, address, phone, and so forth. A record represents a collection of attributes describing an entity.

Redundant arrays of inexpensive disks (RAIDs): Groups of inexpensive hard-disk drives related or grouped together using networks and special software. They improve performance by expanding external storage.

Refresh rate: How often a displayed image is updated or redrawn on the monitor.

Relation: A table in a relational database in which data elements are stored in rows and columns.

Relational database: A widely used database structure in which data is organized into related tables. Each table is made up of rows called records and columns called fields. Each record contains fields of data about a specific item.

Repetition structure: *See* Loop structure.

Reports: Can be lists of fields in a table or selected fields based on a query. Typical database reports include sales summaries, phone lists, and mailing labels.

Research: The organizational department that identifies, investigates, and develops new products and services.

Resolution: A measurement in pixels of a monitor's clarity. For a given monitor, the greater the resolution, the more pixels and the clearer the image.

Reverse directory: A special telephone directory listing telephone numbers sequentially, followed by subscriber names.

RFID tag: Information chips that are embedded in merchandise to track their location.

Ribbon gui: An interface that uses a system of ribbons, tabs, and galleries to make it easier to find and use all the features of an application.

Ribbons: Feature of Microsoft Office 2007 and 2010 that replaces menus and toolbars by organizing commonly used commands into a set of tabs.

RIM OS: Mobile operating system originally designed for the BlackBerry handheld computer.

Robot: Robots are computer-controlled machines that mimic the motor activities of living things, and some robots can solve unstructured problems using artificial intelligence.

Robot network: *See* Botnet.

Robotics: Field of study concerned with developing and using robots.

Rogue Wi-Fi hotspot: Imitation hotspot intended to capture personal information.

Roller ball: *See* Trackball.

ROM: *See* Read-only memory.

Row: A horizontal block of cells one cell high all the way across the worksheet.

S

Sales order processing: Activity that records the demands of customers for a company's products or services.

Satellite: This type of communication uses satellites orbiting about 22,000 miles above the earth as microwave relay stations.

Satellite connection services: Connection services that use satellites and the air to download or send data to users at a rate seven times faster than dial-up connections.

Scam: A fraudulent or deceptive act or operation designed to trick individuals into spending their time and money for little or no return.

Scanner: *See* Optical scanner.

Schema: *See* Data dictionary.

Search engine: Specialized programs assisting in locating information on the Web and the Internet.

Search services: Organizations that maintain databases relating to information provided on the Internet and also provide search engines to locate information.

Secondary storage: Permanent storage used to preserve programs and data that can be retained after the computer is turned off. These devices include hard disks, magnetic tape, CDs, DVDs, and more.

Secondary storage device: These devices are used to save, backup, and transport files from one location or computer to another. *See* Secondary storage.

Sector: Section shaped like a pie wedge that divides the tracks on a disk.

Secure file transfer protocol (SFTP): *See* File transfer protocol.

Security: The protection of information, hardware, and software.

Selection structure: Logic structure that determines which of two paths will be followed when a program must make a decision. Also called IF-THEN-ELSE structures. IF something is true, THEN do option one, or ELSE do option two.

Semiconductor: Silicon chip through which electricity flows with some resistance.

Serial port: Used to connect external devices that send or receive data one bit at a time over a long distance. Used for mouse, keyboard, modem, and many other devices.

Server: A host computer with a connection to the Internet that stores document files used to display Web pages. Depending on the resources shared, it may be called a file server, printer server, communication server, Web server, or database server.

Shared laser printer: More expensive laser printer used by a group of users to produce black-and-white documents. These printers can produce over 30 pages a minute.

Sheet: A rectangular grid of rows and columns. *See* Spreadsheet or Worksheet.

Signature: Provides additional information about a sender of an e-mail message, such as name, address, and telephone number.

Silicon chip: Tiny circuit board etched on a small square of sandlike material called silicon. Chips are mounted on carrier packages, which then plug into sockets on the system board.

Slate computer: *See* Slate PC.

Slate PC: A tablet PC that contains a thin system unit, most of which is the monitor. The best-known tablet PCs are Apple's iPad, Motorola's Zoom, and HP's Slate.

Slide: A PowerPoint presentation is made up of many slides shown in different views and presentation styles.

Slot: Area on a system board that accepts expansion cards to expand a computer system's capabilities.

Smart card: Card about the size of a credit card containing a tiny built-in microprocessor. It can be used to hold such information as personal identification, medical and financial knowledge, and credit card numbers. Information on this card is protected by a password, which offers security and privacy.

Smartphone: A type of cell phone that offers a variety of advanced functionality, including Internet and e-mail.

Snoopware: Programs that record virtually every activity on a computer system.

Social networking: Using the Internet to connect individuals.

Socket: Sockets provide connection points on the system board for holding electronic parts.

Soft copy: Output from a monitor.

Software: Computer program consisting of step-by-step instructions, directing the computer on each task it will perform.

Software development: *See* Programming.

Software engineer: Programming professional or programmer who analyzes users' needs and creates application software.

Software environment: Operating system, also known as software platform, consisting of a collection of programs to handle technical details depending on the type of operating system. For example, software designed to run on an Apple computer is compatible with the Mac OS environment.

Software piracy: Unauthorized copying of programs for personal gain.

Software platform: *See* Software environment.

Software suite: Individual application programs that are sold together as a group.

Solid-state drive (SSD):   Designed to be connected inside a microcomputer system the same way an internal hard disk would be, but contains solid-state memory instead of magnetic disks to store data.

Solid-state storage: A secondary storage device that has no moving parts. Data is stored and retrieved electronically directly from these devices, much as they would be from conventional computer memory.

Sony/Philips Digital Interconnect Format (S/PDIF): *See* Optical audio connection.

Sort: Tool that rearranges a table's records numerically or alphabetically according to a selected field.

Sound card: Device that accepts audio input from a microphone and converts it into a form that can be processed by the computer. Also converts internal electronic signals to audio signals so they can be heard from external speakers.

Source code: When a programmer originally writes the code for a program in a particular language. This is called source code until it is translated by a compiler for the computer to execute the program. It then becomes object code.

Spam: Unwelcome and unsolicited e-mail that can carry attached viruses.

Spam blocker: Also referred to as spam filter. Software that uses a variety of different approaches to identify and eliminate spam or junk mail.

Spam filter: *See* Spam blocker.

Speakers: Audio-output devices connected to a sound card in the system unit. The sound card is used to capture as well as play back recorded sound.

Specialized applications: Programs that are narrowly focused on specific disciplines and occupations. Some of the best known are multimedia, Web authoring, graphics, virtual reality, and artificial intelligence.

Specialized search engine: Search engine that focuses on subject-specific Web sites.

Specialized suite: Programs that focus on specialized applications such as graphics or financial planning.

Speech recognition: The ability to accept voice input to select menu options, and to dictate text.

Spelling checker: Program used with a word processor to check the spelling of typed text against an electronic dictionary.

Spider: Special program that continually looks for new information and updates a search server's databases.

Spike: *See* Voltage surge.

Spotlight: An advanced search tool on the Mac OS X operating system for locating files, e-mail messages, and more.

Spreadsheet: Computer-produced spreadsheet based on the traditional accounting worksheet that has rows and columns used to present and analyze data.

Spy removal programs: Programs such as Spybot and Spysweeper, designed to detect Web bugs and monitor software.

Spyware: Wide range of programs designed to secretly record and report an individual's activities on the Internet.

Stand-alone operating system: Also called desktop operating system; a type of operating system that controls a single desktop or notebook computer.

Star network: Network of computers or peripheral devices linked to a central computer through which all communications pass. Control is maintained by polling. The configuration of the computers looks like a star surrounding and connected to the central computer in the middle.

Stock photograph: Photographs of a variety of subject material from professional models to natural landscapes.

Storage area network (SAN):   An architecture that links remote computer storage devices such as enterprise storage systems to computers so that the devices are available as locally attached drives.

Storage device: Hardware that reads data and programs from storage media. Most also write to storage media.

Strategic model: A decision model that assists top managers in long-range planning, such as stating company objectives or planning plant locations.

Strategy: A way of coordinating the sharing of information and resources. The most common network strategies are terminal, peer-to-peer, and client/server networks.

Streaming: *See* Webcast.

Structured program: Program that uses logic structures according to the program design and the language in which you have chosen to write the program. Each language follows techniques like pseudocode, flowcharts, and logic structures.

Structured programming techniques: Techniques consisting of top-down program design, pseudocode, flowcharts, and logic structures.

Structured query language (SQL):   A program control language used to create sophisticated database applications for requesting information from a database.

Styles: A feature found in most word processors that quickly applies predefined formats.

Stylus: Penlike device used with tablet PCs and PDAs that uses pressure to draw images on a screen. A stylus interacts with the computer through handwriting recognition software.

Subject: Located in the header of an e-mail message; a one-line description used to present the topic of the message.

Subject directory: Organizes information according to categories or topics.

Supercomputer: Fastest calculating device ever invented, processing billions of program instructions per second. Used by very large organizations like NASA.

Supervisor: Manager responsible for managing and monitoring workers. Supervisors have responsibility for operational matters.

Surf: Move from one Web site to another.

Surge protector: Device separating the computer from the power source of the wall outlet. When a voltage surge occurs, a circuit breaker is activated, protecting the computer system.

Switch: The center or central node for other nodes. This device coordinates the flow of data by sending messages directly between sender and receiver nodes.

Syntax error: Violation of the rules of a language in which the computer program is written. For example, leaving out a semicolon would stop the entire program from working because it is not the exact form the computer expects for that language.

System: Collection of activities and elements designed to accomplish a goal.

System board: Flat board that usually contains the CPU and memory chips connecting all system components to one another.

System bus: There are two categories of buses. One is the system bus that connects the CPU to the system board. The other is the expansion bus that connects the CPU to slots on the system board.

System chassis: *See* System unit.

System flowchart: A flowchart that shows the flow of input data to processing and finally to output, or distribution of information.

System software: "Background" software that enables the application software to interact with the computer. System software consists of the operating system, utilities, device drivers, and language translators. It works with application software to handle the majority of technical details.

System unit: Part of a microcomputer that contains the CPU. Also known as the system cabinet or chassis, it is the container that houses most of the electronic components that make up the computer system.

Systems analysis: This second phase of the systems life cycle determines the requirements for a new system. Data is collected about the present system and analyzed, and new requirements are determined.

Systems analysis and design: Six phases of problem-solving procedures for examining information systems and improving them.

Systems analysis report: Report prepared for higher management describing the current information system, the requirements for a new system, and a possible development schedule.

Systems analyst: Plans and designs information systems.

Systems audit: A systems audit compares the performance of a new system to the original design specifications to determine if the new procedures are actually improving productivity.

Systems design: Phase three of the systems life cycle, consisting of designing alternative systems, selecting the best system, and writing a systems design report.

Systems design report: Report prepared for higher management describing alternative designs, presenting costs versus benefits, and outlining the effects of alternative designs on the organization.

Systems development: Phase four of the systems life cycle, consisting of developing software, acquiring hardware, and testing the new system.

Systems implementation: Phase five of the systems life cycle is converting the old system to the new one and training people to use the new system. Also known as conversion.

Systems life cycle: The six phases of systems analysis and design are called the systems life cycle. The phases are preliminary investigation, systems analysis, systems design, systems development, systems implementation, and systems maintenance.

Systems maintenance: Phase six of the systems life cycle consisting of a systems audit and periodic evaluation.

t

T1: High-speed lines that support all digital communications, provide very high capacity, and are very expensive.

T3: Copper lines combined to form higher-capacity options.

Tab: Used to divide the ribbon into major activity areas, with each tab being organized into groups that contain related items.

Table (in database): The list of records in a database. Tables make up the basic structure of a database. Their columns display field data and their rows display records. *See* Field and Record.

Tablet PC: *See* Traditional tablet PC and Slate PC.

Tablet PC system unit: Similar to notebook system units. Two basic categories are traditional tablet and slate. A stylus, pen, or gesture is used to input data.

Tactical model: A decision model that assists middle-level managers to control the work of the organization, such as financial planning and sales promotion planning.

Tape library: Device that provides automatic access to data archived on a large collection or library of tapes.

Task-oriented language: Programming language that is nonprocedural and focuses on specifying what the program is to accomplish. Also known as 4GL or very high-level language.

Technical feasibility: Making sure hardware, software, and training will be available to facilitate the design of a new system.

Technical writer: Prepares instruction manuals, technical reports, and other scientific or technical documents.

Telephone line: A transmission medium for both voice and data.

Telephone modem: Used to connect a computer directly to a telephone line.

Telephony: Communication that uses the Internet rather than traditional communication lines to connect two or more people via telephone.

Text entry: In a worksheet or spreadsheet, a text entry is typically used to identify or label information entered into a cell as opposed to numbers and formulas. Also known as labels.

Thermal printer: Printer that uses heat elements to produce images on heat-sensitive paper.

Thesaurus: A word processor feature that provides synonyms, antonyms, and related words for a selected word or phrase.

Thin film transistor (TFT) monitor: Type of flat-panel monitor activating each pixel independently.

Third-generation language (3GL): *See* Procedural language.

Toggle key: These keys turn a feature on or off, like the CAPS LOCK key.

Toolbar: Bar located typically below the menu bar containing icons or graphical representations for commonly used commands.

Top-down analysis method: Method used to identify top-level components of a system, then break these components down into smaller parts for analysis.

Top-down program design: Used to identify the program's processing steps, called program modules. The program must pass in sequence from one module to the next until the computer has processed all modules.

Top-level domain (TLD): Last part of an Internet address; identifies the geographical description or organizational identification. For example, using www.aol.com, the .com is the top-level domain code and indicates it is a commercial site. *Also see* Domain name.

Top management: Top-level managers are concerned with long-range (strategic) planning. They supervise middle management.

Topology: The configuration of a network. The four principal network topologies are *star, bus, ring,* and *hierarchical.*

Touch pad: Used to control the pointer by moving and tapping your finger on the surface of a pad.

Touch screen: Monitor screen allowing actions or commands to be entered by the touch of a finger.

Track: Closed, concentric ring on a disk on which data is recorded. Each track is divided into sections called sectors.

Trackball: Device used to control the pointer by rotating a ball with your thumb. Also called a roller ball.

Traditional cookies: Intended to provide customized service. A program recording information on Web site visitors within a specific site. When you leave the site, the cookie becomes dormant and is reactivated when you revisit the site.

Traditional keyboard: Full-sized, rigid, rectangular keyboard that includes function, navigational, and numeric keys.

Traditional Tablet PC: A type of notebook computer that accepts handwritten data, using a stylus or pen, that is converted to standard text and can be processed by a word processor program.

Transaction processing system (TPS): System that records day-to-day transactions, such as customer orders, bills, inventory levels, and production output. The TPS tracks operations and creates databases.

Transfer rate: Or transfer speed, is the speed at which modems transmit data, typically measured in bits per second (bps).

Transition: Used to animate how a presentation moves from one slide to the next.

Transmission control protocol/Internet protocol (TCP/IP): TCP/IP is the standard protocol for the Internet. The essential features of this protocol involve (1) identifying sending and receiving devices and (2) reformatting information for transmission across the Internet.

Tree network: Also known as a hierarchical network. A topology in which each device is connected to a central node, either directly or through one or more other devices. The central node is then connected to two or more subordinate nodes that in turn are connected to other subordinate nodes, and so forth, forming a treelike structure.

Trojan horse: Program that is not a virus but is a carrier of virus(es). The most common Trojan horses appear as free computer games, screen savers, or antivirus programs. Once downloaded they locate and disable existing virus protection and then deposit the virus.

Troubleshooting program: A utility program that recognizes and corrects computer-related problems before they become serious. Also called diagnostic program.

TV tuner card: Contains TV tuner card and video converter changing the TV signal into one that can be displayed on your monitor. Also known as video recorder cards and video capture cards.

Twisted pair cable: Cable consisting of pairs of copper wire that are twisted together.

Twitter: The most popular microblogging site that enables you to add new content from your browser, instant messaging application, or even a mobile phone.

Unicode: A 16-bit code designed to support international languages, like Chinese and Japanese.

Uniform resource locator (URL): For browsers to connect you to resources on the Web, the location or address of the resources must be specified. These addresses are called URLs.

Uninstall program: A utility program that safely and completely removes unwanted programs and related files.

Universal instant messenger: An instant messaging service that communicates with any other messaging service programs.

Universal Product Code (UPC): A barcode system that identifies the product to the computer, which has a description and the latest price for the product.

Universal serial bus (USB): Combines with a PCI bus on the system board to support several external devices without inserting cards for each device. USB buses are used to support high-speed scanners, printers, and video-capturing devices.

Universal serial bus (USB) port: Expected to replace serial and parallel ports. They are faster, and one USB port can be used to connect several devices to the system unit.

UNIX: An operating system originally developed for minicomputers. It is now important because it can run on many of the more powerful microcomputers.

Uploading: Process of transferring information from the computer the user is operating to a remote computer.

USB drive: The size of a key chain, these hard drives connect to a computer's USB port enabling a transfer of files.

User: Any individual who uses a computer. *See* End user.

User interface: Means by which users interact with application programs and hardware. A window is displayed with information for the user to enter or choose, and that is how users communicate with the program.

Utility: Performs specific tasks related to managing computer resources or files. Norton Utility for virus control and system maintenance is a good example of a utility. Also known as service programs.

Utility suite: A program that combines several utilities in one package to improve system performance.

V

Vector: A common type of graphic file. A vector file contains all the shapes and colors, along with starting and ending points, necessary to recreate the image.

Vector illustration: *See* Vector image.

Vector image: Graphics file made up of a collection of objects such as lines, rectangles, and ovals. Vector images are more flexible than bitmaps because they are defined by mathematical equations so they can be stretched and resized. Illustration programs create and manipulate vector graphics. Also known as vector illustrations.

Very high-level languages: Task-oriented languages that require little special training on the part of the user.

VGA (Video Graphic Adapter) port: A type of port that provides a connection to an analog monitor.

Video editing software: Allows you to reorganize, add effects, and more to your video footage.

Videoconferencing system: Computer system that allows people located at various geographic locations to have in-person meetings.

Virtual environment: *See* Virtual reality.

Virtual keyboard: Displays an image of a keyboard on a touch screen device. The screen functions as the actual input device, which is why the keyboard is considered virtual.

Virtual machine: A software implementation of a computer that executes programs like a physical computer.

Virtual memory: Feature of an operating system that increases the amount of memory available to run programs. With large programs, parts are stored on a secondary device like your hard disk. Then each part is read in RAM only when needed.

Virtual private network (VPN): Creates a secure private connection between a remote user and an organization's internal network. Special VPN protocols create the equivalent of a dedicated line between a user's home or laptop computer and a company server.

Virtual reality: Interactive sensory equipment (headgear and gloves) allowing users to experience alternative realities generated in 3-D by a computer, thus imitating the physical world.

Virtual reality wall: An immersive experience whereby you are viewing simulations in stereoscopic vision.

Virtualization: A process that allows a single physical computer to support multiple operating systems that operate independently.

Virtualization software: Software that creates virtual machines.

Virus: Hidden instructions that migrate through networks and operating systems and become embedded in different programs. They may be designed to destroy data or simply to display messages.

Voice over IP (VoIP): Transmission of telephone calls over networks. *See also* Telephony.

Voice recognition system: Using a microphone, sound card, and specialty software, the user can operate a computer and create documents using voice commands.

Voiceband: Bandwidth of a standard telephone line. Also known as low bandwidth.

Voltage surge (spike): Excess of electricity that may destroy chips or other electronic computer components.

VR: *See* Virtual reality.

W

WAN: *See* Wide area network.

Wand reader: Special-purpose handheld device used to read OCR characters.

Warm boot: Restarting your computer while the computer is already on and the power is not turned off.

Web: Introduced in 1992, and prior to the Web the Internet was all text. The Web made it possible to provide a multimedia interface that includes graphics, animations, sound, and video.

Web auction: Similar to traditional auctions except that all transactions occur over the Web; buyers and sellers seldom meet face-to-face.

Web authoring: Creating a Web site.

Web authoring program: Word processing program for generating Web pages. Also called HTML editor or Web page editor. Widely used Web authoring programs include Macromedia Dreamweaver and Microsoft FrontPage.

Web-based e-mail client: A special program that communicates with the e-mail service provider and must be installed on the computer first.

Web-based file transfer services: A type of file transfer service that uses a Web browser to upload and download files, allowing you to copy files to and from your computer across the Internet.

Web bug: Program hidden in the HTML code for a Web page or e-mail message as a graphical image. Web bugs can migrate whenever a user visits a Web site containing a Web bug or opens infected e-mail. They collect information on the users and report back to a predefined server.

Web directory: *See* Subject directory.

Web log: A type of personal Web site where articles are regularly posted.

Web page: Browsers interpret HTML documents to display Web pages.

Web page editor: *See* Web authoring program.

Web utilities: Specialized utility programs making the Internet and the Web easier and safer. Some examples are plug-ins that operate as part of a browser and filters that block access and monitor use of selected Web sites.

WebCam: Specialized digital video camera for capturing images and broadcasting to the Internet.

Webcast: An Internet delivery medium that uses streaming technology, in which audio and video files are continuously downloaded to a computer while the user is listening to and/or viewing the file content.

Webmail: E-mail that uses a Webmail client.

Webmail client: A special program that runs on an e-mail provider's computer that supports Webmail.

Webmaster: Develops and maintains Web sites and Web resources.

WebOS: A mobile operating system that supports Hewlett-Packard's smartphones and tablet computers.

WEP (Wired Equivalent Privacy): One of the best-known wireless encryption protocols.

What-if analysis: Spreadsheet feature in which changing one or more numbers results in the automatic recalculation of all related formulas.

Wheel button: Some mice have a wheel button that can be rotated to scroll through information displayed on the monitor.

Wide area network (WAN): Countrywide and worldwide networks that use microwave relays and satellites to reach users over long distances.

Wi-Fi (wireless fidelity): Wireless standard also known as 802.11, used to connect computers to each other and to the Internet.

Wiki: A Web site that allows people to fill in missing information or correct inaccuracies on it by directly editing the pages.

Wikipedia: An online encyclopedia, written and edited by anyone who wants to contribute.

WiMax (Worldwide Interoperability for Microwave Access): Technology that extends Wi-Fi networks to operate over greater distances.

Window: A rectangular area containing a document or message.

Windows: An operating environment extending the capability of DOS.

Windows 7: The newest version of the Windows operating system, released in 2009.

Windows Phone 7: Mobile phone operating system designed for users actively involved in social networking and instant messaging.

Windows Update: A utility provided in the Windows platform that allows you to update the device drivers on your computer.

Windows Vista: An upgrade to Windows XP with improved security, three-dimensional workspace, and filtering capabilities.

Wireless access point: Or base station. The receiver interprets incoming radio frequencies from a wireless LAN and routes communications to the appropriate devices, which could be separate computers, a shared printer, or a modem.

Wireless keyboard: Transmits input to the system through the air, providing greater flexibility and convenience.

Wireless LAN (WLAN): Uses radio frequencies to connect computers and other devices. All communications pass through the network's centrally located wireless receiver or base station and are routed to the appropriate devices.

Wireless modem: Modem that connects to the serial port but does not connect to telephone lines. It receives through the air.

Wireless mouse: *See* Cordless mouse.

Wireless network card: Allows computers to be connected without cables.

Wireless network encryption: Restricts access to authorized users on wireless networks.

Wireless revolution: A revolution that is expected to dramatically affect the way we communicate and use computer technology.

Wireless wide area network (WWAN) modem: *See* Wireless modem.

Word: The number of bits (such as 16, 32, or 64) that can be accessed at one time by the CPU.

Word processor: The computer and the program allow you to create, edit, save, and print documents composed of text.

Word wrap: Feature of word processing that automatically moves the cursor from the end of one line to the beginning of the next.

Workbook file: Contains one or more related worksheets or spreadsheets. *See* Spreadsheet.

Worksheet: Also known as a spreadsheet, or sheet; a rectangular grid of rows and columns used in programs like Excel.

Worksheet file: Created by electronic spreadsheets to analyze things like budgets and to predict sales.

Worm: Virus that doesn't attach itself to programs and databases but fills a computer system with self-replicating information, clogging the system so that its operations are slowed or stopped.

WPA and WPA2 (Wi-Fi Protected Access): A more secure encryption protocol currently replacing WEP.

WYSIWYG (what you see is what you get) editors: Web authoring programs that build a page without requiring direct interaction with the HTML code and then preview the page described by the HTML code.

Z

Zombie: A computer infected by a virus, worm, or Trojan horse that allows it to be remotely controlled for malicious purposes.

Photo Credits

Preface

Page xvii Copyright © 2011 sendspace.com. Used with permission.; **Page xxi** Reprinted with permission from International Business Machines Corporation Copyright IBM Corporation, © (2009). IBM is a trademark of International Business Machines Corporation, registered in many jurisdictions worldwide. Other product and service names might be trademarks of IBM or other companies. A current list of IBM trademarks is available on the Web at www.ibm.com/legal/copytrade.shtml.; **Page xxi** Copyright 2011 DailyTech LLC.; **Page xxi** Copyright © IFPI. All rights reserved. Used with permission.

Chapter 1

2 Bettmann/CORBIS; **3** Steve Rawlings/Photodisc/Getty Images; **4** (tl)Inti St. Clair/Taxi/Getty Images, (c)Sydney Shaffer/zefa/Corbis, (r)Microsoft product screen shot(s) reprinted with permission from Microsoft Corporation.; **5** (bl)Courtesy of Hewlett-Packard, (br)Guy Crittenden/Stock Illustration Source/Getty Images; **7** (tl)Juice Images/Alamy, (tr)Juice Images/Cultura/Getty Images, (br)Juice Images/Alamy, (bl)B Busco/Photographer's Choice/Getty Images; **9** Microsoft product screen shot(s) reprinted with permission from Microsoft Corporation.; **10** Copyright © 2011 Apple, Inc.; **11** Courtesy of IBM; **12** (desktop)Courtesy of Apple, Inc., (notebook)Courtesy of Toshiba, (media center)Courtesy of Hewlett-Packard, (notebook) PRNewsFoto/RadioShack Corporation, (handheld)Courtesy of Apple, Inc., (tablet)Courtesy of Apple, Inc.; **13** (t)Courtesy of Hewlett-Packard, (b)© Willis Technology; **14** (l)© 2010 Samsung Electronics America-All Rights Reserved, (r)© Willis Technology; **16** (tl)Courtesy of Blackberry/Research in Motion, (tc)Courtesy of HTC, (tr)Courtesy of Samsung, (bl)Oleksiy Maksymenko Photography/Alamy, (br)Courtesy of Hewlett-Packard; **17** Inti St. Clair/Taxi/Getty Images; **18** Colin Anderson/Blend Images/Getty Images; **19** (l)Sydney Shaffer/zefa/Corbis, (r)Juice Images/Alamy; **20** (l)Microsoft product box shot reprinted with permission from Microsoft Corporation, (r)Courtesy of Hewlett-Packard; **25** Simon Winnall/Digital Vision/Getty Images; **26** Geri Lavrov/Photographer's Choice/Getty Images; **27** Corbis Flirt/Alamy; **28** Olena Mykhaylova/Alamy

Chapter 2

30 SuperStock/Getty Images; **31** Corbis Bridge/Alamy; **32** Photosindia/Alamy; **33, 59** Copyright © 2011 Qlipso Media Networks Ltd.; **34, 55, 66** Copyright © 2011 Apple, Inc.; **35, 47, 53, 59, 61–62** Copyright © Google, Inc.; **37** Allison Rocks! Photography; **39, 60** Microsoft product screen shot(s) reprinted with permission from Microsoft Corporation.; **41, 60** Copyright © Facebook, Inc.; **44–45, 66** Copyright © Twitter; **51, 61** Copyright © 2000–2011 Shopping.com; **52** Copyright © 1999–2011 PayPal. All rights reserved.; **55** Jose Luis Pelaez Inc/Blend Images/Getty

Images; **56** © 2001–2010 ContentWatch, Inc., All rights reserved.; **57** (b)Photosindia/Alamy, (screenshot) © 2003–2011 McAfee, Inc; **58** George Gutenberg/Beateworks/Corbis; **67** Copyright © domain.com. All rights reserved.; **68** © DigitalDivide.org 2010. All Rights Reserved.; **69** Copyright© 1996–2011 The Pew Charitable Trusts. All rights reserved., Copyright ©2007–2011. I Commit To Green is a property of WinBach Marketing Images. All rights reserved.

Chapter 3

70 Bert Hardy/Hulton Archive/Getty Images; **71** Colin Anderson/Photographer's Choice/Getty Images; **72** Comstock/Getty Images; **73–75, 83–84, 89–90, 96, 98, 103** Microsoft product box shots reprinted with permission from Microsoft Corporation; **89** Copyright © Apple, Inc.; **90** Reprinted with permission from International Business Machines Corporation Copyright IBM Corporation, © (2009). IBM is a trademark of International Business Machines Corporation, registered in many jurisdictions worldwide. Other product and service names might be trademarks of IBM or other companies. A current list of IBM trademarks is available on the Web at www.ibm.com/legal/copytrade.shtml.; **92–93, 102** Copyright © Google, Inc.; **94** Comstock/Getty Images; **95** Colin Anderson/Blend Images/Getty Images; **98** Comstock/Getty Images; **103** Copyright © 2011 Adobe Systems Incorporated. All rights reserved., Copyright © 2011 Tucows, Inc.; **104** © 2000–2011 Business Software Alliance; **105** Copyright ©1996–2011 **Ziff Davis Enterprise Holdings Inc.** All Rights Reserved. eWEEK and Spencer F. Katt are trademarks of Ziff Davis Enterprise Holdings, Inc. Reproduction in whole or in part in any form or medium without express written permission of Ziff Davis Enterprise Inc. is prohibited. ZDE Cluster 8

Chapter 4

106 Terry O'Neill/Getty Images; **107** Design Pics/SuperStock; **108** (t)Ciaran Griffin/Lifesize/Getty Images, (iLife)Courtesy of Apple, (Expression)Software product photo courtesy of Microsoft, (Photoshop)Copyright © 2011 Adobe Systems Incorporated. All rights reserved., (Director)Copyright © 2011 Adobe Systems Incorporated. All rights reserved.; **110, 124** Copyright © 2011 Adobe Systems Incorporated. All rights reserved.; **111** Courtesy of Corel; **111, 114,121, 124, 125** Copyright © Apple, Inc.; **112–113, 124, 130** Microsoft product screen shot(s) reprinted with permission from Microsoft Corporation.; **118** Chris Salvo/Getty Images; **119** (l)AP Photo/Steve Pope, (r)Photo by Koichi Kamoshida/Getty Images; **120** Romilly Lockyer/The Image Bank/Getty Images; **121** QR Code is registered trademark of DENSO WAVE INCORPORATED; **122** Ciaran Griffin/Lifesize/Getty Images; **123** John Lund/Blend Images/Getty Images; **126** Photo by Koichi Kamoshida/Getty Images; **132** © NPPA 2011. All rights reserved.; **133** Courtesy of opbnews.org/http://news.opb.org/article/hanford-workers-training-robot-arm-clean-tank-waste/

Chapter 11

Subject Index

a

A6 Compiler, 351
ABS, 80
AC adapter, 183
Access, 295
Access speed, 235
Accuracy, 295
ACI, 153
Acquiring software, 72, 104
Acrobat Reader, 54, 55
Active-matrix monitor, 211
Ad-Aware, 303
Ad network cookie, 300
Add a Device Wizard, 148
Address, 36
Adobe, 84
Adobe Dreamweaver, 117
Adobe Flash, 130
Adobe Illustrator, 110
Adobe Photoshop, 110
ADSL, 266
Advance fee loans, 309
Advanced graphics card, 176
Advanced Research Project Agency
    Network (ARPANET), 32
Adware cookie, 300
Age of connectivity, 356–359
Agent, 95
AJAX, 37
Altair, 354
ALU, 173
Amazon, 51
Amazon.com, 358
American Standard Code for
    Information Interchange
    (ASCII), 170
Analog, 169
Analog signals, 265
Analytical graph, 80
AND, 80
Android, 143
Android Market, 121
Animation, 87, 88
Anticipating disasters, 314
Antispyware, 302, 303
Antivirus program, 144, 148
AOL Search, 47
App store, 121
Apple App Store, 121
Apple GarageBand, 114
Apple iMovie, 111
Apple iPhone, 143
Applet, 37
Application software, 70–105
    common features, 72–73
    DBMS, 84–86
    integrated package, 89

presentation graphics, 87–88
software suite, 90–91
specialized applications. *See*
    Specialized application software
spreadsheet, 79–83
word processor, 76–78
Apps, 72. *See also* Application software
Arithmetic-logic unit (ALU), 173
Arithmetic operations, 173
ARPANET, 32
Artificial intelligence (IA), 116–120
Artificial reality, 118
ASCII, 170
Asimo, 119
Ask, 47
Aspect ratio, 210
Asymmetric digital subscriber
    line (ADSL), 266
Athlon, 173
Athlon Opteron, 173
Atom microprocessor, 359
Attached WebCam, 207
Auction fraud, 309
Auction house sites, 50, 51
Audio and video clips, 104
Audio and video devices, 217
Audio editing software, 111
Audio-input devices, 207
AutoCorrect, 78
Automated teller machine, 330
Autonomic computing, 153
Autonomic Computing Initiative
    (ACI), 153
Avast Free Antivirus, 148
AVERAGE, 80
Avira AntiVir Personal, 148

b

Background, 138
Backup, 325
Backup and Restore, 145
Backup program, 144
Bandwidth, 267
Bar code, 205
Bar code reader, 205
Base station, 271
Baseband, 267
Basic applications, 72. *See also*
    Application software
B2B e-commerce, 50
B2C e-commerce, 49, 50
Bebo, 41
Binary numbers, 194
Binary system, 170
Bing, 47
Biometric scanning, 312

BIOS, 161
Bit, 170
Bitmap images, 109
BitTorrent, 55–56, 288
BlackBerry App World, 121
BlackBerry OS, 143
Blocking cookies, 301
Blog, 42, 115
Blog creation site, 42
Blogger, 357
Blu-ray disc (BD), 239, 240
Blue Gene, 11
Bluetooth, 263
Boot Camp, 141
Booting, 138, 161
Botnet, 308
Broadband, 267
Broadway, 76
Browser, 35
Built-in WebCam, 207
Bulleted list, 76
Bus, 177
Bus lines, 171, 172, 177, 180
Bus width, 177
Business-to-business (B2B)
    e-commerce, 50
Business-to-consumer (B2C)
    e-commerce, 49, 50
Button, 72, 114
Buyer's guide, 360–364
Byte, 170

c

Cable modem, 266
Cable service, 266
Cables, 182
Cache memory, 174
Calibri, 76
Cambria, 76
CAN-SPAM, 39
CAN-SPAM Act, 358
CAPPS, 326
Caption, 78
Card reader, 204–205
Carder, 51, 306
Careers
    computer support specialists, 152
    computer technicians, 183–184
    computer trainer, 94
    cryptography, 317
    desktop publishers, 122
    network administrator, 279
    software engineer, 246
    technical writer, 219
    webmaster, 57
Carnivore, 262

Carrier package, 172
Cathode-ray tube (CRT), 211
C2C e-commerce, 50
CD, 238, 240
CD-R, 238
CD-ROM, 238
CD-RW, 238
Cell, 79, 81, 173
Cellular services, 267
Center-alignment, 77
Center for European Nuclear Research
    (CERN), 32
Central processing unit (CPU), 172
CERN, 32
Chain letter, 309
Character and mark recognition
    devices, 205–206
Character effects, 76, 77
Character encoding, 170
Character encoding standards, 170
Chart, 80, 82
Chart title, 82
Chart types, 82
Chase Bank, 331–332
Chip, 172
Chip processing capacities, 173
Chrome OS, 142
Cisco, 280
Cisco TelePresence, 280
Citation, 78
Civil strife and terrorism, 311
Classroom Clipart, 111
Client, 269
Client-based e-mail account, 38
Client operating system, 139
Client/server network, 276
Clip art, 110
ClipArt.com, 111
Clock speed, 173
Cloud computing, 52–53, 91, 241
Cloud printer, 216
Cloud storage, 241–244
Cloud storage devices, 255
Cloud suite, 91
Clusty, 47
Coaxial cable, 262
Cold boot, 138
Column, 79
.com, 36
Combination input and output devices,
    217–218
Combination keys, 200
Communication channel, 262–264
Communication system, 261–262
Communications and networks, 258–291
    bandwidth, 267
    communication channels, 262–264
    communication systems, 261–262
    connection devices, 265–267
    connection service, 266–267
    connectivity, 260–261
    data transmission, 267–268
    modem, 265–266
    network architecture, 273, 276
    network security, 277–278
    network types, 270–272
    networks, 268–270

organizational networks, 277–278
    physical connections, 262–263
    protocols, 267–268
    wireless connections, 263–264
    wireless revolution, 261
Compact disc (CD), 238, 240
Compadre, 220
Computer Assisted Passenger
    Pre-screening System (CAPPS), 326
Computer competency, 4, 335
Computer crime, 307–310, 311
Computer criminals, 306
Computer ethics, 315–316. See also Ethics
    copyright, 315–316
    DRM, 316
    plagiarism, 316
Computer Fraud and Abuse Act, 307, 310
Computer monitoring software, 302
Computer network, 268–270
Computer-related articles, 335
Computer support specialist, 152
Computer technician, 183–184
Computer trainer, 94
Computer virus, 148, 307
Connection devices, 262, 265–267
Connection service, 266–267
Connectivity, 260–261
Consumer support sites, 51
Consumer-to-consumer (C2C)
    e-commerce, 50
Content template, 87
Contextual tab, 73
Control unit, 172–173
Cookie, 300, 301
Coprocessor, 174
Copyright, 72, 152, 238, 315–316
Cordless mouse, 201
CorelDRAW Graphics Suite, 111
CounterSpy, 303
CPU, 172
Cracker, 306
Cross references, 78
CRT, 211
Cryptographer, 317
Cryptography, 317
Custom system unit, 193
Customized desktop, 161
Cyber-bullying, 309
CyberPatrol, 56
Cybersitter, 56
Cylinder, 235
Cynic, 333

d

Dashboard widget, 141
Data, 15
Data label, 82
Data manipulation, 310
Data security, 314
Data transmission, 267–268
Database, 84
Database files, 15
Database management system
    (DBMS), 84–86
Database manager, 84

DBMS, 84–86
Demodulation, 265
Denial of service (DoS) attack, 308
Density, 235
Design template, 87
Desktop, 138
Desktop operating system, 139
Desktop publisher, 122
Desktop publishing programs, 109
Desktop system unit, 166, 167
Device driver, 136
Diagnostic program, 144
Dial-up services, 266
Dialog box, 72, 139
Dictionary attack, 312
Digital, 169
Digital camera, 206, 229
Digital cash, 51, 52
Digital divide, 68
Digital media player, 217
Digital Millennium Copyright Act, 316
Digital photo manipulation, 109, 132
Digital rights management (DRM),
    289, 316
Digital signals, 265
Digital software distribution, 73, 105
Digital subscriber line (DSL), 265, 266
Digital subscriber line (DSL) service, 266
Digital versatile disc (DVD), 239, 240
Digital video camera, 206–207
Digital video editing, 112–113
Digital video interface (DVI) port, 181
Digital whiteboard, 212
DIMM, 175
Directory server, 269
Disaster recovery plan, 314
Disk caching, 237
Disk Cleanup, 146
Disk defragmentation, 160
Disk Defragmenter, 147
Display screen, 210
Distributed computing, 287
DNS, 268
Document, 76
Document files, 15
Document scanner, 203, 204
Document theme, 88
Dogpile, 47, 48
Domain name, 36
Domain name server (DNS), 268
Domain registration, 67
Dot-matrix printer, 216
Dot pitch, 210
Dots per inch (dpi), 214
Downlink, 263
Downloading, 55
dpi, 214
Drawing programs, 109
Driver, 148
DRM, 289, 316
DS3, 266
DSL, 265, 266
DSL service, 266
Dual in-line memory module
    (DIMM), 175
Dual-scan monitor, 211
Duplex printing, 215

DVD, 239
DVD players, 239
DVD-R, 239
DVD-RAM, 239
DVD-ROM, 239
DVD-RW, 239
DVD+R, 239
DVD+RW, 239
DVI port, 181

e

E-book, 212, 213
E-book reader, 212, 213
E-commerce, 49–51
E-mail, 38–39
E-mail address, 38, 39
E-mail attachments, 38
E-mail encryption, 313
E-paper, 212
eBay, 51
EBCDIC, 170
ECash, 52
Eckert, J. Presper, Jr., 351
Editing, 76
.edu, 36
802.11a, 263
802.11b, 263
802.11g, 263
802.11n, 263
Electronic commerce, 49–51
Electronic interpreter, 220
Electronic mail, 38
Electronic monitoring, 262, 289
Electronic paper, 212
Electronic profile, 296
EliMT, 220
Embedded operating system, 139
Encryption, 312, 313–314
Encryption key, 313
ENIAC, 351
Enterprise storage system, 245–246
Entertainment site, 33
Environment
    CDs and DVDs, 50, 69
    digital software distribution, 73, 105
    disposal of old machines, 11
    GPS, 263, 290
    green PC, 168, 195
    green software utilities, 105
    power management, 140, 163
    printer cartridges, 215, 231
    printing, 214, 231
    robots, 119, 133
    scams, 308, 327
    solid-state storage, 241
    spam, 38, 69
Environmental robot, 119, 133
Environmental scams, 308, 327
Erasable optical disc, 238
Ergonomic keyboard, 199
ERMA, 352
ESPN, 120
Ethernet, 270
Ethernet cable, 262
Ethernet port, 181

Ethics, 315. *See also* Computer ethics
    audio and video clips, 104
    copyright, 72, 152, 238
    digital divide, 68
    digital photo manipulation,
        109, 132
    electronic monitoring, 262, 289
    free speech online, 43, 68
    open source, 152, 162
    plagiarism, 315, 327
    RFID, 174, 194
    software acquisition, 72, 104
Evolution of computer age, 350–359
    first generation (vacuum tube age), 351
    second generation (transistor age), 352
    third generation (integrated
        circuit age), 353
    fourth generation
        (microprocessor age), 354–355
    fifth generation (age of connectivity),
        356–359
Expansion bus, 180
Expansion card, 176
Expansion slot, 176
Expert system, 119
Explorations
    Adobe, 84
    artificial intelligence software, 116
    domain registration, 67
    e-mail service, 39
    encryption, 312
    ergonomic keyboard, 199
    flat-panel monitor, 211
    hard-disk space, 237
    HDTV, 212
    history of Internet, 32
    IM, 67
    laser printers, 215
    MFD, 218
    microprocessor, 17
    Microsoft, 76
    multimedia authoring company, 114
    password, 314
    privacy legislation, 299
    shareware, 103
    sharing data between applications, 103
    Snort, 278
    spam filters, 67
    speech recognition, 103
    system unit components, 171
    utility software, 148
    Web filtering, 54
    wireless home networks, 270
ExpressCard, 177
Extended Binary Coded Decimal
    Interchange Code (EBCDIC), 170
External hard drive, 236–237
Extranet, 277

f

Facebook, 40, 120
Facebook group, 41
Facebook pages, 40
Facebook privacy controls, 310
Facebook profile, 40, 41

Family Educational Rights and Privacy
    Act (FERPA), 303
Fax machine, 217
FedEx, 332
Feelix Growing project, 123
FERPA, 303
Fiber-optic cable, 263
Field, 84, 85
File, 139
File compression, 237, 255
File compression program, 144
File decompression, 237
File encryption, 313–314
File server, 245
File transfer protocol (FTP), 55
File transfer utilities, 55
Filter, 54, 56, 84
Find and replace, 76
Fingerprint scanner, 312
Firewall, 277, 313
FireWire bus, 180
FireWire port, 181
Flash, 55, 116, 130
Flash drive, 241
Flash memory, 175
Flash memory card, 240, 241
Flat-panel monitor, 211
Flatbed scanner, 203, 204
Flickr Creative Commons, 111
Flora Photographs Web site, 115–117
Folder, 139
Font, 76, 77
Font size, 76, 77
Footer, 78
Footnote, 78
Foreground, 138
Foreign language translation, 220
Form, 84, 85
Format, 76
Formula, 80, 81
4G cellular network, 267
Fragmented, 147
Freedom of Information Act, 298
Friend, 39
Frustrated person, 333, 334
FTP, 55
Function, 80, 81
Fuzzy logic, 119

g

Galleries, 73
Game port, 182
Games.com, 120
Gates, Bill, 355
GB, 175
Gbps, 265
Gestures, 142
GetJar, 121
Gigabyte (GB), 175
Global positioning system (GPS),
    263–264, 290
Gmail, 120, 358
Goal Seek, 83
Google, 47, 52
Google Apps, 53, 244

Google Cloud Print, 216
Google Docs, 92–93
Google Street View, 297, 318
.gov, 36
GPS, 263–264, 290
GPU, 174
Gramm-Leach-Bliley Act, 303
Grammar checker, 76, 77
Graphic suites, 111
Graphical map, 116
Graphical user interface (gui), 72, 73
Graphics coprocessor, 174
Graphics Factory, 111
Graphics processing unit (GPU), 174
Graphics programs, 109–111
Grayscale, 214
Green PC, 168, 195
Green software utilities, 105
Group, 73
Guest operating system, 142
gui, 72, 73

h

Hacker, 306
Handango, 121
Handheld computer system unit,
  167, 168
Handwriting recognition software,
  203, 229
Hard copy, 214
Hard disk, 235–237
Hardware, 6, 10–14
HDMI, 181, 182
HDTV, 212
Head crash, 236
Header, 38, 78
Headset, 217
Health Insurance Portability and
  Accountability Act (HIPAA), 303
Help, 139
Hexadecimal system (hex), 170
Hi def (high definition), 239
Hierarchical network, 273
High definition multimedia interface
  (HDMI), 181, 182
High-definition television (HDTV), 212
HIPAA, 303
Historical overview. See Evolution
  of computer age
History file, 299
Hits, 46
Hoff, Ted, 354
Home network, 270–271, 274–275, 287
Home software, 89
Hopper, Grace, 351
Host, 269
Host operating system, 142
HotJobs, 336
Hotspot, 271, 288, 358
Household robot, 120
HTML, 36
HTML coding, 117
HTML editors, 116
Hub, 269
Human error, 311

Hyperlink, 36
Hypertext Markup Language
  (HTML), 36

i

i5, 173
i7, 173
IA, 116–120
IBM, 153
IBM Lotus Symphony, 90
Icon, 72, 138
Identity theft, 297, 309
IDS, 277
IF, 80
Illusion of anonymity, 299
Illustration programs, 109
IM, 39–40, 208
Image capturing devices, 206–207
Image editors, 109
Image galleries, 109–111
Immersive experience, 118
Impact, 76
Indeed, 336
Industrial robot, 119, 120
Information broker, 296
Information reseller, 296
Information technology (IT), 6
Infrared, 264
Infrared Data Association (IrDA)
  port, 182
Ink-jet printer, 215
Innovative opportunities, 338
InPrivate browsing, 301
Input, 198
Input and output, 196–231
  audio and video devices, 217
  audio-input devices, 207
  combination input and output
    devices, 217–218
  definitions, 198, 210
  image capturing devices, 206–207
  keyboard entry, 198–200
  monitor, 210–212
  pointing devices, 200–203
  printer, 214–216
  scanning devices, 203–206
Instant messaging (IM), 39–40, 208
Integrated circuit, 172
Integrated circuit age, 353
Integrated package, 89
Intel 486, 355
Interactive whiteboard, 212
Interactivity, 114
Internal hard disk, 236
Internet
  access, 35–37
  cloud computing, 52–53
  communication, 38–43
  content evaluation, 48
  crime, 308–309
  e-commerce, 49–51
  movies/TV shows, 34
  origins, 32
  privacy, 299–303
  search tools, 46–48

security, 51
  uses, 32–33
  utilities, 54–56
Internet2, 358
Internet bank, 330, 331
Internet Cash, 52
Internet protocol address (IP)
  address, 268
Internet scam, 308–309
Internet security suite, 56
Internet service provider (ISP), 35
Internet telephone, 218, 229
Internet telephony, 218
Internet worm, 308
Intranet, 277
Intrusion detection system (IDS), 277
iOS, 143
IP telephony, 218
iPad, 359
iPhone, 291, 359
iPhone OS, 143
iPod, 255
iProtectYou Pro Web filter, 56
IrDA port, 182
Iris scanner, 312
ISP, 35
iStockphoto, 111
IT, 6
iTunes, 358
iTunes Music Store Web site, 316
Ixquick, 47

j

JavaScript, 37
Job search sites, 336
Jobs. See Careers
Jobs, Steve, 354
Join, 86
Joystick, 202, 203

k

Kbps, 265
Key, 313
Keyboard, 198, 199
Keyboard entry, 198–200
Keyboard features, 199–200
Keyboard port, 182
Keystroke logger, 302
Kilobits per second (Kbps), 265
Knowledge base, 119
Knowledge-based systems, 118–119

l

Label, 80
LAN, 270, 271
Land, 238
Language translator, 136
Laptop, 167
Large databases, 295–296
Laser printer, 215
Launchpad, 141

LCD, 211
Legacy ports, 182
Legend, 82
Link, 36, 114
LinkedIn, 41
Linux, 142, 356
Lion, 141
Liquid crystal display (LCD), 211
Local area network (LAN), 270, 271
Location, 36
Logical operations, 173
Low bandwidth, 267

m

Mac OS, 140–141
Mac OS 10.7, 141
Mac OS X, 141, 358
Machine translation (MT), 220
MagicJack, 218
MagicJack adapter, 218
Magnetic card reader, 204
Magnetic character recognition
    (MICR), 205
Main board, 171
Mainframe computer, 11
Malicious programs, 307–308
Malware, 307
MAN, 272
Mass storage, 245
Mass storage devices, 245–246
Mauchly, John W., 351
MAX, 80
MB, 175
Mbps, 265
McAfee Antivirus, 57
McAfee SecurityCenter, 151
Mechanical mouse, 201
Media center system unit, 166–167
Medium band, 267
Megabyte (MB), 175
Melissa, 357
Memory, 169, 174–175
Memory capacity, 175
Menu, 72, 139
Menu bar, 72
Mesh network, 273
MetaCrawler, 47
Metasearch engine, 47
Metropolitan area network (MAN), 272
MFD, 217–218
MICR, 205
Microblog, 42
Microcomputer, 11–12
Microcomputer system, 13
Microprocessor, 169, 172–174
Microprocessor age, 354–355
Microprocessor chip, 173
Microsecond, 173
Microsoft, 76
Microsoft desktop operating system, 140
Microsoft Office, 90
Microsoft Security Essentials (beta), 148
Microwave, 263
MIDI, 182
Midrange computer, 11

.mil, 36
Minicomputer, 11
Mission Control, 142
Mistaken identity, 298, 326
Mobile applications, 120
Mobile apps, 120–121
Mobile browser, 37
Mobile digital television
    (mobile DTV), 217
Mobile OS, 143
Mobile robot, 120
Modem, 265–266
Modulation, 265
Molecular storage, 247
Monitor, 210–212
Monitor resolution, 210
Monster, 336
Mosaic graphical Web browser, 356
Motherboard, 171
Mouse, 200–201
Mouse pointer, 200
Mouse port, 182
MS Office clip art, 111
MT, 220
Multicore chip, 173
Multifunctional device (MFD), 217–218
Multimedia, 114
Multimedia authoring programs, 114
Multitasking, 138
Multitouch screen, 202
Music files, 238, 256
Musical instrument digital interface
    (MIDI), 182
MySpace, 40, 359

n

Naive people, 333
Nano, 173
Nanosecond, 173
Napster, 357
NAS, 245
Natural hazards, 310–311
.net, 36
Net Nanny, 56
.NET platform, 358
Netbook, 167, 168
Netbook system unit, 168
Network adapter card, 176, 268–270. *See
    also* Communications and networks
Network administrator, 270, 279
Network architecture, 273, 276
Network attached storage (NAS), 245
Network gateway, 270
Network interface card (NIC), 176, 269
Network operating system (NOS),
    139, 269
Network security, 277
Network server, 139
Network types, 270–272
Newton MessagePad, 356
NIC, 176, 269
Node, 268
Norton 360, 148
NOS, 139, 269
Notebook system unit, 167

Numbered list, 76
Numeric entry, 80
Numeric keypad, 199
Numeric representation, 170

O

OCR, 205
Office 97, 357
Office 98, 357
Office 2000, 357
Office 2010, 359
Office for Mac, 90
Office software suite, 90
Office suite, 90
Office XP, 358
OLED, 211
OMR, 206
Online banking, 50
Online identity, 303
Online job hunting, 336–337
Online office suite, 91
Online shopping, 50, 51
Online stock trading, 50
Online storage, 241
Ooma, 218
Open source, 142, 152, 162
Operating system, 136
Optical carrier (OC), 266
Optical-character recognition
    (OCR), 205
Optical disc, 238–240
Optical disc drive, 238
Optical holography, 247
Optical-mark recognition (OMR), 206
Optical mouse, 201
Optical scanner, 203–204
Organic light-emitting diode (OLED), 211
Organizational change, 338
Organizational cloud storage, 246
Organizational networks, 277–278
Organized crime, 306
Orkut, 41
Output, 210. *See also* Input and output
Output devices, 210
Overstock, 51

p

Packet, 268
Page, 87
Page layout programs, 109
PAN, 272
Panda Cloud Antivirus, 148
Parallel port, 182
Parallel processing, 173
Passive-matrix monitor, 211
Password, 312, 314
PayPal, 52
PC card, 177
PC Card slot, 177
PCI Express (PCIe), 180
PCIe, 180
PCMCIA slot, 177
PDA, 168

PDA keyboard, 199
Peer-to-peer (P2P) network, 276
Pentium Pro microprocessor, 356
Perception system robot, 119
Person-to-person auction site, 50
Personal area network (PAN), 272
Personal backup, 325
Personal digital assistant (PDA), 168
Personal firewall, 325
Personal information, 296–298
Personal laser printer, 215
Personal software, 89
Personal Web site, 131
PersonalFirewall, 151
Phishing, 309
Photo editor, 109
Photo printer, 216
Photoshop Express, 120
Physical connections, 262–263
Physical security, 314
Picosecond, 173
Pit, 238
Pixel, 109, 210
Plagiarism, 315, 316, 327
Plagiarist, 316
Platform, 140
Platform scanner, 205
Platter, 235
Plotter, 216
Plug and Play, 177
Plug-in, 54, 55
PMT, 80
Podcast, 42–43
Pointer, 72, 138
Pointing devices, 200–203
Pointing stick, 201, 202
Port, 180–182
Portable media player, 217
Portable printer, 216
Portable scanner, 204
Portable voice recognition system, 210
POST, 138, 161
Power management, 140, 163
Power supply, 183
Power supply unit, 183
P2P network, 276
Presentation files, 15
Presentation graphics, 87–88
Preventing data loss, 314–315
Primary key, 85
Primary storage, 234
Printer, 214–216
Printer cartridge, 215, 231
Privacy
    Internet, 299–303
    large databases, 295–296
    legislation, 303
    online identity, 303
    personal information, 296–298
    primary issues, 295
    private network, 298–299
Privacy mode, 301
Private browsing, 301
Private network, 298–299
Proactive person, 333–334
Procedure, 5–6
Processing speeds, 173

Processor, 172
Productivity suite, 90
Property, 295
Protocol, 267–268
Proxy server, 277
Public webcam, 318
PV, 80

q

Query, 84, 86
Query criteria, 86
QuickTime, 54, 55
QWERTY, 199

r

Radio frequency (RF), 263
Radio frequency card reader, 205
Radio frequency identification
    (RFID), 205
RAID, 237
RAID system, 246
RAM, 174–175
Random-access memory (RAM), 174–175
Range, 80
Raster images, 109
Read-only memory (ROM), 175
RealPlayer, 54, 55
Recalculation, 80
Record, 85
Redundant arrays of inexpensive disks
    (RAID), 237
Refresh rate, 210
Relational database, 84
Remote deposit (via mobile computer),
    331–332
Report, 84, 86
Resolution, 210, 214
Restricting access, 312–313
Resume advice, 337, 348
Reverse directory, 295
Reverse directory Web site, 295
RF, 263
RFID, 174, 194, 205
RFID tags, 174
Ribbon, 73
Ribbon gui, 73
RIM OS, 143
Robot, 119, 123
Robot network, 308
Robotics, 119–120
Rogue Wi-Fi hotspot, 310
Roller ball, 201
ROM, 175
Row, 79

s

S/PDIF, 182
Safe Eyes Platinum, 56
SAN, 246
Satellite, 263
Satellite connection services, 266

Saya robot, 123
Scam, 308
Scanner, 203
Scanning devices, 203–206
Search, 47
Search engine, 46, 47
Search services, 46
Secondary storage, 232–257
    characteristics, 235
    cloud storage, 241–244
    hard disk, 235–237
    mass storage devices, 245–246
    optical disc, 238–240
    solid-state storage, 240–241
Secondary storage devices, 234
Sector, 147, 235
Secure file transfer protocol (SFTP), 55
Security, 306–315
    anticipating disasters, 314
    computer crime, 307–310
    computer criminals, 306
    e-commerce, 51
    encryption, 313–314
    network, 277–278
    other hazards, 310–311
    preventing data loss, 314–315
    restricting access, 312–313
SecurityCenter, 151
Self-healing computers, 153
Semiconductor, 172
Serial port, 182
Server, 269
SFTP, 55
Shared laser printer, 215
Shareware, 103
Sharing data between applications, 91, 103
Sheet, 79
Sheet name, 83
Shockwave, 54
Silicon chip, 172
Silverlight, 55
SiteAdvisor, 151
Skype, 218
Slate computer, 168
Slide, 87
Slot, 171, 172
Smart card, 174
Smartphone, 168
Smith, David L., 357
Snoopware, 298
Snort, 278
Social networking, 40–41
Social networking risks, 309
Socket, 171, 172
Soft copy, 210
Software acquisition, 72, 104
Software engineer, 246
Software environment, 140
Software piracy, 316
Software suite, 90–91
Solid-state drive (SSD), 240
Solid-state storage, 240–241, 257
Sony/Philips Digital Interconnect
    Format (S/PDIF), 182
Sort, 84, 86
Sound card, 176
Spam, 38, 39

Spam blocker, 39, 40
Spam Buster, 40
Spam filter, 39, 67
SpamEater, 40
SPAMfighter, 40
Speaker, 217
Special-application ink-jet printer, 215
Specialized application software,
    106–133. *See also* Application
    software
  artificial intelligence, 116–120
  audio editing software, 111
  desktop publishers, 109
  graphic suites, 111
  graphics, 109–111
  illustration programs, 109
  image editors, 109
  image galleries, 109–111
  knowledge-based systems, 118–119
  mobile apps, 120–121
  multimedia, 114
  robotics, 119–120
  video editing software, 111
  virtual reality, 118
  Web authoring, 115–116
Specialized ports, 181–182
Specialized search engine, 47–48
Specialized suite, 91
Specialty, 335
Specialty processors, 174
Speech recognition, 73, 74–75
SpeechGear, 220
Spelling checker, 76, 77
Spider, 46
Spike, 311
Spotlight, 141
Spreadsheet, 79–83
Spy Doctor, 303
Spy removal, 302–304, 304–305
Spyware, 301, 325
SSD, 240
Stand-alone operating system, 139
Standard ports, 181
Star network, 273
Staying current, 334–335
Stock photograph, 110
Storage. *See* Secondary storage
Storage area network (SAN), 246
Streaming, 42
Streaming multimedia, 131
Streaming multimedia players, 130
Styles, 76
Stylus, 202–203
Subject directory, 46
SUM, 80
Supercomputer, 11
Surf, 35
Surge protector, 311
Switch, 269
Symbian, 143
System/360 line of computers, 353
System board, 169, 171–172
System bus, 180
System chassis, 166. *See also* System unit
System unit, 164–195
  bus lines, 177, 180
  cables, 182

categories, 166–168
components, 169
defined, 166
electronic data and instructions,
    169–170
expansion slots and cards, 176–177
memory, 174–175
microprocessor, 172–174
ports, 180–182
power supply, 183
system board, 171–172
System unit component, 169

t

T1, 266
T3, 266
Tab, 73, 139
Table, 84, 85
Tablet PC, 167, 168
Tablet PC system unit, 168
Tape library, 246
TB, 175
TCP/IP, 267
Technical writer, 219
Technological failures, 311
Telephone line, 262
Telephone modem, 265, 266
Telephony, 218
Telepresence, 280
Template, 88
Terabyte (TB), 175
Terrorist, 306
Text entries, 80, 81
TFT monitor, 211
Theft, 310
Thermal printer, 216
Thesaurus, 76
Thin film transistor (TFT) monitor, 211
Three-dimensional storing, 247
3D HDTV, 212
3G cellular network, 267
Timeline. *See* Evolution of computer age
Toggle key, 199
Toolbar, 72
Top-level domain (TLD), 36
Topology, 273
Torvalds, Linus, 142, 356
Touch pad, 201
Touch screen, 202
Track, 147, 235
Trackball, 201
Traditional cookie, 300
Traditional keyboard, 199
Traditional table PC, 168
Transfer rate, 265
Transferring files (chatting), 209
Transistor age, 352
Transition, 87, 88
Translating foreign languages, 220
Transmission control protocol/Internet
    protocol (TCP/IP), 267
Tree network, 273
Trojan horse, 308
Troubleshooting, 144
Turnitin Web site, 316

TV tuner card, 176, 178–179, 193
Twisted-pair cable, 262
Twitter, 42, 44–45

U

Unicode, 170
Uniform resource locator (URL), 36
Uninstall program, 144
UNIVAC, 351
Universal instant messenger, 40
Universal product code (UPC), 205
Universal serial bus (USB), 180
Universal serial bus (USB) port, 181
UNIX, 142
UPC, 205
Upgrader's guide, 365–368
Uplink, 263
Uploading, 55
URL, 36
USB, 180
USB drive, 241
USB port, 181
USB storage devices, 254
User interface, 72, 137
Utilities, 136
Utility suite, 91, 148

V

Vacation prize, 309
Vacuum tube age, 351
Vector, 109
Vector illustrations, 109
Vector image, 109, 110
VGA port, 181
Video editing software, 111
Video graphics adapter (VGA) port, 181
Virtual environment, 118
Virtual keyboard, 199
Virtual machine, 142
Virtual memory, 175, 193
Virtual private network (VPN), 278, 314
Virtual reality, 118
Virtual reality wall, 118, 119
Virtualization, 142
Virtualization software, 142
Virus, 148, 307
Virus protection, 148, 150–151
VirusScan, 151
Voice over IP (VoIP), 218
Voice recognition system, 207
Voiceband, 267
VoIP, 218
Voltage surge, 311
Vonage, 218
Vonage adapter, 218
VPN, 278, 314
VR, 118

W

WAN, 272
Wand reader, 205, 206

Warm boot, 138
Wearable computer, 185
Web, 17, 32. *See also* Internet
Web-accessible home appliances, 58
Web auction, 50, 51
Web authoring, 115–116
Web authoring programs, 116
Web-based e-mail account, 38
Web-based file transfer services, 55
Web bug, 301, 326
Web directories, 46–47
Web image galleries, 109–111
Web log, 42
Web page, 36, 117
Web page editors, 116
Web site design, 115–116
Web site encryption, 314
Web utilities, 54
WebCam, 206–207, 209, 230
Webcast, 42
WeBidz, 51
Webmail, 38
Webmaster, 57
WebOS, 144
WEP, 314
What-if analysis, 80, 83
Wheel button, 201
Wi-Fi, 263
Wi-Fi protected access (WPA), 314
Wi-Fi standards, 263
Wide area network (WAN), 272
Wiki, 43

Wikipedia, 43
WiMax, 263
Window, 72, 138
Windows, 140
Windows 3.0, 355
Windows 7, 140, 141, 359
Windows 95, 356
Windows Defender, 303
Windows Media Player, 54
Windows Phone 7, 144
Windows Phone Store, 121
Windows Update, 149, 160
Windows utilities, 144–147
Windows Vista, 140, 359
Windows XP, 140, 358
Wired equivalent privacy
    (WEP), 314
Wireless access point, 271
Wireless adapter, 272
Wireless communication devices, 16
Wireless connections, 263–264
Wireless home network, 288
Wireless keyboard, 199
Wireless LAN (WLAN), 271
Wireless mobile devices, 287
Wireless modem, 266
Wireless mouse, 201
Wireless network card, 176
Wireless network encryption, 314
Wireless revolution, 261
Wireless wide area network (WWAN)
    modem, 266

WLAN, 271
Word, 173
Word processor, 76–78
Word wrap, 76, 77
Workbook, 83
Workbook files, 79
Worksheet, 79, 81
Worksheet files, 15
Worldwide Interoperability for
    Microwave Access (WiMax), 267
Worm, 307–308
Wozniak, Steve, 354
WPA2, 314
WWAN network, 266
WYSIWYG editors, 116, 117

X

Xeon, 173

Y

Yahoo!, 47

Z

Zombies, 308
Zone Alarm, 303
Zoom Web content, 37

Tips Index

b

Buying a computer, 166

c

Clock speed, 173
Connection to wireless networks, 271

d

Defragmentation, 236
Digital camera, 206

i

Identity theft, 297
IP address, 268

m

Microsoft Access templates, 84

o

Optical disk, 239

p

Phishing, 297
Printing from the Web, 216
Privacy on the Web, 41, 303
Protecting your microcomputer, 314

s

Search, 144
Searching the Internet, 46

Shopping online, 49
Spam, 40
Spreadsheet, 80

t

Technical support, 177

u

Updating the operating system, 141

v

Virus, 308

w

Web site design, 118